William Wilkinson

Memorials of the Minnesota Forest Fires in the Year 1894

With a Chapter on the Forest Fires in Wisconsin in the Same Year

William Wilkinson

Memorials of the Minnesota Forest Fires in the Year 1894
With a Chapter on the Forest Fires in Wisconsin in the Same Year

ISBN/EAN: 9783337249205

Printed in Europe, USA, Canada, Australia, Japan

Cover: Foto ©ninafisch / pixelio.de

More available books at **www.hansebooks.com**

REV. WM. WILKINSON.

MEMORIALS

OF THE

MINNESOTA FOREST FIRES

IN THE YEAR 1894

WITH

A CHAPTER ON THE FOREST FIRES IN WISCONSIN

IN THE SAME YEAR

By

REV. WILLIAM WILKINSON

Rector of St. Andrews Church, Minneapolis, and Former Chaplain of the
House of Representatives of Minnesota.

—

PUBLISHED BY

NORMAN E. WILKINSON,
1325 Girard Ave. No.
MINNEAPOLIS
1895

Crown-Litho Publishing Co

PREFACE.

The question with which a man has to do, who writes memorials of events, which are worthy to be had in remembrance, is one of accuracy what really took place; when, where, how and what were the results.

To depart from what is the strict truth is to do violence to history, to invent, not narrate events, and the writer who descends to it finds to his cost that "Fiction entices and deceives, and sprinkled o'er her fragrant leaves, lies poisonous dew."

It is my aim in these memorials to set in order the suffering nobly endured, the great losses sustained, and the prompt and generous help given so freely by men in every walk of life, professors of all religions and of none, saint and sinner, rich and poor alike. In the doing of this, it is my hope to further the ends of Christian charity, and the mutual regard man owes to his fellow man as being members of one common family, the children of one loving Father. In all historic time the heroic men who have added glory to their age, have been held in high esteem; for them anthems have been sung, monuments raised, processions and gala days arranged; the sweetest poets have sung their fame, and the loftiest prose has told their praise; all this has not been, it is not now, for sentimental purposes; it has a firm foundation, and serves a far reaching and useful purpose. It is by the recital of daring and unselfish deeds that high ideals are kept before the public mind, that youth, in its ardor, in its desire of achievement, may rise to the opportunities presented in all their moral splendor, and thus renew the valor, and conquests their fathers won. It is one of the very first principles which comes into operation in the assimilation of ideas, that men grow like the patterns they set before themselves. All the great writers on morals have pointed this out: every page in books like Mr. Lecky's History of European Morals, proves its truth, and never failing incidents. Whatever ideals men have had they have sought some personifi-

5

GOVERNOR KNUTE NELSON.

INTRODUCTORY.

MEMORIALS OF MINNESOTA FOREST FIRES.

"O Lord, how manifold are thy works! In wisdom hast thou made them all ; the earth is full of thy riches."—King David.

"The heavens are the Lord's, the earth with all things therein and thereon, hath he given to the children of men. Everything in its proper place is good. Nature and natural law know no mistakes. Nothing exists but for wise purposes. It is man's duty to find what those purposes are, and then obtain all the good he can from them. The ancient seer probably wrote much better than he knew, when he said of trees, "Their fruit shall be for meat, and their leaves for medicine." In malarial countries, this has been proved true.

Since the time Adam and his wife were in the garden of Eden, trees, woods and forests have been objects of study, admiration and known usefulness. It is, however, doubtful whether even our wisest and most cultivated men know the most important things about them. Many questions are engaging the closest attention of our most alert thinkers, careful watch is being kept, notes taken and comparisons made in different lands respecting the influence of trees on climate, how they grow, and what all the purposes they serve in the economy of nature are. It appears certain that historic man lived in the midst of trees, amongst them he said prayers to his gods, offered burnt sacrifices, from them he cut wood to make his bows and arrows, so they helped him in killing wild animals, and from them, ever since fire was known to savage man, he has taken fuel on which to cook his food. It was in the secluded shelter of the trees he found a hiding place from his enemy, and a refuge from the keen storms of wind which swept over the open ground when all was still in the woods. It was amongst the trees, he saw the birds and heard them sing their songs of love, which, no doubt, filled his breast with delight.

It is a delusion of self opinionated civilized men, that their rude brethren take no pleasure in the refined aspects of life in the woods. Long before man knew how to make a microscope or a telescope, he understood many mighty truths, stern experience had taught him, both in joy and sorrow in the forest.

What had been learned in a general way, our age, which demands exactness and clearness of statement, has sought the reason for and placed in words which, "He who runs may read." Amongst the great industries of the world stands that of agriculture, the farmer and the gardener must work that the clerk and philosopher may live. The life of the world, so far as man is concerned, depends upon the cultivation of the field. How important, then, it is that we all know what helps and what hinders the growth of plants. A keen cold wind retards, often stops growth, and shade from such wind increases growth. Experiments have shown that a board fence, six feet high, makes its presence for good felt six rods away. What influence, then, must the mighty trees of the forest have in stopping strong wind and in lifting it up from the earth, and also in preventing the moisture that is in the ground from being too quickly evaporated by the hot winds of summer. Perhaps they have powerful influences, in such winds, upon the earth itself.

The earth as a conductor of sound and of motion, is being investigated now with as much care by the seismologists as the heavens are by the astronomers. The things these scientific men find out, the lessons they learn, are not more surprising than the instruments they make with which to record what is taking place. Waves are known to spread in the ground. In a paper on recent science, by P. Kropotkin, published in the Century Magazine, and reproduced in Littell's Living Age, Jan. 10th, 1895, he says: "By means of a seismometrograph at the Collegio Romona, in Rome Italy, it was possible to observe the earthquakes which took place in Greece, India, and in Turkestan, and also to see three distinct waves, coming from the three distinct shocks in Japan. These waves had traveled a long distance at a speed of 2,750 yards in a second, and yet were visible in the tracings of the instrument. Wonderful as this is, it is eclipsed by a new Bifilar pendulum, invented last year by Mr. Horace Darwin. It will measure the disturbance of the earth's surface, if it is only the one-thousandth part of an inch in a mile.

All this has opened a new world to scientific men, and they hope to foretell the conditions under which earthquakes take place, just as they have been, and are, able to tell when an explosion in a coal mine is likely to come. It is in the light of instruments and facts like these, and of the knowledge already gained, that trees of the forest, by causing vibrations in the earth may serve purposes, which are as yet unknown. We are only just beginning to understand the susceptibility of the earth to sound and to motion. Old theories are being discarded, and the things Humboldt, the most learned man of his time, taught in Cosmos, are now known to be inaccurate. In the Royal Observatory, at Greenwich, it is well known that the crowds which assemble in the town on a holiday, are reported to the astronomers by the levels they use in their work, and this, though the crowds are far away. What man knows today about the exquisite relations of cause and effect, and of the mechanism of the universe, is not a speck, probably, in comparison with what he will know.

In these western states of America, we are dependent upon the Gulf of Mexico, the great lakes, and I think, also upon the Hudson Bay for our rain. From these great waters there is constantly much evaporation. The air above them becomes wet, it is blown by the winds over our continent, and falls upon the ground in fruitful showers. There are few questions more curious than are those connected with the falling of rain. In some parts of the world, it is never known to rain, in others it rains nearly every day, in others at two seasons of the year. In England, the largest rainfall is in the fall and winter; in Minnesota, we do not look for rain in winter, we expect frost and snow, as the weather is so cold there is little evaporation. In the spring and summer, when the weather is warm, and as it grows hotter, we have rain and more rain. No arrangement could be wiser than this, because of our hot climate. For more than fifty years, the average rainfall in the months of June, July and August has been ten inches. It takes one gallon of water to cover two feet of ground one inch, so that on every two feet of ground, ten gallons of rain falls in the three summer months of Minnesota. Whatever is lacking of this tends to make a drouth. It is not alone, however, the quantity of rain which falls, but how it falls, and what are the conditions of the earth upon which it falls, that determine how much of the water remains for use. Trees retard the water from being taken too rapidly into the rivers, and so to the sea. While the tree is lifting its branches to the sunlight, it is also sending its roots deep into the earth, and the fibers of these, in forests, become one mass of intricate network, every part of which is a sponge and also a hand. The wind rocks the trees on the outer edges of these forests, and loosens the soil, but the storm which rocks the trees without blowing them down, only makes the roots take a firmer hold upon the earth, and at the same time opens drains from the surface of the ground so that when the next rain falls, it follows the course of the roots and thus lets the water into the earth a depth it would not otherwise penetrate. The earth thereby becomes full of water, and the tree in hot weather, long after the surface of the ground has ceased to give much moisture to the sun's hot rays, draws from the supply of water deep in the earth, and thus evaporation is, even in the hottest days, constantly going on. There seems to be no means of testing exactly how much evaporation from a single tree is given, but that the quantity is large, is well known. Competent authorities state that over six acres of leaf surface is exposed to the heat of the sun by some trees, in one summer. Any man who has tried to keep the air in his room damp, by means of a pan of water placed upon the stove, tries to do in a rude way what the trees do with great effectiveness in the long, hot days of summer.

It is considerations like these, which make forest fires and forest destruction so terrible. Those who have not given attention to the subject, do not know what is involved. All forest countries suffer by fires, and if we do not hear as much of the disaster, it is because, usually human life is not lost. In New Brunswick, in October, 1825, a fire occurred which laid 10,000 square miles waste. The Maj.-Gen. Sir Howard Douglas, Bart., lieutenant governor of the Province, speaks of it as follows:

FREDERICTON, October 17, 1825.

For some days previous to the 7th inst., the temperature of the air and the state of the atmosphere, much charged with smoke, indicated that fires of vast extent were raging in the woods, but no serious apprehension seems to have been entertained on account of the prevalence of conflagrations, which are so commonly put in action to commence clearances in the forest.

On the day I have named, however, at about 11 o'clock in the forenoon an alarm was conveyed to the town, that the residence of the commissioner of crown lands, about a mile and a half distant, was on fire. The garrison, and the greater part of the population, ran immediately thither, and succeeded in saving Mr. Baillie's house from the flames, which were spreading through the adjoining woods with tremendous fury.

Whilst there, accounts were brought to me, that the town was on fire, and before I could reach it, though mounted on a fleet horse, the streets were in a blaze.

At that time it blew a gale of wind from the northwest, and however incredible it may have appeared, that the flames should have been communicated to the town from the woods in the vicinity, the sequel of this dispatch will show, from what has occurred elsewhere, that there is every reason to believe such was the case.

The fire raged with a degree of fury which no exertions (and those used were very great) could for a moment check, and the whole population abandoned their houses, making what efforts they could to save their effects.

When the fire had consumed all that part of the town which lay in the direction of the wind, it took a lateral course, threatening the barracks and other buildings, which, had they taken fire, must have led it to the total destruction of what has remained of the town of Fredericton.

As evening advanced the woods, which had continued to burn throughout the day, were now distinctly seen to be everywhere burning. and vast clouds of smoke, rising in the distance, accompanied by extraordinary noises, as of furious explosions of flame, and the fire reflected on the distant sky, portended other calamities which I now report.

On the very same day and about the hour when this place suffered most, the town of Newcastle, 120 miles distant, together with all the mercantile establishments on that bank of the Miramichi river, and some on the opposite side, were consumed by a violent torrent of fire, which issued from the woods in the rear at about 9 o'clock p. m. Thus the destructive element which was causing such devastations in other parts of the Province, appears to have been driven thither by the gale which was experienced here, but which the mighty action of such extensive and rapid conflagration increased as it proceeded, to the most impetuous hurricane, and the very wide range it has taken leads me to fear that we have much yet to learn of its dreadful effects, when reports shall come in from the numerous gangs of woodmen dispersed in the various parts of the forest.

At the same time that the flames and showers of burning embers poured upon Newcastle, they reached the establishments similarly placed upon the banks of the river, and others in the rear, and in fifteen minutes all were consumed.

I wish I could report that life had been spared, but so violently driven were the flames and embers from the blazing woods, well prepared for the most active combustion by the longest season of heat and drought ever known, that men, women and children in great numbers have perished in the houses and in the woods, in exertions to save property, or in attempts to save life; and when driven in terror to seek safety on the water, greater numbers still appear to have suffered in attempts to cross the rivers in boats or in canoes, on rafts or on logs of timber, which were alike incapable of resisting the fury of the storm. Many vessels were at the same time cast on shore, several set on fire, and three entirely consumed by the drift of embers from the land.

The fatal effects of the awful calamity cannot yet be estimated. Fredericton has lost about 80 habitations or stores, and property to the value of at least $165,000. On the rivers Orounvctoo and Renderjonish, tributaries of the St. John, several lives and many habitations have been lost and destroyed, and some of these ravages accompanied by terrific circumstances. On the Miramichi river the loss of life cannot, I fear, be estimated under 300 souls. Great numbers of the destitute survivors had collected in the village of Chatham for relief, and as so many of the provision stores of the merchants had been consumed (the settlement depending almost entirely upon imported food), severe apprehensions were entertained of approaching famine. So soon as I learned this, I assembled His Majesty's council to consider what measures it would be expedient to adopt, and an agent has been sent to Quebec to purchase supplies and to proceed with them to Miramichi."

This fire, so frightful in its results, left, as it appeared, the very earth burned, yet, my friends, Mr. M. B. Turner and Mr. Harvey Turner, of this city, whose father lived in the fire district of New Brunswick, tells me that in thirty years, such are the reproductive and recuperative forces at work in nature, large areas of forest trees were growing with surprising vigor. The Middle, Western and Northwestern states of America have had sad experiences of forest fires, but as yet not much has been learned in a practical way.

One of the most terrible fires ever seen by civilized man in the forests of America, was that at Peshtigo, in Wisconsin, in October,

1871, when millions of dollars worth of property were lost and more than seven hundred persons burned to death. All the summer the heat had been great, and the rainfall small. The pine was thick, and dry slashings, dead timber, wind falls, lay upon the earth, which was baked by the hot rays of the sun. The pools had in them no water, the wells were dry, and the streams very low. No rain had fallen for some time, the fires were in the forests, and when they increased in volume, the hot air quickly ascended, a current was caused, the wind rose, and the dire calamity followed which made Peshtigo prominent in the annals of disaster.

In 1881, Michigan was the scene of terrible fires, which laid waste four counties and killed 125 people. These fires, at the time, were said to be the direct result of atmospheric conditions. This being the case, the United States Signal Service authorities deemed it wise and useful to send Sergeant Wm. O. Bailey, who had charge of the station at Port Huron, to investigate the whole matter.

This he did, and in so doing went over all the burned district and made a map of it, saw what the fire had done, marked the course it had taken, asked questions of whoever could give him intelligent information. All this was done under the instruction of Brig. and Bvt. Maj. Gen. W. B. Hazen, whose report, published by authority of the secretary of war, has been kindly furnished me by the present secretary of agriculture. It is in many respects a model of what such documents ought to be. From it, I learn that the fires which did the damage, began their work of destruction Sept. 5th. There had been fires for a long time, the newspapers had called attention to their danger, little heed had been paid, and no effort to stop them or get out of their way had been made by the settlers, until it was too late for many, so $2,000,000 worth of property went into the clouds in smoke. For weeks before the fire, the earth in many places had cracked, the swamps were baked into hard clay, the heat of the sun was hotter than it had been in that locality for years; not since the fires of Wisconsin, in 1871, had such weather been known. All was ready for one terrific fire. It came, and history tells its story. On Sept. 5th, the wind was strong enough to blow or break down trees thirty feet high and eight inches through. It has been said and it is believed by Sergeant Bailey, that in Huron, some distance from the scene of the fires, the temperature was 99 degrees in the shade at 7 a. m. It was a southeast wind which blew the flames into Huron township. It appears that the winds which prevail in forest fires generally come from the southwest. In forest states it should be made a crime for men recklessly to start fires in hot seasons, when no man can tell where they will stop. There are many reasons for this. Our forests are being used up at an alarming rate. The supply of timber is limited, and as our population is growing at a rate which has increased the people five times in about sixty years, the demand for lumber is in proportion. The need of care and prudence in seeing that no waste by fire takes place which can possibly be prevented is great.

Wet and dry periods appear to go in cycles covering 34 to 37 years, if we may take the statements of experts in countries where weather reports have been longest and most accurately kept. We appear, at the present time, to be in the dryer division. Why these periods should be, man with all his wondrous capacity, is not able to give a probable explanation. The earth and its affairs are connected with other worlds, and larger knowledge would doubtless put us in possession of facts needed to explain the mystery. The great authorities on meteorological questions are of opinion, that the day is coming when scientific knowledge and discovery will enable them to foretell what the weather will be, with all the accuracy with which they can now predict an eclipse of the moon. The day of this achievement may be distant; it is, however, a well defined hope in the minds of philosophers. When that day comes the farmer will know what next year's crops, under given cultivation, will be. Meanwhile we have to read life's riddle and agricultural and commercial duty in the light of past averages, and act accordingly.

The following statement has been kindly prepared for me by my friend, Mr. E. K. Smith, than whom no man in this state is more competent. Its absolute accuracy is certified to by Mr. Edward A. Beals, director of the state weather service.

Speaking in general of the drouth of 1894, the editor of the August, 1894, Monthly Weather Review, published by authority of the secretary of agriculture, says that, "From an agricultural point of view, a drouth is not merely a deficiency of rainfall, but a deficiency of water available for the use of the growing crops, whether grass, grain, fruit, or forest trees. As the water supply stored up in the soil is often sufficient to tide the plant over a long interval without rain, therefore the contents and nature of the soil are important features. Again, as the dryness of the air, the velocity of the wind and the temperature, are the principal factors in the evaporation of water from the soil, as well as from the surface of the leaves, these features must be considered. Thus a drouth affecting agriculture is a complex result of many considerations. The drouths that affect the water supply of cities, navigation of rivers, and irrigation, depend upon a similar complexity of considerations, among which is the direct influence of the consumption of water by the vegetation growing on the soil. Evidently, therefore, both from an agricultural and engineering point of view, it is impracticable to define the intensity of a drouth in general and exact terms. On the other hand, from a purely meteorological point of view, the term drouth is usually considered as referring only to the quantity and distribution of rainfall, omitting all consideration of the humidity of the air, the amount of cloudiness, the strength of the wind, but taking full account of the normal quantity and distribution of the rainfall for the given locality. The great drouth of 1894 so far as concerns agriculture, has been but the culmination of a long period of deficient rainfall. The tables of accumulated precipitation published monthly, show that the whole region in which the crops have suffered during August, reports a steady and generally an increasing deficiency in the accumulated rainfall since the first of January. The drouth is, therefore, not merely the drouth of July and August, but that of several months."

In the upper Mississippi Valley the accumulated deficiency of rainfall at the close of the year 1893, was 4.4 inches. At the end of August, 1894, the deficit had increased to 9.5 inches, or only 63 per cent. of the amount we should have received. The temperature showing an excess, above the normal, of 2.7 degrees since January 1st, and during the month of August, 3.1 degrees."

In Minnesota the longest rainfall record is one kept at Fort Snelling, beginning in July, 1836. A few years during the war, and just previous to that period, the post was temporarily abandoned, and no record kept. By combining this record with one taken at St. Paul only a few miles distant, it is made practically continuous to date. Its examination shows, that for this vicinity, the average yearly rainfall during the last 58 years amounts to 26.24 inches.

The spring rainfall (March, April and May) to 7.06 inches, and the summer rainfall, (June, July and August) to 10.40 inches.

Referring to the conditions existing in the immediate location of the fires between St. Paul and Duluth, we find the local conditions as follows:

THE SOIL.

The soil is rather light, and covered, originally, with heavy timber of pine, spruce and hard woods, except in certain locations, consisting of pine barrens, swamps or lakes. During the past 25 years much of the timber has been cut off, leaving a large accumulation of dead and down timber, stumps and brush, inflammable material.

RAINFALL.

The records of the weather bureau at St. Paul show a normal rainfall for the period covered by the drouth, or from May 16 to Sept. 10, of 13.61 inches. For the same period during 1894 the records show a rainfall of but 2.20 inches, a deficiency of 11.41 inches, or 84 per cent. of the normal, a rainfall per square acre of 59,738 gallons as against a normal of 369,565 gallons. During the time in question, (nearly four months) no soaking rain, but a number of light showers were reported, amounting in July to but 0.13 inch, and 0.36 inch in August, as against a normal of 2.99 and 2.98 inches for the same months.

One inch of rain falling upon an area of one square mile is equivalent to 2,323,200 cubic feet, or nearly 17,500,000 gallons, and this quantity of water will weigh 145,200,000 pounds, or 72,600 tons.

TEMPERATURE.

The reports of temperature for the same period of time, show an accumulated excess of 427 degrees, a daily excess of 4.2 degrees above the normal. The mean temperature at St. Paul was the highest ever recorded for July, and in July, 26 degrees, the highest for at least 33 years.

HUMIDITY.

The relative humidity of the atmosphere is best shown in the following table for the years 1891-2-3-4, during the months of June, July and August.

	1891.	1892.	1893.	1894.
June.	77 per cent.	71 per cent.	64.3 per cent.	60.5 per cent.
July.	81 per cent.	70 per cent.	60.5 per cent.	48 per cent.
Aug.	74 per cent.	72 per cent.	63.2 per cent.	59.6 per cent.

Thus it will be seen that as compared with 1892 (in which year the rainfall was somewhat above the normal) the year 1894 showed a marked decrease of humidity for the time under consideration, and as between the same months of 1891 and 1894, a steady and continuous loss of humidity from the air.

WINDS.

The winds both as to direction and velocity, show but little variation from the normal up to Sept. 1st.

Evaporation is constantly adding moisture to the air from moist surfaces of the earth, water and plants, the rate increases with the increase of the temperature, and is highest at times of greatest heat combined with the dryest air and strongest winds." During the period under consideration, there was a combination of all the essentials for the greatest evaporation except the winds, which until Sept. 1st, were not strong. These conditions, i. e., great lack of rainfall, high temperature, dry air and light winds, were persistent for a period of nearly four months, resulting in parched earth, crops destroyed, vegetation of all kinds dried up and down timber and brush but tinder ready for the match. Fires had been started in August in various places throughout the timber regions of Minnesota, Wisconsin and Michigan, and smouldered or sprung into life as the winds arose. Such was the condition up to the 1st day of September, which ushered in "High, hot winds, that fanned the fires into fierce flames, themselves also creating a strong upward draft, increasing with the increase of the fierceness of the fires which caused such destruction of life and property."

From all this it is very clear that for a considerable time terrible fires in the forest parts of Minnesota had been not only possible, but feared.

As early as July 16th the Minneapolis Tribune had a report from Hinckley, which read as follows:

Fires in the Northwest—Damage being done in the vicinity of Hinckley.—Section men get to work to fight the flames.—Hundreds of tons of hay destroyed.

Hinckley, Minn., July 16.—The forest fires in this vicinity continue, and along the lines of the Eastern Minnesota the property of the country is threatened to such an extent that the section men are all out fighting the flames. So far no reports have been received of any damage to buildings, although in several instances the fires have approached very closely, and have only been driven back after hard fighting.

Along the line of the St. Paul and Duluth, between this place and Mission Creek, the next station south of here, there has been considerable loss from the fires in the meadows, hundreds of tons of hay having been destroyed. It has not yet been necessary for the company to take any steps to protect its property, as the fires have been some distance from its right of way. Unless a heavy rain comes soon there will be great loss sustained, as the fires are spreading rapidly, and everything is as dry as tinder.

As we look back, in the light of our experience, we wonder, that with such warning so little heed was paid to the imminent danger the people were in, and by the facts one more illustration is given of the old truth, that men become so accustomed to great peril, that it loses its terrors.

MISSION CREEK.

NOTHING in all the history of the fire deserves observation better than the conduct of the people who live at Mission Creek. All had the good sense to follow their leader's advice, and to stay in a piece of cleared ground upon which potatoes were being grown.

Around this little village much of the pine had been cut off. The heat, consequently was not as intense as at some other parts of the districts in the region where the fire burned, but death came very near to every one of those who were at Mission Creek. As the reader goes north, if by the St. Paul & Duluth line, at Mission Creek he may see on the left hand side of the train a log house a little way from the tracks. The potato ground was in front of this house, and to the left of it, that is, nearer White Bear. It was on this land, perhaps two acres in area, that the persons named below saved their lives. From that little log house they set out to reach the train at the bridge, two miles and a half nearer Pine City, and when they got to it were soon taken to a place of comfort in Pine City. Thus these dwellers in this little nook of earth, who every day did their share to build up their part of the state, helped to make history. It is far more important to a nation to know how the working people live, how they escape danger, who helps them in time of trouble and loss, than it is to know about some political intrigue. It is in scenes like and allied to those at Mission Creek that first day in autumn that all which is best in human action is called into full play.

A Resident of Mission Creek writes:

Dear Sir:—Your letter of the 16th to Mr. Markham has been handed to me by him to answer. It was my intention to call on you and report personally about the fire, but have had sickness in my family and could not do so as yet, but will give you the information you ask herewith.

19. WRECK OF THE SAW MILL—MISSION CREEK.

Mission Creek was a small saw mill town owned by Laird & Boyle, who also owned general store, hotel and saw mill, blacksmith shop, etc. The saw mill had shut down about a month before the fire and a great many of the people went to Dakota harvesting.

At that time there were seventy-three people here who were working on their lands near town. They had been fighting the local fire for a month before the fatal day, trying to save what hay and wood, etc., they had put up on their places. At noon September first, they became more or less uneasy, as great clouds of smoke could be seen in the southwest. By two o'clock the wind became a hurricane and at three o'clock it was almost as dark as night. The people all came to the store wanting Mr. Boyle to telegraph for a train to take them away. By this time the whole place was a-fire and Mr. Boyle ordered everyone to the potato patch, which was in the rear of the store, and at the same time gave his men orders to take a couple of barrels of water along which were standing on a wagon.

Some wanted to start to Hinckley, and did so, but only went a few rods and then returned to the potato patch, where we lay fully two hours with our faces to the ground, until the worst was over. The heat was intense and the children were all crying from the heat and ashes which nearly blinded us. After the worst was over, Mr. H. S. Rice counted up our crowd and found one short and we turned out to hunt for him in the field. He (Mr. Hamilton) was found all by himself a few rods from the rest of us all right, and in looking for him, we found the log house which we could not see before for the smoke and ashes. At six o'clock we got the women and children to this house and the men watched the outside, fearing sparks would set fire to it. The women and children got their faces washed and felt relieved that the worst was over.

Several deer were seen running around us for shelter and one large one got caught on a wire fence and some of the men brought it over to the only house on the place. We dressed and cooked it and dug up some potatoes and roasted them and partook of supper about 8:30.

About this time Andrew Nelson, who came from Pine City on foot, going to Hinckley, informed us a train was at the bridge about two and one half miles south of us, repairing the bridge which was burned, and would reach us probably about eleven o'clock.

He went to Hinckley where his family lives. Mr. Boyle told him to have Mr. Young, agent at Hinckley, send the train down for us, stating the condition we were in. Little did we then think that Hinckley had met its doom as we heard later on. Our crowd walked over the burnt ties until we reached the work train, which took us to Pine City. Everybody lost all they had, except that a few saved a little wearing apparel which they had in satchels.

The village contained twenty-six houses, one store, one hotel, a mill, a blacksmith shop and school house. There were thirty-eight head of stock burned. Laird & Boyle lost twenty-two oxen and four horses. Other stock was burned belonging to farmers.

All of our people have gone back on their lands and are getting along as well as can be expected.

Peter Nyberg and Gust Johnson were a mile east of town in the hay meadow, watching the hay from the fire when a big fire struck them. They lay in the creek until the worst was over and then came in Sunday morning, and were horrified to find our little place completely cleared out and not a person to be found in the town.

Our people are thankful to think they did not meet the same fate as our neighbors north, even if they did lose all their worldly effects.   Yours truly,

                                    ED. J. BOYLE.

BROOK PARK.

AT the time of the fire this place was called on railroad maps Pokegama; but the post office was Brook Park, and the Great Northern road has since changed its name so as to make it the same as the post office.

Here, at the time of the disaster, was a thriving community of happy people. They were away from the noise, strife and vice of large towns, and in every day affairs knew and cared nothing about the style, emulation and deceit of much that is known as society. For them the clear brook ran its silvery course through the woods, the birds sang glad songs of love, the cows roamed at will and enjoyed themselves as well behaved kine should. The rising sun dispelled the darkness and the silent moon spread its rays o'er all the landscape. The whole scene was such as brought joy to the hearts of men and women who had no ambitions except to do their daily duty, and make an honest and comfortable living.

The boys and girls—happy children of nature—in the spring and summer time plucked flowers and fruits, went to school, and said their prayers, never dreaming of the world outside their enchanted groves. This spot was to their young hearts a paradise—a very gate of heaven.

The winter brought to them its stern, but not sad realities; the treasures of the snow gave peculiar opportunities for enjoyment, which they were quick to take advantage of. Thus the charmed years passed, full of pleasure, full of work and of play, of prayer praise and service.

Brook Park had no police court, needed no jail, no saloon; not one of the abominations known in modern crowded city life in connection with the tenement houses, crowded, narrow thoroughfares, squalor, rags and dirt.

Enough to eat, drink and wear, a good school, plenty of work, and all things necessary for life and godliness. Here each and every public improvement was the concern of every one, and all

BROOK PARK—THE POOL IN WHICH MORE THAN THIRTY PERSONS SAVED THEIR LIVES.

desired to see everything possible done to advance the public interests and the general good.

When the foundations of the new school house were laid, it was a high day; and when a thousand dollars had been spent upon it, and it stood on the day of the fire complete, and was that very day accepted from the hands of its builders, it was the pride of the place. In less than one hour it was gone; the fire had consumed it!

Mr. Berg was postmaster, Mr. Nelson was section foreman on the Eastern Division of the Great Northern railroad. Dr. Kelsey was medical practitioner, and represented the Kelsey-Markham Land Company, in which are four partners: Dr. Kelsey's brother, who is a banker at Kenyon, Minnesota, the doctor himself, J. D. Markham and his brother George, both of whom reside at Rush City. These men own fifteen thousand acres of land at and near Brook Park.

The firm of Seymour and Baty had a saw mill, which would cut thirty thousand feet of lumber a day.

Mr. Carver and wife kept the boarding house. It is said that Mrs. Carver was a model in neat housekeeping and good cooking.

Among the settlers were Mr. Joseph Frame and his wife—typical westerners—with their family of six sons. This family have a taste for music, and amongst its household treasures was a violin, which Joseph made do duty often at home to the delight of the boys, and in the evenings he made it discourse sweet music for the pleasure of his neighbors. This violin was a general happiness dispenser, and great indeed was Mr. Frame's sorrow when he found that it was turned to ashes, while he had not a cent in all the wide world with which to buy another. He said: "There is nothing I have lost I so much regret as my fiddle. It was my daily companion many years. I feel lost without it."

I told this story to my good friend, Mr. Dyer, music dealer in Minneapolis, who promptly gave me a new violin for Mr. Frame. I wonder if ever a violin in the world produced such pleasure in the heart of man as this did in the mind of him who received it! It is almost certain that the first musical instrument taken into the burned district after the fire was this violin.

In the fire, Mrs. Frame had a thrilling experience. She was away from her home with her family and a neighbor, Mrs. W. W. Braman, picking cranberries in a marsh. Her husband left them, thinking them safe, to go and look after his hay. Alas! the fire came in a way, and at a time they looked not for it! They took refuge in a creek and by prudence and courage all escaped with their lives; but it was a miracle, almost, that they did so.

Mr. Frame escaped by staying on a piece of land which had been burned over before. They saved a team; all they owned beside was lost.

When the fire had passed, they stood but thinly clad, in all the garments they possessed.

In this, however, they were as well off as any of their neighbors, for all had suffered like and many greater ills.

There were twenty-three dead; and those who were living were scattered.

Dr. Kelsey was severely burned, so was Joseph Gonyea, who was taken to the St. Raphael hospital in St. Cloud, where he had to remain a long time.

There were two box cars on the railway tracks which had escaped the violence of the fire. Into these the settlers gathered, till help came, which soon reached them.

The St. Cloud people, when they knew of the disaster, began to relieve the suffering. They sent out a train on Sunday the second of September, which reached Brook Park, and took the many sufferers to Mora, where the Methodist Episcopal church had been made into a hospital. On Monday they sent a special train to Brook Park, which took large quantities of useful things. For this and other generous deeds of love, the St. Cloud people deserve high praise. The names of the persons who went on this train are in the report of the work done by the people of St. Cloud.

The good people of Mora, also, must not be left without due and ample recognition for their noble help, led by the Rev. Mr. Thomson, Methodist Episcopal minister. They behaved as men and brothers should. Verily they will have their reward.

To the people of Mora and St. Cloud belongs the credit of being the first on the ground to render assistance to the afflicted at Brook Park.

A report of the work done by them is given in this book.

While this was being done from the south side of the fire at Brook Park, earnest souls at the north side did not sit down with folded hands. Rather they designed noble plans to get to their fellows, whether they were living or dead.

On the Monday night at Hinckley in the railway yards, piles of wheat were burning, and the ties under the rails blazed. All the landscape for miles was clouded with smoke. A party of gentlemen, headed by J. D. Markham, on Monday, September third, procured a hand car, at Hinckley, and loaded it with two army tents, thirty pairs of blankets, food of various kinds, axes and several shovels, a flour barrel full of useful things, and, like men who have set their hearts to face any danger, determined to reach Brook Park that night. The names of these gentlemen are: J. D. Markham, Dr. H. B. Allen of Cloquet, Dr. C. W. Higgins, Minneapolis, B. J. Kelsey of Kenyon, Alexander Berg, W. W. Braman of Brook Brook Park, Mr. Thomson, New Brighton, Minnesota, Rev. Mr. Fosbroke, Protestant Episcopal minister at Sunrise, Minnesota, and the writer. Around this car at its start stood many well known men to wish the party good speed, amongst whom were Senator McMillan, Dr. Kilvington, Dr. Nippert, Dr. Fitzgerald and Alderman Gray, all of Minneapolis. All these men I knew, but did not know any of the many others from different parts of the state.

We had two lanterns and set out, little knowing the difficulties and dangers ahead. The car was so crowded that I had to sit on the top of blankets piled up on the barrel.

Dr. Higgins and Dr. Allen sat in front of the car, each with a lantern, and filled the office of watchmen. Every man kept his ears open and his mouth closed. It was not a time or place for idle talk.

As the darkness gathered, far as the eye could reach, the blazing stumps of pine lighted up the distant scene, and gave to it an air of peculiar beauty. But we were not on the lookout for grand scenes, or picturesqueness. All felt the sadness of the hour, and the importance of our mission.

We had not gone far when rang into the silent air: "Stop! rails spread!" On went the brake like a flash, and every man had to get off the car, and by much trouble the damaged rails were passed, and again we went on our way; and soon "Burned culvert," was the cry; and we not only had to get off the car, but to unload it and carry the goods over, as well as the car. Not a man shirked his share of the work. Every one took hold with a will. Few words well ordered action, and in the course of half an hour all was ready to proceed.

Now, it was needful to have some one walk ahead with a lantern.

Dr. Kelsey, Brook Park.   Alderman De Leo, St. Cloud.

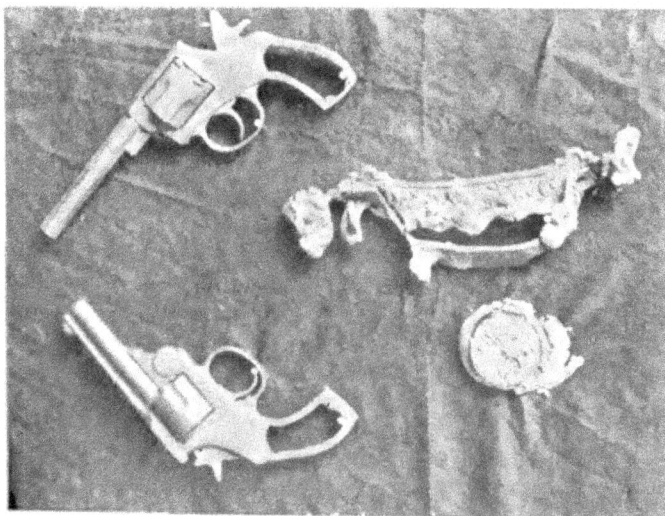

Relics from the Fire.

All offered to do this. Dr. Higgins took his first turn. The rails were terribly warped, and in many places the atmosphere was stifling, a peculiar thing being, that the density of the smoke in the air was like streaks of fat and lean in bacon—now dense, then clear. At last we came to a place where nature and destiny appeared to say: "Gentlemen, so far you may come; farther you shall not, with that hand car, go!" The culvert—if it could be called one—I should call it a bridge, was long and high. In the bottom was burning earth. One said: "This is a terror! We shall find it hard to get over this place even a-foot!" In the hour last passed quite a little wind had begun to blow, and the whole surrounding country was like a fairy creation; flames of all sizes, and burning embers of all kinds could be seen. The moment the peat was reached and a man's foot placed upon it, the danger was manifest. We held a short council of war. One gentleman said: "There is not more than two or three yards of smoldering fire between us and firm ground. The shovels we brought are made for such a time as this." In a trice those shovels were throwing the burning earth to the winds. We carried all the blankets over the path thus made; the tents and all our food also; then took in hand the car. It ran down the slope, I thought, beautifully. At the bottom it came to a sudden stop, and so did those who had to carry it up, often before they got it to the top. It seemed to weigh a ton; the hill was very steep, the ground very hot, and the air full of hot, flying ashes. Resolution never failed; at last the railway track was reached and all were thankful.

The journey was continued, and we reached the burned bridge at Brook Park after twelve o'clock, so it was, in fact, Tuesday morning when we got there. We had to leave the car at this place and go on foot up the line. We found the two cars and the people who had been through the fire, and also the St. Cloud working men. It was a time of joy. Dr. Kelsey, who was reported dead, was alive, but had a burned face and sore eyes. We distributed the blankets, which the people needed, said our prayers and lay down on the floor of a box car till five o'clock, when we all got up.

There was no stove or fireplace nearer than Mora, eight miles away; but the people of St. Cloud had thoughtfully brought kettles and frying pans, knives, forks and spoons, bread, coffee, tea, condensed Swiss milk, eggs, bacon, beef and other things. We had no table. We made a fire in the open air and prepared breakfast.

There was little style at Brook Park during the first week of September, but what was lacking in style was made up in appetite; and there was plenty of good living and good fellowship.

On that day and the next we found seventeen dead. In several cases we had to carry heavy wooden boxes long distances in which to put the dead.

The settlers, the St. Cloud men, the party who came on the hand car and Mr. Barnes, a divinity student, who preached at Milaca, all did their best. Not one of the dead had a vestige of clothing upon them; all were sadly disfigured. Many could not be recognized, except by circumstantial evidence. Twenty-three are known to be dead. I saw the bodies of nineteen, only one of which I could have identified, no matter how well I had known the departed. All the dead buried at Brook Park that were found were placed in graves on Molander's farm. Several bodies were sent away for burial.

The Rev. Mr. Fosbroke read a part of the service at several of the funerals. I took charge of the funerals in so far as the church service was concerned, and gave an address at each and all. Over each grave was placed a cross made of wood, and upon it was written the name of the dead who rests beneath.

On Tuesday, September fourth, in the morning search for the dead, we passed twenty-nine dead cows, oxen and horses. These were later burned under piles of charred pine, gathered from the course of the fire. One of the latest bodies found was that of Mr. Jaw W. Braman, who was twenty-seven years old, and was at the time of the fire with his father hauling hay. They were driving to Brook Park from north of the town, when the father said: "The fire is upon us; the hay will soon be ablaze. Let us leave the horses and wagon, and escape for our lives!" he son replied: "Father, you go; I can make a place of safety; you look out for yourself."

Vain hope! Mr. Braman made for the pool of water in the shadow of the railway embankment, near the bridge, where more than thirty people were saved. See photograph.

On Wednesday, September fifth, I was out with a searching party. We found the tires of the burned wagon, part of the harness, remnants of the team driven by the Bramans on their ill fated journey; not far from these the charred bodies of the two horses, burned almost past recognition; and near, the young man lay in the stillness of death. He had evidently unhitched the horses to give them a chance for their lives, and in doing this had stayed too long and sacrificed his own life. He was the only son of his mother, a good young man, her comfort and hope. His body was that day buried on F. Molander's farm. I read the service of the book of common prayer over it, gave an address, and marked the spot with a wooden cross inscribed with his name. Later his remains were removed to the new burial ground in the cemetery. I was present at the re-interment. This was the first body placed in God's acre at Brook Park. When this funeral took place, the sun was shining, the settlers stood around—all sad at this death, sad at the knowledge of their own great losses, and desolate prospects. Willing hands had dug this grave; around it stood Mrs. Nelson and her family, the Kelseys, the Wards, the Frames, Mr. Racine, the Johnsons, John Powers, who had distinguished himself at a time when all men and women had done their very best. No work was too disagreeable or too difficult for John. He had put bodies long dead into coffins; helped to dig graves and had done all love could prompt a man to do.

This burial scene was one to captivate the mind of an artist, who desires to portray love and service, life and death in their very best forms.

On this day, October seventeenth, Fred Molander was found in a well, but in such a state that those who knew him in life knew him just as well in death. This well was thought to be empty, at the time of the fire, and when looked into from the top, appeared to be covered with cinders and ashes and to contain nothing more. When Frank Lepingarver went to rebuild on his land, which is near that upon which Fred Molander resided, and went down into Molander's well to clean it out, to his surprise he found six feet of water, and the body of Molander. He quickly came to the top and reported the facts.

Dr. Kelsey, W. W. Braman, John Powers, David Frame and others went to the well, taking a box which had been made by the St. Cloud men, and left to use in the event of finding any more dead. Dr. Kelsey descended the well, fastened a rope about the body, by which it was lifted to the surface, where it was reverently placed in the box, conveyed to the grave left vacant by the removal of Jay Braman's remains, and buried there. I was present here also, read the church service and gave an address. This was the last

VANDERLUCE, NEWS AGENT, ST. CLOUD.

NORMAN E. WILKINSON.

NORTH MINNESOTA BEFORE THE FIRE.

body found. Fred Molander rests in his own inheritance;that is to say, in the land upon which he lived.

He had been in the well from September first until October seventeenth following, being the same date upon which the re-interment of Jay Braman took place.

At Brook Park, there were many striking scenes at the time of the fire, and many wonderful escapes. The fire came from Quagma, and began at the north end of the railway switch at that place; coming north to Brook Park, it swept away in its hot flames everything burnable in its path.

The people made as quickly as possible for places they thought would hide them from the storm.

C. W. Kelsey and his wife, author of "The September Holocaust," and their children got into a well. They had a blanket which they kept wet. Mrs. Kelsey is a God fearing woman, and an old fashioned believer in Providence. Mr. Kelsey stood on a ladder in the well. They could hear the roar of the fire: the smoke was dense, and they knew the destruction raging all around, and that if spared at all, all they would have left would be their family. The children cried; their mother comforted them with: "Don't cry, Earl, God will take care of us!" And so He did. "Madie, what is the matter? Don't faint; you will fall into the water! Allen, give your sister a drink." The little boy Earl began to talk in his childish way: "We will go to hebben," said he. Mr. Kelsey replied, "We must pray to God to save us; our house is on fire."

The heat was nearly unbearable, but the water in the well helped them to endure it. The wind took the flames from the house away from the well.

The mother said: "Let us sing." And the two older children joined their mother in singing sweetly,

> "Jesus loves me; He who died
> Heaven's gate to open wide:
> He will wash away my sin;
> Let His little child come in."

Could anything be more beautiful than this? It was from this well which had become holy ground, that this family came, only to witness such desolation as few people ever beheld.

It was now that the work of reconstruction had to begin in earnest. The living cannot forever dwell upon the dead; life hath its active duties, which no disaster can put an end to, and the dwellers at Brook Park looked those duties fairly in the face. They examined the damage done by the fire, and asked, "What can we do and how can we best do it, to repair the loss?" The many friends of the residents came with words of cheer and generous deeds of help from Stillwater, sent words which brought joy to the hearts of the settlers, and substantial aid also. From Mrs. W. C. Kelsey's brother, Dr. Allen, in Cloquet, came men and material to build for her a new house, much better than the one burned. This he gave them with a most cheerful will. The state commission offered to help the settlers to a new start. They placed Norman E. Wilkinson in charge as their representative. Careful inquiry was made into every man's loss, and present need. The Kelsey, Markham Company gave to each man, for whom the state commission built a house, two acres of land, so that every family stands in the position of having a good house and a garden, all free from debt, and the land adjoining it in such a state that as much can be cleared this year as could have been cleared in four, before the fire.

Many persons sent help in various ways, which did not go through the hands of the state relief commission. Mr. George D. Turner, of Minneapolis, who was for years engaged in the lumber trade on Kettle river, sent a car which contained many tools and things used in farming, to Brook Park. In this way and by the skill of experienced heads and the deftness of willing hands the conditions in eight months since the fire have been rapidly changed and all are full of confidence and zeal. There are many who think that except for the sacrifice of life, that which at first looked so awful and such a terrible calamity, will be a means of stimulating the progress and growth of Pine county, in which Brook Park is located, by leaps and bounds.

What Dr. C. A. Kelsey says:

The first settler went to Brook Park in 1893. Amongst them William Thomson, James Riley, James Smith, Joseph Coblin. When I went to live there in June of 1894, there were one hundred and thirty-five persons in the settlement. All through the month of August these fires had burned south and west of us. On the day of the great fire the wind blew a gale from the southwest and swept the fire, which seemed formed in a line about three miles long, over the town. The buildings in Brook Park at this time, belonged to Messrs. Rafel, Johnson, Supero, Missel, Hans Nelson, A. Berg

(store building), a boarding house owned by Bousher and Racine,
Ward, Thompson, Collier, Anderson, Raymond, C. W. Kelsey,
Whitney, Goodsell, C. H. Ward, W. W. Brenman and myself. The
fire came from the southwest and proceeded toward Hinckley, and
I suppose it was the same fire that burned Hinckley and that country, for it was about two o'clock when it reached us, and it struck
Hinckley about four, giving it time to travel about that distance.
It would be interesting to call attention to the fact that on a clear
day a fire that is a long distance off appears to be very near. When
the fires first began, they were burning all around the country. I
was greatly alarmed one day by a fire which appeared to be very
near us, but upon investigation proved to be about six miles away.
The day of the great fire the atmosphere was filled with smoke, but
none were aware of their danger until it was upon them. The
question among the people was "Is there danger?" One was running to the other asking, "Where is the fire?" and no one seemed
to be able to answer the question. The people gathered together
near the Pokegama creek. My own family, a short time before the
fire, was scattered, one little boy having gone to the store and another unloading lath; but a few minutes before the fire came, we
were altogether in our home. Mrs. Kelsey's first impression was
to go to the boarding house to see if there was danger, but after
leaving the house she went up through the garden toward the mill.
This proved providential, for had she gone by the school house,
she would probably have been in danger, for it was bursting into
flames by the time she would have been near it. Upon reaching
the railroad she first thought that the greatest safety would be to
go down the railroad track. Some influence changed this impression and she turned and went toward the mill and arrived on the
banks of the creek just in time to save herself and the children by
getting into the water, where she found the majority of the neighbors. They were in a small pond near the railroad bridge.

The fire swept in through the old logging dam, setting fire to a
pile of edgings which had been dumped over a steep bank by the
mill company. This made an intense heat which drove them to
the opposite side of the pond, a distance of about 100 feet. The
next great heat came from the burning section house and lumber
yard, to the east of them. When this in a measure had subsided
the railroad bridge took fire. This increased their danger, for had
it fallen toward the people, it would have placed them in great peril.

They moved as far away as they could and watched the burning structure, which fortunately did not fall toward them. This little pond was about fifteen feet deep in the center, allowing only the edges to be used by the people, and the danger was increasd by getting beyond their depth in the water. The people huddled together, giving such assistance to each other as neighbors could under the circumstances, throwing water upon each other and assisting in care of the children. The heat was so intense they were obliged to stand in the water and barely leave their mouths and noses exposed so as to breathe, and were obliged to keep their heads constantly wet.

Among others was Mrs. Collier, whose baby was only three weeks old. The little one came through bravely, and seemed as happy after the experience as though nothing had happenede.

The people were kept in this pond by the heat from two until six o'clock in the afternoon.

By six o'clock Mr. Ward had explored up the track and found two box cars, untouched by the fire, that had been left that afternoon. One was loaded with brick and the other with lath. They were directly opposite a piece of land whach had been burned clear, and so nothing was left upon it to be burned and they thus escaped. A part of our people went immediately to these cars for shelter. Quite a number of people were in these cars for two nights, without any change of clothing after coming out of the water.

Our breakfast Sunday morning after the fire, consisted of boiled potatoes without any salt, and roasted eggs which were found where two cases had been unloaded the day of the fire. The boxes were burned and some of the eggs, but some in the inside were nicely roasted.

Sunday afternoon the good people of Mora came to us upon two hand cars. They immediately returned bringing to us a supply of food, but they were unable to bring bedding, so that the second night was spent without bedding, and the people slept upon piles of lath or brick.

Monday afternoon the relief train from St. Cloud reached us, bringing a supply of food sufficient to satisfy all our wants, and a train load of kind hearted people who were anxious and glad to do all in their power to add to our relief.

Monday night a party consisting of Rev. Wilkinson, of Minneapolis, B. J. Kelsey, from Kenyon, Dr. C. W. Higgins, from Minneapolis, Dr. Allen, from Cloquet, and J. D. Markham reached us on a hand car, by way of Hinckley, after exposing themselves to great danger of being dashed to pieces by being precipitated into some of the creeks where the bridges were burned, in the darkness of the night, and after carrying their hand car and its contents around these burned bridges, in some instances being obliged to shovel the burning earth to make a path through. They brought with them a supply of blankets, the first we had received, medicines, bandages, food and tools, and still more, kind hearts and willing hands to assist us. Rev. Wilkinson remained with us after the remainder of the party had returned to their homes, helping us to find our dead, pronouncing burial services, and with his own hands assisted us in burning up stock which had perished and was endangering our health, and in many other ways working heroically while offering us kind words of encouragement and sympathy.

Immediately after the fire nearly half of our settlers took the first train and their departure. This removed from us all of the timid ones and left with us a band with bravery and courage to stay and continue the development of our villages. They have all been enabled to remain through the kind assistance so nobly rendered by voluntary subscriptions, and the state assistance granted through the legislature, and wisely expended by able business men, who were willing to neglect their own business to superintend the disposal of the fund placed in their hand for our relief.

The terrible loss of our friends and neighbors, (twenty-three perished), can never be repaired. The destruction of timber was great, but the service rendered by the clearing of the land will result in a benefit in future development into a farming country, which will fully repay all financial losses. Since the fire twenty-four different families have purchased land, and have arranged or are arranging to make Brook Park their future home. The work of clearing up and making farms is progressing at a rapidity that surprises us. Some farmers will be able to put in forty acres of crops this year, providing the seed can be obtained. Our homes have been rebuilt, a school house erected, in which we are now having school, a Sunday school organized; and our ladies have gone to work to raise funds for the first payment on an organ which is now being used for the Sunday school and day school.

Our present settlement is one in which we take great pride, being composed of intelligent and energetic people. While laying

J. D. MARKHAM, BROOK PARK.

foundations for future prosperity, our numbers are being augmented constantly and the quality of the land, being a rich clay loam, naturally adapted to successful growth of all tame grass, and all crops usually raised in this latitude, and the reasonable price of land and favorable terms given by the land company of Kelsey & Markham, continue to bring rapidly, continuous additions to the settlement. Steps have been taken for the organization of a Baptist church, there being thirteen members now on the ground. Other religious denominations are well represented, but we all join heartily and pleasantly in the support of a union Sunday school. Thus we are working together, endeavoring to help each other in every way. I believe that the future development of the country will demonstrate that the expenditures made by the state in the way of furnishing seed and assistance to this farming community are wisely placed and will bring returns in the way of an increase of taxable property.

Mrs. Joseph Frame, her six children and husband and Mrs. W. M. Branman, were about three miles northwest, gathering cranberries at the time of the fire. The husband, becoming alarmed at the dense smoke for the safety of his hay which was in that vicinity, remained to care for it, while Mrs. Frame and her six children and Mrs. Branman started to return to the village. They were cut off by the fire, about a mile from the village, and took refuge first in an old cellar but the heat and smoke soon drove them from this, and they saved their lives by reaching the creek, which was near. The two ladies and six children spent the night in the creek, with only one blanket as protection, reaching the village the next morning. We were greatly alarmed for the safety of Mr. Frame, who had not yet returned, but our suspense was relieved by his reaching us the next Sunday after the fire. He had saved his life by getting on a piece of ground which had previously been burned over.

The two room school house which had been accepted the day of the fire, was burned. It cost $1,000.

In the village was a saw mill, owned by Baty & Semour, which had been erected in the spring. It cut 25,000 feet of lumber a day, purchasing the logs from the settlers.

The postmaster was Mr. Berg, who kept a store.

Mr. **Hans Nelson**, who lived here near the railroad track, was section master on the Great Northern line, and had four children. He lost his home and everything he had except his family.

Mr. Raymond, wife and three children; Chas. Anderson, wife and three children; Fred Molander, wife and two children and the wife's brother and sister, were all found dead.

The fire started three miles southwest of Brook Park.

John Powers, William Thompson and Frank Lepengarver were about two miles south, cutting hay. They saved their lives by getting in the center of the meadow, back firing and covering themselves with wet horse blankets. Mr. Powers heroically declined to turn his horses loose and saved them also, by covering their heads with wet blankets. After the intense heat had subsided Mr. Powers groped his way through the smoke about five rods to the creek for a pail of water; when coming up from the bank, he put his hand, in the darkness and the smoke, upon a deer, which, instead of fleeing from him with fear, followed him to the center of the meadow and stayed some little time near them.

Mr. John Gonya, Joe Chipris, and M. C. Anderson were with me a mile and a half northwest of the village, endeavoring to save Chas. Collier's building. We felt safe from the fact that there was a large potato patch south of the house, in which we could take refuge if the house burned, but when the fire reached us, the heat was so great that it drove us immediately to the sheltering side of the house, and to our dismay the entire house immediately burst into flames. We jumped into tubs of water, filled our shoes, wet our clothing, and made a dash, during the first ten rods of which, the heat was so intense that it seemed almost impossible for us to breathe and live to get through it. From this time on the heat and smoke continued to be almost unbearable. The road led through green tamaracks, which we felt certain would not burn, but upon reaching them, we found to our horror that they were in flames. Trees had fallen across our road, through the burning tops of which we were obliged to clamber as fast as we could. While in the midst of this, we became so exhausted we had to lie down, burying our faces in our hands, close to the ground in the water to breathe. Soon after starting from our rest, I fell and was passed by Mr. Anderson and Mr. Gonya, who I insisted should go on and save themselves, leaving Joe Chipris and myself. After resting and proceeding a short distance farther, Mr. Chipris became so exhausted he could not go on, but by words of encouragement, he continued for a short distance, and then insisted he could not go another step. I gave him my hand, saying we would stay together and that we would yet come out all right, as we were nearly through with the smoke, and I felt certain that upon reaching the green meadow, a short distance ahead, we could lie down and get our breath. As we emerged from the smoke on to the meadow, we could see nothing but smoke and flames burning as far as the eye could see. Feeling it would be impossible for us to save ourselves by continuing in that direction we turned at a right angle to the west, and reached the creek, where we dropped down and found to our intense relief that the heat and smoke was not so overpowering but that we could breathe. We remained in the creek bed until nearly night, and reached the village about half past ten, yet found no village there, but our families saved in the box cars before mentioned. Messrs. Gonya and Collier made the run of a mile and a half through a continuous line of fire, but were terribly burned, Mr. Gonya being in the St. Cloud hospital several months before he was able to walk, owing to the dreadful burns on his feet. When near the pond they became separated. Mr. Gonya saved himself by reaching a moist piece of ground, into which he, as much as possible, buried himself in the water. Mr. Collier succeeded in reaching the pond to the intense relief of his wife and mother who were there.

The fallen trees fell to the northeast from the southwest, and the green saplings were bent nearly to th ground by the wind, and were fixed in that position by the heat, thus giving positive evidence remaining after the fire that it came from the southwest to the northeast.

Rev. Wilkinson was subsequently appointed by the commission to look specially to the needs of Brook Park. His assistance, and that of his son, Norman, have been of great value to us, and their kindess and self sacrifice will ever be remembered by our people with feelings of deep gratitude. They have assisted us in many ways and have brought much elp to us by their personal efforts, entirely independent of the state commission.

End of Brook Park

It was found that the section lines had been destroyed by the fire, and the city engineer of Minneapolis, Mr. F. W. Cappelen, kindly sent one of his most competent assistants to run new lines. This Mr. David H. Forneri did with accuracy. He stayed nearly a week at Brook Park and did good work.

HINCKLEY REBUILT.—From a Photo by Miller.

HINCKLEY.

IT IS often thought in Europe, and possibly other places, that new Western towns are rough, that the dollar is the principal thing. Hinckley was a typical place, and it may be well to give an idea of how the town looked before September last. It had a public school, in which were four teachers. Mr. D. S. Collins was principal, assisted by Miss Vaughan, Miss Maggie Hawley and Miss Craig. There was a town hall, Odd Fellows' hall, three churches, five hotels, eight stores, and restaurant, two railway depots and a railway round house. Which shows that neither culture nor religion had geen forgotten. The saw mill would cut two hundred thousand feet of lumber a day. Mr. John Owen was president of the mill company, H. D. Davis vice president, Mr. Putnam, treasurer, Mr. E. B. Putnam, secretary. The postmaster was Mr. P. Lawless.

Its town officials were as follows: Le Webster, mayor, John K. Anderson, Nels Parsons and John Merrigan, trustees; Andrew Stone, recorder, S. W. Anderson, treasurer, and R. J. Hawley, policeman.

Hinckley was one of the lumbering towns in the county of Pine, and had last year more than twelve hundred people. The St. Paul and Duluth railway, and the Great Northern railway both go through it, each had helped in the development of the town. Grindstone river has its rise in the Grindstone lake, and flows through Hinckley. The mill, which was a large one, employed in various ways about three hundred persons, and this industry brought money into the pockets of Hinckley people.

For years Pine county had been renowned for its timber and kings in the lumber business had operated here and in the surrounding county. The Brennan Mill Company is know all over the west for their operations here. Geo. N. Turner, Minneapolis, in years gone by, cut large quantities of logs in this locality and on land adjacent to Kettle river.

The Lairds and Nortons of Winona, the Staples of Stillwater, and many others, all had had large interests in the fire district. It is

7. HINCKLEY — THE SAND PIT WHERE MANY FOUND SHELTER

said that one firm in the first week in September, had a loss in damage to its standing pine of three hundred thousand dollars. The loss total in the period covered by the fire and the time of reconstruction was not less than three million dollars. It may have been much more.

There is something in different localities, both in sea and land, which man has not been able satisfactorily to explain. Why a tree, or a certain kind of trees, will grow and flourish in great luxuriance in one part of a state, and will not grow to be of any account in others parts of the same state, is not easy to understand. See map showing the pine region of Minnesota. This map was made by the geological survey, and kindly lent me by my friend Mr. Beals, who has charge of the weather reports in the northwest. A glance at this map will show how an all wise God has designed northern Minnesota, by nature, to grow pine, and this it does in great plenty. The lines marked show that in the south of the state pine does not naturally grow. Left alone, the north will be covered with pine, while other parts of the state will have no pine worth speaking about, and if any, it will be poor and stunted. The curious may find things analogous to this in the sea. There have been in this age few more observant men than that prince of naturalists Frank Buckland, in his "Curiosities of Natural History," second series, page 295, says: "As my readers are probably aware, the great sperm or spermaceti whale is found south of the equator only, and according to Maury's 'Physical Geography of the Sea,' there is a line (marked in his map) across which ths sperm whale cannot pass. Nevertheless, I have a well authenticated case of a sperm whale (phycester macrocephalus) appearing in the Bristol channel. I have also a good engraving of a whale which was cast ashore near Antwerp, A. D. 1576. This creature is also a large sperm whale." So we see whales now and then are found out of their natural home; so are pine trees.

Hinckley is in the geographical situation where pine is at its best, best for all purposes for which pine may be used, and so when found in large quantities and gets on fire, the heat is intense.

All round Hinckley, the woods were as dry as a kiln, and ready for one terrible bonfire, which came, driven by a fierce wind; no power wielded by man could by any possibility have stopped it in its onward course to and past Hinckley. The danger of fire had been long seen and warning had been given of possible damage to the town.

The inhabitants had come to think that no danger was at hand, but on Saturday, September first, the fire reached Mission Creek and swept onwards toward the north. By the time it had followed the direction of the St. Paul and Duluth railway tracks to the Great Northern tracks at Hinckley, nothing but certain doom was in store for Hinckley; every intelligent man in the place saw and felt this. It is as possible to stop the Gulf stream, or an eruption from Mount Vesuvius as it would have been to stop the fire.

It was the fire then from Mission Creek direction, which struck Hinckley, and everything found to burn added to the heat of the flames and air. Soon the fire which had laid Brook Park in ashes joined the fire which at Hinckley had laid that town in ashes, in one avalanche of flame, wind, heat and storm, all of which did their death dealing and destructive work. The depots, hotels, the city public buildings, schools, etc., simply melted down in a few moments and kegs of nails which had been on sale in hardware stores, were found one melted mass. The earth and air, the very heavens above men's heads appeared to be on fire; it was only in flight, water, or on the train that escape could be looked for; and how little flight could help many is to be read in the ghastly finding of the dead, and in the sights and sounds which made strong men weep and women faint. On the Monday after the fire, all day long, Mr. Webber, of Rush City, with a band of helpers, dug trenches and placed in them the dead. More than one hundred that day were laid thus to rest.

Mr. Chris Best, who still lives at Hinckley, lost his father, mother, sister and brother, a nephew and niece, and with his own hands dug one large grave, all the while speaking not one word. He was alone on one side of the cemetery, all available men being at work in the long trench, and each man intent either upon the sorrows of others or of his own. I found two men to take up the work Best was doing and offered to pay them. They said, "We should despise ourselves if we took pay to help this man." The hot scalding tears ran down his face. For weeks he looked for his brother whom he hoped to find. Alas! No such providence for him could be, as without a doubt he was amongst the unknowable dead. Seven persons of the name of Best met death. C. Best escaped to tell in part the story, and to his latest day mourn the loss.

It was in this cemetery on that Monday night, when the blackened bodies were being brought in on wagons that Rev. Feethan, M. E. minister, Rev. Mr. Peterson, Rev. Mr. Knudsen, Rev. Father Burke, Rev. Father Bajec and the writer all joined as one in the common grief with one common purpose. The Bible was read, prayer offered and an address given. Not a word was spoken which could jar on the mind of any reverent man. This beautifully shows how much religionists of all names have in their great heritage of faith, hope and love, and it furthers the ends of Christian charity. One touch of nature makes the world akin. Sorrow, pain and death were not invented by priests, nor by atheists, and they cannot be prevented by either or by both.

Death speaks all languages; it comes and brings sorrow into the souls of the bereaved, no matter what their faith or lack of faith. In this dark day, when the Methodist minister said, "Lord bless us in our deep sorrow," the Roman priest said, "Amen," when the Presbyterian read "Now is Christ risen from the dead," and went on to say "Death shall be swallowed up in victory," every heart felt the need of this. When the Angelican minister, at the close of his address said,

> "The sky is flushed with gold,
>   In glad celestial warning,
> The purple clouds are backward rolled,
>   All gloom and shadows scorning.
> O'er pain and grief victorious
> Above all glories, glorious,
> There comes an Eastern morning."

every heart replied through tears that ought to be true. We turned away from these scenes and walked in different directions. Joseph Manix, of Minneapolis, and I walked to a grave where were being laid Mrs. Martinson and her four children. Her husband and little son stood by. The lad told his experience at the Grindstone river. John is a bright lad about eleven years old. He with his mother and four other children were in the river, and he someway got to the gravel pit, after he had seen the other members of his family fall in the river. John said: "I was in the river with my sister. I could swim well. I used to go swimming nearly every day. She said, 'Come, hold me up.' The heat was so great I could not get to her. She fell in the water. My mother was with us. Someone said, 'Go to the pit.' I do not know how I got there. I was saved, they died."

REV. P. KNUDSEN.

MRS P. KNUDSEN.

I gave a Swedish Bible to Martinson, which had been found by me. It was partly burned. Afterwards I tried to buy it to give to the Minneapolis Public Library, he set too much store by it to let it go. The gravel pit has a history. Before the fire the Great Northern railway needed to fill in a long piece of ground to level their track, and dug this pit, which is over three acres in extent. The dwellers at Hinckley ever since have said it was a damage to their town, and ought never to have been made. Some of the people who had often said this found it a place of refuge from the fire, and thus saved their lives; so little do men know what may be of the greatest use to them. We passed the gravel pit on our way to the railway, in the early evening, where I met the gntlemen who were going to Brook Park on the hand car, joined them and did not return till the Friday after.

The Rev. Father Lawler is a Master of Arts and a Bachelor of Science. He is a Roman Catholic priest in the burned district, which is in the diocese of Duluth, of which James McGolrick is bishop. It is one of the five dioceses forming the archdiocese of St. Paul, over which John Ireland presides as archbishop, thus being the metropolitan.

Father Lawler had services at Mission Creek and at Sandstone. By his diligence and faithfulness, by minding his own business and doing good as he had opportunity, he had gained the respect and lived in the love of all sorts and conditions of men. Ever since he went to Hinckley he had taken an active interest in all that concerns the public good of that place. The fire department had been an object of his special attention, he knew perfectly its workings, its available power and its needs. It is well known that the alarm bell never rung when he was in town but he promptly answered it.

On September first, just after noon, the gong was rung, which meant that the firemen were to meet at the engine house. Promptly that call was answered, and Father Lawler was as usual on hand. The chief said, "It looks threatening in the south and in the southwest. I do not think there is any danger, but it is well to be prepared for an emergency." And it was decided that if the fire came, it would come by way of Mission Creek, along the St. Paul and Duluth road, cross the Eastern Minnesota tracks and then strike the town. It was agreed that the place to stop the fire if it should come, was at this point.

The fire came. All was in readiness; the entire available force of the town concentrated here. The wind blew so strong that it was impossible to throw water any considerable distance against it.

Father Lawler saw that Hinckley was doomed. He said, "Escape for your lives, Hinckley will be destroyed!" He ran toward the town, and on his way he came to a number of of men who were hitching up teams. He said, "For heaven's sake, leave all you have! Get to the gravel pit, run to the river! Hinckley will be destroyed!" One man, in his excitement, said what in other times he probably would not have spoken, "To hell with advice of that sort!" Not one of that party who took the old post road to Sandstone are known to have escaped. The priest ran on shouting as did Jonah in Nineveh of old, "The city will be destroyed! Escape for your lives! Run to the gravel pit; run to the river! Leave all you have, save your lives!"

Had it not been for this thoughtfulness, the loss of life, great as it was, would have been greater. The people, hearing the priest and knowing who he was, as fast as possible gave heed to his warning; and soon mothers with their little children were hurrying to a place of safety. Having warned all he could of danger and directed them to places of safety, and being nearly exhausted, (he was just recovering from a severe attack of typhoid fever), and almost blind with the smoke, having done al lhe could, he himself got to the river, where he stayed until the relief party came.

Such words and such deeds require no comment; they tell their own story.

THE REV. PETER KNUDSEN.

The Rev. Mr. Knudsen was a Presbyterian minister of the church in Hinckley, who did missionary work in all the country round. He is a Dane by birth. On the day of the fire he saw the danger coming, but had no idea that the disaster would be as great as the fact have proved.

Grindstone river has its rise in Grindstone lake, and flows from east to west. A little north of the town of Hinckley two railroad bridges span this river. One is on the St. Paul and Duluth road and is north-west of the town, the other is on the Eastern Minnesota railway and is north-east of the town. Between the two railway bridges, is another bridge over which foot passengers and teams cross. It was over this bridge that so many persons sought safety in flight. Here they crossed, alas, never to return. Death overtook them before they could reach a place of safety. Grindstone river is shallow, being from eighteen inches to perhaps five feet deep, and many who sought safety in its shelter lost their lives. Near to the Eastern railway was an open space in which many persons took refuge. In ordinary forest fires, it would have been a wise thing to do, and they would have saved their lives; but in this fire, the heat of which in some parts of the Eastern railway yards at Hinckley was sufficiently fierce to melt steel, open places were of no avail. Ninety persons, on and near this spot, laid down their lives.

It was a hurricane of fire which swept up from Mission Creek and Brook Park, eight miles away, and the fire had gained great strength before it burned Brook Park, having come from the south several miles ere it reached that fated town. At Hinckley, the current of fire was met by another which was probably as strong, which had swept up from Mission Creek, when the two forces joined, having traveled on two sides of a triangle to a point.

Nothing in the town of Hinckley escaped, except a little closet north of the Eastern tracks, not far from the round house, the round house itself and the water tank. They were standing in the yards where were a number of cars which were filled with wheat. These all took fire. So great was the heat two hundred paces north of the round house, that the rails and steel wheels of the cars were melted and some of them ran liquid steel.

It was near this spot that the freight train, going north, and the passenger train, going south, met. This (passenger) train was run by conductor H. L. Powers, W. B. Best, being engineer, Geo. J. Ford fireman, and C. Beach, brakeman. Freight train No. 23, going north to Duluth, was run by Conductor W. D. Campbell, Edward Barry was engineer, A. R. Thistle fireman, Charles C. Freeman, G. W. Gilham and A. McLaughlin, brakemen.

Several merchandise cars were standing on the track, which were then coupled to the passenger train. Best was not in front of the train. Best had taken in water at the water tank and, backing to the train, was in its rear.

It is one of the rules of the service on the Eastern Minnesota road, that when difficulties arise, if two train crews have to join forces, the conductor of greater rank assumes charge, direction and hence responsibility, which is shared by the engineers and the other conductors. It was in this way that Conductor Powers became the man in authority on this mixed train, but it must not be forgotten that these crews had an exceedingly difficult and dangerous task in a

Round House and Water Tank at Hinckley.

time of high excitement, with the forests burning north and west, and everything in that part of the country burned south and west, and the wind blowing a gale, and the north, the only way of escape, and that likely to be cut off in an incredibly short time, the flames south seeming to reach to the heavers, the smoke increasing every moment, and burnig brands being carried through the air and showers of hot cinders falling; surrounded by men, women and children, some of whom were almost frantic, many in great desperation, others who felt that the last hours had come. These men required not alone strong nerve, they needed a clear eye, firm purpose and unerring judgment, which should inform them how long to stay so as to save the largest possible number of lives. Events proved that these two crews were equal to the occasion. It may be safely said that if the days of mystics are passed, the days of heroism are indeed here. All this speaks well for the discipline and exact direction upon the Eastern Minnesota railway, that no fatality occurred at that time and place.

The old Hebrew prophet said, "The lame shall take the prey." It is singular, yet well attested, that the first man who got on board this historic train was Mr. Hogan, well known in Hinckley as the man who wheels himself about in his chair, being paralyzed. He had seen the danger—living near the tracks—and his brother, seeing him in his chair, carried him to the train. Hogan's mother, running to the train, saw her son's chair and pulled it along with her, and the train men, with that sympathy which always goes out to the helpless, put it on board. He has it now and nothing in the world could be more useful to him.

The last man who got on this train was Mr. Douglas Greeley. It will stand as one of the brightest facts in connection with all this disastrous fire that four hundred and seventy-six souls were saved. The work of Best and Barry has been told in glowing words. There were two men whose names have been little heard, who deserve to be held in honor. Their names are O. L. Beach and Peter McLaughlin, brakemen. There was no headlight in the front of the tender of this train, and these men stood on the tender, each with a lantern, their eyes almost blinded, the heat intense, the danger of death imminent, and the knowledge of that fact in their minds was clearly defined. Never for an instant did they falter, duty with them was supreme, and no small share of triumph of that fateful day, belongs to them.

Ford, Thistle, Gilham, and Campbell all deserve the admiration of high minded men. Mr. Best is not only a prudent, fearless, cool headed man, but he is one of the most accomplished engineers in America. His skill is well known and generally acknowledged in the railway world of the Northwest.

Powers, the conductor, has long been in the employ of the Eastern road and by the authorities is highly respected. On the testimony of competent judges, he displayed rare qualities in this fire. It is the opinion of Judge Geo. B. Young, St. Paul, and District Judge Seagrave Smith, and J. Jamison, of Hennepin district court, who were going from Duluth to Minneapolis on his train, that he acted a noble part; never for an instant did he lose his self possession. He advised every one to keep perfectly cool; saw nothing but harm could come of excitement; helped the people onto the train; kindly but firmly refused to delay for a moment to take baggage on board; said to women who frantically demanded delay that they might secure some household goods, "Mrs. we cannot wait for that baggage. We will gladly take you, get on board. It is your only chance. Lifted the children on board with the deftness and tenderness equal to that of a mother's love.

It was in recognition of this service that Mr. Samuel Hill, president of the Eastern road, gave to Mr. Powers a gold watch such as few railroad presidents carry, inscribed as follows: "Presented to H. D. Powers for his heroism on September first, 1894." On the tenth day of that month, the Minneapolis Times had the following:

CONDUCTOR POWERS.

Entitled to Great Credit for His Actions at the Hinckley Fire.

An eye witness of the scene at Hinckley describes it as follows:

"To understand the situation," he began yesterday, "one must know of the exact movement of the trains at Hinckley on the fateful day. The passenger, consisting of six coaches containing the steamship passengers from the Northwest, pulled into Hinckley at 3:30 Saturday afternoon. The fire was then raging in the east end of the Hinckley freight yard and a switchman reported the fact to Conductor Powers. On a side track, with the engine at the farther end of the train consisting of three freight cars and a caboose, stood the freight train, the locomotive in charge of Engineer Barry and the train controlled by Conductor W. D. Campbell. The engine was headed down, but had the right of way over the track towards Duluth. Conductor Powers recognizing this fact, decided upon a coup to se- cure the right of way back to Duluth for the passenger, as well as the freight. He was the conductor in authority and he ordered Con- ductor Campbell of the freight to couple the two trains together. This was done, but by this time, the smoke had become blinding and the fire was making rapid headway toward the train. Engineer Barry whistled to back up, but Conductor Powers would not permit him to do so, and the train remained in the yard at Hinckley until the bridge over the Sandstone river caught fire and escape was nearly cut off. Then it was that Conductor Powers ordered the train back towards Duluth, but by this time many of the Hinckley refugees had gone on board. On the other side of the creek it was stopped again and more persons were taken aboard, the total number saved being 478. Brakeman Freeman, of the freight, acted in an heroic manner by stopping the train by means of the air brake when it was started once, through a misunderstanding of the signals. Brakeman Beach was the man who rode on the rear end of the locomotive when it was backed towards Duluth, at the imminent peril of his life."

The train stopped long enough at Hinckley to take all who could get to it. It departed at the last moment it could have left safely. There were not a few on board who blamed the train men for stay- ing so long. Experience of danger of many kinds in long years of service, had taught them what was wise to do and how to do it. It must be a great satisfaction to everyone on board that train to feel that none were left behind, who possibly could have been saved.

Pastor Knudsen, a Dane by birth, and a Presbyterian by convic- tion, the minister in charge of the church at Hinckley and missionary to the districts round, with his wife, did remarkable service this September day. It is not without deep meaning that a man like Father Lawler, Roman Catholic priest, said to me, "Pastor Knudsen is a royal man. I firmly believe that he would lay down his life to serve another, without a thought that such a deed deserved any special credit." He and his wife stood together when the fire came towards Hinckley. "We are only two," said he (they have no family), "let us stand together and help these poor women with little children onto the train." They did so. The train was crowded, but there was room for this man and his wife. He said, "No, others are left in the village, we must go back if possible and help them to the gravel pit." And so the train moved through blinding smoke. They went their

ENGINEER WM. BEST.

FIREMAN FORD.

way toward the town. Twice she fell and then she said. "Let us lie down and die together here." Just then, through a rift in the smoke, she saw a wagon, and by one desperate effort crept under it. They were sheltered from the falling, burning cinders until the wagon took fire, when they crept to the gravel pit hard by. The owner of the wagon, his wife and several members of the family were burned to death.

The gravel pit is an excavation made by the Eastern Minnesota Railway when that road was built. To fill up the valley near Hinckley, they took the gravel and left a hole probably three acres in extent, in the bottom of which is said to be a spring. At the time of the fire there was about one acre of water. The people of Hinckley ever since the earth was taken from this spot, have said it disfigured and was an injury to the town. In the day of greatest stress, it was as the "shadow of a great rock in a weary land," it was a "shelter from the storm" of fire. Not one who got into it perished, and as if by unerring instinct, many animals sought shelter there and saved their lives. When the fire was passed, a tin pail was found at a water tank on the Eastern Railway. Mrs. Knudsen, like most Western missionary's wives, is a woman of practical sense; she milked a cow. A number of musk melons were found at the edge of the gravel pit. They cut the insides out and make cups and the children drank from them, the first food they had after the fire. Mr. Knudsen and his wife lost their home and all they had which could be lost; but hope, faith, love and character they did not lose. Their record is on high and their judgment is with the Almighty who does not forget the deeds of his servants.

The subjoined letter gives a good idea of several scenes through which the parties mentioned passed:

PINE CITY, MINN., Feb. 25, 1895.

Rev. William Wilkinson, Minneapolis, Minn.:

Dear Brother: Pardon my delay in answering yours of Feb. 7th. I have been away from home. The Methodist minister's name who took part in burying the dead at Hinckley, Monday, September 3d, is Rev. T. H. Feetham; at present he is in Duluth. I have asked the Reverends Peterson, Finstrom, and Father Bajec, of Rush City, to write you and send photographs. In explanation to your question concerning myself and wife, permit me to say. I found the watermelons in a garden just above the gravel pit and brought them with me down to the survivors in the pit. Some of the rinds were hollowed out and served for cups, out of which we drank water while in the pit. My wife milked the cow in a pail found in the Eastern Minnesota Railroad pumphouse, and the depot agent, Mr. George Turgeon held the cow while she did the milking, and together they carried the milk to the children and others. It would pay you for the trouble to come to Pine City some day and get the experience of the survivors that live here,—Messrs. Barden, Russell, Wright, Cameron, Wingren and others. Had I time I would write it up for you. Be kind enough to see that our names (my wife's and mine) are spelled right in your book. Yours, in great haste,

P. KNUDSEN.

P. S. The cow my wife milked belonged to Mr. Wingren.

REPORT OF J. W. STOCKHOLM.

I was working at the Brennan Lumber Company's store. We were engaged in supplying the teams with empty barrels, as all the teams were hauling water in barrels along the Snake River Road, intending to fight the fire back from the lumber yard and that part of the town. It was burning very badly in the west part of the town all the forenoon in the swamps. At 2:30 things began to look pretty bad, yet we did not think it serious.

I went to my home, one block east of the gravel pit and told my people to act quickly if it should come to look pretty bad, and have a few barrels of water ready if the fire should attack the fence from the woods. I went back to the store,—the way through the woods over the crossing of the St. Paul & Great Northern Railway. The wind commenced to blow very hard, and going along the way I could hardly keep my eyes open. Upon reaching the crossing, I commenced to realize to some extent that the town was in danger. The wind was still rising, bringing into my face a hot air like standing before a furnace. I turned back just as the Great Northern passenger train pulled into the yard by the pump house. I met Mr. Richner of the Eastern Hotel, and he said he thought the train would never get through. (That was the same train which later brought us out of the burning town). I went up town along the front street towards the store, meeting on my way the Brennan Company's typewriter, S. Mason, and Charles Anderson, bookkeeper of the Pine City Bank, who both perished near the St. Paul & Duluth depot. I met Widow Resbery and her four children. She asked me what to do and where to go. I told her to go toward my home, and as soon as I had been in the store I would follow up. I entered the store, Mr. Albricht, the bookkeeper, and I being the last of the employes left. We made up our minds the time had come to get out. I went out of the front door, finding Mrs. Resbery there yet where I had left her. I saw the time for argument was getting short, and at the same moment my nephew, Hans Hanson, from Chicago, a boy of sixteen years, visiting us at that time, came on his bicycle, telling us everything was taking fire over at my home, and to get over there as fast as possible. I then took Johnny Resbery, a boy of three, in my arms, told Hans to take the baby, and Oscar, a boy of eleven, and Mrs. Resbery and her daughter, a girl of nine, followed up, and we went toward the Eastern Depot, which is on the way toward my home.

Arriving there the people were crowding in to get on the train which had just pulled into the depot. Leaving the boy there, I went across the gravel pit to my home and found that my wife, three children and two sisters were not there. The fire was rolling over the place and I got out at once, and running back across the pit, inquired for my family and found out by Asel Hanson, who perished, that my wife was going north on the Great Northern tracks. Running after them, I got them turned back and calculated to go to the gravel pit. The wind was now blowing fearfully and the fire and cinders were blackening our faces, as we had to come back against coal. We backed up to Skunk lake, and just before I got to the Knudsen and Mrs. Knudsen.

We agreed to go to the pit, but at that time my people got so much ahead of me that they secured the first box car on the train on the Great Northern, which was then coming along side of the gravel pit. The train brought us safe to Duluth where we were all received with open arms, and all our needs supplied. If honor be due to any men who stand by their posts, firm and collected in the hour of danger, a goodly share is due the two crews of trainmen who took the refugees from the burning town of Hinckley to Duluth over the Great Northern Railway.

Mr. G. I. Albricht, who was bookkeper for the Brennan Lumber Company, says that he lived in Hinckley over five years.

"Three years ago there was talk about the possible burning of Hinckley, but all the summer of 1894 I never thought it probable that Hinckley would ever burn up, and not until after 3 p. m., on Satur-

day, September 1st, did I think for an instant that the town would go, although I sent my wife and two children to Pine City by the train which left Hinckley about 1 o'clock. I thought it would be better for them to go, lest the worst should happen.

At about 3, I looked south and west and saw the whole surroundings were terrible. The air grew hotter and dryer every moment. The smoke was by this time being driven by the wind. I saw by 3:30 it was not possible to save the town. I went for my wife's sister who had put up trinkets, silverware and other things; her name is Annie Wescott. I said, "Annie, leave those things and come along with me, if we save our lives that is all we may expect to do." I intended to send her to Pine City on the train due about 4 o'clock. While we stood waiting near the depot, the fire appeared to come in a sheet of flame over the town and to drop on our left hand side, as we faced Pokegama. It appeared as if the very air was on fire. We made a rush, reached the Eastern train and were saved."

What Mr. DOUGLASS GREELEY says:

I kept the Morrison Hotel at Hinckley, which was the largest hotel there, and had 50 bed-rooms; kept 6 girls and 4 men at the time of the fire. Had resided six years at Hinckley, was elected county auditor in November, on the Democratic ticket. I had a family of one child, my mother, Mrs. Hannah P. Greeley, was visiting me on September 1st, with my sister and her two children.

September 1st, at noon, it began to look scarey; in the south, toward Mission Creek, it looked bad. There was a very hot smoke, densely black, and a light wind. The train from Duluth to St. Paul was more than an hour late. I sent all my relatives away on the train. I did not go to bed and fall asleep you may be sure. I went south several times to the Eastern tracks. It kept getting worse every moment. The sun broke through the smoke, and I thought the worst had passed. William Ginden, who was ex-mayor, and at this time was a member of the board of supervisors, stood on the corner. I stood near my hotel. He had been down near the round house, when his son, a lad in his early teens, came up and said, "Father, do you want mother to leave home and seek a place of safety? She wants to know." He replied, "Willie, run home and tell mama the danger is passed." He ran north to his home to tell his mother. William Ginden and all his family perished.

I went into the hotel; all the girl help were excited. One of them,

Ida Janda, who worked in the dining room, asked, "What shall we do, what shall we do?"

I said, "Stay here till I tell you to leave. You will be all right. I will go out and will tell you presently what is the best to do." I went to view the situation and saw that hope was gone, and went back quickly and said: "Now is the time to save ourselves." We all left the hotel by the front door, seven sad souls. We met at the corner John Brodie, who used to board with me; he said, "There is a train on the Eastern line waiting." I said, "Go with Mr. Brodie;" and ran back, put my money into the safe, locked it, and when the fire was over, it was there with all my papers. The safe was the property of William O'Brien, who was engaged in lumbering, and I kept his books and had done so for six years. I left the hotel, knowing the desperation of the situation, and as I passed the gate at the back of the barn yard, at the rear of the hotel, I saw D. Fortin, C. O. Carlson, Albert Nudewood and Otto Skamser, all of whom worked for me, turning my two driving horses and four cows out of the barn. I began to help them and we got the horses into the street. Nudewood, Skamser and Carlson now left. Fortin and I now were joined by Charlie Nehland, who helped us to get the remaining cows out. Just then the horses came back at full speed. They had become frightened. I took one horse and Fortin one, and put bridles on them. Nehland took a buggy and ran with it to the gravel pit, and saved himself and it; I have it now.

Fortin and I rode up north a block on the front street and turned east, leaving town. As we got to the Eastern track, we saw the flames from the houses east of the track and had to turn back to the wagon bridge over Grindstone river, which was about eighty feet long, but there was hardly any water in the river here. We made for the train on a bee line.

"As we went through some willows, I said to Fortin, 'We are gone now.' He said, 'Yes, I guess we are.' I at this moment heard some-one call. I looked and saw Nudewood, on hundred feet away in the door of a box car, and I never heard a sound so welcome. Barry, the engineer, had seen us and stopped. We were the last men on that train, and near that spot over one hundred dead were found. The two horses we left were burned to death near there. The next morning the four cows turned up all right. They had not a hair singed; it is probable they escaped in the gravel pit. From the box car door in which I stood, as the train moved off, I could see the roof of Brennan's mill fall in.

"From that time on, darkness enveloped the train. In the car some were on their knees praying, some crying, and some asking for relatives. The children did not realize what was taking place, or how much the fire meant to them. At Sandstone we stopped. At Partridge the citizens brought water, lamps and lanterns. None of the residents left on our train and in fifteen minutes their city was aflame and soon in utter ruins. We reached Duluth safely and received a royal welcome. I went to the house of my brother, John Greeley, who is general manager of the Keystone Investment Company.

"I got on the Eastern train which left September 2d, at 5 o'clock in the morning. On it were Mr. Thorne, superintendent; Mr. Devlin, roadmastetr; Dr. Stephan, Mr. Albright, Mr. Dunn and Mr. Murphy.

"We came slowly along, every now and then a burnt tree had fallen over the line. In the afternoon, early, we found the first bridge burned out, about one mile north of Partridge. We all walked to Sandstone, except as many traveling men as could get upon a hand-car. They preceded us to that town; when we walked there, we saw the desolation of the place. In our journey, we had passed many dead animals, rabbits, deer and birds. We now stood on the north bank of the Kettle river, and saw on the south side the poor- homeless, helpless, penniless people who were left. We forded the river a mile below the bridge, and came thus into Sandstone. We saw the ruin, and before we had left had seen forty-five dead bodies,—age and youth, women and children, mingled in one common death.

"We came out on the other side and journeyed, sad men, to Hinckley. All the others went back north. We were the first parties to get back to Hinckley of all who left that ill-fated spot on Saturday.

"It was now past 5 o'clock Sunday night, and we saw what the disaster here was: there was not a house or building left standing north of the Cushing, and nothing south of it except the water tank, coal shed and round house. The relief train had come in from the south and had brought all kinds of help from Pine City, Rush City, and points on the line. Many of the dead had been picked up and some had been placed in boxes and coffins which had been sent up. Engineer Barry behaved well, as did all the trainmen.

FREDDY ROBINSON.

This boy was rescued by his aunt, Mary Robinson. His mother died two years ago, and his father, Peter Robinson, and

C. H. STROMBERG

CHR. ARVOLD.

GEO. C. DUNLAP.

PAUL JAMES DULUTH CROCKER.

uncle, Nels Robinson, both perished in the fire September 1st. The dwelling of Peter Robinson was on the west side of town, and as the fire broke in over the place from the woods, he took his only boy in his arms, rescued him, and gave him to his aunt, and told them to start. He and his brother, Nels Robinson, yet lingering, for some reason unknown to Mary Robinson (which proved to be fatal, as they both perished). Mary Robinson took the three-year-old boy in her arms and carried him through the burning town and reached the Eastern depot just in time to board the train pulling out from the depot, and reached Duluth in safety.

CHARLES M. STOMBERG.

His father, mother, two brothers and two sisters lived at Hinckley at the time of the fire. They came out on the St. Paul & Duluth train and started up track. In dense smoke he lost them and found refuge in a section well. Next morning he found the corpses of the rest of the family burned to a crisp altogether, being recognized only by watch, jewelry, etc.

He is nineteen years old, lives at Duluth, and the local relief committee are taking an interest in him.

B. C. BARTLETT.

Proprietor of Eating House, Hinckley, prior to September 1st, 1894.

I have been keeping the St. Paul & Duluth Railroad Eating House about fifteen years. The day of the Hinckley fire, September 1st, 1894, my family and myself decided about 5 or 10 minutes before 4 o'clock p. m., to leave our house. At that time everything in sight, fences and buildings, were taking fire. The heat had been very intense and it had been very dark for some time before, and the air as high as we could see seemed to be on fire; the wind blowing a gale and a terrible noise as of a great many wagons driven over a rough road.

We got the members of our family together and attempted to go to the gravel pit, but in consequence of heat from the burning buildings, which lined the street leading to it, and the strong wind, we decided we could not get there. We then started with the wind and with our backs to the heat, north on the St. Paul & Duluth Railroad tracks. About one and one-half miles from Hinckley, we met the Limited train, Conductor Sullivan and Engineer Root, and after telling them the situation at Hinckley, we got on the train and rode back to Skunk Lake. We then got off and walked about eight miles to

Finlayson, where we were picked up by the relief train from Willow River. When we got on the train near Hinckley the train was on fire the whole length of it, and by the time we reached Skunk Lake, the windows on the west side were nearly all broken out by the heat, and the cars were burning very fast. The coal in the tender was blazing high. We decided we could not live to go into the shallow water at Skunk Lake, so we walked on again.

Of the party of about fifty persons that left Hinckley when we did, about thirty-three perished between Hinckley and Skunk Lake, and without doubt we would have lost our lives had we not had the ride on the Limited train to Skunk Lake, and also that we determined from the start not to get outside of the iron rails. We had to avoid inhaling the heated air, and could not open our eyes, and our only guide was to keep inside the rails on the track. Three girls employed by us in the eating house were separated from us at the start and were burned; three kept with us and were saved. One of my sons, George D. Bartlett, got out on the Eastern Minnesota Railroad train with Conductor Powers and Engineer Best; two sons, H. S. and T. W. Bartlett, went to the gravel pit and were saved.

THE REV. FATHER BURKE.

The Rev. Father Burke, who was active in his ministry of help to the living, and who also took part in the burial of the dead, is a man with a history.

In 1872, he went to St. Hyacinthe's College, Canada, for the diocese of Rochester, New York: there he became acquainted with Cardinal Vaughan's work amongst the colored people of the South, and was one of the first American youths who set out for England to prepare for that glorious mission. For five years he was trained in the College of St. Joseph's, London. He was ordained priest by Cardinal Vaughan on December 21st, 1878. Whilst arrangements were being made for departure to America, he was sent over the Irish Channel to the Emerald Isle, to make known to the faithful and others the work of the missions, and raise money for them. He was there but a few days when Cardinal Vaughan was asked to send priests to Afghanistan as chaplains to the British forces engaged in war in that wild land, and after the fighting had ceased they were to tell the story of the gospel to the natives. So he and others started, by authority, to the field of work in Asia. This was the first Christian mission among the Afghans.

They left London, England, on the 15th day of April, 1879, and journeyed through India all that summer, in the midst of heat and cholera and suffering, too great for pen to tell. The party got to Kandahar in August.

A priest died in the Khyber Pass and Father Burke had to go and take his place and work; whilst on the way, campaign number two began, so he had to go on with the soldiers and join General Roberts, who was on his way to Kabul. It was October 4th when the father got to the famous pass at Khyber. No tongue can tell the hardships of the nine months passed, at night on the saddle, over deserts, mountains and passes, heat one hundred and thirty in the coolest bungalow at the foot of the Himalaya Mountains; here cholera was holding sway on all sides. Not even a native of the country was allowed to travel for three months. No food but hard tack, and muddy water for drink, with the hot ground for a bed, in danger of being stabbed by Patan scimetars, as were many soldiers in the sixty-sixth regiment.

For distinguished services, this priest received a bounty of five hundred rupees and the Victoria medal. The next five years were spent in the presidency of Madras, as missionary amongst the Teleger population, to whom the Afghan priests were sent when they had to quit Afghanistan. For seven years he was at work amongst the colored people of Washington, D. C., U. S. A. It is surprising how many men who have a record for service on many fields, met in this Pine County disaster. The following letter shows how the Rev. Father Burke looked at Hinckley, when he stood there in his readiness to do all in his power as man and priest. It is such men as he who are an honor to the churches at whose altars they minister.

WHITE BEAR, MINN., Jan. 10, 1895.

My Dear Mr. Wilkinson:

I am very glad that you are to write a history of the great forest fires. I am sure that you will do justice to the subject, though no pen can describe the horrors of those early September days. I never shall forget the evening when we stood in the Hinckley cemetery, before the long trenches in one part of which men were digging, and in another part men were reverently placing the poor charred remains of the dead, while a little in the distance were small groups of persons burying their lost and longed for. How beautiful and comforting the words of Holy Scripture of prayer and praise. The night was coming and nothing could be seen except the blackened landscape and the burned pine stumps all black and bare. I saw the horrors of the Afghan war and passed through them, but never beheld a sadder scene than this.

Do you know that my friend Jim Root drove the engine which took Gen. Sherman on his famous ride to the sea? This would make an interesting fact to place in your book. When it is published, please forward me two copies, for which I will promptly send the money. I may want more.

With kindest regards, I am very truly yours,

R. T. BURKE.

SANDSTONE.

SANDSTONE is a well-known town on the eastern division of the Great Northern Railway. It was surrounded by dense pine forests, from which vast quantities of logs had been cut; yet more remained to grace the landscape and bless and enrich the lumberman.

A hardy class of settlers had taken up their abode in the town and upon the lands adjacent, in the hope—not only of making a living, but of becoming well-to-do.

Kettle river, in its winding course, adds peculiar beauty to the place, and the high steep banks on either side, give to it a rugged appearance, which rises almost into the majestic and picturesque.

In these banks and under the town lies what may be fairly named one of the very best varieties of building stone in the land. And in the quarries, men who desire, can find work during the greater part of the year. This stone is in such quantities, that it is certain no man now living will see the day when the supply will be exhausted.

From all this, it will be seen that Sandstone possessed means of obtaining money such as few towns are privileged to have, and this gave hope and promise of happy and prosperous years.

The school edifice, which for a place like Sandstone, was a worthy, even splendid building in its ruins, testifies to the fact that those who built it, hoped to see a place of two or three thousand inhabitants. It was here that the persons who met their death and those who escaped with their lives only, had laid plans for years of work, and happy useful lives, from which they might reap due reward.

The fire has changed many things in Pine county, and at Sandstone; but it has not blotted out the hopes or plans of the men who yet reside here, and who are interested in its growth.

The Great Northern Railway Company are making it a division on its eastern branch, and will build a roundhouse.

This summer—1895—The Minneapolis Trust Company are to

BRAKEMAN GILHAM.

F. A. THISTLE.

BRAKEMAN MCLAUGHLIN.

NEWS AGENT MANHART.

work the quarries, and have designs for their development of the stone business which will make everything which has been done in the past seem small indeed.

The Protestant Episcopal Church secured two lots, the gift of the Trust Company; here will be a church and rectory.

The Presbyterians also have a house of prayer.

There is a good public school and hotel, "The Northern," and an air of confidence pervades all lives and gives brightness to all hearts. Even now the fire is looked upon as a thing of the past, and at the same time, as having given a sacredness to the town which nothing else ever could have imparted. The place where imminent danger was passed ,where sad trials were bravely borne, and where death came to the loyal and the loved ones, now lost to human ken,—all have left an impress never to be effaced.

EXPERIENCE OF JOHN FALK.

My home is at Sandstone Junction, and on the day of the fire I was there alone, as my wife and children were at Sandstone. I began to get uneasy about 1 o'clock, when the clouds of smoke could be seen overhead, showing plainly that a large fire must be burning in our immediate vicinity. About 2 o'clock it became so dark that one could not see without a lamp. I thought it best for me to be with my family, so I started for town, which was four miles away. I reached it just in time, as the fire had commenced its work of devastation before I arrived there. I found my family all right and sent them down to the river; I followed soon afterwards. We stood in the river about three hours, and the next morning were taken to Duluth.

EXPERIENCE OF M. W. W. JESMER, BRIDGE WATCHMAN, EASTERN MINNESOTA RAILWAY.

About 2 p. m., on Sept. 1st, I was at my house, which stood about two hundred feet from the bridge that crosses the Kettle river at Sandstone. The sky had been cloudy and the air full of smoke since about 10 o'clock a. m. About 2:15 p. m. I noticed a reflection in the sky as if from a large fire. I was standing on the bridge, which is about one hundred and fifty feet above the water, and I could see that in the direction of Hinckley a large fire was burning. I could also hear a rumbling noise, as if the wind were blowing a gale. It got so dark about 3 o'clock that the lamps had to be lighted.

The train passed over the bridge at about 3 o'clock p. m.; the head-light on the engine was burning. I had to carry my lantern to get the number of the engine, this being part of my duty as bridge watch-man. I remained at my post on the bridge till about 4 o'clock, when a fire started in the woods on the west side of the track. The wind had risen meantime, and many sparks were carried over my house; at 4 o'clock I sent my little boy down town to ask for help, as I was afraid it would catch fire. I also told him to tell the section foreman to send his men up, in case they should be required to save the bridge. Mr. Bullis, the railway agent at Sandstone, ran up to the bridge and told me that the south-bound train, which had passed at about 3:05, was backing up from Hinckley, as it was unable to proceed any farther. The train backed over the bridge loaded with passengers and refugees from Hinckley, and as many more as they could pick up on the way. The sparks from the fire were falling thick and fast; they came down just like hail-stones; the bridge was burning in twenty or thirty places when the train passed over. I told my wife to go down to the rocks under the bridge and remain there until I came.

The train had not gone more than two thousand feet from the bridge when the two bents on the east side were blown over. I knew then that the bridge was doomed, and so I went back to my house to try and save what I could. I carried my trunk out of the house and left it in a potato field near by, then started down the bluff under the bridge where my family were waiting.

The night watchman, W. W. Damuth, was standing about half way between the house and the bridge. I called him to come with me, as there was no use in staying there any longer; he seemed dazed and did not answer, but kept walking toward the bridge. That was the last I saw of him alive.

When I joined my family I thought that we should be safer in the quarry, which was only a short distance away. We tried to reach it, but could not, the heat was so intense. I then made up my mind to go into the river, as I thought drowning preferable to being burned to death. I took my wife and four children into the water; we were followed by Thomas McCoy and Nels Flygt, and they helped me to keep my wife and children from drowning as the water near the bridge is very deep.

When I went over the bridge for the last time my dog followed me, but would not come off the iron spanning the middle, I tried to catch him but could not. He remained on the bridge during the whole time and howled. At first I thought it was Mr. Damuth as it sounded like a human being. He had to stay on the bridge until Monday morning, when a bridge builder climbed upon the supports and lowered him with a rope. The bridge was so hot on Sunday that nothing could be done to rescue him. The poor brute was badly burned, but is all right now. We remained at Sandstone until Monday night, when we were sent to Duluth.

EXPERIENCE OF PETER BILADO.

I was staying in town with my wife's sister, and had one of my little girls with me. My sister's house stands in the center of a clearing fully 200 yards from any timber. It grew so dark about 2 o'clock that I thought a cyclone was coming, and we had to have the lamps lighted. We could see the reflection of a fire in the sky, and could hear a peculiar sound like thunder in the air. The fire came on us very suddenly. It seemed to come from above with a roaring sound something like a large body of falling water. Balls of fire seemed to be bursting in the air.

My sister and her children ran from the house, and I took my girl by the hand and ran with her to a ditch about fifty yards away. The fire was so close to us that it set fire to our clothes. I must have lost my senses, for as soon as we got into the ditch I fell. The long grass on each side was burning. Both my hands were burned, which brought me to my senses.

I told my little girl that we could not stay there. She jumped up, looked about her, and ran towards the fire. She must have been out of her mind. She ran about 10 yards, calling out, "Papa, papa!" I lost sight of her in the smoke, and did not see her again until I saw her dead body.

I do not know how I escaped being burned to death, as I was completely out of my mind. Both my hands and lower limbs were burned, and nearly all my clothes. The fire beat down, and it seemed as though the air was full of hot sand which fell like fine hail.

EXPERIENCE OF MRS. BILADO.

I was living on our homestead, about four miles from Sandstone; my husband and one of the children were at Sandstone. I heard that a forest fire was burning near Hinckley, but did not give it much thought. On the afternoon of September 1st, I was sitting on the doorstep, with my baby in arms, waiting for the children to come

QUARRY AT SANDSTONE.

home, they having gone to the pasture to bring the cattle; it was about 5 o'clock p. m. when they came. We went in to supper at about 5:15; it was so dark that we had to light the lamps, and I began to feel a little uneasy, especially as my husband was in town.

I came out of the house at about 5:30 o'clock and could see the woods burning about a quarter of a mile away. I thought it would be best to let all the stock loose in case the fire should come upon us. The wind began to freshen and I could see the rapid approach of the fire; I though that we could fight it with buckets of water, and so remained about the house, but the flames made such headway that I decided at once to leave the house and everything else to its fate.

I told my children that we would have to go to McKay's Lake. I took the baby in one arm and a pail of water in the other hand. Flora, my oldest daughter, fourteen years old, carried a sheet and two blankets, and the other two little girls clutched hold of my dress. The flames were now quite close to us; we had not gone more than fifty yards when I told my children that we could never reach the lake. I decided at once to lie down in a rutabaga patch a few yards off. Just as we crossed the fence, burning cinders began to fall on us, like flakes of snow or hail stones. I wet the sheet with the water which was in the pail, left my children on the plowed ground, and went back to the house for more water. When I was going back a blazing tree fell and knocked the pail out of my hand, but I managed to pick it up before the water was all spilled. I hurried as quickly as possible, and just as I reached the fence, a frightened deer ran up to me as if looking for protection. The poor animal appeared to be dazed, and in a few minutes dropped dead. I went to where my children were, and wet the blankets. We all lay down in the turnip patch. The wind was blowing like a cyclone, and the heat was something awful.

Flora asked me if I thought we should perish. I told her to trust in God, that he would do what was best for us. I tried to spread the sheet over the children but the wind carried it away. I tried the blanket, but the same thing happened to it. I spread the second blanket over them. I then got under it—Flora and myself on either side and the children in the middle. The flames were roaring all around us with a noise like thunder; they seemed to come from the sky and beat on everything.

Just then, Flora got up from under the blanket to try and find the blanket which had blown away. I called to her not to go, but she either did not hear me, or did not understand what I said; she ran about one hundred yards towards the fire and fell down, her clothing burning. I screamed out in my agony for her, but I dared not go to her assistance. My hair caught fire and my dress across my shoulders. By this time, the flames were all around us. The heat was so intense that it soon dried out our blanket; I tried to put some clay on it as it was burning in places where the sparks had fallen.

My baby was lying across my breast, and I could hear him gasping for breath as if he were suffocating. I blew in his mouth and that seemed to revive him; the other two children never moved and I did not know whether they were dead or alive. At first I could hear them gasping as baby did, but I am thankful to say they were safe. It it had not been for the wet blanket we should all have perished. When the fire had passed, I got up to see if anything was left. Nothing was to be seen; fire everywhere. I thought of my poor Flora and wondered if she had suffered much. We remained in the turnip field all night. The next morning I searched everywhere for Flora's body, but could not find it. I took the children to the well, and with water in an old tin washed our eyes. We all walked to Sandstone over burning stumps, and found that Sandstone had suffered the same fate. I found my husband, his hands, arms and legs being badly burned, and I learned from him that my other little girl had also met a terrible death.

EXPERIENCE OF MRS. DAVID LIFEBRER.

The 1st of September is a day which I shall never forget. My husband was in Dakota; living with me were my five children, the youngest five months old. My brother-in-law, Mr. Bilado, and his little girl had stayed with us all day. I noticed that about 2 o'clock in the afternoon the sky became cloudy, and smoke was coming as if from a fire in the woods. It grew darker and darker; lamps had to be lighted at 4 o'clock. We could see the reflection of the fire in the sky, and knew that the woods were burning.

I thought we were safe, as our house stands in the middle of a clearing. At about 5:30 we heard a noise like lumber piles falling; we supposed that the lumber piles at Sandstone Junction were on fire; it sounded just like thunder.

The wind came up suddenly and sparks flew in all directions. Still we thought we were safe. We did not leave the house until it caught fire; we then ran for a piece of plowed land about thirty yards from the house, I carrying the baby and a shawl, which I had dipped in a barrel of water; my oldest girl, seventeen, carried the next youngest, three years old. The flames were coming down as if from the sky, and the air seemed to be full of hot sand. We buried ourselves as best we could in the onion patch and covered ourselves with the shawl. One cat came running from the woods, mewing in a most piteous manner and crawled under the shawl. I did not know until afterwards where my brother-in-law and niece were. We remained under the shawl for about an hour, until the fire had passed.

The experience was an awful one, the sky seemed to be full of balls of fire which would explode, keeping up a constant noise like heavy peals of thunder.

My eldest boy had a narrow escape, he was driving from Sandstone Junction when the fire overtook him. He cut the horses loose but they did not escape, he ran into a corn field, and so saved his life. I had sent my youngest boy to the post office, and the people there would not let him go home. He saved himself by going into the river.

We are thankful to have escaped with our lives. We lost everything we had, but thanks to the relief committee, we shall not starve. They are taking good care of us, and we are especially grateful to Mr. Miller, the relief agent, for all his kindness.

EXPERIENCE OF PATRICK REGAN.

I was working in the quarry, and I first noticed the smoke in the air about two p. m. I left the quarry about 2:15 to go to my house which was about half a mile distant, and when I reached the house it was so dark I had to light the lamps. The sky got so dark about 3:30 that I thought I would go over to a neighbor's house close by and ask him what he thought was the matter. He said it was only an eclipse of the sun which would soon pass over; I told him it was either fire or a cyclone, and advised him to get his family out of the house.

We soon found out what was the cause of the darkness. We could see the sky getting red. I decided at once to move my family into some place of safety. There was not much time for thought, so I told them the safest place would be in the river, which was about eight hundred yards distant from the house. They went for the river. It was then about 3:30. I remained at the house, pouring

REV. A. RYAN. D. C. L.

water on the two stacks of hay which were close by, and which I thought I could save. I did not leave the place until I saw three houses burnt around my home. I decided then to run at once for the river.

I could see coming from the sky what looked like large balls of fire; wherever they fell they would explode and set fire to whatever they touched. I had gone about one hundred and fifty feet from the house when I remembered one of the cows was tied up in the barn. I ran back and cut the rope which held her. The poor brute was almost mad with fright; the barn was on fire. I had hard work to get the cow to go out the door, but I finally got her out and she made a run for the river, and I followed her.

While I was running, I saw a woman coming from another direction, evidently making for the river. I thought I would wait for her and try to help her along, but the flames traveled faster than she did; they soon overtook her and she dropped in her tracks, her clothing all on fire. I did not go to her assistance, as it would have meant death for me to do so, but made the best of my way to the river. Before I reached the bank my clothing was on fire in several places. I could not see my family, so I supposed they had gone into the water. I looked again up and down the bank, and at last discovered them with about fifty people, all huddled together, who were afraid to go into the water. I made the four oldest go in first and pour water with their hands on the others as fast as they went in, and when I thought I had them all safe in the water, I discovered that two of my own children were missing. They had in some way got separated from the others and were crouching on the bank unable to move, they were so frightened; one I carried into the river and asked the other to follow, but she would not, and I could not go back to her, as the child I was caring for would not let go my arms.

I saw my dog Prince in the water and told him to go and bring Lizzie into the river and hold her there until I came to her rescue. He did what he was told and dragged her into the water. I came and released her. I can thank that dog for saving Lizzie's life. If she had remained on the bank one moment more she would have been burnt. We all stayed in the water until the most of the fire had passed, about two hours and a half.

The smoke was still very dense, but I thought I would venture upon the bank and see if I could find a house that had escaped the flames. I discovered an old powder house in which were four large

THE RIVER AT SANDSTONE.

kegs of powder. I picked up an old empty powder can, filled it with water and threw it upon the burning sticks which were lying about. I made everything safe outside, then went in and carried out the powder kegs and threw them into the river. I then wet the floor of the powder house so that there might not be any danger there.

I then went down to the river and brought up as many women and children as could crowd into the powder house. Two men got in and would not come out. The women and children were all wet and cold, so I thought if I could only find a few potatoes and cook them, the poor people might like it. I picked up an empty powder can, filled it with water, put it to boil on some live cinders and very soon had some nice warm potatoes ready. There were not enough to go around, so I cooked more until all were satisfied. About 9 o'clock Sunday morning I found a pig which had been partly burned. I cut it up, made a pan out of some old sheet iron, and soon had some nice roast pork for breakfast. I helped as many as I could in that way.

My family and I were taken to Duluth, and I am thankful to say through the kindness of the relief committee and their agent, Mr. Mr. Miller, we are very comfortable today.

EXPERIENCE OF PETER PETERSON, SUPERINTENDENT MINNEAPOLIS TRUST COMPANY'S QUARRIES.

My men and I were at work on September 1st at the quarry about 2 p. m. The sky grew so dark that I sent my men home. I knew there was a forest fire off toward Hinckley, but I had no idea that it would touch our town. I went to my store where it was so dark that the lamps had to be lighted and almost every man outside was carrying a lantern, as if it were night. At 3 o'clock, I went to the depot to meet the train from Duluth, and try to find out what they knew about the fire. When I left the depot, a small fire had started about six hundred feet away. I then ordered some of my men who happened to be there to go down to the quarry and take the horses out of the barn, and also bring out some barrels of water and try to save as much of the property as possible.

I went back to my house and remained there a short time; I could see no signs of a large fire, and thought Sandstone would escape. I was soon disappointed, as the bridge watchman's son came running down from the bridge, and asked me to bring some men up, and try to save his father's house which was threatened. When I reached

LEROY THOMAS.

W. D. CAMPBELL.

N. J. MILLER.

GEO. VAN PELT.

his house, the flames had got pretty headway, a fire having started
north of the bridge and the wind was blowing a fresh gale from the
north. I told him to leave his house and bring his family into town.

Just before I left the bridge, the Eastern Minnesota train No. 4 from
Duluth, being unable to go any farther than Hinckley, was backing
up with a train load of refugees from Hinckley, and other places
along the line between Hinckley and Sandstone. The bridge was
not burning when the train passed over, but the woods on the north
side of the bridge were burning fiercely, and the sparks were being
carried by the wind towards the bridge. When I saw the train backing from the town, I thought it was time to try to save what I could.

Just then, I heard a rumbling noise which I thought was thunder.
I could see the fire in the sky across the river; it looked as though
a cyclone were coming upon us, carrying everything before it, then
it died down and I thought the danger had passed. Shortly after
that, a strong wind came up from the southwest; I then realized that
there would be no chance of saving the town.

I went into the store and blew out the lights, and found my wife
and two children standing outside. The wind by this time was blowing a hurricane, and the flames were burning up everything before
them; millions of sparks were falling and setting fires.

While we were standing outside, undecided what to do, a man
came running past, shouting, "Make for the river!" He said that
Hinckley was all burned up and that Sandstone would share the same
fate. At the time, I did not understand what the man said as the
noise of the storm was so great it was impossible to hear. We made
up our minds at once to go to the river, which was about eight hundred yards away. When we were on the main road which led to it,
the people of the town were coming from all directions, and before
we got half way down to the river, the brush, trees and houses on
both sides of the road were burning. I thought we could find sufficient protection behind a pile of small stones on the river bank, but
the heat was so intense that we did not stay there longer than three
or four minutes. We all went into the river, which is, at this place,
about two feet deep. It was impossible to stand in the water and
face the wind and heat and we commenced throwing water over each
other.

We remained in the water until the air had cooled a little—it may
have been an hour and fifteen minutes. The smoke was still very
dense; a man on the bank shouted to me that the quarry office had

escaped the fire, though a stone mill not twenty yards from the office was a total wreck. I then told as many as could to go to the office, away from the flying cinders and smoke, and soon the building was filled; the women and children, suffering from cold and wet, were glad to find protection.

About 11 p. m. the wind went down, and the smoke cleared away so that the men of the party were able to go to town. A more desolate sight could not be imagined than that which met our gaze—not a house was left, nothing but a few smoking tree stumps, to show where, an hour before, the thriving little town of Sandstone had stood. Here and there, could be seen the half charred bodies of men, women, children, horses and cattle.

The 1st of September, 1894, is a day that will never be forgotten by the survivors of the disastrous fire at Sandstone.

EXPERIENCE OF MR. ANDERSON, CONGREGATIONAL MINISTER AT SANDSTONE.

Sandstone and Hinckley had been enveloped in smoke many times during the summer. On the first of September at two o'clock p. m., we could not see the sun on account of the smoke. The evening before I had been in Hinckley to preach my farewell sermon, expecting to return to the Chicago Theological Seminary on the 10th of September, where I had a year's work yet to finish.

After my farewell sermon I should have stopped at Hinckley until the next morning, but some way or other, I was so uneasy that I could not be still, although I did not know of any danger. There was, so to speak, a voice within me saying that I should go back to Sandstone that night. After having decided to obey this voice, I took the St. Paul and Duluth train at three o'clock in the morning for Sandstone Junction. But not more than four minutes later the train stopped because of the fire on both sides of the road, although it did not stop very long before it started through the fire, and so, about four o'clock I was in Sandstone Junction, and from there I had to walk three miles that dark night to Sandstone, where I arrived at five o'clock in the morning.

I wish to write especially about Sandstone. The Swedish Congregational Church of which I was pastor, had prepared to give an entertainment on the first of September, especially for my benefit before I should leave them. And at this entertainment I was expected to speak. I had worked hard about two weeks to prepare myself for

this address, but had not succeeded, so I thought I would try it
this last day, and I worked and worked with it all forenoon, but did
not get anything out of it. I speak of this because it seemed to
be a warning of the great danger that was coming.

About two o'clock in the afternoon the skies turned red, and all
the earth looked as if it had been dipped in blood; we were all
amazed. And what would happen? All works stopped and every
one went to his home. Oh what a sight! This condition of things
continued about two hours, and then we had to light the lamps, and
the light of the lamps looked like electric lights. Then two men
were sent to see if the fire was so near as it seemed to be; returning, they reported that the fire was about three or six miles away.
Then the fire apparatus was taken out, and the water works were set
in order so that all was ready if the fire should come. The train
on the Great Northern Railway passed Sandstone at three o'clock
p. m., and when it came to Hinckley the greater portion of the village was already in flames, and four or five hundred people were
gathered around the station waiting for the train. But the conductor on the train saw that it was no use trying to go any further.
He gave orders to the brakeman to switch off on the side track, and
pick up all the empty box cars so as to prepare room for all the
people who were standing round. When this was done, the fire
was so close by that some of the cars began to catch fire, but the
cars were filled with people in a moment, though there was not room
for all who were standing ready to flee for their lives. The train
started at full speed for Superior, leaving many behind. While
this train was in Hinckley, a telegram was sent to us in Sandstone,
saying, "If you love your lives, try to save them." The redness of
the skies had turned black at this time, and it was very dark. The
wind began to blow furiously. All the time before it was very calm.
This was about four o'clock in the afternoon. I went to see the
man in charge of the water works, and told him that he better
go home and take care of his family, but he said he did not dare
to, because if he did he might lose his place. It was so dark that he
could not see to attend to his machine, so sent his little eleven-
year-old boy home to get a lamp, and when he came back the fire
was very near.

Before he went to get the lamp I had left the water works, and
hurried around in the city to warn the people of the impending
danger, telling them to run to the river and save themselves.

Among the people that I warned was one man who said he had plenty of water without going to the river, enough to save both his family and his house; though his whole water supply consisted of five or six barrels and three or four washtubs of water. With the water in the barrels he would save the house and himself, and with that in the tubs his wife and children could save themselves.

The next day we found his wife and children lying around the empty water tubs in the midst of the street, and the husband lying about thirty feet below—every one of them burned to death. There were also a great many others who did not heed the warning and likewise perished.

I am now ready to speak about the great fire. It turned out to be a veritable cyclone of flames. There came, as it seemed to me, great balls of fire from the sky, and when they were within twenty feet of the ground, they burst, sending down a heavy rain of flashing sparks, like a mighty sky rocket exploding with brilliant display of flashing light. Having warned as many as I possibly could, I stopped for a moment to think if I had forgotten anyone with whom I was acquainted. Looking around I saw a light in a cellar window under a house where a family lived that I was acquainted with. Only a few moments and I was there, burst in the door and told them to run for the river. There were three families, and immediately they all started out, but one of the men became so excited that he left his wife behind with her little six months' old child and ran all alone to the river with the rest. When the wife came out she stood there bewildered, not knowing what to do, and while standing there a gust of the cyclone picked her up and carried her about twenty-five or thirty feet where she was dropped among some corn-stalks. The reason that I was not picked up by the same storm was, that I stood on the other side of the house, out of reach of the sweeping elements. After the worst shock of the hurricane was over, I started for the river, not knowing but that the rest were already there, but on my way I heard a cry from the small corn fields near by. There I found that wife with her little child. I wanted to take the child but she would not let me. She finally yielded after I had promised to save her child if I could save myself. I then told her to run for the river as fast as she could.

When I started with this little child in my arms, the house was already on fire, and in another moment it was seized by the storm and carried away. I was then behind a house down below a hill, or else I would have been carried off that time. From this place I started off down hill toward the river. Everything around me was on fire. Coming down to the house where the deacon of my church lived, the fire had not yet come thither; there I saw a light through the kitchen window. The kitchen door was open but not a living soul could be found in or about the house. Looking around, I saw a watch and some money on the table, but did not stop to take it, for there was no time to lose. I started through the kitchen door and was met by fire, so I ran back through the house, aiming for the front door, but found it locked. It soon yielded to my vigorously applied push, and out I rushed, straight for the river. But, alas, when I came out in the midst of the street I was picked up, with the little child in my arms, by the storm, and carried a distance of about 1,000 feet, where I was laid down all safe—neither I nor the child was hurt in the least. This storm took us right down toward the river, and only a short way from where we were dropped by the storm we found the mother of the child. My clothes had now caught fire, but the river was close by; I ran and threw myself right into the water, still having the little child in my arms. There were not yet very many in the water, but the banks of the river were lined with people, ready at any moment to throw themselves headlong into the water. On the west side of the river were large boarding houses, and on both sides of the river were a number of haystacks, all in flames. The fire seemed to soar sky high. The people in the river were all under water but their heads. The air that we had to breathe was so hot that it burnt way down into our lungs. When the people who had stood on the river bank were come into the water, we heard the awful cries and wailings from the poor perishing people up in town who had not heeded the warning.

In this, our great common despair, we were all praying people; Christians or non-Christians. The ungodly of all kinds prayed now to the living God, if they never had prayed before.

But, on account of our great anxiety and weariness we were all (especially the women, even I, myself,) getting very weak and tired.

I had not seen the mother of the child that I had in my arms since I was let down by the storm, and now I was so tired and weak that I began to sink to the bottom of the river, but for a man who happened to see me sinking and braced me up, I would have drowned.

REV. E. ANDERSON.

I had sunk so deep that the water had commenced to cover the little child, and when that man lifted me up, I heard the poor little baby cry. Then I remembered the promise to its mother, and this seemed to strengthen me, and then they led me over to a log near by, against which I could rest myself a little while, and here another man kept throwing water over me and himself, to keep our heads from being burned by the flames flying around us.

While standing there, the father of the child happened to find me; recognizing his little child he took it in his arms and kissed it, and a short time afterwards we found the mother. I was now getting a little stronger so that I could go about and help others. We had been in the water about two hours when we found a great block of stone out in the river. On this rock we tried to put all the weak and tired ones, as many as we could, and then all the rest who could find room went up on the rock, in all about one hundred people. On that rock we had the most blessed prayer-meeting I have ever attended. Then we all joined in praising God with the following hymn:

THE MIGHTY FORTRESS.

1. To the rock that's higher, take me
From the flames across Jordan's stream.
Take me to that mighty fortress,
Which in every storm shall stand.

CHORUS: O, thou blessed Rock of Ages,
Let us rest in peace in thee;
Who remaineth firm, unshaken,
Firm to all eternity.

2. Tho' around that mighty fortress
Billows high as mountains roll;
All their angry threatening voices
Shall not move my peaceful soul.

3. Oh, what joy that fortress mighty,
Gives me while the moments fly;
Oh, what peace and strength is flowing
From its fountain rising high!

4. Every day that fortress mighty
Fills my heart with hope and cheer,
Lifting higher, soul and spirit,
To a holy, boundless sphere.

5. O, thou blessed Rock of Ages,
Life and all I have in thee;
Perish every worldly treasure,
Thou my own shall ever be.

6. Rock of Ages, give, oh, give me,
Strength to sing the praise of love;
With the roaring flames around me,
'Till I rest in peace above.

Translated from Swedish, freely, by K. E. LARSEN.

This prayer-meeting lasted about a half hour. All combustible things about us were now consumed, we having been in the cold water about three hours, this being about eight o'clock P. M., everything dark about us, except now and then a flash of light from the burning ruins. Being in this awful condition, shivering, cold, wet, hungry, tired and almost naked, we finally found near by the river, a sand bank, whither we betook ourselves for rest. While staying here the stronger men went in search of a temporary shelter to which we might bring the poor, suffering mothers, with their little babes, and others who were severely burned. They found a small house, having been used for an office, standing all alone, with everything about it burned down, miraculously saved, as it were, from fire, with not a scorch on it. This we turned into a hospital, and brought thither our fellow-sufferers, until the whole floor was covered. The rest of us had to stay on the sand bank all that cold and dismal night.

We found a half burnt boat by the river side, which we made use of as a kind of shelter against the raging whirlwind of sand and ashes. Thus, we remained during the night.

The next morning the sun looked down upon the black desert of destroyed homes. Families had been broken up, never to unite again; the lost were missed and those that remained sought them with tears. Here was a husband asking "where is my wife?" Here is a mother crying in despair, "where is my child?"

What a sight the sun beheld as he looked down this beautiful Sunday morning upon the ruins of former Sandstone.

Here lay scattered, all about, the burnt corpses of my beloved friends. Amongst these I recognized some of my own church-members, and about half the children who used to attend our Sunday-school. About ten feet from her own house a mother was found, burnt to a black corpse, with her two little children by her side, one under each arm. The feeling I had, confronted with this sight, cannot be translated into words. Tears drowned the power of utterance, and not a word could I speak.

BREAKFAST ON SUNDAY MORNING.

Not having had anything to eat for over twenty-four hours, we naturally felt weak and hungry. But where should we find anything to eat when everything was burnt. We found some pails and went into the gardens near by and digged up potatoes with our hands, roasted, and all ready to use. I never ate potatoes that tasted so good.

We also found a calf and three cows, providentially saved, as it seems, for they too had run into the river. We killed the calf and milked the cows, and thus provided food for the little babies and others who could not relish their potatoes as some of us did.

Realizing that we were cut off as to all communications with the rest of the world—the telegraph and railroad being burnt—we sent two men on a five-mile walk to Hell's Gate, to find out what the conditions were there. They found that the boarding house was saved with provisions on hand for about one day, and returned with orders to us to walk thither, as many of us as could. Thus we started off for Hell's Gate barefooted and scantily clad. Fortunately enough, our friend Mr. Hysler, of Sandstone, had succeeded in saving his two horses and wagon, and they now came to our service.

Those who were unable to walk and could stand to ride, were taken over by him, while some stayed behind to care for those who were too weak to be moved. In passing through the town we were almost choked by the stifling air.

REST AND REFRESHMENT AT HELL'S GATE.

Having arrived at this place about one o'clock we enjoyed a much-needed wash, a hearty dinner, and a refreshing rest.

At midnight I was aroused by two men from Miller's Station sent by the relief train, with orders for as many as could to walk to that place. It was my task to awaken the people. In spite of all precautions, they rushed up crying, "Is there fire in this house also?" Thus, almost trampling each other down, until I succeeded in quieting them and convincing them that there was no danger.

Thus we set out, as many as dared, and felt able, in pitch dark midnight, from Hell's Gate to Miller's Station, on a five-miles' walk. But, oh what a terrible walk! Many were without shoes. Their feet were burnt, sore and bleeding; almost without clothes, cold, tired, and heavy-hearted; while the stronger of us carried the little children in our arms until we were well nigh weighed down.

Arriving at the train, we were taken in hand by kind and sympathetic friends and refreshed with food and tender care. The doctors dressed our wounds, and experienced, tender nurses cared for our

16. HINCKLEY. AMBER ST. AFTER FIRE.

sick. We felt glad and grateful, both to God and man for this timely relief, for now we felt that we were out of the reach of those terrible devouring flames.

This train took us to Duluth, where we arrived on Monday morning at seven o'clock. From the depot we were taken to Armory Hall, where we found a temporary resting place. Here tables were stretched from wall to wall, spread with all manner of good things, by kind and loving friends.

Having myself received food and clothing, I returned with the relief train which left Duluth at 10:30 A. M., Monday, for Sandstone and Hinckley, to assist in picking up the dead bodies. We arrived on the ground of devastation about 2 P. M., and assumed our terrible work at once. Here we found whole families where the family ties had been broken by the merciless foe, and father and mother and children lying scattered about in wild confusion in the field of death and horror.

Thus we continued our work of picking up the poor unfortunate ones all along the track and its vicinity. At Sandstone Junction we divided ourselves into different groups. I was with a group that went out to the neighboring farms. At one place we found a family of six and only one had escaped. They had all sought refuge in the cellar, but no shelter there against the penetrating heat. The husband tried to get them all out and bring them to the well. But ere he succeeded in doing so the cruel flames seized his wife, and his five children and he, himself, escaped barely with his life, badly burnt, without home and alone in the world. We found the little children lying but a short distance from their mother, as it seemed just as they had been playing, not very much burned, but life was gone.

At another place we found thirteen people scattered about a little potato field, all having perished by a like fate. One of the most remarkable cases was a babe which we found yet clinging with its little arms about its mother's neck, not very much hurt, though its mother, lying face down, was burnt in front to a black fire brand.

Many other cases might be mentioned but we will now proceed to Sandstone. There I found the man in charge of the water works, whom I had told before of the impending danger to his family, ten feet down in the ground at the water connection, leaning over his eleven-year old boy, with clasped hands, as if praying; in that attitude he had gone from this world of sorrow, misery and woe. True to his charge, he left his beloved family and died on his post.

At another place we found eighteen bodies in one well, of whom about twelve were children—my little Sunday-school children—all dead. But the odor that arose from that well was beyond human endurance; it cannot be related.

We found one woman sitting in the well on a mattress, stooping forward a little, with her hands on her knees, apparently alive, but, alas, no. Thus the husband found his wife that awful Sunday morning; overcome with grief he cried out in despair, "Nothing further for me to live for," and went and drowned himself in a creek.

Only a little ways from here, on a farm, we found a whole family in the cellar, standing together, with arms clasped around each other, leaning against the wall—all dead. While a neighbor, in a similar place, saved himself and family by having a great supply of milk on hand whereby the greedy flames were quenched.

From here I returned to the relief train and went with it to Hinckley, assisting in picking up the dead bodies along the track. In Hinckley the ruins were still burning, and the bodies in hundreds were scattered about the town. Here we worked until nine o'clock in the evening. The corpses were left here for burial on the following day while those belonging to Sandstone and vicinity were buried at the Sandstone cemetery.

On our way to Hinckley we were joined by a little calf that came up to the train seemingly to plead for relief. We pitied the defenceless creature, took him into the train, and gave him milk, which he evidently swallowed with good appetite, but how he escaped the fire no one can tell. He was joined a little further along the road by another fellow-creature of his own kind. That one stood alone in the gravel pit, having alone escaped the horrid death to which hundreds of mortals had fallen victims all about him in that pit; we also took him into our train.

I don't know whether the calves enjoyed it the better, or we. Everybody seemed to be their friends and enjoyed their company. These two calves were taken to the county farm where they will be tenderly cared for and in due time put on exhibition as choice relics of the few escaped.

We returned thence to Duluth at three o'clock A. M., all tired out with this sickening work.

As a crowning event at the close of this eventful time, and as a delightful change, I had the privilege of marrying a couple that had saved themselves out of that all-absorbing conflagration. This young couple seemed to be cheerful and hopeful, in spite of the fact that they possessed not a single dollar.

These experiences have sunk deep into my heart. This conflagration is wider in its sweep and more terrible in its results than any one can imagine who has not been an eye-witness of the actual scene.

During all these terrible experiences I was not afraid, for, in the very flames, I only waited the time, evidently near at hand, when I should see Jesus, and enter into His rest.

EMIL A. ANDERSON.

SANDSTONE QUARRY STORE HOUSE.

PARTRIDGE.

P REVIOUS to the fire, Partridge, although not a large town, was doing a heavy business, largely lumbering interests centering there.

It contained several dwellings, owned by H. Hogenson, J. Johnson, Mrs. May Boyington and R. L. Saunders (night operator for the Eastern Minnesota Railway Company), two stores, one owned by T. O'Neal, the other by T. C. Kelly; one hotel owned and managed by D. Boyington.

The Eastern Minnesota railway station, together with the day telegraph work, had been successfully run by May Boyington (wife of D. Boyington), for five years previous to the fire.

When Partridge was threatened, Mrs. Boyington bravely kept to her post; even when the train arrived bearing the Hinckley refugees, she refused to leave, waiting until the fire was upon them. Then leaving her own property she remained to gather up such valuables as she could carry belonging to the company, barely escaping with her life.

The fire left most of the Partridge people homeless and without money. O'Neal Brothers, J. Fleming, D. Boyce and Welch, Donevan & Co., were heavy losers.

The residents consider their escape from the fire miraculous, as it burst upon the town with sudden fury.

GEORGE VAN PELT.

On the first day of September, 1894, I left West Superior on extra at 2:30 p. m., with engine 206, Fireman Albert McMahon, Conductor J. C. Cardle, Brakeman Joe Allen, and Kid Nelson, who lost his father in the fire. We got as far as Dedham, which is about fifty-three miles from Hinckley, where we received orders to lay up on account of fire, and if the fire got so close as to endanger the train, to come back to West Superior.

REV. PROF. POOLE, M. A.

On the arrival of the passenger train from Hinckley, we got orders to take five empty box cars from our train, proceed toward Hinckley, and rescue all we could of those unable to get on the passenger train. While waiting at Dedham, I had a few minutes conversation with Engineer Best, of the passenger train, who told me the condition of things along the line toward Hinckley. I stopped two or three times between Kerrick and Partridge (the latter place fourteen miles from Hinckley) and cut trees off the track, which had blown down.

When I got within three miles of Partridge, I met people running, they knew not where, only trying to get away from fire. I stopped and they told me that the people of Partridge had run to a little lake about a quarter of a mile north of the track. Partridge consisted of a lumbering camp, general store, depot, hotel and a few dwellings. The only relic of the place left is the water tank.

Then I proceeded toward Hinckley until I came to a bridge on fire, when I could go no farther, and started back, picking up people as I went, and when opposite the lake, I whistled, and they came toward the track as fast as they could, as the woods were then all on fire. We got all but three or four people, who were overcome with heat and gave up, so they could not be saved. All told we brought about two hundred refugees in on our train."

ALBERT H. McMAHON.

The following is a correct statement of the work of our trainmen at the time of the great fire, to the best of my knowledge and belief.

"On Saturday afternoon of September first, 1894, we left West Superior, Wisconsin, about 2:30 p. m. for St. Cloud, Minnesota, with an extra freight train in charge of J. C. Cardle, conductor, and George Van Pelt, engineer. The weather was hot and smoky. When we arrived at Boylestown, six miles from West Superior at 3:30 p. m. we had to light our head light and cab lamps, as well as others.

"We reached Dedham, which is fourteen miles from West Superior, at five p. m. We had in the meantime received instructions from headquarters to tie up at Dedham, until further orders, as the fire was so close to the track that it was dangerous to proceed with the train any further. We side tracked our train until the arrival of passenger and local freight from Hinckley with the rescued on board. At 8:30 p. m. we received a message to take five cars and the way car and go to Partridge to rescue what people were there alive. From Dedham we went to within half a mile of Partridge. The fire was very bad, and the air was hot and oppressive, almost to suffocation. Between Mansfield and Partridge we stopped our train three or four times to chop the burned and fallen trees from off the track.

"When within one-half mile of Partridge, we came to a burning bridge and found it was not safe to pass over. Some one informed us that the people had fled to a lake in the woods some distance from Partridge; so we backed up the train slowly to a logging road and sounded the whistle to let the people know we were there. This was about one o'clock, the morning of Sunday, September second. We were about one hour loading the poorly clad people on our train, which backed up slowly to West Superior, arriving at six a. m.

"There were about sixty families as near as I can judge, numbering, all told, about two hundred.   ALBERT H. McMAHON,

"Fireman on 'Extra.'"

> "Though oft depressed and lowly"
> "All my fears are laid aside"
> "If I but remember only
> Such as these have lived and died."—Longfellow.

"Through envy of the Devil came death into the world. But the souls of the righteous are in the hands of God, and there shall no torment touch them. In the sight of the unwise they seemed to die; and their departure is taken for misery, and their going from us to be utter destruction; but they are in peace. For though they be punished in the sight of men, yet is their hope full of immortality, and having been a little chastened they shall be justly rewarded for God proved them and found them worthy of himself. They that put their trust in God shall understand the truth, and such as be faithful in love shall abide with him; for grace and mercy are to his saints, and he hath a care for his elect."—THE WISDOM OF SOLOMON.

FOREST FIRES OF SEPTEMBER 1, 1894.

DEATH LIST.

1. Abbey, Cora—Age 27, wife of Albert Abbey, residence, I mile north of Hinckley; identified by X. Sherman; no valuables found except I locket and a few trinkets; has sister in Langford, S. D.
2. Abbey, Albert—Age 33, married, husband of Cora Abbey, residence I mile north of Hinckley; found near his home and identified by X. Sherman; has father and mother in Michigan.
3. Abbey, Floyd—Age 7, son of Albert and Cora Abbey; found with his parents.
4. Abbey, Lloyd—Age 9, son of Albert and Cora Abbey; found with his parents.
5. Arndt, Miss Mattie—Age 18, single, residence Hinckley, parents live near Montrose, Minn.; unidentified; nothing found but buttons, etc.; reported by B. C. Bartlett.
6. Anderson, Anthony—Age 62, married; residence, Sandstone.
7. Anderson, Mrs.—Age 58, wife of Anthony Anderson.
8. Anderson, ———Male, age 6, son of Anthony Anderson.
9. Anderson, ———Male, age 10, son of Anthony Anderson.
10. Anderson,———Male, age 12, son of Anthony Anderson.
11. Anderson, John G.—Age 48, residence Hinckley, husband of Mrs. Emily Anderson; not identified.
12. Anderson, Mrs. Emily—Age 45, wife of J. G. Anderson; not identified.
13. Anderson, Chas. G.—Age 21, son of John G. Anderson, was found I mile north of Hinckley, identified by C. Vanhoven, H. S. Bartlett, and others; buried in Hinckley cemetery.

14. Anderson, Emily—Age 18, single, daughter of J. G. Anderson, was not identified; has uncle in Moorehead.

15. Anderson, Frank—Age 35, married, residence Sandstone, husband of Mrs. F. Anderson, No. 16.

16. Anderson, Mrs.—Age 32, wife of Frank Anderson, above described; residence, Sandstone.

17. Anderson, ———Boy, age 6, son of Frank Anderson.

18. Anderson, ———Boy, age 7, son of Frank Anderson.

19. Anderson, Mrs. Engla—Age 32, married, wife of August Anderson; residence, Sandstone; found in Halvorsen's well with 17 others; identified by August Anderson.

20. Anderson, ———Female, age 9, daughter of August Anderson, found in well with her mother.

21. Anderson, ———Female, age 7, daughter of August Anderson, found in well with her mother.

22. Anderson, August—Age 36, married; residence, Sandstone.

23. Anderson, Mrs.—Age 36, wife of August Anderson; residence, Sandstone.

24. Anderson, Chas.—Age 35, married; residence, Brook Park.

25. Anderson, ———Child, age 4, son of Chas. Anderson; residence, Brook Park.

26. Anderson, ———Child, age 5, daughter of Chas. Anderson; residence, Brook Park.

27. Anderson, ———Child, age 8, son of Chas. Anderson.

28. Anderson, Mrs.—Age 35, wife of Chas. Anderson.

29. Burke, John—Age 40, married; residence, Hinckley; wife living in Sandstone; John Burke was not identified.

30. Bilado, Emma—Age 8, daughter of Peter Bilado; residence, Sandstone; parents living in Sandstone; this girl was found near her home.

31. Bilado, Nora—Age 13, daughter of Peter Bilado, found near her home; identified by her mother.

32. Berghaln, Magnus—Age 24, single; residence, Sandstone.

33. Brodd, Alfred—Age 29, married; residence, Sandstone.

34. Brodd, Mrs.—Age 26, married, wife of Alfred Brodd.

35. Brodd, ———Age —, daughter of Alfred Brodd.

36. Brodd, ———Age 8, son of Alfred Brodd.

37. Burns, Robert—Age 35, single; residence, Sandstone.

38. Brayman, James W?—Age 27, single; residence, Brook Park; found in woods east of the section house; identified by his father; father's residence Brook Park.

39. Barnes, James—Age 35, single; residence, Pokegama; son of Robert Barnes, Pokegama; identified by his father.

40. Barnes, James—Age 25, single, found on wagon road, 2 miles south of Pokegama; identified by his father, Robert Barnes.

41. Best, John—Age 63; residence, 2 miles south-east of Hinckley; found on road, 60 rods west of his house; identified by his son Christian; buried at Hinckley; identified by a jack knife which he carried.

42. Best, Eva—Age 60, married, wife of John Best; found with John Best in the road west of the house; identified by Christ Best.

43. Best, Bertha—Age 18, single, daughter of John and Eva Best; identified by Christ Best.

44. Best, William—Age 21, single, son of John and Eva Best; not identified.

45. Best, Fred—Age 23, single, son of John and Eva Best; not identified.

46. Best, George—Age 25, single, son of John and Eva Best; not identified.

47. Best, Victor—Age 8, son of John and Eva Best.

48. Bean, James—Age 48, married, wife living in Eau Claire, not identified; perished in swamp north of Hinckley.

49. Burke, John, Sr.—Age 65, father of John Burke, No. 29; residence, Hinckley, with his son; his body was not identified, supposed to have gone across the river, north of Hinckley.

50. Blanchard, Mrs.—Age 29, married, wife of John Blanchard, of Hinckley, body found at St. P. & D. round house; identified by her husband; buried in Hinckley.

51. Blanchard, Frank—Age 11, found with his mother at round house.

52. Bee, Stephen—Age 16, son of Alex and Hannah Bee; residence, south of Hinckley; could not be identified.

53. Curry, Michael—Age 38, married; residence, 1 mile north of Hinckley; all of family burned; has brother in Michigan; found three-fourths of a mile north of his home; identified by N. Sherman and Jos. Tew; buried at Hinckley.

54. Mrs. Curry—Age 30, wife of M. Curry, found 1 mile north of her home; identified by N. Sherman and Jos. Tew.

55. Curry, Willie—Age 12, son of Mike Curry, found with his mother; identified by his being with his mother.

56. Cain, David—Age 54, married; residence, Rock Creek; was in Hinckley on visit; found in swamp 1 mile north of Hinckley; buried at Hinckley.

57. Cain, Mrs.—Age 50, wife of David Cain, found with husband in swamp north of Hinckley.

58. Chambers, Louis—Age 24, married, came from Illinois to Hinckley; found on Section 12, Town of Hinckley; identified by N. Sherman, by his personal appearance, and knife and buttons.

59. Crowley, Jerry—Age 59, widower; residence, Hinckley; found in gravel pit north of Hinckley; identified by Dr. D. W. Cowan, of Hinckley; buried at Hinckley.

60. Corbett, Thos—Age 57; residence, Hinckley; burned in the woods north-east of Hinckley, near Kettle River.

61. Costigan, William—Age 50; residence, Hinckley; not identified; supposed to have perished in swamp one-half mile north of Hinckley.

62. Costigan, Mrs. Effie—Age 41, wife of William Costigan.

63. Costigan, Miss Effie—Age 15, daughter of William Costigan.

64. Costigan, Irma—Age 15, daughter of William Costigan.

65. Costigan, Myrtle—Age 10, daughter of William Costigan.

66 Costigan, Jennie—Age 7, daughter of William Costigan.

67. Costigan, William—Age 5, son of William Costigan.

68. Costigan, Hazel—Age 2, daughter of William Costigan.

69. Conniker, Jas.—Age 50, single; residence, Hinckley; has sister living in Pine City; was not found.

70. Donahue, Ellen—Age 37, married; residence, Hinckley; found in swamp one-half mile north of Hinckley; husband lives in Hinckley; she was identified by him, and buried in Hinckley.

71. Donahue, Esther—Age 8, daughter of Dan Donahue; found in swamp with her mother; burned beyond recognition.

72. Donahue, Katie—Age 10, daughter of Dan Donahue, found in swamp with her mother; identified by Dan Donahue.

73. Donahue, Mary—Age 12, daughter of Dan Donahue; found with her mother.

74. Dunn, Thomas—Age 25; residence, Hinckley; son of Michael Dunn, of Hinckley; was recognized by appearance and jewelry; was buried at Pine City.

75. Demet, William—Age 26, single; residence, Sandstone.
76. Dagerstrom, Chas.—Age 20, single; residence, Sandstone.
77. Erickson, Mrs. Mary—Age 42, wife of O. Erickson; residence, Sandstone.
78. Eck, Nels—Age 39, married; residence, Hinckley; not identified.
79. Edstrom, Sophie—Age 60, widow; residence, Sandstone.
80. Edstrom, Mrs.—Age 30, wife of Ed. Edstrom; residence, Sandstone.
81. Edstrom, ————Age 8, daughter of Ed. Edstrom.
82. Edstrom, ————Age 6, son of Ed. Edstrom.
83. Edstrom, ————Age 4, son of Ed. Edstrom.
84. Edstrom, ————Age 2, daughter of Ed. Edstrom.
85. Frisk, Caroline—Age 42, married; residence, Hinckley; burned in swamp north of Hinckley, but not identified.
86. Frisk, John—Age 10, son of Mrs. Nels Frisk; was burned with his mother.
87. Frisk, Richard—Age 2, son of Nels Frisk; burned with his mother.
88. Frisk, David—Age 7, son of Nels Frisk; burned with mother in swamp, one-half mile north of Hinckley.
89. Englund, ————Age 3, son of Peter Englund; residence, Sandstone.
90. Englund, ————Age 5, son of Peter Englund.
91. Englund, ————Age 7, daughter of Peter Englund.
92. Englund, ————Age 9, son of Peter Englund.
93. Englund, ————Age 11, son of Peter Englund.
94. Englund, ————Aged 12, daughter of Peter Englund.
95. Englund, ————Age 14, daughter of Peter Englund.
96. Englund, Mrs.—Age 43, wife of Peter Englund.
97. Englund, Peter—Age 44, married; residence, Sandstone; found in well with others on Halvorsen's lot; the entire family was burned at Sandstone.
98. Fitzgerald, Pat—Age 47, married; residence, Hinckley; not identified.
99. Fitzgerald, Mrs. Mary—Age 42, wife of Pat. Fitzgerald; not identified.
100. Fitzgerald, John—Age 14, son of Pat. Fitzgerald; not identified.
101. Fitzgerald, Mary—Age 13, daughter of P. Fitzgerald; not identified.

102.   Fitzgerald, Pat—Age 12, son of Pat Fitzgerald.

103.   Ginder, William—Age 47, married; residence, Hinckley; supposed to have burned across the river; not identified; has brother living near Hinckley.

104.   Ginder, Mrs. Winnie—Age 45, wife of William Ginder; recognized and buried in Hinckley.

105.   Ginder, William, Jr.—Age 9, son of William Ginder; was not identified.

106.   Ginder, James—Age 9, son of William Ginder; not identified.

107.   Grissinger, Mrs. C.—Age 35, wife of William Grissinger; residence, Hinckley; identified and buried by her husband.

108.   Grissinger, Miss C.—Age 10, daughter of Mrs. Grissinger; identified by William Grissinger; buried with her mother.

109.   Grissinger, Mabel—Age 8, daughter of William Grissinger; identified by her father; buried in Hinckley.

110.   Granstrum, Mary—Age 7, daughter of Andrew Granstrum; residence, Hinckley; was burned in swamp, one-half mile north of Hinckley; not identified.

111.   Ginder, Winnie—Age 8, daughter of William Ginder.

112.   Greenfield—Age 7, son of M. E. Greenfield; residence, Finlayson; identified by his father.

113.   Greenfield, ———Age 15, daughter of M. E. Greenfield.

114.   Greenfield, ———Age 8, daughter of M. E. Greenfield.

115.   Greenfield, ———Age 5, daughter of M. E. Greenfield.

116.   Greenfield, ———Age 3, daughter of M. E. Greenfield; the Greenfield children were identified by the locality where they were found.

117.   Goodsell, David—Age 25 single; residence, Pokegama; has parents living in Polk county, Wisconsin.

118.   Guhldahl, Andrew—Age 30, single; residence, Sandstone.

119.   Hanson, Mrs.—Age 20, wife of Ed. Hanson, No. 2; residence, Hinckley; burned in swamp one-half mile north of Hinckley; not identified.

120.   Hanson, Mrs. Clara—Age 30; residence, Hinckley; burned in swamp, one-half mile north of Hinckley; not identified.

121.   Hanson, Axel—Age 39, married; residence, Hinckley; burned in swamp one-half miles north of Hinckley; identified by Otto Kowalke, of Pine City, and others; buried in Hinckley; leaves wife living in Hinckley.

122. Hanson, Henry—Age 35, married; residence, Hinckley; identified by watch, etc.; buried at Hinckley; leaves wife and 6 children in Hinckley.

123. Hanson, Ed.—Age 45, married, family in Duluth; not found; burned in swamp north of Hinckley.

124. Hanson, Mrs. Sophie—Age 44, married, burned in swamp one-half mile north of Hinckley; not identified.

125. Hathaway, Mrs.—Age —, married, found one-half mile east of Hinckley; reported by A. G. Perkins.

126. Hjerpa, Karin—Age 62, married, mother-in-law of Nels Frisk, burned in swamp one-half mile north of Hinckley; identified by the locality in which she was found.

127. Henderson, John—Age 12, son of Thos. Henderson; residence, Pine City; burned in the woods north of Hinckley; identified by the father and buried in Pine City.

128. Henderson, Sandy—Age 13, son of Thos. Henderson; found with his brother.

129. Hopps, Mrs—Age 48, married; residence, Sandstone.

130. Hoffman, Henry B.—Age 81, married; residence, Sandstone; was burned near his home; identified by his son, Robert Hoffman, of Pine City; buried at Sandstone.

131. Hoffman, Mrs.—Age 79, wife of H. B. Hoffman, found with her husband

132. Jones, Thos.—Age 45, widower, found on top of Hinckley Hill; buried in Hinckley.

133. Johnson, Mrs. Annie—Age 31, wife of Peter Johnson, found on St. P. & D. Ry. track; buried in Hinckley; identified by Nels Frisk; address of friends, John Pearson, Hinckley.

134. Jensen, Peter—Age 33, husband of Mrs. Annie; residence, Hinckley; burned in swamp north of Hinckley.

135. Jensen, Albert—Age 10, son of Annie and Peter Jensen, found with his mother on railroad track; identified by Nels Frisk; buried in Hinckley.

136. Jensen, Annie—Age 12, daughter of Peter Jenson, found with her mother on the railroad track north of Hinckley.

137. Johnson, Alfred—Age 29, single; residence, Hinckley.

138. Johnson, Ernest—Age 27, married; residence, Sandstone.

139. Johnson, Mrs.—Age 25, wife of Ernest Johnson.

140. Johnson, ———Age 1, daughter of Ernest Johnson.

141. Kelly, Jas.—Age 43, single; residence, Hinckley; burned near Kettle River; identified by Ernest Hogan, who was with him; buried in Pine City.

142. Kjellen, Peter—Age 29, married; residence, Sandstone.

143. Kjellen, Mrs.—Age 28, wife of Peter Kjellen.

144. Kjellen, ———Age 10, son of Peter and Mrs. Kjellen.

145. Kjellen, ———Age 8, daughter of Peter Kjellen.

146. Kjellen, ———Age 6, son of Peter Kjellen.

147. Lind, Mrs.—Age 32, wife of ——— Lind; residence, Sandstone Junction.

148. Lind, — ———Age 10, daughter of Mrs. Henry Lind.

149. Lind, ———Age 8, son of Mrs. Henry Lind.

150. Lind, ———Age 6, daughter of Mrs. Herry Lind.

151. Lind, ———Age 4, son of Mrs. Lind.

152. Lind, ———Age 1, son of Mrs. Lind.

153. Lovell, Thos. J.—Age 38, married; residence, 1 1-2 miles north of Hinckley; found 60 rods south-east of his house; came from Pierpont, S. D.; identified by N. Sherman.

154. Lovell, Louise—Age 35, wife of Thos. J. Lovell; found with her husband; buried with rest of family in Hinckley.

155. Lovell, Esther—Age 14, daughter of Louise Lovell; identified by being near her parents.

156. Lovell, Chester—Age 11, son of Thos. J. Lovell; identified by being found with his parents.

157. Lief, Lottie—Age 18, single; residence, Hinckley; not identified; reported by B. C. Martlett.

158. Larson, Erick—Age 22, single; residence, Pokegama; found 1 mile east of Pokegama section house; identified by Hans Nelson; thought to have relatives at Mud Creek, Pine county.

159. Martinson, Mrs. I.—Age 36, wife of Martin Martinson, of Hinckley; found in river at Hinckley, near the wagon bridge; identified by husband; buried in Hinckley.

160. Martinson, Ida—Age 9, daughter of Martin Martinson; found in river near her mother.

161. Martinson, Emma—Age 7, daughter of M. Martinson; found with the mother.

162. Martinson, Hilda—Age 5, daughter of M. Martinson; found in Grindstone river, with her mother; identified by her father; buried in Hinckley.

163. Martinson, ———Age 2 months, daughter of M. Martinson; found with mother in the river.

164. Murphy, Mike—Age 40, husband of Mrs. Nancy Murphy, of St. Paul; residence, Hinckley; was not found; supposed to have been burned in the mill yard at Hinckley.

165. McDonnell, John—Age 27, married; residence, Hinckley; was seen to go over the railroad bridge with others; none returned; was not identified; has father, Jas. McDonnell, in Wauzeka, Wis.

166. McDonell, Bertha—Age 27, was seen to cross St. P. & D. Ry. bridge, with her husband; was not identified; reported by Michael Dunn.

167. Molander, Fred—Age 25, married; found in well near his house.

168. Molander, Mrs.—Age 25, wife of Fred Molander; found in her house; identified by proximity to her house, and having children in her arms.

169. Molander, ———Age 3, daughter of Fred Molander.

170. Molander, ———Age 1, son of Fred Molander; identified by A. Berg.

171. Mattison, Hans W.—Age 20, single, burned in swamp one-half mile north of Hinckley; not identified; has parents living in Eau Claire, Wis.

172. McNamara, Mrs.—Age 48, wife of John McNamara of Rutledge; found on railroad track, north of Hinckley; identified, and buried at Hinckley.

173. McNamara, John—Age 14, son of Mrs. McNamara; found on track with his mother.

174. McNamara, James—Age 12, son of Mrs. McNamara; found and buried with his mother.

175. McNamara, Michael—Age 8, son of Mrs. McNamara; found and buried with his mother.

176. Nelson, Mrs. Betsy—Age 42, married, wife of Nels Nelson; residence, Hinckley; not found; burned in swamp one-half mile north of Hinckley; reported by her husband.

177. Nyberg, Maggie—Age 20; residence, Hinckley; not identified; has relatives in North Branch, Minn.; reported by B. C. Bartlett.

178. Nesbit, William—Age 38, single; residence, Hinckley; burned in swamp, one-half mile north of Hinckley; Albert Frazer, of Hinckley, saw him die; identified after death by watch, jewelry, etc.; has brother in Eau Claire, Wis.
179. Nelson, John—Age 26, single; residence, Sandstone.
180. Newstrom, Gust—Age 33, married; residence, Hinckley.
181. Newstrom, Mrs.—Age 31, wife of Gust Newstrom.
182. Newstrom, ———Age 3, daughter of Gust Newstrom.
183. Nelson, William—Age 25, single; residence, Hinckley.
184. Nelson, Louis—Age 28, married; residence, Hinckley.
185. Nelson, Mrs. P. M.—Age 32, married; residence, Hinckley.
186. Olson, Otto—Age 38, married; residence, Hinckley; not identified; supposed to have burned in the swamp, one-half mile north of Hinckley; has wife left.
187. Olson, ———Age 1, son of Otto Olson; found in the river.
188. Olson, ———Age 9, daughter of Otto Olson.
189. Olson, ———Age 4, son of Otto Olson.
190. Olson, Miss Lena—Age 18, single; residence, St. Paul; found with the Molander family at Pokegama; was a sister of Mrs. Molander; identified by being found with Molander family.
191. Olson, Chas.—Age 22, single, brother of Mrs. Molander, of Pokegama; identified by A. Berg; buried at Pokegama.
192. Olson, Nora—Age 14, sister of Chas. Olson; found with Molander family; buried at Pokegama.
193. Olson, Oscar—Age 16, brother of Chas.; found with sister; identified, and buried at Pokegama.
194. Peterson, Emily—Age 12; residence, Sandstone.
195. Peterson, Emil—Age 29, single; residence, Sandstone; found in the village of Sandstone; identified by C. Staples; has brother, Gust Peterson, in Sandstone; buried in Sandstone.
196. Pennoyer, William—Age 24; residence, Hinckley; found on railroad track; fell from the train that was burned; identified by Walter Gray.
197. Raymond, Thomas—Age 35, married; residence, Pokegama; found one-half mile north-east of his residence; identified by pipe, etc.; has friends in West Superior; buried in Pokegama.

198. Raymond, Mrs.—Age 35, wife of Thos. Raymond; found with her husband; identified by purse; buried with her husband; reported by W. Brayman; friends at Grand Forks, N. D., and Fond du Lac, Wis.

199. Raymond, Edward—Age 10, son of Thos. Raymond; found one-half mile north-east of village; buried with his parents.

200. Raymond, ———Age 2, daughter of Thos. Raymond.

201. Raymond, ———Age 6, son of Thos. Raymond.

202. Ricketson, E.—Age 71, father of William Ricketson; residence, Hinckley; found in Hinckley; buried in Hinckley; came from Minneapolis.

203. Riley, Dennis—Age 40; residence, Hinckley; found north of his home, between the two tracks; identified by L. S. Miller and Conductor Sargent; address of friends, J. McNamara, Rutledge; had $2,000 insurance in Oskosh Accident; has 1 boy left.

204. Riley, Mrs. Winifred—Age 35, wife of Dennis Riley; supposed to have been burned in swamp, one-half mile north of Hinckley.

205. Riley, Thos.—Age 15, son of Dennis Riley; not identified.

206. Riley, ———Age 5, daughter of Dennis Riley; not identified; supposed to have burned with her mother; buried in Hinckley.

207. Rodgers, John—Age 39, married; residence, Hinckley; born in Canada; found in Hinckley, near railroad track; identified by W. DeLong.

208. Rodgers, Mrs. R.—Age 26, wife of John Rodgers; found near her husband; identified by being near husband; buried with rest of family in Hinckley.

209. Rodgers, Mary—Age 4, daughter of John Rodgers; found with mother.

210. Rodgers, Minnie—Age 2, daughter of John Rodgers; found with parents.

211. Rodgers, ———Age 7 days, son of John Rodgers.

212. Rowley, Otto—Age 43, found near Skunk Lake; identified, and taken to Duluth.

213. Robinson, John—Age 44; (no further information.)

214. Robinson, Mrs—Age 40, wife of John Robinson.

14.—HINCKLEY.—BROUGHT IN FROM THE OUTSKIRTS.

REMAINS OF T. J. LOVELL AND FAMILY.

215. Robinson, ————Age 13, son of John Robinson.
216. Robinson, ————Age 11, son of John Robinson.
217. Robinson, ————Age 9, son of John Robinson.
218. Reynolds, L.—Age 54, married; residence, Hinckley; born in Maine; not identified; burned in swamp, one-half mile north of Hinckley.
219. Reynolds, Mrs.—Age 40, wife of L. Reynolds, burned on a wagon with rest of family; not identified.
220. Reynolds, ————Age 9, daughter of L. Reynolds; not identified; burned in swamp north of Hinckley.
221. Reynolds, ————Age 6, daughter of L. Reynolds.
222. Reynolds, ————Age 6, daughter of L. Reynolds.
223. Reynolds, ————Age 2, daughter of L. Reynolds.
224. Rustin, Swen—Age 29, married; residence, Hinckley; not identified.
225. Rustin, Mrs.—Age 27, wife of Swen Rustin.
226. Rustin, ————Age 7, daughter of Swen Rustin.
227. Rustin, ————Age 4, daughter of Swen Rustin.
228. Rustin, ————Age 2, son of Swen Rustin.
228. Stromberg, Chas.—Age 45; residence, Hinckley; not found; probably burned in swamp, one-half mile north of Hinckley; entire family burned except 1 son, Charles, who is now in Sioux City.
230. Stromberg, Mrs.—Age 36, wife of Chas. Stromberg; not found; supposed to have burned in swamp, one-half mile north of Hinckley.
231. Stromberg, ————Age 8, son of Chas. Stromberg; burned with rest of family.
232. Stromberg, Victor—Age 10, son of Chas. Stromberg.
233. Stromberg, ————Age 8, son of Chas. Stromberg.
234. Stromberg, ————Age 4, daughter of Chas. Stromberg,
235. Stromberg, ————Age 2, daughter of Chas. Stromberg.
236. Stromberg, Joseph—Age 43, married; residence, Hinckley; (nothing further known.)
237. Stromberg, Mrs. Mary—Age 42, wife of Jos. Stromberg.
238. Stromberg, Oscar—Age 13, son of Jos. Stromberg.
239. Stromberg, Albert—Age 11, son of Jos. Stromberg.
240. Stromberg, Mary—Age 9, daughter of Jos. Stromberg.
241. Stromberg, Augusta—Age 6, daughter of Jos. Stromberg.
242. Swanson, August—Age 38, married; residence, Sandstone.

8. HINCKLEY.— A FUNERAL PROCESSION — BRINGING THE BODIES IN.

UNKNOWN DEAD.

243. Swanson, Mrs.—Age 32, wife of August Swanson.
244. Swanson, ————.Age 10, daughter of August Swanson.
245. Sanderstrom, Thos—Age 56, nothing certain of his being identified; buried in Hinckley.
246. Sherman, Fred—Age 31; residence, 1 mile north of Hinckley; found 80 .ods from house; identified by knife, etc.; reported by N. Sherman.
247. Sherman, Mrs. Eva—Age 24, wife of Fred Sherman; found in root house; buried in Hinckley.
248. Sherman, Ralph—Age 7, son of Fred Sherman; found with his father.
249. Sherman, Earl—Age 6, son of Fred Sherman; found near his father; buried at Hinckley.
250. Sherman, George—Age 4, son of Fred Sherman; found near his father.
251. Sherman, Bina—Age 2, daughter of Fred Sherman; found with parents; identified by N. Sherman.
252. Sherman, William—Age 1, son of Fred Sherman; found with his parents; buried in Hinckley.
253. Sherman, Albina—Age 26, wife of Noble Sherman; residence, Hinckley; found near the house; identified by breast-pin and other jewelry; reported by N. Sherman, her husband.
254. Sherman, Flora—Age 7, daughter of Noble Sherman; found near her mother; identified by N. Sherman, her father, who is going to Riversdale, Mich.
255. Sherman, John—Age 5, son of N. Sherman; found with his mother.
256. Sherman, Leslie—Age 3, son of N. Sherman; identified by his father; buried in Hinckley.
257. Sherman, Romanzo—Age 1, son of N. Sherman; found with his mother; the entire family was buried in Hinckley.
258. Schlano, Paul—Age 26, single; residence Hinckley; burned in swamp, one-half mile north of Hinckley; identified by his uncle, P. Leake, of Taylors Falls; was taken to Taylors Falls, and buried there.
259. Stromberg, Chas.—Age 28, married; residence, Hinckley.
260. Stromberg, Mrs.—Age 28, wife of Chas. Stromberg.
261. Turgeon, Mr. T.—Age 26, married; residence. Hinckley; not identified; leaves family living in Hinckley.

262. Westby, Thos.—Age 38, married; residence, Hinckley; not identified.
263. Westby, ————Age 34, wife of Thos. Westby; not identified.
264. Westby, ————Age 1, daughter of Thos. Westby; not identified.
265. Westby, Thos., Jr.—Age 10, son of Thos. Westby.
266. Westby, Sophie—Age 8, daughter of Thos. Westby; unidentified.
267. Westby, ————Age 5, son of Thos. Westby; unidentified.
268. Westby, ————Age 3, son of Thos. Westby; this entire family was burned in the swamp, one-half mile north of Hinckley; none were identified.
269. Weigle, Anton—Age 33, married; residence, Hinckley; not found, but supposed to be among the unidentified bodies taken from the swamp, one-half mile north of Hinckley; reported by Christ Best.
270. Weigle, Eva—Age 22, wife of Anton Weigle; was burned with her parent, John Best; was not found.
271. Weigle, Winnie—Age 4, daughter of Anton Weigle; not identified.
272. Weireter, Mrs.—Age 24, wife of Geo. Weireter; residence, Hinckley; not identified; husband lives in Hinckley.
273. Whitney, Albert—Age 30, married; residence, Pokegama; found on railroad track, by William Wilkinson and D. Markham; buried where found.
274. Wall, John—Age 38, married; residence, Sandstone.
275. Wall, Mrs.—Age 37, wife of John Wall.
276. Wall, ————Age 6, son of John Wall.
277. Wall, ————Age 4, son of John Wall.
278. Wall, ————Age —, daughter of John Wall; this family was buried in Sandstone.
279. White, Thos.—Age 33, married; residence, unknown; found near Hinckley; was an explorer.
280. Webster, Mrs. Belle—Age 26, wife of Lee Webster, mayor of Hinckley; not identified; former home in Iowa.
281. Wallace, Anna—Age about 35; residence, Hinckley; died in hospital from burns; reported by M. Garity.
282. Wacke, Mrs. Sophie—Age 20, married; residence, Hinckley.
283. Wacke, ————Age —, infant daughter of Sophie Wacke.

284. Westlund, Mrs.—Age 29, married, wife of John Westlund; residence Hinckley.

285. Westlund, ———Age 2, daughter of Mrs. Westlund.

286. Westlund, ———Age 4, daughter of Mrs. Westlund.

287. Wold, Louis—Age 44, married; residence, Hinckley; identified by John Pearson; buried in Hinckley; burned in swamp, one-half mile north of Hinckley; buried in Hinckley.

288. Wold, Alfred—Age 12, son of Louis Wold; not identified; burned with parents in swamp, one-half mile north of Hinckley.

289. Wold, Mrs. L.—Age 35, wife of Louis Wold; burned in swamp north of Hinckley; not identified.

290. Wold, Ida—Age 11, daughter of Louis Wold; not identified.

291. Wold, Christ—Age 6, son of Louis Wold.

292. Wold, ———Baby, about 1 year old, son of Louis Wold; the entire family was burned in swamp, one-half mile north of Hinckley; none of them were identified, except Louis.

293. Wold, Louis, Sr.—Age 72, father of Louis Wold; burned one-half mile north of Hinckley, in swamp.

294. Westlund, John—Age 39, married; not identified; his wife is now in Duluth.

296. Westlund, ———Age 2, daughter of John Westlund.

297. O'Brien, Belle—Age 20, single; residence, Hinckley.

298. Dolan, Emma—Age 24, single; residence, Hinckley; not identified.

299. Anderson, Andrew—Age about 23; residence, Hinckley; worked in saw mill for Brennan Lumber Co.; not identified; reported by William Bruce.

300. Dahlgren, John—Age 19; residence, Hinckley; worked in saw mill; not identified.

301. Hopkins, Nathan—Age 50; residence, 1 1-2 miles west of Hinckley; found in Hinckley; not identified.

302. Hopkins, Mrs.—Age 40, wife of N. Hopkins; burned in Hinckley; not identified.

303. Hopkins, Walter—Age 13, burned with rest of family in swamp one-half mile north of Hinckley; unidentified.

304. Peterson, Peter—Age 24, single; residence, Hinckley; not identified; probably burned in swamp north of Hinckley.

305. Parrish, Jos.—Age 21, single; residence, Hinckley; not identified; burned in swamp, one-half mile north of Hinckley.

306. Evans, Chas.—Age 38, married; residence, Hinckley; not identified.

307. Campbell, ———Age, 47: (nothing further known.)

308. Paulson, Mrs. Hans—Age 33; residence, Hinckley; not identified; burned in swamp north of Hinckley.

309. Paulson, ———Age —, daughter of Hans Paulson.

310. Paulson, ———Age 4, son of Hans Paulson.

311. Paulson, ———Age 5, son of Hans Paulson.

312. Paulson, ———Age 7, son of Hans Paulson; none of this family were identified.

313. Hopkins, Bertha—Age 8, daughter of N. Hopkins; not identified; burned in swamp north of Hinckley, with her parents.

314. Hopkins, ———Age 3, son of N. Hopkins; burned in swamp, one-half mile north of Hinckley.

315. Unknown—Male; height, 5.10; weight, 165; wore heavy laced shoes, woolen ribbed socks; nothing on body; found in swamp, one-half mile north of Hinckley.

316. Unknown—Boy; age about 12; knee pants; long, black ribbed stockings; shingle nails found in pocket; found one-half mile north of Hinckley.

317. Unknown—Girl; age about 13; weight, 90; found on railroad track, near the round house, in the village of Hinckley; burned beyond recognition.

318. Unknown—Man; age about 24; weight, 160; wore Bloucher laced shoes and Bedford cord pants; small silver watch, case No. 25107; $3 in silver; 1 Yale padlock key; hair burned off; probably sandy.

319. Unknown—Man; weight, 170; body well formed; no clothing on; found on top of Hinckley hill.

320. Unknown—Female; age about 45; dark hair, tinged with gray; plain gold earrings; height, 5.02; wore low gaiter shoes; 2 plain gold rings on finger of left hand, also ring set with red stone; found in swamp, one-half mile north of Hinckley.

321. Unknown—Male; weight, 160; short, gray beard; checked shirt; heavy shoes; 40 cents in silver; jack knife.

322. Unknown—Male; age about 25, wore low gaiters; 73 cents in silver; door key No. 14; pencil with rubber; large jack knife, and plug of Spear Head tobacco. Hinckley.

323. Unknown—Male; age about 40; found on country road, 1 mile from Hinckley; burned beyond recognition; nothing but shoes left on his body; weight about 150.

324. Unknown—Male; age about 40; weight about 140; height, 5.08; had on striped woolen shirt; silver watch and chain, with bull's head engraved on case; body found in swamp, one-half mile north of Hinckley.

325. Unknown—Male; found in mill yard; only bones and a few buttons left; buried in Hinckley.

326. Unknown—Male; age about 35; found near Skunk Lake; evidently a passenger from the train; nothing left on body but a pair of shoes; buried in Hinckley; reported by E. Stephan, C. Vanhoven and J. G. Howard.

327. Unknown—Male; found in lumber yard; only jack knife, watch and buttons left; not enough found to be buried.

328. Unknown—Found in engine room of saw mill in Hinckley; only a few bones.

328. Unknown—Female; age about 25; found in swamp, one-half mile north of Hinckley.

330. Unknown—Female; age about 20; dark hair; gold breast pin; nothing further known; found on top of Hinckley hill.

331. Unknown—Male; age about 38; found in swamp, one-half mile north of Hinckley; nothing to identify him.

332. Unknown—Male; age about 40; weight, 160; sandy hair; wore low gaiter shoes.

333. Unknown—Female; age about 18; gold hair pin; found on top of Hinckley hill; buried in Hinckley.

334. Unknown—Female; baby, about 1 year old; found in swamp, one-half mile north of Hinckley.

335. Unknown—Male; age, 28; found in Hinckley.

336. Unknown—Age about 50; found near Skunk Lake; supposed to be a passenger from burned limited train.

337. Unknown—Age about 50; weight, 150; height, 5.09; taken from ruins of Hans Paulson's house in Hinckley; buried in Hinckley.

338. Unknown—Girl; age, 12; found in Hinckley.

339. Unknown—Girl; age, 10; found on railroad track, near Hinckley; buried in Hinckley.

340. Unknown—Male; age, 35; weight, 170; well built; webbing belt around waist; gray trousers, with longitudinal stripe; 1 door key and 5 cents in silver, trunk key and Swedish newspaper.

341. Unknown.

342. Unknown—Male; age, 60; weight, 200; sandy hair; wore heavy buckle shoes; found near Hinckley.

343. Unknown—Boy; age, 16; found near Hinckley; burned beyond recognition; buried in Hinckley.

344. Unknown—Male; age, 12; found near Hinckley; buried near Hinckley; nothing to identify.

345. Unknown—Female; age, 12; found in Hinckley on railroad track; buried in Hinckley.

346. Unknown—Female; age about 6 months; found in swamp, one-half mile north of Hinckley.

347. Unknown—Only buttons and bones left; found near Eastern Minnesota track on the north side of the river.

348. Unknown—Male; age, 25; found at Pokegama; not identified; buried in Pokegama.

349. Unknown—Girl; age about 5; found near track at Pokegama; buried at Pokegama.

350. Unknown—Man; age about 30; found near the place where the limited train burned; buried in Hinckley.

351. Unknown—Female; age about 20; weight, 120; found in swamp, one-half mile north of Hinckley.

352. Unknown—Male; burned beyond recognition; found 2 miles north of Hinckley; buried where found.

353. Unknown—Girl; age, 3; found in swamp, one-half mile north of Hinckley; buried in Hinckley.

354. Unknown—Girl; age about 18; found 1 mile north of Hinckley, on railroad track; nothing else to identify; buried in Hinckley.

355. Unknown—Female; age, 26; found north of Hinckley.

356. Unknown—Female; age, 16; found near Hinckley.

357. Unknown—Girl; age, 6; found in swamp, one-half mile north of Hinckley.

358. Unknown—Male; age about 27; found on top of Hinckley hill; burned beyond recognition; buried where found.

359. Unknown—Male; age, 14; found north of Hinckley; nothing to identify; buried in Hinckley.

360. Unknown—Female; age about 60; found near Hinckley; nothing further known.

361. Unknown—Male; age, 13; found near Hinckley.

362. Unknown—Male; age, 24; found 1 mile north of Hinckley, near Eastern Minnesota railroad track.

363. Unknown—Male; age about 19; found in Hinckley.

364. Unknown—Male; age, 2; found where limited train burned; buried in Hinckley.

365. Unknown—Nothing but particles of bones left; found in the woods north of Hinckley.

366. Unknown—Male; age, 45; found near Hinckley.

367. Unknown—Female; age about 45; height, 5.03; weight, 140; found on top of Hinckley hill; buried in Hinckley.

368. Unknown—Girl; age, 10; wore black cashmere dress; button shoes; black stockings; found in swamp, one-half mile north of Hinckley.

369. Unknown—Female; burned beyond recognition; found on Ernest Hogan's place, 3 miles east of Hinckley; buried where found.

370. Unknown—Female; burned beyond recognition; found 3 miles east of Hinckley; nothing to identify; buried where found.

372. Unknown—Boy; age about 12; knee pants, white waist; found in swamp, one-half mile north of Hinckley.

373. Unknown.—Male; only bones left; found between St. Paul & Duluth and Eastern Minnesota tracks, north of Hinckley.

374. Unknown—Female; age, 7; found north of Grindstone river, just outside the village.

375. Unknown—Male; age, 25; found 100 yards from St. Paul & Duluth track, north of Hinckley.

376. Unknown—Male; age about 30; found in swamp north of Hinckley; watch with hair chain and locket; weight about 150; buried in Hinckley; nothing but shoes left on body.

377. Unknown—Male; age, 25; burned beyond recognition; buried in Hinckley.

378. Unknown—Baby; age about 1 year; found in road, one-half mile north of Hinckley.

379. Unknown—Male; age, 7; found on track 1 mile north of Hinckley; wore laced shoes; body burned beyond recognition.

380. Unknown—Female; age, 6; found near the river in Hinckley.

381. Unknown—Infant; found near baby carriage in swamp, one-half mile north of Hinckley.

382. Unknown—Woman; age about 30; gray woolen dress; found in the woods one-half mile north of Hinckley.

383. Unknown—Woman about 40; weight about 160; found beside track, one mile north of Hinckley hill.

384. Unknown—Male; age about 1 year; found on road, one-fourth mile north of Hinckley.

385. Unknown—Girl; age, 10; burned beyond recognition; found one-half mile north of Hinckley.

386. Unknown—Male; age, 25; found on county road; buried in Hinckley.

387. Unknown—Male; age, 40; found on county road.

388. Unknown—Male; sandy complexion; age, 40; weight, 160; height, 5.08; blue blouse, striped pants, silk handkerchief and tobacco pouch; thought to be a lumber piler for Brennan Lumber Co., Hinckley; found one-half mile north of Hinckley.

389. Unknown—Male; age about 40; weight, 190; height, 5.10; wore heavy buckled shoes; found on bank of the river, near the saw mill, Hinckley.

390. Unknown—Male; age about 25; found on track at Pokegama; burned beyond recognition.

391. Unknown—Male; age about 70; found near old gravel pit; buried in Hinckley.

392. Unknown—Baby; female; age about 3 months; found in swamp north of Hinckley.

393. Unknown—Boy, age, 6; found 1 mile north of Hinckley, near railroad track; burned to a crisp; buried in Hinckley.

394. Unknown—Boy; age about 12; found 1 mile north of Skunk Lake; burned beyond recognition.

295. Unknown—Woman; found in Hinckley; burned beyond recognition.

396. Unknown—Child; age about 4; only bones left.

397. Unknown—Male; height, 5.10; found one-half mile northeast of where train was burned; buried in Hinckley.

398. Unknown—Woman; found north-east of Hinckley; burned beyond recognition.

399. Unknown—Child; found north-east of Hinckley; burned beyond recognition.

400. Unknown—Man; only bones and buckle of heavy shoes left.

401. Unknown—Female; age about 50; weight, 130; found in swamp, one-half mile north of Hinckley.

402. Unknown—Child; age, 2; found in swamp, one-half mile north of Hinckley; buried in Hinckley.

403. Unknown—Lumberman; age, 45; weight, 170; height, 5.10; buried in Hinckley.

404. Unknown—Girl, age, 17; found one-half mile north of Hinckley; buried in Hinckley.

405. Unknown—Girl; age, 7; found with body of Mrs. William Costigan.

406. Unknown—Girl; age, 5; found with Mrs. William Costigan; burned beyond recognition.

407. Unknown—Girl; age, 14; found north of Hinckley, near Great Northern railroad track.

408. Unknown—Man; age, 40; weight, 150; buried in Hinckley.

409. Unknown—Boy; age, 3; found in swamp, one-half mile north of Hinckley.

410. Unknown—Girl; age, 6; found in swamp, one-half mile north of Hinckley.

411. Unknown—Lumberman; age about 30; wore blue mackinaw suit, heavy shoes; found 2 miles north of Hinckley.

412. Unknown—Girl; age about 16; found 1 mile east of Pokegama; buried in Pokegama.

413. Unknown—Male; nothing but bones and jack knife found; burned in mill yard.

HINCKLEY, MINN., Nov. 24, 1894.

This is to certify that the foregoing death list is correct to date, to the best of my knowledge and belief.

D. W. COWAN, M. D.,
Coroner, Pine County.

REV. FATHER BURKE, M. A.

"THE NO. 4 LIMITED."

THIS is one of the few trains which in the northwest, and in the railway world, will become historic from the fact that it was in the greatest fire Minnesota ever had and that it was all burned except the engine and tender, and its passengers had to escape for their lives. All were saved except one. The heroism of those in charge of the train has been told wherever English is spoken, and will live in song and story as long as knowledge of the fire exists. It is easy for men who were not there to say what could have been done, which was not, but it will ever stand, clear as a mountain peak in sunlight, that no man left his post or was untrue to his trust at a time when it looked as if the heavens would pass away and the earth melt with fervent heat.

The St. Paul and Duluth Railway Company runs a train daily on fast time from Duluth to St. Paul. It usually starts from Duluth at 1:55. Such trains are always officered by men of known character, skill, and experience. The risks are far too great to place them in any other hands. On the day of the fire No. 4 was in charge of Thomas Sullivan, conductor, Beaumont street, St. Paul, who had been seven years in the company's service: James Root, of White Bear Lake, engineer, who had been in their employ more than 22 years. J. McGowan, St. Paul, fireman, seven years in the service; J. W. Blair, St. Paul, porter of chair car, seven years in the company's employ. The news agent was Herman J. Mawnhart, St. Paul. These were the men who passed the fiery ordeal with such distinction. Only one passenger was lost, Mr. Rowley, and he no doubt was bewildered and thus parted from the other passengers.

ST. PAUL, MINN., April 20. 1895

REV. WILLIAM WILKINSON, DEAR SIR:

Replying to your favor of the 17th inst, please note the information you ask entered at the bottom of your letter. A. L. Thomson was agent at Miller at the time of the fire, but has since been transferred to Hugo.

Your letter of the 17th inst. to Mr. Brooke has been referred to me and in answer thereto I beg to say that we had about 22 miles of main track badly damaged, being obliged to replace about 22,000 ties in the above length of track. We lost one open culvert of about twelve foot span and two pile trestles, one 30 feet long and the other 70 feet long. In addition to this all of the ties were burnt on our steel through span bridge over the Grindstone river at Hinckley, the length of this bridge being 90 feet. In addition to the above loss all of the company's buildings at Hinckley consisting of the following: Station building, two section houses, tank and pump house, coal bin, turn-table, and engine house, were destroyed. All the tracks in Hinckley yard were made impassable by the fire. The station building at Miller was also destroyed.

As I believe I have already advised you all of the coaches in our train No. 4, of September 1st, were burned, the train consisting of one combination car, one day coach, and two chair cars; engine was badly damaged. In addition to the above 32 freight cars were destroyed and about 18 miles of fence. Yours truly,

L. S. MILLER.

Ass't. Gen'l. Manager,

WHITE BEAR LAKE, Feb. 3, 1895.

REV. WILLIAM WILKINSON, DEAR SIR:

I am glad to learn you are to write up the Hinckley episode, to which, I feel sure, your graphic pen will do ample justice.

During the Anglo-African war of 1879, journeying in India, almost every night for nearly a year I witnessed many a scene of death and disaster, but never anything so appalling as what you and I saw at Hinckley that dread Monday evening, when, standing between the living and the dead, we spoke words of consolation and religion. Shall we ever forget those tragic scenes of clouds of fire and smoke, of charred men and beasts and trees? Was it not a magnificent panorama in miniature of the end of the world?

I never realized so vividly this great event described in Holy Scripture as I did during the four days I spent in the burnt district tending the sick, consoling the desolate and burying the dead, in company with my dear friend, Father Bajice, pastor of Rush City. We buried the dead at Hinckley, Pine City and Rush City, not to mention that we also attended the hospital and the homes of the unfortunate ones.

I served as a member of the general and burial committees.

Yours truly, T. BURKE.

JAMES ROOT IN THE FIRE.

The St. Paul & Duluth Limited, No. 4, left Duluth September 1st, 1894, at 1:55 p. m. The day was rather cloudy and very sultry. As we started out, I remarked to my creman that we were liable to have a storm. We continued without any special experience until we reached what was known as the junction, where it got very dark and very warm. After we left Carleton we lighted our cab lamp (to see the water glass), and the lamps in the coaches were all lighted, I understood. We continued our journey, seeing nothing unusual in regard to forest fires, but were running through total darkness about forty miles.

Just before I came to Hinckley hill the smoke (or cloud) had cleared away so I could see Hinckley very clearly, and I discovered a number of men and women running towards the track, from all directions. I said to my fireman, "There is something wrong," and I applied the air brake and stopped the train. The first three females to approach were an old lady and two daughters. I got off the the engine and asked what was the trouble. The only reply was, "For God's sake, will you save us?" I told them to get aboard the train. People kept coming, but there was no fire that I could see, in any direction. The people kept climbing in. Mr. Bartlett and his wife, who kept the eating house, were about the last couple that came. I asked Mr. Bartlett to tell me what was the trouble at Hinckley. He said "Every thing is burned up! Everything is on fire, including the depot and track house." I said, "Get aboard the train and we will go back to Skunk lake." I said to Sullivan, the conductor, "Look after the end of the train. I am going back to Skunk lake." He said, "We will never get there alive." I said, "Then we will die together," and I pulled the engine out and started. Mr. Bartlett and his wife got aboard the engine and just as I got on and was reversing the lever, the wind arose, I looked towards Hinckley and saw a small cloud of smoke or dust at the bridge. Before I opened my engine there came an explosion and it broke the cab window and carried a piece of the glass to the further end of the engine cab. That fell and struck me on the side of the head and cut a gash in my neck and on the forehead. The left side of my head and face were pretty well cut up, although I didn't feel anything the worse. The cut in my neck bled a great deal—pretty much all the blood in my body, I should think. The end of my train ignited at that moment, and the fuel car—even the top of big Hinckley hill I heard a hollering and saw three men flee-

JAMES ROOT.

ing. I shut the engine off and applied the air. I took a second thought and said to myself "If I stop the windlass it will stop the train and we shall all be burned alive." I opened the throttle. Two of those men got onto the pilot. One man caught onto the pilot for a short distance and fell off and was burned. The other man rode to Skunk lake on the pilot. There he got off. After we got over the top of Big Hinckley hill it appears that I fainted and fell back in my engine. I presume my engine must have run a mile or a little more, probably nearly two miles; when I came to again I looked up at the gauge. The engine was going very slow; I was just approaching Little Hinckley Hill, within a mile of the Hinckley line. I had only 95 of steam. I had my hand on the throttle. I presume that in leaning over I had shut the steam off to a certain extent, but not wholly. It was very dark. I didn't think we were at our destination, so I opened the throttle again. Nobody was on the engine but myself. I saw my fireman stick his head out of the water hole of the tank. When, or in what position I was when he left I don't know. I presume I must have been on the seat, but I don't know anything about that. He came out of the water hole. When he got to me my head was swinging back and forth again. He put out his hand to stop me from falling. The water dripping from his coat sleeve spattered my face and I said, "My God! give me some more of that." It seemed to revive me. I said, "Go and draw a pail of water," and he did so and I dipped my hands right into the pail. I said, "My hands are all burnt. I don't dare rub them for fear of rubbing the flesh off." My hands were all puffed up. He says, "Mine are burnt, too," and he dipped his in the water also. Then I took the pail and said, "Let me have it and put some more water in." He said he didn't know where it was. I brought a light and showed him a little water at the side of the track. I knew there was none for fifteen miles except this. I stopped on Skunk lake bridge. We were a little too far and I said I would pull ahead about a car length. I did so, and then fell again, through weakness. I said, "Leave me alone and go help the passengers into the water." He said, "You can't live here." I told him to go, that I was all right. I concluded I could take care of myself. He left me and took the pail and undertook to throw water onto the cars so the passengers could get out of the coaches. He came back to help me, and he and another man assisted me onto the ground and I hurried myself into the water and laid there, I don't know how long —probably three or four hours. I became very numb—had no feeling from my hips down. I pulled myself onto the land and laid there awhile. Feeling came back to me and I commenced to chill. I said, "I am going to get warm, somehow. I am going back to the engine." It was along towards ten or eleven o'clock—I don't just know what time. He says, "You can't live on the engine for the coal is all on fire." He assisted me and I laid down on the deck of the engine. I told him then to get the men to come help shovel the coal out of the tank. He came back and said, "I can't. It is too much." I says, "Get down under the engine and let the engine off and we will run away." We did so and stayed the balance of the night. Everything about the coaches burned up.

During the night Mr. Anderson, of Minneapolis, came to me and wet my eyes with a cloth. The great difficulty seemed to be with our eyes.

The first relief crowd came from Duluth. I started to go with the crowd back that way, but I was too weak; I saw I would take up the room of three or four, so I let the other folks go and I remained there for another train. An hour and a half or two hours afterwards there came a relief crowd from Hinckley with hand cars and push cars. I got on one of those push cars, and with the assistance of Saunders, who supported my head, stayed there until we got to Hinckley. There we found a relief train waiting to convey us to Pine City and thence to St. Paul. I got off at White Bear, where I lived. Dr. Francis Clark came and dressed my wounds.

Robert M. Bell, superintendent and secretary of Duluth Union Depot and Transfer Co., at Duluth, twenty-five years a railroad man with St. Paul and Duluth all the time, writes:

We left Duluth on train for the south at 1:55 p. m., September 1st, 1894. No danger apparent till within a mile of Hinckley, at a few minutes past four, was due there at 4:10. Here the refugees began to appear which caused us to stop. The passengers saw the flames coming from a southwest quarter, driven by a strong wind. They saw at once what the conditions were; the glass was all broken and driven in from that side, and they at once took the middle aisle and called for water. A little fellow who was with his father shouted, "O father, we are dead!"

I was at the end of the car. Blair and I began to pass out water from the ladies' toilet room. Blair was a colored porter on the chair car. At this time the car was on fire underneath. This was kept up until the train stopped. Hinckley Big Hill is two miles from Hinckley proper; after this is another hill called Little Hinckley Hill; the top of this is about four miles from Hinckley proper, and about a mile and a half from South Skunk lake. This was a race for dear life to get to the lake. One woman took on badly; she fainted and some of the passengers bathed her face, etc. I got out and tried to put out the fire under the car; it was useless. The porter brought down a fire extinguisher; it could not be used. I called my daughter and started to walk the track, to the north. We got to the hand car house and broke it open; "necessity knows no law." We got a hand car which had a keg of water on. How the people did gulp that down! We filled the car with people and made for the station house.

Sullivan, the conductor, went in to see what he could find out by telegraph, but the wires south of Miller were all down and I was called to come in. Sullivan was sitting on a bench and some of the people were bathing his head with water. He said, "O, Mr. Bell, all the passengers are burned!" When he was quieted down I asked the agent what the chance was for a train from the north. He said Roper had orders to come from Willow river and was expected to be here in fifteen minutes. I was thinking whether it would be safe to proceed with our hand car. The agent, Mr. Thomson, said that it certainly would not be safe, because Roper with his train was liable to come any time; and besides, the woods were on fire just north of us on both sides of the track. This was the safest place anyhow, this part of the country was all burned over, nothing more remained to be burned except the station house and a few cars. We decided that he was right. We then threw the hand car off the main track onto the siding. The flames soon began to come again, and in sheer self defense we began to walk north. We walked probably two and one-half miles, to near Finlayson depot, which is three and six-tenths miles from Miller. Here we were met by Roper's train. He was conductor, Peter Kelly was the engineer. They were the first people we had seen, and of course wanted to know all they could be told about the disaster. We told them all we knew. They said, "You go to Finlayson, which is near; we will go as far as we can, help all we can, come back sure and pick you up on our way home to Duluth." This is what we did. We found water and had an opportunity to wash, and we found a pitcher of milk and drank it. Soon the hot waves began to reach

ROOT'S ENGINE.

us. We were not going to take any more chances we could avoid, and wo set again north. There were twenty-one persons in this party in all, Mrs. Bartlett, my daughter Josie, fourteen years old, and Freight Conductor Wellman's daughter, May, about the same age. We kept on walking until we came to a big cut, about two miles north of Finlayson. We sat down and heard Roper's train on its way toward us; no sound could be more welcome. They took us on. This train brought us to Willow River station. It had on the refugees they had picked up from Root's train. Here we met the first relief train from Duluth, in charge of David H. Williams, who is yard master on the St. Paul and Duluth road at Duluth.

We had a doctor on board our train, who attended to our eyes; the smoke, heat and cinders had made our eyes too painful to endure and hard to see. Several of our party had to be led by the hand.

Mr. Williams, yard master, Mr. Vance, general agent of the St. Paul and Duluth railroad at Duluth, asked us what the extent of the calamity was and what was the general situation. I told them all I knew. The relief train returned with Mr. Vance in charge, Mr. Williams, with Roper's engine, tender and box car. We went to Miller, found three trestles burnt out. These we repaired with supplies we had with us in the box car. We went on half a mile, found a trestle, twelve feet wide and twelve feet deep, burnt out, and had not material enough to repair it. Took the hand car and started on, leaving engine.

We had Dr. Magie (who is the company's regular surgeon,) and Dr. Codding, Conductor Roper and part of his crew, and at a point near old Sandstone Junction we found the corpses of a lady and four children near two other children, all beside the track, bodies nude. With the second two children was a lady's traveling bag, leather, one of the old style. We tried to open it to see if it contained anything to show who the dead were, but we could not open it. We threw it on the hand car and started on our way to Skunk lake. When daylight came, we broke open the bag; it contained $3,500 in currency certificates of deposit. It was the property of Mrs. McNamara, the wife of section foreman at Hinckley, and it was his wife and family who lay in the stillness of death. It was given to the owner.

We kept on till we got to Skunk lake. Here we saw the coal of Root's train afire; all was still. I said to Dr. Magie, "Can it be they are all dead? Let us holler." We did so, and were promptly answered by many voices from the swamp. We ran toward the people. The first man we reached was Senator Dougherty, of Duluth, next Mr. Blades, manager of Crown Hardware Co., Duluth, John Blair, the colored porter, who told us all he could. The two doctors began to treat all who suffered. One man had a cut in his leg from glass flying from the window in the car; all had trouble with their eyes. We found how many could walk three miles; some said they could; most said we will stay till a train can be got here. We left the doctors in charge of the people and made our way to the engine we had left. Then we went to Rutledge, about nine miles, woke up the mill men of the mill company, got timber, tools and mill hands, and took them to the burned out culvert to repair it. We got it fixed in the early morning. I never saw men respond quicker than those Rutledge men did, or work harder. The culvert repaired would not have taken a gold medal for beauty, but it was good, and firm as a rock.

We went to the people at Skunk lake, loaded them on and also an old greyhound. I took care of him, helped to keep him, but when well, he left me. He is a tramp now about town here. We got back to Miller but could go no further, because of its being a single line to Duluth, and I had telegraphed from Rutledge when I went for the supplies and men, to start another relief train and to fetch the people to Duluth, and told them to come to Miller regardless of me. The wires were down from Miller to Rutledge, so in the interests of safety I had to wait at Miller with my train and people, and here we had to stay half an hour, then had men take hand cars and flag me to Rutledge. Met the Duluth train and placed the refugees on this train. Wellman was in charge as conductor and Engineer Killroy. My conductor, Roper, I instructed to follow to Carlton, this being a coal and water station. I came on with Wellman, but when I got to Willow River, I found the settlers and citizens alarmed for their safety should fire break out, so I had Roper stay with his train at that place to take the people away if need be. We got to Duluth about 12:30 Sunday noon. Went back after dinner with another train to repair the track: worked all day and night clearing wreck and repairing trestles, and met Assistant General Miller and Master of Transportation Mr. Brown, about 10 a. m. Monday, September 3d. They had come from the south on a hand car. Traffic was resumed over all the road on the afternoon of that day.

STATEMENT OF HON. FRANK B. DAUGHERTY.

I was one of the passengers on the St. Paul and Duluth Limited on September 1st and had with me my son, Otto, a lad about ten years old. It had been smoky for several days and this had annoyed us from the start, but at Barnum it grew so dense that the porter lit the lamps. The lights, however, for some reason, seemed but very dismal attempts at illumination. At Miller this darkness became less heavy, the densest smoke seemed to have been lifted into a cooler stratum of air and this lit up the atmosphere in a very peculiar way—into a sort of dull, glowing, yellowish twilight, which had a brilliant but at the same time unnatural effect on things within range of vision.

Of course the kind and extent of the danger we afterwards ran into had not been anticipated, but it could not be denied that things wore an exceedingly ugly outlook ahead. At one time I fancied I saw a great mass of flames, "a sea of flame," in fact, some miles ahead over the timber, but my apprehensions, and I think those of my fellow passengers generally, were confined to the danger we might run into in going through the forest region. It had never occurred to me, at least, that we might be compelled to run back. Nothing more startling happened on the "run" from Miller toward Hinckley, than that the smoke increased as we approached, until we were "flagged" a mile or so this side of that place by the people coming to meet us. This took place in an old clearing or meadow, and here the smoke lifted again so much that it was made a subject for remark, for we seemed to breathe freer and could see clearly through it the people streaming along toward us. As they were assisted into the cars we gathered from them that the whole surrounding country seemed to be on fire and that Hinckley was burning up.

The brightening of the atmosphere was but a cruel illusion, probably due to the smoke being driven forward to give place to the destructive element itself in its living force, for even while the poor people were yet coming, a stream of fire struck the train from the southwest, leaving it ablaze underneath and in other more inflammable parts. At this the train commenced to move backward and the poor unfortunates who did not reach us in time must have perished in a peculiarly cruel way within the very sight of relief, and yet the laws of self preservation could not have permitted the saving of another life, for in less than the minute the train itself, the fancied haven of refuge for so many, was in the midst of a terrific struggle

MR. BARTLETT.   MRS. BARTLETT

BRAKEMAN MONAHAN.   R. BELL.

for existence, it was in fact running "a cheek and jowl" race with death. The run to Skunk lake has been described so often that I do not care to enter into the details minutely again. That the unprecedented occurrences should create a commotion among the passengers need not be said. Several gentlewomen fainted from shocks of terror in the car my son and I occupied, and that both men and women became strongly excited in different ways and to different degrees, goes without saying. Those who, like myself, had somebody else to see to, were probably the best off, as their solicitude for the loved ones would to a certain extent take the mind from self and so rob the situation of some of its terrors. Thus Mrs. Saunders, of St. Paul, had seven young charges—some of them her own—to care for, and I do not think there was a lady on the train that showed more self command. My son Otto became alarmed at the unusual occurrences and the excitement prevailing, and turned his frightened face up to me with, "Have we got to die papa, have we got to die?" I summoned all my strength for his sake and undertook to assure him as well as I could that it would be best for him to keep very still and quiet, for as long as the cars were moving all would be well. In this way, or some such way, I succeeded in quieting him, when a great big fellow, evidently a religious fanatic, with eyes bulging out of his head went through the car shouting, "We are all going to heaven together." I was very angry with him for undoing my work and frightening all the children and passengers as well, and said to him very decidedly, that it might be so, but I wished he would keep his pious opinions to himself.

The apprehension that something would stop the train, hung very heavily on my mind; in fact we did experience several severe lurches as if it had struck obstructions and cleared them with difficulty. These lurches may have been due to the sinking of the track over burning culverts or to branches from burning trees fallen across it, or it may have been to passing over bodies of flesh, brute or human; whatever the cause was, had the obstruction been heavy enough to stop the train, no power on earth could have saved us. I knew nothing of Skunk lake at this time or of any attempt to get there. I supposed we were simply running to get out of the fire, and I have since been thankful that I did not know, for it would have added to the hopelessness of our situation. That our engine was running short of water at this time, that we could not have got farther than that place from this cause alone. But there was

ARTHUR T. BROADY.

MR. BLAIR.

yet another reason that would have made it impossible to proceed farther; the train was burning up. The day coach was entirely enveloped in sheets of flame so that most of the people in leaving it had their clothing or wearing apparel caught and their hands or faces singed or blistered. The rear chair car was not yet burning so badly but that it might have been saved, and I suggested to Conductor Sullivan that it be uncoupled and shoved back; my idea was to occupy it as long as possible as a shelter against the flames in the hopes, of course, that they would soon pass over. A few of us, about a dozen, were at the rear of train when I made this proposition; but Sullivan said something about another train coming, he evidently had in mind Roper's, and started up the track, the others following. That is, I presume the others had followed, for while I had stepped back into the St. Paul car for my boy's skull cap they had disappeared. The other passengers had all disappeared too, having been conducted by the porter, Blair, and News Agent Manhart into the marsh which I had neither knowledge of nor power to see, so my son and I found ourselves quite alone on a burning train and in a sea of smoke.

I tied up Otto's head with some linen furniture coverings and left the track on the west side, groping for some place of shelter. We found some tall grass on low ground (this was on the edge of the marsh, although we did not know it), but was afraid this would simply add more fuel to the general combustion and went to higher ground in a potato patch.

Here we fell in with two gentlewomen, one, Mrs. Minne Spriggs, of Duluth, with a baby in her arms some six months old, and her sister, Annie Kernan, of St. Paul, and without any design on the part of either we were compelled to keep together, for we had only just met when a sheet of flame came and compelled us simply to drop where we were. I laid my body over that of my son as much as possible and we were doing fairly well under the circumstances, when one of our neighbors screamed that her clothes were on fire. This threw me into a terrible state of mind; I was afraid to leave my boy, but the woman screamed that she was burning up and it was then that Otto encouraged me. "Don't let the poor lady burn up, papa, I am all right," and I busied myself at once and succeeded in tearing the fire out of their dresses.

There seems to have been three distinct sheets or streams of fire passing over us, the two following very like the last, and each time the dresses of the poor women would catch and the operation of "putting it out" had to be repeated.

At the end of what might be called this third "baptism of fire" we witnessed a very curious phenomenon (I speak of it here because I have not heard it mentioned by others). It resembled nothing so much than I can think of as a heavy snow fall, with this difference, that instead of snow, the flakes were of glowing coals and cinders. A whirlwind of flame and heat had evidently swept from the burning district a cloud of burning particles, which had burst over us in a cooler stratum of air and myriads of "fire flakes" were thus let loose to fall at will over our heads. It was a wonderful sight, at once interesting and awe-inspiring, but not at all dangerous because accompanied by no wind. I was curious enough to note the time of the passing of the phenomenon; by my watch it was 5:07 p. m.

After this a decided improvement in the atmospheric conditions became perceptible, the air grew cooler, we could breathe freer, and we dared to take the cloths from our heads and look about. The chair car porter, Blair, came up to us about this time and through him I learned how the other passengers had been saved.

The story that Conductor Sullivan had thrown a child out of the window is not true, but a little girl had been placed in his charge, and anxiety as to her fate may have affected his mind in connection with the other terrible experiences he had gone through. The girl was saved with the others in the marsh.

STATEMENT OF WM. H. BLADES, OF CRANE, ORDWAY & CO., OF DULUTH.

We left the Duluth Union Depot by the St. Paul and Duluth Limited September 1st, anticipating no special danger, though the atmosphere was dense with smoke as it had been for days, owing to the forest fires prevailing and an unusually dry season. The smoke kept increasing in density as we proceeded, and at Miller, sixty-six miles from Duluth, got to be very bad. From Miller to Hinckley it thickened into a sort of unnatural twilight, with cinders falling through it like black snow, and the air became overheated as if blasts from a hot oven were blowing spasmodically. The train was flagged at a little bridge about a mile and a half this side (north) of Hinckley, and there being an open space, an old clearing or meadow, we could see clearer and breathe easier here.

A crowd of men, women and children were running across this

open space towards the train, and we gathered from them that Hinckley
was burning up, and that fearful fires were sweeping through the forests from every direction. There were between two and three hundred of these people, and all were taken aboard. Things had commenced to look very serious by this time and I had some thoughts of
trying the little body of water under the bridge for shelter, for I had
noticed that the cars were even then blazing underneath in spots,
where, being bespattered with axel grease, the woodwork was made
more inflammable; but when Conductor Sullivan sang out "All
aboard," I instinctively swung myself back on the train. The train,
besides engine and tender, was composed of a baggage, express and
mail, a smoker, a day coach and two chair cars, which were now well
filled with the people from Hinckley, and we had brought 110 passengers from Duluth. One great source of danger, I have since
learned, was that the supply of water for the engine was getting very
low and so overheated that it is doubtful if the train could have been
moved in many minutes more. This accounts for the painfully slow
time that was made on the backward move to Skunk lake, which
has been estimated as much as twenty minutes.

The train must have burst into flames very soon after we started
and we had not run far before things became extremely wild, as
live fire enveloped the cars and broke the glass in the windows, and
transoms commenced to crack and burst, thus letting tongues of
flame through the splintered openings. At this sight, which was
in itself extremely terrible, many of the women would scream and
cower away from it as much as possible. The windows on the west
side were the first to break, those on the east remaining longer, so
that all the passengers crowded to the east side as much as possible
in an instinctive effort to keep farther from the flames. That the lady
passengers particularly should recoil with horror at a sight so awful
is not to be wondered at; indeed it only seems strange that such an
experience could be gone through with by them at all, and still retain their normal faculties of mind. As I now see those events,
the conclusion is forced upon me that a more cool and composed
set of passengers than were on this train, it would be impossible to
conceive of under any circumstances, for except when the senses
were startled by some new phase of the horror, there was no unusual
commotion. I do not think the large majority realized the full horror of the situation until later. As for myself, I seemed to appreciate fully the fearfulness of the danger and the hopelessness of the

H. D. POWERS.

EDW. BARRY.

situation, for I had given up the idea of ever getting out alive, and yet I must have been in a sort of daze, for the nearness of an extremely shocking death did not disturb me as much as it might have done, and I presume it was very much the same with those around me.

During most of the run I was in the lavatory of the St. Paul chair car, with half a dozen other gentlemen. We were wetting towels and cloths and passing them in to the passengers in the main body of the car. The nearest approach to a panic I came in contact with during the whole ride was when a stranger put the question to me, "What chances do you think we have of getting out of this?" and I replied, "About one in twenty thousand!" at which he made a dive for the platform, and would have left the train had I not pulled him back into the car and held the door on him.

As for my recollection of the run back to Skunk lake, as a whole I can only say that it seemed a long one, during which, extraordinary things were happening and coming upon each other in quick succession and that each thing than happened seemed more terrible than the preceding one, and that each seemed designed more surely than the last to give assurance of a speedy and inevitable destruction. The smoke and cinders, the occasional glimpses of great whirls of flame in masses of forest, the stifling heat, the bursting of glass and the tongues of flames lapping hungrily through the empty car windows, the bursting out of flames in new places, the stifled shrieks and the recoils of terror by the women, the frozen stare of horror among the men, I certainly saw and heard and understood all, and yet, as I have mentioned before, with something less than a full realizing sense. When the train stopped and some said "This is the place!" it seemed natural enough that we should stop here, but it was not coupled with exquisite sense of relief, which is supposed to be experienced by those who have escaped a very great danger.

The male passengers bestirred themselves to take out the women and children from the burning coaches. A barbed wire fence was kicked off the staples and everybody ran for, or were helped into, the deepest part of the miry, muddy water, which was at most only eighteen inches deep. Here I sat down with the rest so that the mire and water came up nearly to the armpits, and when sheets of flame swept over us, as they seemed to do periodically, we would crouch down as much as possible, keeping our heads entirely covered with wet clothing.

Of the many mysteries connected with the extraordinary adventure, the most inexplicable is that the sheets of flame, which had before and did afterwards sweep over us, should at this particular juncture have ceased to play on this spot long enough to allow, practically, all the passengers to reach the water.   Had one of those great whirls of fire caught us here that afterwards passed over us, we must have perished, everyone.   As it was, we were, as one might say, let in between two great heats.

How long we were in the marsh is uncertain; several successive sheets of flame passed over us and when they ceased or became fewer and less terrible, the people gradually crawled up to higher ground.   Considerable suffering from cold was then experienced by almost everyone, for after the heat of the flames had passed over, the air became quite cool, and being entirely wet through, this air had all the effect of a raw winter wind.   That reaction from extreme heat to severe cold should have been experienced so suddenly, may be singular, but there is no mistake about the recollection of this fact.

Conductor Sullivan was in his right mind, or appeared to be, as long as I saw him.   I knew nothing of the time of the incident with the child.   This is likely to have happened, however, and that the child should have been saved is not strange, for there were plenty outside to catch it in their arms or pick it up as the case might be. The last glimpse I had of him he was with a pail in hand trying to put out the fire on the rear car which was burnt the least.   This was when the people were crawling toward the marsh, but the flames and smoke soon shut everything from sight.   I heard of him afterwards through R. S. Farrell, a man in my employ, and who had also been a passenger.   Farrell saved himself by running up the track, and arrived at Miller Station at the same time that Sullivan did.   He saw no indication of derangement of mind in him, but on the contrary, says he handed a dispatch to the operator.

The railroad embankment cuts the marsh called Skunk lake in two at that point.   The smaller portion on the west side being the one wherein our people were saved, the longer sheet of water on the other side, strange to say, seems to have experienced a much heavier visitation from the flames than we did.   When Dr. Codding and I walked out to examine it the next morning, we found the wet, spongy soil converted into a thick layer of ashes, as far as we could see.   Afterwards the remains of three people were found, who had evidently crawled into it for protection and perished. There is no doubt in my mind that if our people had been directed into the larger body of water on the east side of the track, that many, if not all of us, must have shared the same fate, on the other hand every one, as far as I know, that sought shelter, so to speak, in the smaller pool came out alive and practically unharmed.

GLADSTONE, MINN., May 7, 1895.

REV. WILLIAM WILKINSON, DEAR SIR:

In reply to yours of recent date regarding my experience in forest fires September first, 1894, as conductor of St. Paul and Duluth Limited train No. 4, I will try to give you as near as possible my own, as well as the experience of some of my passengers.

Train No. 4, known as the fast limited, left Duluth at 1:55 p. m., consisting of a baggage car, smoking car, two coaches and two chair cars, pulled by Engineer Root and Fireman John McGowan; Baggageman Morris, Brakeman Manahan and Porter Blair. Leaving Duluth and arriving at Carlton, there was nothing to indicate the fearful disaster that was our fate to encounter later on.

Arriving at Barnum on time, thirty-nine miles from Duluth, I noticed it was growing dark and very smoky, but paid little attention to it, as we had become accustomed to this condition of affairs during the previous two months. We still proceeded on schedule time, nothing more to indicate any danger ahead until arriving about three-fourths of a mile north of Hinckley station where we came to a stop. I opened the baggage car door and jumped to the ground to ascertain what the trouble was.

Upon looking ahead I discovered the fire coming in the shape of a cyclone. I said to my engineer, "Jim, we cannot stay here long; we will have to go back to a place of safety." Looking around we could see people coming from all directions making for the train, and to the best of my knowledge I had received in the neighborhood of one hundred and fifty or one hundred and sixty men, women and children. Thinking all safely on board the train, I was about to signal to start back, when screams to my right attracted my attention. It proved to be a mother and her three little children running for their lives, and the flames grasping like a demon behind them. Those were the last people that I loaded on my train. I then sprang into the first class coach and gave the engineer the bell twice, the third pull felt to me as though the bell cord were burned off. I ran into the smoking car and gave the

BARRY'S ENGINE.

bell cord one more pull and we started back. Our train at that time was all on fire, with between three and four hundred lives beneath its roofs. We had only gone a quarter of a mile when a mighty wave of flame struck us at a terrific rate of speed, I should think between sixty and seventy miles an hour. It took every window out of the west side of the train. While standing in the smoking car, a gentleman whom I did not know, raised his foot and put it through the window on the east side of the train; he had no sooner withdrawn his foot than one of the refugees, who had sought the train for safety, jumped through the window into the flame outside, before I could make any attempt to stop him. He had no sooner gone through the window when another man started to do likewise, and whom I caught and pulled back on his feet almost severing one of his hands from his wrist upon the broken window glass. Turning to me the poor fellow said, "Can you do anything for my hand?" to which I replied I could not, having no means at hand to relieve his suffering.

I then left the smoker and went to the first class coach, which was crowded to its utmost capacity with men, women and children screaming at the top of their voices and which I think was the hardest sight I have ever seen. With all my might I shouted to the people to keep quiet, as everything was going to be all right, and as soon as I succeeded in making myself understood it seemed to restore them to splendid order. Arriving in the north end of the car, I beheld a six-weeks-old baby lying upon the seat protected by its loving mother. The lady asked me if we were going to get out alive, which I assured her we were, advising her to keep the smoke away from the baby as much as possible and everything would be all right.

Passing through the next coach, I entered the chair car and came in contact with Mr. C. D. O'Brien, who asked me how we were going to be. Saying to him that things would be all right, I hurried through the chair cars, giving the same assurance of safety that I had in other parts of my train.

Standing there administering to the wants of the passengers, was Porter Blair of the chair car, who I must say is as brave a man as I ever saw. On our backward ride from Hinckley to Skunk lake I saw one of the pluckiest women I ever met. She stood inside the door of the chair car and handed me saturated towels from the washstand in the car, which I used to prevent the end of the car from burning.

On my arrival at Skunk lake I jumped from the train, first meeting Fireman McGowan holding an empty pail in his hand, which I took from him and got into the lake and filled it with water, then went back to put the fire out on the platform of the coaches so as to get the passengers off.   When that was done Porter Blair was still at his post helping and relieving those people in his charge. When the train was relieved of its load of human freight, I contemplated making the awful trip to the next station called Miller. When I thought everything else was secure I then thought of getting some report to my superior officers, so as to get some assistance for those suffering people.   I started on my perilous walk through smoke and heat.   The smoke was so dense that I could not see my open hand before me.   I kept, all this time, between the rails of the track, lest I should wander away from it and be burned.   I had to lie down at various times on the ground in order to get a breath of air, and suffered intense pain with my eyes.

Arriving at Miller Station, I went to the operator, Mr. Thompson, who sat bravely at his post of duty, operating his key.   I asked him then where No. 12 was—the local freight that was following me, of which I feared so much on our backward ride—and he said they were at Willow river and ready to come this way.   I then asked him if he could get Rutledge and find out how the bridges were at this side, and see that we were not cut off.   A portion of a message I delivered to the operator, which he sent to Duluth for help.   We then had to leave again as the fire was coming up to us and had only left there about three or four minutes when the station was consumed.   Continuing on my walk four miles further to Finlayson Station, I heard the noise of an aproaching train; it was our No. 12, pulled by Engineer Kelly and Conductor Roper.   I shouted and said, "John, is that you?" and he came to my assistance and I asked him for God's sake to give me some water, which he did.   I asked him at the same time where he was going and he replied, "I am going to your train."   I said, "I am afraid you cannot do it."   At this time I went into the station and remained there a little while until I got rested up.   The heat was again getting intense and I could hear the fire coming.   I then started out again and walked two miles further, which made my walk in all about ten miles.   I got to a gravel pit and stopped and said to my companions, "I am afraid we are cut off, as I see fire ahead." We then made up our minds to take chances and remain where we were until the return of Conductor Roper's train.   We remained there about one hour, thinking it to be a year, when I heard the whistle of the returning train, which was very encouraging to us at that time. They picked us up and the next stop was made at Rutledge Station. I went into the station and inquired of the operator, Kallis, on duty, what he had heard from my train, if anything, and he said "Nothing; but they are sending a relief train from Duluth." I then was taken back to the caboose, when I completely broke down from exhaustion.

The next stop made was at Willow River. I was taken from the caboose and was taken in charge by the citizens of that little town. They did everything that could be done to relieve our suffering until the arrival of the relief train from Duluth. I was put aboard that train and taken to Duluth. One thing more I would like to add in connection with this experience, that one lady who was aboard my train at the time of the disaster, Mrs. Saunders, had with her seven children whom she managed to protect and care for during this awful time. I can assure you of the fidelity of the entire train crew during this terrible ordeal, and I hope the public were satisfied with the manner in which they conducted themselves. I certainly hope we will never be called upon to render the same services, under such circumstances, for every moment to us all was a most trying one. All that we could see, and as it looked to me, the heavens and earth were like a sheet of flame.

I will say in conclusion that any one man deserves no more credit than another, as none of us did any more than our duty, which we owe to our employers and to the public in our charge. This is my experience during the awful forest fire of September first, 1894.

Yours respectfully,   THOS. SULLIVAN.

GEORGE C. DUNLAP, OF ST. PAUL, PASSENGER ON THE DULUTH LIMITED.

At 1:55 on the afternoon of September first, 1894, we left Duluth on the south bound "limited" for St. Paul. The day was dry and sultry. A strong wind was driving the smoke of forest fires across the skies, so that after a time the sun became totally concealed as behind a dark mantle.

As we approached the town of Carlton we noticed that the trees and stumps were burning on each side of the track, but as yet we had little apprehension of danger. After we passed that station, however, the signs of disaster became apparent. The heat grew more intense, the black smoke thickened, until at three o'clock

D. W. COWAN, M. D., CORONER.

GEO. D. HOLT.

day had changed to night and it was necessary to light lamps and headlight. Breathing became more difficult every moment and the danger of suffocating seemed imminent. On we went, running at lightning speed, hoping to pierce the almost impenetrable gloom. As town after town was passed in quick succession, the anxious inhabitants were seen collected in small groups, and evidently much alarmed. Soon a bright red illuminated the heavens. The black forms of trees became blazing firebrands. Then followed the crash of falling timber and the accompanying shower of sparks.

At last the light of day again appeared and the passengers gasped a sigh of relief. It was said that the fires were local, and that we should soon be out of all danger.

Suddenly the train came to a stop about a mile from Hinckley bridge. Men, women and children half naked, partly burned, and covered with ashes and dirt, came groaning and crying on board. Still others made all haste to reach our train. In all there were about one hundred and fifty refugees. They told the trainmen that Hinckley and the bridges were burned and that a great fire was approaching us. The engineer, finding that the heat was becoming unbearable and that his passengers were in the greatest danger, decided to back up at full speed to a pond known as Skunk lake. When this was made known, many a poor, homeless settler begged piteously for a little time to go back and get his dear wife and children.

Almost instantly a great hurricane of fire bore down and struck the train. Blazing embers of all shapes and sizes were hurled upon the cars. The burning forest around was fanned by the gale, and the heat and smoke became well night unbearable. It seemed as though a huge mountain of flame was rolling upon us. The baggage car took fire and thus our destruction seemed to be made certain. Then began the immortal race for Skunk lake, a race lasting only seven minutes, although it seemed like seven hours. The window glass melted, curtains vanished and the fire swept through the cars at will. The passengers stood huddled together in the aisles, some praying, some crying, others dazed. To breathe was torture. The heroic porter, John Blair, was constantly trying to alleviate the suffering of the women and children, who, almost choking, gasped for water. Once the train gave a sudden lurch and we feared that the cars had left the track and that the end had come.

But we were still permitted to rush backward, though it seemed strange that so violent a wind did not derail the train.

At last we arrived at Skunk lake, none too soon, for scarcely had the coaches been deserted when they became completely enveloped in flames and were destroyed in a few minutes. The majority of the passengers sought safety in the water, while many wandered about, they knew not where. A few of us were unable to reach the lake on account of the blinding smoke and intense heat. We ran up the track and came to a culvert; into this large wooden box we crawled, foolishly thinking that in it we might escape the scorching wind. In a short time we were driven out, but returned again and again, staying long enough to get fresh air. At last we were forced to leave the culvert and seek safety elsewhere. After roaming about aimlessly, we sat down in a place where there was nothing inflammable. There we remained with our heads covered with coats, while the storm of fire brands, cinders and ashes swept over us. Thus we escaped suffocation. Our eyes filled with dust and weakened by heat, began to cause us intense suffering.

The wind was now shifted from the west and all further danger was averted. Our party, consisting of Miss Scarvy, of Merriam Park, Mr. Hayden, of West Superior, and myself, returned to the place where the "limited" had stopped. There, in place of the elegant coaches, were found the bare trucks covered by a mass of iron work and debris. The Skunk lake district was found to be a large clearing with a small lake, and low meadow lands on each side of the track. Under the circumstances, such a place was most desirable. We met a Scandinavian, who kindly brought us to a place where were two dugouts, each holding at least a dozen persons, in one of which he had saved himself and family. There we spent a long, dreary night.

We were kept busy passing up the muddy water of a spring to many a thirsty survivor, who, as he drank, would falter out the story of his miraculous escape.

On the following morning we returned to the wreck, where we found that relief had arrived from Duluth, and that many of the passengers had left at an early hour for Hinckley, where they were to take a special train to St. Paul. We immediately set out hoping catch the same train, but when we reached Hinckley we found that we were two hours late. We were then obliged to wait several hours before a second relief train arrived.

The sights beheld that morning were horrible in the extreme. The dead bodies of men, women, children and cattle lay around in heaps on every side. I cannot dwell on the sickening spectacle.

We went to the Great Northern round house, the only building in the town, and patiently waited, suffering all the time the most intense pain from our eyes. At last the welcome whistle of a train was heard. It was the long looked for relief. A large number of survivors, who had come in from all parts, were taken on board, and provisions were distributed among them. On arriving at Pine City we were taken to the hospital, where our eyes were treated and our wants ministered to. Had it not been for the keen foresight and high sense of duty of the noble James Root, coupled with the indomitable courage and the valuable assistance of his no less noble helpmate, John McGowan, Skunk lake would never have been reached. To these two men—these two heroes—all honor and praise are due for having saved the lives of so many, when the chances for doing so were so very, very few. We cannot pass over the name of our brave conductor, Thomas Sullivan, he who revived the drooping hopes of his passengers by his encouraging words and who, though choked and blinded, fought the flames at every point. The citizens of Pine City, and especially Mr. J. Y. Breckinridge and James Hurley, deserve the highest praise for the very hearty way in which they received and waited upon the hundreds of sufferers, who were constantly pouring in.

JUDGE SEAGRAVE SMITH DESCRIBES THE FIRE.

MINNEAPOLIS, MINN., Feb. 9, 1895.

REV. WILLIAM WILKINSON,

Dear Sir: Yours of the 7th inst. is at hand and contents noted. In compliance with your request please find hastily and briefly written some of the things observed on that terrible day. You can use so much of it as you see fit, if you think it worthy of using. Hope you can read it.   Yours Respectfully,

SEAGRAVE SMITH.

Sept. 1st, 1894.—Train left Duluth 1:30 p. m. for Minneapolis. About twenty miles this side of West Superior fires were seen on each side of the train, mostly off at a distance, but occasionally coming near to the railway track. There was but little wind and the fires were burning slowly and quietly. The sky was being obscured by smoke, as we came along it became more dense. After we passed the 29th mile post it became so dark that when we reached the next one I was unable to see it or any other object outside dis-

WRECKING CREWS CLEARING THE TRACKS.

tinctly. The cars were soon lighted and the darkness increased until it was as dark as midnight in a cloudy night. This condition continued until we arrived within a few miles of Hinckley. During this time silence reigned and anxiety was depicted on the countenances of the passengers. As we approached Hinkley the cloud of darkness lifted. It lighted up so we could see the sun. The countenances of the passengers changed and many exclaimed, "We are out of danger." During our ride through the dense smoke and darkness we could see fires blazing on either side of the road, sometimes quite a distance off, at others near the track.

At one place near a wood station the ties on a side track were burning quite briskly near the main track. When we arrived at Hinkley the train stopped at the station a minute or two and started on again. It had not gone but a short distance when it stopped again. I went out of the car to learn the cause of the stopping.

Looking ahead of us I saw the round house and a number of freight cars on fire. It appeared to be an extremely hot fire. As I was looking at it, in an instant, a fierce wind blew from it a volume of hot dust and sand. It came with such force and was so hot it burned our faces. The conductor at once ordered the train back to the station. Before we had stopped at the station the people from the village, men, women and children, came running toward the train with their trunks and bundles. Others were running with their effects and locating themselves in a large and deep gravel pit on the east side of the station, the bottom of which was nearly all covered with shallow water. When the train stopped at the station there was a short consultation between the conductor, myself and a few others as to what should be done. It was decided best to stay there as long as it would be safe and prudent—get on all the people we could in that time, and get away before the fire should entirely surround us. While we were thus waiting I watched the progress of the fire and the doings of the people who were trying to save themselves from destruction. Many got on to the train; others sought for safety in the gravel pit referred to—all frightened. It was a heart rending sight to behold—the wind was blowing a fearful gale. The flames of fire were leaping high and consuming every thing it came in contact with almost instantaneously. I saw on the west side of the village a volume of flame strike a small house and shed, wipe it out in an instant, and leap from there over a number of other buildings without touching them, strike a saw mill beyond

with such force that it was moved bodily from its foundations
in a second, and went floating in the air a burning mass; every stick
of timber in it seemed to be on fire. On turning to the other side,
I saw that the fire had burned around the gravel pit and was fast
getting in front of us. The people of the village, during this time,
were running from every direction, and getting in the cars or into
the gravel pit with such effects as they could carry along with them.
I saw one man who carried nothing with him but his gun. The
conductor in the meanwhile had attached some freight (box) cars
to our train, into which many of the people got. The train staid
there as long, and it seemed to me longer, than it was safe. The
fire had passed around the gravel pit and got ahead of us. It was
burning furiously as far as could be seen on each side
of the track. The bridge immediately in front of us was on fire.
The train started through this double wall of fire. Just as it started
I looked to the rear of the train, saw a woman leading a child, with
another in her arms. She was hurrying to get on the train. She
was only a few feet away when it started. She was left. She went
toward the gravel pit; before she reached there I saw a flame of
fire strike her down to the ground. It was too much to behold; my
eyes turned away from the awful sight. We went on in the darkness
through the walls of fire, which heated the windows of the car on
the side where I was so it was painful to place my hand on them. We
were passing over burning bridges, and cut-outs with walls of fire on
each side for a long distance—no hope of escape should our car
get on fire. Nothing in my opinion prevented our car from taking
fire, excepting that the right of way on each side was very well
cleared of combustible matter and the wind was blowing directly in
the line of the track. Had it been blowing across the track nothing could have saved us. All must have perished.

The refugees apparently felt safe, but the passengers were in
breathless suspense for hours, knowing not what moment we would
drop through a burning culvert or bridge, or our cars, ignite and
burn. No pen can adequately describe the awful scene, or the feelings of those who witnessed it. It was an event never to be forgotten.

After many stoppings we arrived late in the evening, at Duluth,
covered with smoke and dirt, our nervous systems terribly strained,
but our lives saved. In that condition we felt happy that we had escaped with our lives and had succeeded in saving many others.

ST. PAUL & DULUTH RAILROAD COMPANY.

St. Paul, Minn., April 1, 1895.

Rev. William Wilkinson, Dear Sir:

In reply to your letter of March 27th I beg to say that our records show that all of the passengers on our train No. 4 of September 1st, 1894, which train was burnt at Skunk lake, were saved excepting O. W. Rowley, whose body was found some four or five hundred feet directly west of the track, he evidently having become dazed and confused after leaving the train, wandered away from the rest of the passengers and was burnt.

Mrs. Miller has asked me to thank you for your letter and to say to you that she will follow my example so far as the photograph is concerned. This is her own wish, and has in no way been influenced by me. Yours truly,

L. J. MILLER.

Ass't Gen'l Manager.

Mr. Miller and his wife did excellent work for the relief of the distressed and bereaved. I should have been glad to place their photographs in this book, but they declined the honor, saying: "We only did our simple duty."

A TRIBUTE TO JAMES ROOT.

The citizens of Minneapolis, while seeking to alleviate the sufferings of the victims of the terrible holocaust which has just swept over Northern Minnesota, pause to pay a fitting tribute to James Root, engineer of passenger train No. 4, of the St. Paul and Duluth railroad, which left Duluth Saturday afternoon September first, 1894.

When one mile north of Hinckley, Engineer Root, having driven his train through miles of the dense smoke and increasing heat of the forest fires of that day, found his train met by people fleeing from the burning town and the flames fast closing in around him and his charge.

Taking on board the panic stricken people, he stood at his post while, through a very sea of fire, he ran his train back five miles to Skunk lake. Here two hundred of his scorched and suffocating passengers found refuge from his now burning train in the waters of the lake, while he, brave man, fell burned and bleeding to the floor of his cab where he was found when the fire had spent its fury.

The loftiest impulse which animates the human breast is that

W. B. BEST'S ENGINE.

which prompts one to self sacrifice for the salvation of others. That impulse controlled James Root on that Saturday afternoon when, writhing in pain and facing death, not thinking of himself but of the lives he had in his keeping, he stood upon the pinnacle of human glory.

The merit of his heroic deed attaches not alone to him, but also to the craft of which he is a member. The lives of thousands upon thousands of people are hourly in the hands of locomotive engineers, and seldom has one proven false to his trust, or failed to rise to the emergencies which confronted him.

Such an emergency which tried the mettle of manhood confronted James Root on this occasion, and he proved himself its master. Two hundred human beings today owe to him their lives. On that Saturday morning he was a locomotive engineer; today he is a hero.

W. D. Washburn, Wayland Hoyt, Eugene G. Hay, R. J. Anderson, special committee.

Chas. A. Pillsbury, chairman; H. W. Brown, vice chairman; P. B. Winston, treasurer; J. H. Sullivan, Citizens' Relief Association.

W. H. EUSTIS, Mayor.

The following is a report given by the St. Paul Pioneer Press, of a meeting held September 13th, 1894.

THE HEROIC JOHN BLAIR.

The colored people of this city held a well attended meeting at Market Hall last night in recognition of the heroism of Porter John W. Blair, whose acts of bravery contributed so much to the safety and comfort of the passengers on the train that was burned at Skunk lake on the night of the terrible forest fire. In honor of his manly conduct the colored people of the city got up a subscription and purchased a handsome gold badge, which was presented to him at the meeting last night. Quite a number of white people were present at the meeting, among them being several of those who were on the ill fated train.

T. H. Lyles presided, and on calling the meeting to order he said that while Engineer Root and the other members of the train crew had been eulogized for their heroism, but little or nothing had been said about the conduct of Mr. Blair, who was really entitled to just as much credit as any employe on the train. He then introduced Mr. C. D. O'Brien, who was one of the passengers on the train.

Mr. O'Brien said that John Blair had done his duty, and this was typical of his race. He was glad the colored people of the city had seen fit to give some testimonial for his bravery. The man who, facing death, does his duty is worthy of some recognition. He said he could not tell the horrors of that night, and no man could. The first they knew of any real danger was when the refugees stopped the train near Hinckley. The train rushed back through a mountain of flame. John W. Blair stood at his post in the burning car passing water as coolly and collectedly as if he were on a summer excursion. When the passengers were lying on the ground with their faces down, Blair stood up in the midst of the flames playing a fire extinguisher on the women and children whose clothing took fire.

"For three-quarters of an hour we stood in a flame that is as indescribable as the flames of hell," continued the speaker. "John Blair might have left the party and sought his own safety, but he was too much of a man for that. He stood there, a willing sacrifice, until the last passenger was safe. It was not the bravery of a trained soldier or a sailor, but that of a poor porter of a chair car, keeping his mind to follow out the dictates of a heart as pure and noble as any that ever beat in a human breast. It is well to honor such men and teach our children to emulate their example. I am proud to be alive to take him by the hand and thank him for his humanity."

With this Mr. O'Brien walked across to where Blair was sitting, and taking him by the hand, shook it with a vim that showed a deep feeling for the colored hero.

G. B. Dougherty of Duluth, and Capt. R. L. O'Gorman and Dr. Curry, of this city, all of whom were on the train, corroborated the statements of Mr. O'Brien regarding Blair's conduct during the terrible ordeal they went through at the lake. And letters giving expression to the same sentiment were read from O. C. Hartman and J. E. Lobdell, both of Duluth, and Anna L. Munson, of this city.

Rev. R. C. Quarles, colored pastor of the Pilgrim Baptist church, was then introduced. The speaker said it was nothing strange when a man could by a little bravery get possession of a large amount of wealth, or by a little military prowess make a name in some military achievement, or even to risk his life for the protection of his own family, but when a man could rise above the thought of everything else, even his own life, and throw himself in the face of death for the sake of protecting men and women who were utter strangers to him, then, indeed, there was something grand and noble about it.

"We have seen in blazing headlines," he added, "the praises of brave Engineer Root and the other members of the train crew, but I have looked in vain for the name of John W. Blair as a great hero of that terrible occasion. I am glad, John W. Blair, that among those who had the coolness and manhood to make a record on that terrible night, that there was a black face with a white heart."

F. L. McGhee, the colored attorney, then presented Blair with a badge. He said that whenever a negro was called upon to do his duty he always did his full duty, but who would expect him to go beyond the law of self preservation to protect his fellow men and women.

"We can not fittingly honor him as it is fitting he should be honored," he went on. "But when called to appear before the judgment seat, John W. Blair, then and only then will you receive your full reward. I have here a little token of recognition of your heroism. It is from the people of that race from which you spring. Wear it. It is but a poor monument to the memory your conduct merits as compared with the honor that conduct has been to us."

Mr. Blair modestly replied that he wished he had command of language to express his gratitude for the many flattering tributes paid him on the occasion.

"All I can say is that on that awful night I did what I thought to be my duty," he added. "The memories of this night and the kindness you have shown me shall always be cherished by me as long as I live."

The badge is quite large and is of a beautiful design, the face being engraved with the picture of a burning train. On the reverse side is an inscription stating that it has been presented to Mr. Blair in testimony of his heroism on the occasion referred to.

The railway authorities gave Mr. Blair a fine gold watch to show their appreciation of his fearlessness and service inscribed as follows:

Presented by the St. Paul & Duluth R. R. Co.

TO JOHN WESLEY BLAIR

For gallant and faithful discharge of duty on Limited train, No. 4,

In Forest Fires, Sept. 1, 1895,

BRIDGE OVER KETTLE RIVER.

THE COMPOSITE TRAIN ON THE EASTERN RAILWAY.

The Lancashire Puffing Billy made by George Stevenson, is known to all railway men, because it was the first locomotive. The train which saved its passengers and 476 who were in imminent peril of death by fire and took all in safety to Superior and Duluth will live in the literature of America as long as this is a book reading people. The conduct of all in charge will be pointed to as a model for all who have the care of life and property in the railway world.

CONDUCTOR H. D. POWERS.

On September first, 1894, I left Duluth on the Eastern Minnesota passenger train, No. 20, at one p. m. bound for St. Paul. On the way to Hinckley we didn't see any more fire than we had seen every day for weeks before, but over part of the distance, the smoke was very thick and it was so dark we were obliged to use our lanterns and the engineer lighted his headlight.

As we approached Hinckley it lightened up. Arriving there it was as light as usual, except that the sun was obscured; there was no fire in the town then. We pulled to our lower yard where I learned that the bridge and cars at the lower end of the yard were in flames and the fire was sweeping into the town with great rapidity. I felt sure the town was doomed, and at once began preparations to get my train to a place of safety and to take as many people out of the town as possible.

The way freight crew from West Superior (W. D. Campbell, conductor) being there, I made arrangements with him to couple into the rear of my train with his engine, also to get three empty box cars (these being all we could procure). We then coupled everything together, engine 105, Barry, engineer, in the rear backing up, my regular engine 125, Engineer Best, on the other end of the train handling the air brake.

Everything being in readiness to make a run for it when the time came. We stood at the old passenger depot and loaded the people as fast as possible, and stayed there until the buildings less than one block away were in flames and the fire was all around the bridge over the Grindstone river. Fearing it would burn and thus cut off our only retreat, we pulled across the bridge and stopped. We picked up forty or fifty people here.

Meantime the fire was advancing in an almost solid wall, driven by a wind that was simply terrific. The Brennan Lumber Company's mill and yard were on fire and the heat was intense. I could see the fire was getting into the woods at the north, through which we must pass to get out, and fearing our only means of escape would be cut off, we pulled out. As it proved, we started none too soon. We found the woods a sea of flame; the very air seemed to be on fire, and we passed over three small bridges that had begun to burn. We got out of the fire about five miles north of Hinckley and had no trouble after that.

The trainmen with me were my own crew, consisting of O. L. Beach, brakeman, M. W. Baker, baggageman, Wm. Best, engineer, and Geo. Ford, fireman. The way freight crew, consisting of W. D. Campbell, conductor, Chas. Freeman, Peter McLaughlin and Geo. Gilham, brakemen, Ed. Barry, engineer and Alex Thistle, fireman.

It is sufficient to say that every man did his full duty. That we escaped with this train load of a little over six hundred souls, is due it seems to me, not to human heroism, but to the mercy of an all-wise Providence.

> I ask not for their lineage; I ask not for their name;
> True manliness is in their heart, they royal blood may claim.
>   —R. Nichols.

The following graphic description is given by Engineer Best, of the Eastern Minnesota railway.

"I presume the public will be surprised to hear from me at this late day, but in justice to myself and others, I certainly think it is time for me to present a few facts concerning the happenings to the train I was running, on the day of the Hinckley fire, September first. From all that has been said and written of the adventurous trip of our train with the forest fires, on that day of horror, my railroad friends in the United States and Canada must think that the train crew, as well as myself, were crazy. For instance, I have seen descriptions of how we ran over burning bridges at the rate of sixty miles an hour, without giving the passengers a chance for their lives. Why not say that I had engine 999 with a record of one hundred and twelve miles an hour; or that I slipped the wheels out from under engine No. 125 and substituted the Ferris Wheel, and all that I had to do was to touch the button and fly? Such fancies are suggested to me by the many exaggerated stories I have heard and read. I will try to give a statement of our trip from Duluth and West Superior to Hinckley, and return, just as near right as possible, and will try to explain a few things in my simple way.

"We left West Superior on time, with train No. 4, Eastern Minesota Limited, consisting of engine and five coaches, for St. Paul. About thirty miles out the smoke became so dense that I had to light the headlight and cab lamps. At the next station, Kerrick, it was very dark and for about thirty miles it continued so. I was still making the regular time of the train as we had no notice of danger from along the line, and I expected the atmosphere would clear up when we ran into the open country near Hinckley. The air did appear to clear somewhat, but the clouds seemed to be on fire, and great sheets of flame shot athwart the heavens with electrical activity.

"When we came in view of Hinckley everything was quiet except the southern extremity of the town, and in the Great Northern yards, where the fire had made its appearance. We arrived at Hinckley on time, 3:25 p. m., and after doing our regular switching, started down to the water tank which is situated in the freight yard. When we stopped at the tank we saw that it would be impossible to get through. It became so hot at that point that my fireman, George Ford, was driven three times from the spout. I called to him to stick until we had secured water and he did, for his grit was good. By this time the freight station and the cars were on fire, and we had to back away from the tank. The wind commenced to blow and it looked as though the town must go.

"Passenger Conductor Powers came to me and said, 'What do you think of putting the freight engine behind us?' The freight was standing on a side track so that we could follow it if necessary. We all thought it was wisest to follow, and we coupled the trains together. We understood each other without talking much. The wind was blowing a gale by this time, and we realized that Hinckley was doomed.

"The people now commenced running from the burning town to the train. In fact, they were running anywhere and everywhere, for they were panic stricken. I jumped down from the engine to talk with Conductor Powers in regard to the length of our stay, as the question at this time was, how much longer can we stay, and get safely away with the train? The people were climbing into the coaches. Engineer Barry whistled off and the train started. I ran to my engine, and, setting the air brakes, stopped it. Conduc-

REV. FATHER LAWLER, M. A.

tor Campbell, of the freight, came to me and said that Engineer Barry
would pull the coupling pin and go. I said that I guessed not, but
a second later was told the same story by a brakeman. But it was
no go, at any rate. We were loading women and children, and
as I had just come over the road, I was determined to stand on my
judgment. But again and again did the freight engine whistle off
brakes, and try to start the train. It was at this juncture that excited men pushed women and children from the coaches in their mad
haste to get in themselves.

"Four men jumped on my engine and said, 'Back up! back up! or
we will all be burned to death.' I told them not to get excited
as we were all right yet. I was constantly implored to go, but
there was still time, and many lives to be saved by the waiting.
Many of our passengers wanted to help in the general cause and
they worked with a will, assisting those who required help and in
making the best possible use of the space in the coaches. Conductors Powers and Campbell and the brakemen worked rapidly, and
to the best apparent possible purpose. The heat had become terrible, and again would freight engine 105 scream out two whistles
as if in agony, as a signal to start. But it was no go yet, and I held
the train in the iron grasp of the brakes. Still the people kept
coming, and at last I turned to my fireman and said, 'Good God,
George, will I sacrifice the train at last?' The heat was awful and
my anxiety was intense, for between the tips of my fingers and
the air brakes lay the destinies of hundreds of people. At last the
mad rush was reduced to a few stragglers. I looked hastily around
and saw that no more people could get to us. The wind whirled
through the streets and men and dumb animals could be seen
falling as they were overcome in the vain endeavor to reach a place
of safety. I realized that I had stayed the limit. I stepped back into
the cab and released the air brake, and we started from ill-fated
Hinckley. Houses were burning so rapidly that one could see
bedroom sets and other contents of the rooms. The fire would
seem to burn the sides right off the buildings, revealing the contents in the glare. Buildings seemed to melt rather than burn in
the fierce glow.

"We backed rapidly away from this scene of ruin and death, and
as we passed the road running north of the station, we saw people
running toward the train, and beckoning us to stop. But it was

useless to think of it, for they were too far away from us, and I turned my head that I might not see them in their distress.

"The next point we reached was Grindstone bridge. Fire was all around us, but we passed it safely. Here was a small company of people to whom life was a matter of minutes. The dump was high and the fires had not yet reached it. At Hinckley it had been the few for the many, but here it was the many for the few. We took the refugees on board. I took a last look at Hinckley. The spectacle was awful, but impressed me as grand in the extreme. The sights and sounds of that day will always occupy a vivid place in my memory.

"Just before starting up, after taking on the last company of refugees, Conductor Powers came to me and said, 'Bill, we have got them all I guess, let's go.' He went back to the cars and then commenced the battle royal. Two brakemen, Wm. Meach and a freightman jumped upon the tank of engine 105. Both engines were backing. Every man was in his place and discipline was perfect. The brakemen on the tank, a very exposed and trying position, signaled to Engineer Barry at the throttle and whistle. Every man was doing his duty and doing it well. The wind was increasing in violence and the danger grew more and more menacing. Trees were thrown down, and terror and death stalked through the forest and clearings. Our train seemed like a sentient thing, but how insignificant in that tempest of wind and flame.

"The brakemen who held the dangerous post of outlook doused themselves with water from the manhole. They never once wavered and their grit was good. As we were approaching each bridge, I would slow the train down till the outlook had signaled to Barry that all was well. Barry would whistle off brakes and I would throw the throttle wide open till we neared the next bridge. I had made up my mind that I would stop at the top of the hill. Just beyond this summit was a bridge about which I had some misgivings. As we neared this structure, which is forty feet in height, I began slowing the speed of the train down. I was anxiously watching and estimating the distance, when my heart was chilled with a sudden call for brakes. In a moment we were standing still, and I turned to my fireman and said, 'George, the jig is up. The train is lost and all that are on board of it.' I could see the face of my faithful fireman when I uttered these words, but it relaxed none of its resolution. Still he thought as I did, though he made no reply. The thought came to me then that I would meet with measureless censure from the public for holding the train at Hinckley in the interest of humanity against so much opposition, and that now it must go. I experienced at that moment what any other engineer would have under like circumstances. The fear of death never entered my mind. There was no room for any other sensation than remorse and self-condemnation for what I then believed to have been my bad judgment. I suffered more in that brief period of suspense than before in all my life. But my ears were soon greeted with the signal to go ahead, and never music gladdened the car like that shrill whistle from 105 signaling to go ahead. Away we went, and soon emerged from the fire into dense smoke, but the fire was following fast behind. The next station was Sandstone, and we stopped there for a few minutes. Engineer Barry came to me and said that the conductors had decided to stop over there. I jumped from the cab and urged them to go right through. None of the people at Sandstone thought at that time that their danger was great, but we all know now how that in less than an hour the town was destroyed and many lives lost.

"Our next stop was at the now famous Kettle River bridge. I had noticed a local fire near this point when I went down that afternoon and was apprehensive. No trains are supposed to pass this bridge until proper signals are given by the watchman, and on this occasion I watched for them with unaccustomed anxiety, as may well be imagined. I received the signal to go ahead and we rolled onto the structure and over it in due time. The south end of the bridge appeared to be on fire, but whether it was or not will never be known, for the watchman had given his last signal, and his charred remains were found not far from where I last saw him.

"From Kettle river we went along all right, making the run from Hinckley to Partridge, fourteen miles, in fifty minutes.

"The next station was Kerrick. I was down oiling the engine at that place when four of the passengers came out of the parlor car, which was right behind the engine. They were very profuse in their expressions of praise and gratitude for all of us. They were safe, and knew it, and their relief was great, of course. We arrived in West Superior in due time and here our engines were put off and others substituted to convey the train to Duluth. It was impossible for either Barry or myself to see after we reached the union depot. I went home and to bed immediately, after bandag-

KINEKEY. SEARCHING PARTY STANDING OF A CABIN IN THE WOODS.

FINDING THE DEAD.

ing my eyes, to allay the inflammation caused by the heat and smoke. It was 4:00 a. m. before the pain in my eyes would permit me to fall asleep.

"A great many people, I am sorry to say, have carped about the conduct of the trainmen, while others are loud in their praise. I, for one, feel a good deal like Actor Frank Chanfrau, whose motto in life—and it was used for his epitaph—was: 'I've did the best I could and I ain't got nothing to take back.'

"West Superior, December Twenty-second, 1894.

"WILLIAM BEST."

FIREMAN GEORGE FORD.

We left West Superior at one p. m. on time on that eventful day, September first, 1894, with Eastern Minnesota limited passenger train No. 4, engine No. 125, having five coaches, en route for St. Paul.

Arriving at Holyoke, a station thirty miles out, the smoke was so thick that we had to light the headlight and cab lamp. The next station was Kerrick. We were making regular running time of train, and not hearing from the general office at West Superior of any danger, we thought it would break away when we came to Hinckley and it did; but the sky was very lurid, although when we turned the curve going into Hinckley everything looked peaceful, except south of the town, where the Great Northern yards were on fire.

We reached Hinckley at 3:25 p. m., and, having done our regular work, we pulled down to the water tank for water. It was so hot that I was driven from the spout three times, and would have given it up had it not been for our engineer, William Best, who called to me in his always pleasant way to fill the tank if I could. The freight station and cars were all on fire. We backed from the tank.

Our passenger conductor, Powers, came up to the engine and said to our engineer: "The local freight train No. 23, is in the yard; how would it do to have them couple on behind us?" Mr. Best said it was just what he wanted, if it did not take too long. By the time they had coupled on it was getting pretty hot; it then looked as though we would have to back away from Hinckley. We were standing at the passenger station, and the wind was blowing a gale. It was not more than five or ten minutes before a sheet of flame shot up to the clouds, and the whole town was on fire.

The people commenced to run toward the train. Our engineer

HINCKLEY—WHERE THE DEPOT STOOD.

consulted with Conductor Powers in regard to how long we could stay. Of course we would stay until the coaches were filled with those poor people who were running for their lives from the fire; but the question was, how long could we stay without burning up the train.

Engineer Barry, of the local train, gave two sharp whistles, a signal to pull out. Our engineer, Best, jumped on our engine and applied the brakes to it and to our coaches. Conductor Campbell, of the local, came up and said to our engineer: "Barry will cut off his engine and pull out!" Our engineer said, "I guess not!" Then a brakeman came up with the same story. As they were leading women and children, again and again did Barry's freight engine scream out those two short whistles, a signal to go ahead; but we had just come over the road and our engineer said he would use his own judgment and not move until he saw fit.

Men pushed women and children away in order to get in themselves. Several men jumped up on the engine and said to our engineer: "Back up! back up! or we will all be burned!" One of them was the section foreman of Hinckley. Best replied, "Boys, do not get excited; we are all right yet!" Some of the passengers wanted to back up; others wanted to help. Our engineer told them to get in the cars, and we would take care of them. But they went to work gladly helping to load the people, and making room for them in the cars; there were some out working with the trainmen.

I could see Conductor Powers running here and there, helping this one and that one, and Conductor Campbell, of the local train, doing the same work of the trainmen; as fast as the people came they were taken into the cars. It was getting awfully hot by this time, and again would the freight engine give that terrible scream to go ahead, but our engineer held the train under his control. He turned to me and said, "God God! will I sacrifice the train at last?" for it was terrible now; but God was watching over us and we were to be saved. The anxiety for me was awful.

At last Engineer Best got down on the step of the engine and looked around to see if any more could get to us. I could see people, houses and cattle, falling around us. To remain longer was death to all. He got back on the engine and released the brakes on the train, and we left Hinckley.

We passed the road crossing just north of the town, then backed over the Grindstone bridge and stopped, and people came running up the track.   We waited and got on all whom we could see, then backed up to Sandstone.   Here again we stopped for a few minutes.

Engineer Barry came up to Engineer Best and said, "The conductors are going to stop here."   Best got off the engine to speak to the conductors and said, "We want to get out as quickly as possible, for the fire is coming on us fast!"   Then we backed up to Kettle River bridge.

There is a standing order to run this bridge at four miles per hour and as an extra precaution the company have a watchman there, and we do not pass without a signal from the watchman. Here we slowed to four miles an hour.   We got a signal from the watchman that everything was all right, which we answered, and rolled onto the bridge.   Our next station was Partridge where we stopped.   The passengers came up to the engine and asked for water; we gave them all they wanted to drink, as they were suffocating from the heat, then we went ahead and were ever so thankful to see West Superior again.

NEWS AGENT GEORGE S. COLE.

In accordance with your verbal request of the 26th inst. I have the honor to submit the following statement, covering my personal experience in connection with the recent forest fires which have destroyed the town of Hinckley and other places in this state.

On Saturday, September first, 1894, the Eastern railway train No. 4, south bound, left Duluth for St. Paul, at one o'clock p. m. in charge of Conductor Harry Powers, Engineer William Best, Brakeman O. L. Beach, Fireman J. Kellock, Express Messenger Massey Baker, and Parlor Car Porter George Goodin.   The train consisted of two parlor cars, two day coaches, and one combination smoking car.

We had a large number of passengers leaving Duluth, and got many more at West Superior and a few at South Superior.   All went well until we got close to Dedham, Wisconsin, which is about fifteen miles from Duluth, and then we discovered the woods on fire, and the atmosphere in the cars became hot and smoky.   In passing through the cars, back and forth, I was questioned by many of the passengers as to the probable danger from fire, and I informed them that I apprehended no danger after the train got out of the woods.

The smoke, heat and darkness continued from Dedham to Sandstone, a distance of about forty-five miles. From Sandstone to Hinckley we did not experience any great inconvenience from smoke or heat, and all on board of the train thought the danger was passed, but upon our arrival at Hinckley we found the whole town in flames and the inhabitants wild with excitement. After stopping at the depot the train ran down to the water tank, a distance of about six hundred yards, where the engine took water, and a short consultation was held by the conductor and engineer. After taking water, the train was backed to the depot, where we found Conductor Campbell and Engineer Ed. Barry with freight train No. 23 north bound for West Superior. Conductors Powers and Campbell then held a consultation, and decided to attach three empty box cars to the passenger coaches, and load them with passengers and such light baggage as the people were bringing to the train.

While at Hinckley I did all in my power to assist the people in their escape from that place. After taking all on board the train proceeded to Sandstone, and upon arriving there Conductor Powers waited for orders from the train dispatcher. After receiving the necessary orders we proceeded slowly toward Duluth, picking up passengers en route, and running through a great deal of fire and smoke, which made it so hot in the cars that the passengers drank all the water that the filters contained, and then ate the ice which remained.

On arriving at Kerrick station we stopped for a few minutes and I got a passenger to accompany me to the engine, when we got a pail from Engineer Best and carried six pails of water to the cars, which satisfied the passengers until we arrived in Duluth.

In justice to all concerned, I deem it only my duty to say that, in my opinion, the heroism, bravery and coolness displayed by the train crews under this trying ordeal, have never been excelled in the history of this state. Respectfully submitted,

GEORGE S. COLE, News Agent.

CONDUCTOR W. D. CAMPBELL.

Yours of February seventh to hand and contents noted. I left West Superior on the morning of September first, 1894, in charge of train No. 24 on the Eastern Minnesota. We arrived in Hinckley about 2:35 p. m. and found fire all along the road. About 1:30 or

ST. MARY'S HOSPITAL, DULUTH.

2 p. m. the wind commenced to blow and fan the fires, which had been burning in this vicinity for some time, into fierce flames.

When we arrived at Hinckley we found the fires burning the ties in the east end of the yard. The residents and fire department were out fighting the fire when we arrived, but the heat was so intense and the smoke so blinding that the people were powerless. We could not leave Hinckley as the wires were down and train No. 4 was due there at 3:25 p. m.

On arrival of train No. 4 we took three merchandise cars with us and coupled into train No. 4, since they could go no further, and prepared to make our escape to West Superior.

At this time the residents of Hinckley had begun to flee for a place of safety, and in making for the gravel pit found our train. All who wished got on the train, but many sought other places of safety. About 75 persons went out on the government road and were found dead near where we last found them. The heat was so intense by this time that we could not remain outside the cars, and everything that we could do being done, we left there.

It was about 4:10 p. m. and the fire was ahead of us and on all sides.

Engineer Barry claimed that he was so blinded he could not see, and as the engine was backing up, Brakemen O. L. Beach and Peter McLaughlin volunteered to ride the back tender and act as lookouts, where they rode to Kerrick, a distance of about thirty miles.

You will understand that both engines were backing up, one on each end of the combination train, and therefore had one of the many bridges that were on fire been gone, the train could not have been saved, as the men could see nothing: we were running through darkness, the smoke having shut out the light of day.

We arrived in South Superior about 7:30 p. m., when I turned my train over to Conductor Powers.

You will understand that the trains I ran, Nos. 23 and 24, only run from West Superior to Hinckley and return. Ed. Barry was engineer, Thistle the fireman, and the brakemen, Gilham and McLaughlin, who will communicate with you. I remain very respectfully,

W. D. CAMPBELL.

ENGINEER EDWARD BARRY.

Yours of the 7th inst. to hand and in answer will say that I left West Superior on train twenty-four on September first, 1894. W. D.

St. Luke's Hospital, Duluth.

Campbell conductor, and proceeded to Partridge where it was so dark, the air being filled with smoke, that I had to light the head-light on the engine and the lights in the cab, and then it was next to impossible to see.

I proceeded toward Hinckley slowly, expecting to find bridges on fire. We arrived there at 2:45 p. m., and found all the people out fighting fire, which was surrounding the town on all sides. We set out our train on the side track, and went to the lower end of the yard. Everything was on fire, the ties under the rails were burning, and the box cars on the side track were on fire. I got back to the water tank as quick as I could, it being impossible to see, and the rails started to warp in the yard. We stood on the side track waiting for passenger train No. 4, which was due at 3:25 p. m., in charge of Conductor Powers and Engineer Best. I notified them that they could go no further, as the rails were warped, everything being on fire east of there and that it was dangerous to go any further.

I was running engine 105 with A. R. Thistle as fireman. We went in on the side track and got three large box cars and a caboose, and pulling out on the main track, coupled onto the rear end of the passenger train, I was regular train No. 23 and had the rights of the road from Hinckley to West Superior, and the passenger train was helpless, as they could get no order to back up.

I pulled my train, with passenger train, down to the depot; it was composed of three box cars, one caboose, coaches and one combination car; and waited for the people to get on, as they were coming from all directions. Some of them failed to reach the train, being overcome with the fire and smoke, and died from the effects in plain sight of me. By this time the storm was a regular cyclone, and it was impossible to see or to stay any longer at the depot.

The conductor, W. D. Campbell, told me to pull across Grind-stone river, which is one-half mile west of Hinckley; the bridge con-sisted of one span; it caught fire while we were standing there load-ing passengers. The ties and bridges ahead of me were all on fire and my only salvation was to pull out at once and head the fire off. I knew if we stayed there any longer we would all be burned. Conductor Campbell gave me a signal to go. I whistled off brakes and started.

When one mile west of Hinckley I saw men, women and children coming from all directions. I called for brakes and re-versed engine, and stopped and picked up the people and then started again and ran as fast as a wheel could turn under an engine. By this time we had about five hundred of the Hinckley people on our train No. 23, who were packed in the box cars, coaches and engine and every available place on the train. Every bridge we crossed between Hinckley and Sandstone was on fire.

When we arrived at Sandstone Conductor Powers wanted to stay there. He thought that everything west of us was burned and that it wasn't safe to go farther. I refused to stay there and said we would better take our chances of crossing Kettle River bridge, even if it were on fire, than to stay at Sandstone, which meant sure death anyway, as the fire had reached there. He said, "All right, go ahead. You are running the engine and have the right of road." I pulled out and hadn't been gone more than fifteen minutes before the people who did not get on the train or get into the river, were burned up. When I got to Kettle river bridge the cold shudders ran through me for I expected to find the bridge burned, and it was on fire at the time. The watchman called to me that it was all right to go ahead, as the fire had just struck it.

We arrived at Partridge and there I found that our supply of coal and water for the engine had almost given out, and that we must have more before we could go further. The people were packed so tight in the cars that they were nearly suffocated. I went with the men to O'Neil's logging camp near by for water pails and cups, and carried water to the suffering passengers to revive them. I finally got started toward West Superior again. I stopped at all stations and notified all the people of what had happened.

Before I arrived at Kerrick my eyesight had become so affected by the smoke and fire that I could not see. I stopped there twenty minutes to bathe my eyes. I got them doctored so that I could see well enough to start again and arrived at West Superior all safe and sound with the five hundred passengers on board.

I failed to state that while I was at Partridge I got orders to run ahead of train No. 3: (train 22 was abandoned to run slowly) and to use my own judgment.

Enclosed find my photograph which you requested. These are the facts as they occurred from the time I left West Superior on train 24 and from Hinckley to West Superior on train 23, pulling passenger train consisting of coaches and engine 125, three box cars and one caboose from Hinckley to West Superior.

Hoping this explanation is what you desire. I am yours truly,

ED. BARRY, Engineer,

BRAKEMAN C. C. FREEMAN.

We left West Superior at seven a. m. for Hinckley on train 24, September first, 1894, and on arriving at Partridge the sun became clouded by smoke, and we knew that there must be a big fire south of us. On arriving at Sandstone it was so dark that we could hardly see to do our switching.

On leaving Sandstone about two p. m. I lighted the side lights of the cab so that they might see the cab from the head end.

When we reached Hinckley, about 2:30 p. m. it was so hot and the smoke so dense, that we could not see half way over the train. We pulled down in the yard and pulled through the M. & M. track No. 2 and left all our train excepting three or four cars, which were for St. Paul, which we set on Eastern Minnesota track No. two or three. The engine then came back to the north end of the yard, where the heat was so intense that they could not get on the turntable to turn it, or get any coal.

I was getting the numbers of some cars that we intended to bring back. I got the numbers of thirty-four loads. The next was a car of merchandise, the number of which I wrote on the book, and then I heard the engine give two whistles, which I knew meant that they were going over the St. Paul and Duluth crossing. I looked up to see which way I should go, and saw that the cars were on fire right in front of me. I then started for the office and nearly suffocated before getting there, when I found that all the trainmen had gone, and that only Mr. Murry, the telegraph operator, and Mr. George Surgeon, the agent, were there. We stayed there as long as we could, then started for the upper office, where we found that train No. 4 from West Superior for St. Paul, had just arrived.

I told Engineer Best that he could not get through the lower yard, as all the cars were on fire when I left there. I then found Conductor W. D. Campbell, of train 23, and we took all the cars that were on the house track, three in number, and our cab, and coupled onto the rear end of the passenger train, and then were ready to come back.

We loaded everybody that we had time to before the fire drove us away, staying there about eight or ten minutes after we coupled to the passenger train, during which time the train was started three or four times, because Engineer Barry thought it perilous to stay longer, as the fire was so near and so hot. We stopped, however, a short time longer.

JOHN G. HOWARD, SUPERINTENDENT OF BUILDINGS.

When we left there we pulled across Grindstone river bridge and stopped again, to pick up what people we could. We waited perhaps four or five minutes, during which time the train was started that many times, and I stopped it until Conductor Powers and Campbell deemed it unsafe to stay any longer. We then started for good. As engine 105 was backing up Brakemen C. Beach, of the passenger train, G. Gillam, P. McLaughlin and myself of train 23, were on the back of the tank to watch for danger. As we were nearing the first bridge, about three-fourths of a mile this side of Hinckley, we could see that it was on fire and slowed up a little, but thought it better to go on than to stop, so we started and did not stop again until we got to Sandstone. Every bridge we crossed over from Hinckley to Sandstone, was on fire.

We got to Sandstone O. K., where we tried to get the residents to get on the train; but the fire was not burning very fiercely there then, and they did not wish to leave their homes, they said; so we started again.

Kettle river bridge was not on fire when we crossed it, or any more bridges from there to West Superior.

On reaching Partridge the poor little ones and the ladies who were in the cars were nearly famished. G. W. Gillam and I with some of the men who were aboard got water for the children and sick women to drink. We were there about twenty-five or thirty minutes.

Mr. G. W. Gillam and myself rode the back of the tank from there to Dedham, where we were not able to see any more from the ashes and smoke. We stopped at all places from Partridge to West Superior, and notified people to look out for fire.

On arriving at West Superior our engines were uncoupled from our train and a switch engine took us to Duluth, where we left all the cars and came back to West Superior and home. From what I have heard and from books that have been printed, there were only one or two men who got any credit for the work done on the first day of last September. If they are the only ones deserving of credit, let it be so, but I do not think there was a man on that train who did not do all in his power to save the lives of every one that he could, and the property of the company as well.

The names of the crews on train 4 and 23 are given below:

On train No. 4, H. L. Powers, conductor; W. B. Best, engineer, engine No. 125; and C. Beach, brakeman.

On train No. 23, W. D. Campbell, conductor; Edward Barry, engineer, engine No. 105, and Charles C. Freeman, G. W. Gilham and A. McLaughlin, brakemen.

FIREMAN A. R. THISTLE.

I was firing engine 105 on September first, on trains 23 and 24 between West Superior and Hinckley. We arrived in Hinckley at 2:45 p. m. and found the yard and town surrounded by fire and everybody out fighting fire. We put the train away with difficulty. We could not make up the train on account of fire and smoke, so we went on the side track and waited the arrival of train No. 4 then nearly due. We did not get our engine turned, as the fire had already caught the telegraph office, and was dangerously near the round house and turn-table.

On arrival of train No. 4, we backed up to the passenger station, along with that train, as they could not get any farther, and took three box cars from the freight house along with caboose, and coupled onto the rear end of the passenger train; then waited until everybody got aboard. We then started for West Superior.

Hinckley was all in flames when we left.

We were signaled to stop at the mile board and did so, taking on a few more people. It was then as dark as night and the ties in a great many places were on fire; also some of the bridges between Hinckley and Sandstone. We stopped at all stations between Hinckley and West Superior.

HEROES REMEMBERED.

The Hinckley fire sufferers feel that they owe a great debt of gratitude to the brave railroad men of the Eastern Minnesota, who rescued 500 of their number from almost certain destruction on that fatal September afternoon, when the fire king in his fury raged through the forest, sweeping towns and farm houses out of existence and destroying many hundreds of lives. They remember how the boys in charge of that train, when the shadow of death was over all, worked rapidly, seriously, and with perfect composure, with the single object of rescuing human life. They remember the terrible experience of the ride through the burning forest, where serpents of flame writhed and clambered and it was an open question whether or not death had intercepted them and waited their arrival a little farther on.

Prominent among the men who distinguished themselves on that memorable day were Engineer Edward Barry and Conductor W. D. Campbell, of the freight train which doubled up with the passenger on that occasion. The Hinckley people have presented to these two gentlemen each a solid gold medal in the form of a six pointed star and which is suitable for being worn as a watch charm. On the face of each charm is inscribed: "Hinckley Fire Sufferers, to ————," mentioning the name of the recipient. On the reverse side appears the following: "In recognition of his heroism and bravery."

BRAKEMAN BEACH.

D. E. WILLIAMS.

PINE CITY.

PINE CITY is the county seat of Pine county, and the town nearest to the scene of disaster. It is bisected by the St. Paul & Duluth Railway; it was from this place that the memorable telegrams telling the world of the great fire were sent, and John F. Stone, the well known proprietor of the Pioneer House, the man who sent them; the operator was Mr. A. J. Armstrong. Not often in the memory of men now living, have any messages gone over the wires, which awakened such world-wide interest. As soon as the work of the fire was known, every one, who in Pine City could help, were glad to do so, and interest to the close of the work never abated for an instant. To tell who helped would be to tell the names of the adult population and many of the children.

To Pine City, telegrams came from near and far like a flood, one man could not have possibly done the work. Telegrams to persons who had relatives in the fire and from relatives to those who had escaped its heat and flames, from all sorts of people offering help and asking questions. Crowds flocked to Pine City on foot, in wagons and buggies, and by trains, the representatives of the state, of the great cities; lawyers, doctors, clergymen and nurses; every rank in society found this a convenient place. The refugees might be seen upon the streets, men upon whose faces the terrible anxiety of the fatal Saturday had stamped an indelible mark; they were too sad to speak; women who had little children in their arms, into whose faces they looked and took a sweet pleasure in so doing, even though they knew that to provide for these little ones meant for them years of dreary work, hard toil and sacrifice; children out of whose lives had departed the comforts of other years. Some of these people had escaped death only by most wonderful providence. There was one common bond of sympathy, and that was that they had all had similar, though different experiences.

Every available place which could be of service to those from the burned localities was used in the way found best. There were never wanting ready hands prompted by loving hearts, to assist to the very

JUDGE NETHAWAY, STILLWATER.

CAPT. HARRIS, SUPERIOR.

uttermost each and all who wanted help. The ladies did a work which they may well look back upon with pleasure. Mrs. J. F. Stone worked long and hard, day and night and many a fire sufferer will carry grateful memories of her kindness to their latest day. Mrs. L. E. Breckenridge was one of the women who counted toil joy and labor sweet if she could, as she did, bring light to many hearts. She was night and day at the drug store, bright hopeful and useful to a degree no words can fully tell. Mrs. Kate Vaughan, Mrs. F. A. Hodge, Mrs. L. H. McKusick and Miss Nannie Monk all did noble work, with many others. Amongst the men who worked incessantly were lawyer S. S. L. Roberts, John Vaughan, Otto Mowalkee and Henry Kath. These men led the crew that went out on hand cars on the Saturday night. A good system of registration had to be adopted, places at which meals could be had provided, steps taken to ensure that all had not only a place in which to sleep, but where they could be sure of plenty to eat. Mr. H. H. Hart was on hand with Mr. Arvold and Mr. J. F. Jackson, secretary of Associated Charities of St. Paul, Mr. J. T. Manix, secretary to Mayor Eustis, Minneapolis, and many other well known people made Pine City headquarters. The following ticket shows how the admission to the dining room was gained:

1	2	3		1	2	3		1	2	3	

GOOD FOR 21 MEALS

TO

STATE RELIEF COMMISSION.

NOT GOOD UNLESS COUNTERSIGNED.

J. F. JACKSON, Agent, Pine City.

1	2	3		1	2	3		1	2	3	

Every one entitled to such a ticket received it freely. The mayor and officials gave the freedom of the town and hospitality of the people to their neighbors in all their trouble. The whole state is debtor to the good citizens of Pine City for what they so self-sacrificingly did in the month of September, 1894. The narrative of Mr. Stone will be read with deep interest.

PINE CITY, MINN., Sept. 1, 1894.

To the PIONEER PRESS and GLOBE, St. Paul, Minn.:

The forest fires north of the town are raging with savage fury, the high winds through the day have fanned every spark into a flame and it has been traveling over the country, sweeping everything before it. Settlers are being driven from their homes to seek shelter in the marshes; hay and buildings consumed, and the air in suffocating condition from heat and smoke. The north bound Limited train with all the passengers, is now laid up at this place waiting to get through to Duluth. Crews are out working on burnt culverts and repairing bent rails to get the trains through if possible, tonight. There is no communication with Hinckley, but it is feared here that the town is in imminent danger. Relief crews are being sent out from town as rapidly as possible to aid the distressed settlers. At this writing (10:30 p. m.) the wind has died away and hope has correspondingly increased. No danger to this town at present.

STONE.

PINE CITY, MINN., Sept. 1, 1894.

To the PIONEER PRESS and GLOBE, St. Paul, Minn.:

Hinckley burned to ashes; many people lost their lives in the fire, balance are homeless and destitute; send relief if possible at once. The little town of Mission Creek entirely wiped out. Engineer Jim Root probably fatally burned. Situation appalling and heart-rending in the extreme.

STONE.

PINE CITY, MINN., Sept. 2, 1894.

To Gov. NELSON, Minneapolis, Minn.:

Relief committee to receive aid for Hinckley sufferers is James Hurley, J. F. Stone, E. A. Haugh, H. Birchers, J. W. Breckinridge, all at Pine City, to whom supplies should be sent.

J. F. STONE.

PINE CITY, MINN., Sept. 2, 1894.

To the PIONEER PRESS and GLOBE, St. Paul, Minn.:

Relief party has gone from here with medical aid for the suffering and provisions for the hungry. Wires are down and no communication since train came down at 12 o'clock. The town is completely wiped out. The Limited train from Duluth, Root, engineer, was caught in the fire and Root standing to his post like a hero, ran his train back to Skunk Lake with it all on fire, and saved his passengers. When last seen, he was lying in his cab, badly burned but breathing. The people of Mission Creek saved themselves by lying down in a potato patch until the fiery indignation was past. The disaster is full and complete and sad enough to dismay the strongest heart. Relief temporary, substantial, and immediate is needed and needed bad.

The Limited passenger train, six miles above Hinckley, is in ashes, and about two hundred people are there in the marsh near Skunk

Lake, with fire all around them. Yard master at Hinckley is badly burned. The relief party is pushing through and hope to get there by 2 o'clock. It was only by the most superhuman effort that the train was backed out of the fire and the passengers saved. Poor Root! he ought to live, such men are always heroes in time of need.

STONE.

ST. PAUL, MINN., Sept. 2, 1894.

To FRED A. HODGE, Pine City, Minn.:

Special train with food and blankets leave here at 3:30 for Pine City. Tents and clothing will follow on later train.

TAMS BIXBY, Governor's Secretary.

ST. PAUL, MINN., Sept. 2, 1894.

To FRED A. HODGE, Pine City, Minn.:

What is needed? Answer quick.

TAMS BIXBY, Governor's Private Secretary.

MINNEAPOLIS, MINN., Sept. 2, 1894.

To FRED A. HODGE, Rush City, Minn.:

You have the unmeasured sympathy of our people in your terrible affliction. Will rush relief; hope to send car of provisions in a few hours. Do you need any medical help. Wire for anything specific you need at once. W. H. EUSTIS, Mayor.

ST. PAUL, MINN., Sept. 2, 1894.

To F. A. HODGE, J. F. STONE and S. L. ROBERT, Rush City, Minn.:

Your telegram received too late or notice of the calamity would have been sent to all the churches in the city. Wire me at once a list of articles most needed and will send today. Will call meeting of citizens tomorrow morning.

ROBERT A. SMITH, Mayor.

REV. WILLIAM WILKINSON, DEAR SIR:

Your kind invitation to contribute some data concerning the Pine county forest fires I deem an honor far greater than my ability to fulfill.

Living as I did, thirteen miles from the immediate scene of the disaster, I can only give you points and facts that came to my personal knowledge after the event transpired.

Pine City was safe. Safety is a great thing in time of danger. Danger is made up of degrees that gradually increase until it assumes the shape of a gigantic calamity, beyond the power of the human mind to understand, or physical ability to avert. Such was the character of the great Hinckley fire. It is said that "Coming events cast their shadows before." This may be true; it is true in many respects. It was true of the Hinckley fire. We read in the Bible that, "The

DEATH ON THE ROAD.

elements shall melt with fervent heat, etc.," a prophetic utterance, relative to a general breaking up of all things. It may not be apparent to all, and it may be scoffed at and criticised by the overwise, but the fact nevertheless remains that our meteoroligical conditions for the last twenty years have been undergoing a gradual, insidious and dangerous change. It is fashionable now, and adds much to our fancied security, to have a convenient root house, or cyclone cellar, to flee to at the first indication of a rising storm. Little innocent clouds, whose former office was only to "drop the gentle rain from heaven upon the place beneath" have learned such dangerous tricks of late, that when they begin to get bigger than a man's hand, the people are filled with apprehension, and vague unrest, which continues until the glad sunshine comes again.

Formerly the seasons were tempered with a very even distribution of precipitation; but now Dame Nature resorts to the curious and unusual freak of emptying it all out in a short period, in the shape of cloud bursts and spiral spouts of electric fury. These periods are followed with severe drought, parching the earth, withering the vegetation, and preparing everything in first class shape for the flames.

The fire at Hinckley was one of the results of causes which are constantly increasing in power and frequency, and which will, in the near or distant future, develop much more disastrous effects. This fire resulted in the constituent elements of the air becoming disintegrated, separated, and leaving one element—an inflamable, dangerously explosive gas, while the other hung like a dark pall over the scene, shutting out the light and rendering the chance for destruction more weird and complete. Literally the air was on fire, exploding in flashes.

Mr. Fraser, who with his family was caught in the vortex of one of these death dealing explosions, saved himself and family by placing his children in the water barrels found on the wagon hitched to a fleeing team, and saved his wife and himself by keeping under a constant stream of water, kept up by his undaunted heroism and bravery in the face of death, and presence of mind in time of imminent and fatal danger. As it was, all his family suffered serious and permanent disfigurement and injury from the hot stifling blasts from the explosions. These gigantic storms, this "melting of the elements with fervent heat" in earlier ages of the world's history produced our primary drift, and in that way have been a wonderful aid to agriculture, civilization and commerce; but a change is taking place which we can know if we try to discern the signs of the times; and while it is not in our power to avert, we can save ourselves, in many cases, by fleeing from the wrath which is sure to come.

Time is divided into periods and cycles, some of which are conducive to human life, its development and prosperity; while others are equally powerful to destroy. To say we are gradually entering such a period now, would only provoke criticism, and lead the learned to raise the cry of "calamity howler;" but cold facts, based on many years of careful calculation, bear out by unimpeachable evidence this important theory. This Hinckley fire was one of those unimpeachable witnesses. Years ago "rocks fell to dust" and mountains melted away before the same supernatural force, only manifested in a greater degree. It is coming again. What did Pine City do in this awful calamity of last September? Only her duty.

When suffering and stricken humanity presents itself to her more fortunate fellows, the better instincts of the human mind predominate, and we help without ever thinking of the right or wrong. It is done unconsciously, and from absolutely pure motives. I could tell you how the scorched, burned, and half-suffocated victims came down through the suffocating darkness on that fearful September night, from that awful holocaust, but that has been and will be told in your valuable book by others. I sent the first message over the wires announcing the sad news to the outside world, through the columns of the St. Paul Globe and Pioneer Press, of which I was the local Pine City correspondent. As fresh news came in it was sent out until it became apparent to the two great dailies that a special correspondent must be sent at once to the field; this was done. I sent out the messages to the governor of the state and to the mayors of the Twin Cities when it became obvious that our resources were entirely insufficient to meet the necessities and pressing needs of the victims. This was done after taking counsel with the leading citizens here, and deciding that such a course was imperatively necessary.

A. G. Parkins, Esq., called a public meeting in Robinson Park early Sunday morning, September 2nd, where the first relief committee was chosen. This committee consisted of James Hurley, chairman; J. G. Breckinridge, secretary; Fred A. Hodge, treasurer; John F. Stone, Herman Borchers, E. A. Hough and A. G. Perkins. Each one then was assigned a part, and in the course of two hours thereafter everything was moving like clock work. The Citizens' Committee from St. Paul and Minneapolis, on their arrival Sunday night, September 2nd, found us in perfect organization, and the immediate necessities of the sufferers fairly well supplied. This committee continued its good work until all the difficult labor of relief had been met and accomplished.

Early in the week, Gov. Nelson appointed a State Relief Commission, who visited our village, met and conferred with us, appointing Secretary H. Hart as their executive officer, to whom, after a few days of joint work, the whole business was turned over. Secretary Hart opened an office here, where he continued the work about four weeks, after which he removed to Hinckley where he could be nearer the center of the district needing their services. Up to this date the commission is still in existence, doing much valuable work.

Not wishing to go into the details for fear of repetitions, as no doubt you have chronicled all the incidents which I could relate, again thanking you, I close. Yours truly,

JOHN F. STONE.

MR. JAMES HURLEY, CHAIRMAN OF THE PINE CITY RELIEF COMMITTEE, SAYS:

"I was sitting on the steps at my neighbor Lambert's at 11 o'clock p. m., Saturday, September 1st. We were talking about the fire—there was considerable uneasiness regarding it—when the marshal, J. E. Netser, came and said, "Hinckley is all burned out, and many lives lost." The news was brought by Augus Hay and Carle Veenhover, two residents who had walked miles through smoke and fire to a construction train that was engaged in repairing a bridge, which had brought them here, and in a little while all Pine City knew what had happened and was astir.

I went into my house, told my family what had happened, got my overcoat and went down town. I met a number of men and women at the park. We called all the young men and boys present and sent them to every house, and gathered all provisions ready for use. Within half an hour, everything carried in this train was at the depot, and a local doctor and two other doctors, had such medicines, drugs, liquor, batting, bandages and all they would be likely to use in that line, together. We started with an engine and two coaches. We went through fire and smoke, and it was a grand panorama to look upon the flames in the distance, eighty feet high, but dangerous to pass through. I should judge seventy-five men were on the train. On our way we stopped three times to take on hand cars and push

THE STOCKHOLM FAMILY.

ALBERT BERG.

cars, to move the sick and the dead. We got to Hinckley about 12:30 or 1 a. m., Sunday, September 2nd. We stopped at the junction of the St. Paul & Duluth and Eastern Railroad. Here we found all who were saved and able to get there from Hinckley. They had come to the round house, and were in and near it. We made no records at that time, there were too many things needing attention; but I am safe in saying there must have been two hundred people.

The doctors at once went to the help of the burned, and as soon as they could be loaded on cars they were taken to Pine City, where all possible preparations had been made to receive them. While the doctors were treating the injured at the round house, and the others were getting onto the train, I with a party of five or six others went to the gravel pit.

We found Rev. D. W. Lawler, partially unconscious. He had been brought from Grindstone river, where he had been during the fire, to the place in which we found him. He knew us well before the fire, but being now totally blind, at first did not understand who we were. We carried him to the train; the others who were with him there, coming with us,—many being just able to walk, and got on the train which now left for Pine City. With lanterns all the adjacent places were searched for the living and dead. It was a gruesome task, some of them being baked, not yet cold. The train came back from Pine City, after leaving its load of desolate sorrowful people there.

The Skunk Lake relief party had got back to Hinckley with all they found at that place. When those, with all we had found, were loaded, the train again went to Pine City. We came back Sunday forenoon. Thus all the living had been looked after, this being the first imperative duty. By this time we saw something of the magnitude of the work before us. The leading citizens met in the park and organized committees; the duties of several were to look after the needs of the living, and care for the dead. Donations had been made and while all had done their best, still it was evident that local gifts could not supply every need, so we ordered out of the stores what was necessary for present use. By this time all the continent knew of the awful calamity, and telegrams in floods came in, of sympathy and offers of help, all of which were gratefully received.

This brings us to Sunday, September 2nd, at 4 p. m.

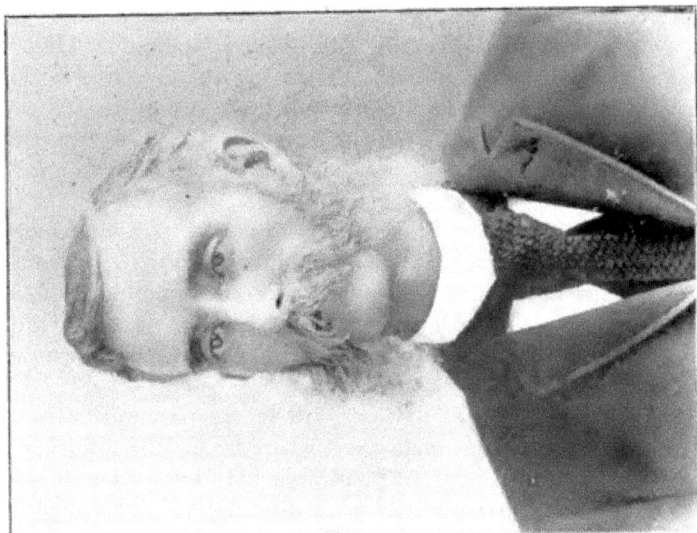

DR. WATSON.

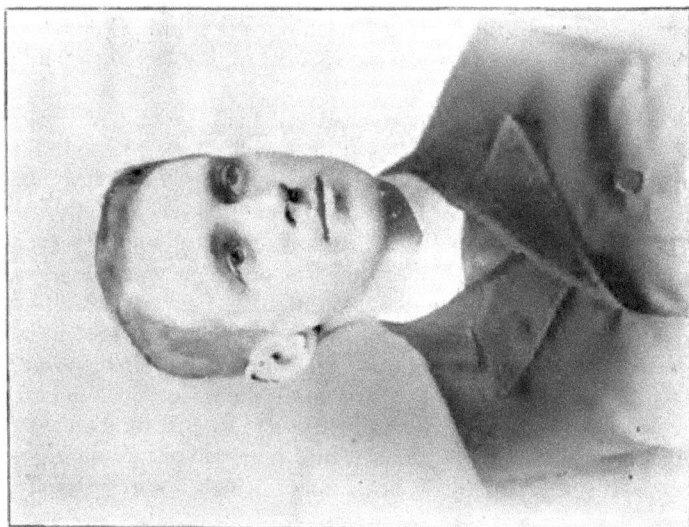

CHARLES F. ROBEL.

PINE CITY, MINN., Jan. 12, 1895.

HON. H. H. HART, Secretary State Fire Relief Committee:

I hand you herewith a statement of receipts and disbursements of the treasurer of the Pine City relief committee, as promised. I will itemize a statement of disbursements if you desire.

Yours truly,

F. A. HODGE.

JAMES HURLEY, ESQ., Chairman Relief Committee, Pine City:

I submit herewith a statement of the funds I have received and disbursed as treasurer of your committee, viz.:

RECEIPTS.

Citizens of Taylor's Falls	$394.60
Dr. Hukins and brother, Iowa	10.00
A. L. Leinman, White Bear	5.00
Rutledge Lumber Company	100.00
Employes of Rutledge Lumber Company	175.00
August J. Anderson, Taylor's Falls	50.00
Village of Rush City	250.00
Citizens of Stillwater	200.00
Citizens of Lindstrom	83.00
L. A. Elbert, West Duluth	25.00
W. A. Bend, from St. Paul committee	500.00
Village of Harris	100.00
Citizens of Harris	37.75
P. H. Stolberg, Harris	100.00
P. Huntoon, Stillwater	5.00
W. G. LeCrone, Faribault	7.00
Citizens of White Bear	196.17
A. P. Noyes	2.50
Rev. H. B. J. Jansen, Alexandria	15.00
George H. Cunningham, Sturgeon Lake	25.00
A. H. Clark	5.00
Citizens of North Branch	100.00
J. A. Guthrie	1.00
Unknown	1.00
W. P. Broughton, St. Paul	25.00
Unknown, Cambridge, N. Y.	5.00
J. Leary, Bald Eagle	1.00
P. E. Foredine	2.00
Citizens of Wyoming, Minn.	83.00
Mr. and Mrs. R. F. Paxton	5.00
Mrs. W. DeHart	1.00
Sunday School, Amora, Ill.	5.00
Sunday School, Big Wood	1.77
F. Chimielewski, Sturgeon Lake	5.00
J. F. Jackson, account State Relief Commission	77.42

Total receipts $2,599.21

DISBURSEMENTS.

Paid orders drawn by State Relief Committee............$1,102.42
Paid orders drawn, Pine City Relief Commission......... 1,372.72
Paid Kenneth Clark, treasurer of State Relief Commission. 124.07
                                                        _____

Fred A. Hodge, treasurer......................$2,599.21

MEMORIAL SERVICE FOR THE DEAD.

After the fire, as soon as men had time to look over the condition of affairs in Mille Lacs, Carleton and Pine counties, it was felt that there should be one great public service, in memory of those who had departed from the life that now is, and gone into that which is on the other side of death. Pine City being the town nearest the scene of disaster and most easily accessible at that time by rail, it was the place selected for the purpose of holding it. The result proved the wisdom of the choice. September 9th was appointed and was probably one of the most memorable services ever held in America since the great Abraham Lincoln was laid to rest. All day the fires near the city had been burning; the very photographs of horrid and alarming experiences endured a week before were stamped upon the minds and hearts of many hundreds of men, women and children, who were either making Pine City their home or had come to the service. They saw anew September 1st, and the sight brought tears to their eyes. They heard again in memory the voices now silent and saw once more the faces gone never again to return.

To this service, which had been made known all over the land through the public press, had come from all parts of the state and many other states as pilgrims to a shrine, throngs of people, and the opera house was the place to which they wended their sorrowful way. All entered into the spirit of the hour, and the words of Christian hope fell on the ears of the people, as the gentle rain falls upon the warm dry earth, softening, refreshing, blessing it. In two solos the deep bass voice of Mr. Albert Berg, who is now secretary of state, sounded through the hall like music from another world. Mrs. Barnum sang a solo, and her soft, clear voice, produced a deep impression.

When Mr. Knudsen read a list of dead, a profound silence pervaded the whole assembly. The Rev. Mr. Feetham, Methodist minister in Pine City, and Rev. Father Bajec, priest of Rush City, spoke with much feeling. The Right Rev. Mahlon N. Gilbert, D. D., assistant bishop of the Protestant Episcopal church in the diocese of Min-

nesota, had been asked to give the principal address. All who heard
it said nothing could have been more tender, beautiful or appropriate.
The Rush City Post reports the meeting thus:

Through the courtesy of Mr. J. D. Markham a number of persons
from this place were taken to Pine City in a private coach Sunday to
attend the services which were to be conducted in memory of the
fire victims. Owing to a report that Pine City was in danger of
being destroyed by the insatiable flames, the car which was due to
leave at 4 p. m., did not start until 6 o'clock. By that time the
greater number of those who intended to go decided to remain at
home. The dreadful report that flames 200 feet high were advancing
rapidly towards Pine City was ample reason for their deciding not to
go.

The services were to have been held in Robinson's Park, but the
confusion which prevailed during the afternoon made it impracticable
to conduct them at that place. The committee wisely postponed the
services and made arrangements to have them in Tierney's hall in
the evening.

The scene at the hall was a heartstirring one. There were those
present who alone represented what remained of a once happy family.
Some were still bandaged; upon others frightful scars were visible,
and the look on the faces of many told only too plainly the story
of the loss of home, loved ones and hope. Sadness pervaded the atmosphere and a heavy feeling seemed to press on the hearts of all
present.

The exercises opened with a few remarks by Chairman Mannix,
who, in closing, presented Rev. Knudsen, pastor of the Presbyterian
church at Hinckley, who read a selection from scripture. Bishop
Gilbert followed with an earnest prayer and then Mrs. Barnum sang
a solo with much feeling. Rev. Knudsen again stepped forward and
read a list of those of his congregation who were dead and buried
and made some comment upon the havoc caused by the flames. He
was a fellow sufferer, and believed the hand of God was hidden beneath the cloud of sorrow.

By request Attorney S. G. L. Roberts read a poem composed by
Mr. Tallman commemorative of the forest fires.

Rev. Feetham ministered words of courage and comfort to the sorrowing and made a point of the lesson that out of all sorrow some
good is sure to be derived.

Father Bajec spoke on the subject, "Is life worth living?" Among

REV. C. C. SALTER, M. A.

other things he said, "When I looked upon the cold, distorted corpses as they lay scattered upon the blackened ground and thought of how suddenly fire had taken them from life; how they had struggled for a foothold upon plenty amidst hardships and discouragements, and how family ties had been rent asunder and grief was all there was left, it certainly seemed that life was not worth living. But, my friends, there is hope beyond, and these persons who are now cold in death were slowly preparing for an eternal home." He dwelt upon this subject in a manner creditable to himself, and his remarks were appreciated by the large assembly.

Attorney Markham gave an account of the expedition party which searched the woods in and about Pokegama and concluded by advising the homeless refugees to again go to the place where home once stood and build. Money should be furnished out of that so generously contributed and assistance would be forthcoming from all directions. His advice was just what was needed, and inspired the forlorn sufferers with renewed hope.

Albert Berg, Republican candidate for secretary of state, was present and sang two of his famous solos. His rich, powerful, wonderful voice was indeed music to the ears of those who had heard naught but sobs and distress during the week.

The address of the evening was delivered by Bishop Gilbert. The bishop was thoroughly impressed with the solemnity of the occasion and seemed inspired with eloquent emotion. From the Pioneer Press we quote the following, which is a brief synopsis of his address:

"I stand before you tonight to give voice to the sympathy which swells up from responsive hearts over the land. This little community, before obscure and scarcely discovered on the map, has for the last week been the nerve center for all the world. Messages of love and sympathy have come throbbing under leagues of ocean from all parts of the world. God must have had some sublime object in bringing about this awful disaster did we only read his purpose beneath the intensest of suffering. Let it not be said that God has thus spoken out of the whirlwind and we have not heard. I know we cannot unravel all the mysteries of God. We are often like babes who can only cry out with pain and cannot understand the cause, but then like children we can learn the lesson taught us. Our eyes fill with tears when we recall the awful agony through which many of you passed when the besom of destruction swept over you and the black cloud of death was illumined only by the lurid flames, but I would have you think not of this, but of those lost friends regained again in a better land. These calamities are all a part of God's plans. The great civil war of thirty years ago is an illustration of this, where sacrifice and suffering wrought freedom and a united land. So it has often been in your own lives where there has been seeming loss. What is the gain? First, we are taught that God is greater than all material things. When we have built up a material fortune and begun to worship it, one sweep of divine justice takes it away, reminding us that God is more powerful than these things; second, our hearts are brought together. You have heard of the great strikes that agitated the country a few weeks ago, arraying man against man, threatening anarchy and social disruption. Like the finger of God this calamity has come and swept away all distinction of rank and class. God used this to cement again the bonds of fraternity which were being rent asunder. I stood last Monday in the chamber of commerce at St. Paul and saw tears moisten the cheeks of the men who rule the finances of a great city as they responded to the appeals made in behalf of those stricken people. They did not know these woodsmen; they did not know these men of toil; but their hearts were touched by the sufferings of common humanity. God thus used the grim surgery of fire to heal the wound.

".Again we must not lose the lesson of personal heroism. When we have met these men as we do frequently on the train they did not look like heroes, but plain men, scarcely worthy of our notice. When the trial came and an awful death threatened hundreds of human lives, they stood up in their divine heroism and taught us a lesson that beneath the humble garb is often concealed a noble manhood, and when we have turned to dust the world will still honor the names of Powers, Best, Sullivan, Root, Campbell and Blair. Such heroism will cover a multitude of sins, and I doubt not God will blot out some of their faults, for they doubtless had faults, and remember that they nobly did their duty in the time of trial. The trial seems hard, but what matter if it makes you better? Look up and let the sacrifice of friends and loved ones make you nobler and purer. Last of all, when the grass has grown green over their graves and your hearts' wounds are somewhat healed, let us not forget that God came down in a chariot of fire one day as he did for Elijah of old to take our better selves up to himself."

The hymn, "Our Great Redeemer Praise Ye," written by J. E. Modin, was sung to music by Mozart, and so added to the memorial service for the dead.

STATE COMMISSION APPOINTED.

By Monday afternoon, September 3rd, all the continent of America, and the most of Europe had heard of the terrible calamity which had befallen the state of Minnesota. It was then seen that the work of relief would have to be taken in hand in a large way, no public sympathy left to work at random would meet the urgent needs of the case. Gov. Nelson consulted with some of the wisest and best men in the state, and at once appointed a commission who received power to ask for money and to use it as it should be needed for the fire sufferers. The relief proclamation is printed in the state commissioner's report in this book, so that there is no need to reproduce it here.

In looking at the end in view, the governor had to keep in mind the fact that large sums of money had to be raised by the gifts of the people at large; that as winter was near it would have to be spent quickly; so it was absolutely needful that the men whom he vested with authority, should be men of known uprightness and of known ability, and also that they should be men in whom the fire sufferers themselves would find kind friends.

As soon as the five names were published everyone felt that we had a commission whose personal acts would be above reproach. The names are: Charles H. Graves, of Duluth; Mathew G. Norton, Winona; Hastings H. Hart, St. Paul; Kenneth Clark, St. Paul; Charles A. Pillsbury, Minneapolis. Mr. Graves is well known, particularly in Northern Minnesota; he is also well known all through the state, having been speaker of the house of representatives. He had the advantage of being in the district where the heaviest part of the work, of dealing with the distressed, had necessarily fallen. He is a man of high character and good ability. Mathew G. Norton is respected and honored wherever known, by noble industry, prudence and honest business methods he has won a reputation which is to be envied. H. H. Hart is secretary of the Board of Corrections and Charities, Minnesota, and thus had an experience which the governor rightly thought would be of much value to the commission in its work. Mr. Kenneth Clark is president of the Capital Bank in St. Paul, a Presbyterian in religion, and interested in many good works in the city. Mr. Pillsbury is head of the greatest milling firm on the continent. Pillsbury's Best flour is known from one end of the land to the other. He is accustomed to large plans and a royal man is he.

These five men were called to their first meeting in St. Paul, Sept. 5th, as the annexed letter shows:

EXECUTIVE DEPARTMENT, ST. PAUL, MINN., Sept. 4, 1894.

HON. C. A. PILLSBURY, Minneapolis, Minn.:

By direction of the governor, I have the honor to inform you that you are appointed as a member of the State Commission for relief of Hinckley fire sufferers, authorized to receive contributions of money and supplies, and to expend and disburse the same.

The commission meets tomorrow (Wednesday) at the capitol at 4 o'clock in the afternoon. Don't fail to be on hand.

Yours very respectfully,

(Signed) TAMS BIXBY,
Governor's Private Secretary.

At this meeting Mr. Pillsbury was chosen chairman, H. H. Hart, secretary, Kenneth Clark, treasurer, and they were made the executive committee because, being the officers of the commission, and living in St. Paul and Minneapolis, they could readily be called and easily meet together. I know the spirit in which their work was entered upon, and the difficulties they had to meet; it is the simplest truth to say that no five men ever entered upon a work of love with higher aims or purer desires. The public will never know all the difficulties they had to encounter and overcome.

The fire had swept through a new piece of country, the people left homeless and penniless, many of them helpless, from many lands and churches. They had had different kinds of training, and they differed greatly in personal character and tastes. The property they had before the fire was held in very many different ways. Some had a contract to buy and had paid part of the cost, others had bought and had mortgages upon their houses and lands. Now the houses, barns, etc., were all gone the mortgages were greater than the value of the property left. In such cases to rebuild on that land was to put money intended for the fire sufferers onto the land which the nominal owners, in all human probability, would lose on foreclosure; others did not know just how their property did stand in regard to title. Some fire sufferers were widows with small children, some old people who had lost those upon whom they depended for counsel and help. To act quickly was to be sure to make very grave mistakes;

to stand still was impossible in the circumstances. It took a little time to comprehend the whole situation. To add to all this there was a large class whom the commission could not effectively keep, who were the well-to-do, and had been, up to the day of the fire, for years, in circumstances which to them were affluent.

The commission was not an insurance society, it could not place such people where they were before the fire, in the commercial world, yet it was this very class, who in all except in the loss of life, lost most. The commission appointed agents, as its report shows, whose duty and pleasure it was to find out the exact facts in regard to loss and need, and the ability of those who came for help to help themselves, and each and every case was taken up, considered with care, and assisted as it appeared wise.

It was soon found that the most ready to press claims, the most clamorous, were not the most needy, nor had they, in many cases, suffered the greatest injury by the fire. On the contrary, many such persons were the least worthy, and had least ground for appeal. It often happened that the retiring and modest, the highly deserving, had to be sought and helped, and made to understand that accepting such aid was not charity, but the common help of man to man in the day when one suffers extraordinary misfortune.

The commission decided that they would not build any houses upon property to which, those for whom it was intended had not a perfect title. They engaged a competent lawyer to see that this rule was strictly complied with. The wisdom of such action is seen at once; it answers two purposes. It sees that the money given by the generous public is not wasted, and that the fire sufferers had at least a home in which to live; both very desirable points.

ANGUS HAY.

J. E. GEMMEL, M. D., C. M.

OLIVE A. BROWN.

FRED ROBINSON.

RUSH CITY.

THE reports printed below give a good photograph of what was done with such heartiness by this town and its people:

MISS OLIVE A. BROWN, DAY OPERATOR AT PINE CITY, WRITES:

At exactly at 11:30 on the night of September 1st, 1894, I was sitting in the office with Mrs. James Root, wife of engineer Root, waiting for the arrival of the south-bound train, No. 4, on which train Mr. Root was engineer, when I was paralyzed to hear the following message sent from Pine City to the dispatcher in St. Paul:

PINE CITY, MINN., Sept. 1, 1894.

To J. MICHAELS, St. Paul, Minn.:

"Hinckley, Mission Creek and No. 4 train are all burned up, except the engine. The passengers on No. 4 train are in Skunk Lake, about six miles north of Hinckley, and about half the people in Hinckley are dead. We want all the assistance possible. Notify both doctors at Rush City, and any others that can be got here at once."

After hearing this, I at once started and notified both doctors.

There being an extra freight train and also a light engine here at that time, they immediately started the light engine north, with the two doctors and six other men to the scene of action.

The citizens here then gathered together provisions sufficient to feed the sufferers for two days, the supply including one hundred and thirty gallons of milk, and loaded it on to the relief train, which was ready to leave in less than forty-five minutes from the time the message was received. The first relief train that reached the sufferers was started from Rush City.

Altogether, there was sent from this place about seven hundred gallons of milk to the sufferers at Hinckley.

OLIVE A. BROWN.

MARSHAL GEORGE B. KNIGHT.

Quite a party from Rush City responded to the telegram from Pine City, the nearest office to the affected region. Shortly after receiving this telegram, which was the first we had heard of the fire, a relief train from the south stopped and took aboard our delegation, together with provisions, blankets and such articles as could be hurriedly thrown together, including a carload of milk.

Arriving at Pine City two hand-cars were procured and manned, the cars going ahead to examine the track and prevent a collision with a relief train which had previously started for Hinckley and which was now thought to be returning, the train following slowly. In this way Hinckley was reached.

We began immediately to care for the suffering and covered the dead. It was while ministering to the affliction of a party of blinded and exhausted trainmen that the question was heard, "Has anybody gone to Pokegama?" "No. Why?" "Our train was wrecked there. The people of Pokegama are in the cars, for God's sake go up!"

No time was lost in procuring another car, and a party consisting of W. S. Chapin, George Knight, Robert O'Leary, Gustaf Lingren, Ed. Farrel and Frank Smith undertook the arduous task of pushing on over the burnt and smouldering road to Pokegama.

One mile out from Hinckley, Smith decided that he had made a mistake in starting and endeavored to persuade the others to turn back. Failing in this, he mournfully sat down on the car and allowed the remaining members of the crew to pump him on two miles farther. Three miles from Hinckley a long trestle over a marsh or ravine had been burned, and the only way to proceed was to carry the car around the smoking ruins. Here two other rescuers stuck, and the party was equally divided as to whether or not they should turn back. The matter, however, was compromised, the three promising to remain with the car while Chapin, Knight and O'Leary, taking a box of biscuits and a can of milk, pushed on afoot.

Two miles from the burnt trestle they found the so-called wreck, which consisted of two passenger cars "ditched," while the engine and one car yet remained on the track. To these cars part of the inhabitants of Pokegama had fled for shelter, and here the rescuers found about sixty burned and blinded sufferers. After finding and relieving in every possible way that sympathetic manhood could devise the sufferings of the unfortunates, a party of about sixteen was organized and the rescuers, each bearing a child upon his shoulders, led them back to the trestle and the car. Rails and boards, which the haste of the fire had left untouched or but partially burned, were collected, the car enlarged and the entire party placed thereon. All six of the crew fell manfully to work, and, notwithstanding that in the short distance of that three miles the car had to be unloaded and lifted around burnt culverts and defective rails no less than fifteen times, Hinckley was soon reached.

As soon as the car could be cleared of its suffering freight, it was again headed for Brook Park, the same crew at the handles. This time none faltered. There were suffering fellow mortals ahead whom they could assist; they would. Arriving at Brook Park, however, they found but two, a man and wife. The others had been reached and cared for in some other way.

Taking these, they returned slowly to Hinckley, being much exhausted, having worked twenty hours without sleep.

Of the heroic and unselfish work of the above Geo. B. Knight in keeping the party to work, too much cannot be said. He carried babies and little children great distances and the rescued said, "Never did anything taste quite so good as that can of milk.

John Powell was section foreman in charge of crew of section No. 10 of St. Paul and Duluth railroad, who writes:

We passed a section crew one mile south of Pine City, in smoke so dense, and No. 3 following so close, we dare not stop and take them on. Kept on until one mile south of Brown's Hill, which is four miles south of Mission Creek. In the cut there we picked up Section Foreman Gustafson and his crew; and found his wife and two children, and sent one man back with them to Pine City, or they would, no doubt, have perished. One-half mile beyond we found a great pile of logs burning close to a bridge and removed them, the men using their clothing to protect themselves while at work.

Engineer Jones took me on the engine to pilot him, it was so dangerous. The men in the caboose wanted to turn back; it was so hot they lay down in the bottom of the caboose. I told Jones of this; but he replied that it was as safe to go ahead now as to turn back.

Three and one-half miles north of Brown's Hill we found Section Foreman Baumchen, of Hinckley, and his crew. They were in the creek bottom and cut off by fire on both sides. They fol-

T. J. MANNIX.

J. F. STONE.

lowed up the creek, coming in to the railroad again at the next bridge, where we picked them up. One-half mile farther on we found a bridge burned out.

Having charge of the crews, I kept five or six men with me, and the train went back to Rush City for bridge timbers, reaching there at 6:15 p. m. and leaving at 6:55, with four cars of timber and rails—which they loaded themselves.

They brought John Gillie, bridge foreman, and his crew and reached us at eight p m. In forty minutes we had that bridge "rip rapped."

While the train was gone to Rush City I sent four men ahead on a hand car to Mission Creek. They picked up a deer on the track that had been smothered, and took it to the people at the Creek, who skinned it, and with it and some potatoes made their first meal.

With the repaired bridge crossed, we went on within one-fourth of a mile of Mission Creek station, where we found a culvert gone. I rode on the engine, and I can tell you we did not know when we might go into the ditch, it was so very dark from smoke, fearfully hot, and we were nearly blinded. Ties were burning all along the line, affording us a little light to see the rails, which in places were badly warped. While this culvert was being repaired I took a few men and walked to Mission Creek, where we found all the settlers— thirty-five to forty—sheltered in a little log house, the only one left in the town, and brought them with us to the train. These were the people who were saved in the potato patch. While waiting for them to get to the train, a hand car from Hinckley came down with Editor Angus Hay, of the Hinckley Enterprise, and a party in search of a physician for the sufferers at Hinckley. We sent this party with others on the train back to Pine City at once.

Through Mission creek we found the main track all burned out and warped out of shape. I kept a crew with me while the train was gone, and repaired passing track, then went with them on to Hinckley, where we arrived at 12:30 that night.

At first it seemed impossible to get through town, or across the bridge. I did not stop to look in the round house, or go to the gravel pit; I only thought of pushing on to the other train on our own road and reach those people.

Passenger Conductor Buckley, of St. Paul and Duluth No. 3 limited train going north, came back from Pine City in charge of a train to take the people back, having Conductor Jim Sargent with him, assisting in looking after supplies, etc.

I succeeded in getting five hand cars and a push car over the burned bridge, which was all iron (as all the ties were burned out), and almost red hot; and we had, at the south end, to carry them about five rods.   At times it seemed impossible to get across, the heat was so intense, and the bridge so long, with the burning mill so near.   But Conductor Buckley, who was there in charge, said: "Those people are over there, somewhere, and we are bound to get to them."

I went ahead and flagged them through on the first hand car and took four men on each car.   We left Hinckley at 2:30 a. m. and reached the burned No. 4 limited at Skunk lake at 4:30 a. m.   We found the rails out in several places, ties all burned and rails warped.

Three miles south of Hinckley we picked up a badly burned man, whose clothes were nearly all burned off, only a part of his under-clothing remained.   The section men gave him some of their cloth-ing.   One-fourth of a mile from the burned train, we found a cul-vert burned out, and had to tramp around these burned out places. We had some provisions on our car.   Conductors Buckley, Sargent and myself walked ahead from this last culvert to the train, which was all destroyed.   The coal in the tender was all afire when we reached it.   We found Engineer Jim Root in his engine on the deck (I mean the floor).   He was propped up and all alone.   I was the first one to see him and said, "Hello Jim!   How do you feel?" He answered, "I am poorly."   He did not know me for awhile. Conductors Buckley and Sargent said, "We have a doctor, Jim."   We now had with us Dr. E. E. Barnum, of Pine City—brought him on with the train.   Some one replied, "A doctor is no good, now!" And we feared so, too.

By this time the hand car came on with provisions, which the conductors distributed among the passengers, who looked pretty hard, I tell you!   They were along the railroad right of way.

I pressed on north and found Section Foreman McNamara, of Hinckley, whom I had promised to look up.   He was so dazed as to hardly realize what he was about.   When I inquired about his family, he said he did not know anything about them, and together we went on north in search of them.   Two miles further on we found three traveling men, one of whom was so bewildered he did not know what to do.   One went north on my car, which I let go on, while the other two walked south with us to Skunk lake.   I stayed there at Skunk lake until the arrival of the relief train under Con-ductor Roper, from the north.   I then went to Rutledge with Mc-

Namara and stayed until the construction train came south, on Sunday afternoon to Skunk lake.

With nine men I walked to Hinckley. We found, I think, ten bodies between the burned train and Rutledge. I saw none dead at Skunk lake.

From Hinckley I took the train and arrived home at Rush City Sunday night at midnight, after one of the most awful experiences and scenes of terror that men ever passed through.

What Dr. A. J. Stowe, of Rush City, says:

I will give you some of the facts as I know them in connection with the great fire in Hinckley, September first. During the afternoon of the above date word was received by the mayor of Rush City, Mr. C. S. Johnson, that Hinckley was in danger of burning, and asking for as much hose as the city could spare. One thousand feet of hose was accordingly sent on the St. Paul & Duluth Limited, which leaves here at 4 p. m. We afterwards learned that the hose never reached its destination as the train went no further than Pine City.

We heard nothing further from Hinckley until about 11 p. m., when a message passed through this office from Pine City on its way to St. Paul, saying that Hinckley was entirely burned, and probably most of the people; that train No. 4 of the St. Paul & Duluth Railroad was totally destroyed, except the engine, and that nearly all the passengers, as well as the train crew, were in Skunk lake, north of Hinckley. The message was sent by Mr. Lobdell, who was a passenger on the train, and had succeeded in walking a distance of sixteen miles to Pine City.

The operator at this place, Miss Olive Brown, acting under orders from the superintendent of the railway, came to my house and requested me to get what assistance I could and go to the scene of the calamity. Dr. Gemmel and myself had soon in readiness surgical instruments and supplies sufficient to meet any demands likely to be made.

A St. Paul and Duluth engine was placed at our disposal, and no less than three hundred people gathered at the depot, many volunteering their services, but were not allowed to go, the engine being already crowded, not only by the relief party, but it also carried quantities of clothing, food, blankets, etc., hastily gathered by willing hands and given by generous hearts. The run to Pine City was made at a speed that was very exciting to say the least. There a long delay was caused by the fact that a train had already gone, on account of which the railway company would not permit our engine to proceed until they returned, the wires all being down above Pine City. The party growing impatient at the delay, secured hand cars and started out in the darkness.

When two miles out of Pine City, the burned district was reached and the progress somewhat delayed by smouldering fires ahead which were constantly mistaken for the returning train. When out about eight miles the train was finally met and boarded by the most of our party, and the work of relieving the suffering began.

The train was loaded with all those who had saved themselves in the gravel pit and round house, as well as a number from Mission Creek station, just south of Hinckley. I do not know how many the train held, but there must have been at least one hundred and fifty persons, all suffering from the effects of heat and smoke, and many from the effects of severe burns, all blackened beyond recognition. As yet nothing had been done to speak of to relieve the suffering, which was intense. Mayor Johnson, Dr. Krogstad, who joined us at Pine City, and myself returned with the train to Pine City, where a hospital was hastily improvised in the skating rink, and the work of washing up and applying surgical dressing began in earnest. Several were so badly burned that their lives were despaired of. No fewer than forty were quite severely burned about the hands, feet and head, and all were suffering from pain in the lungs and eyes, the effects of heat and inhaling the smoke. The work steadily progressed from 3 a. m. until long after daylight, before all had received attention.

Great credit is due the ladies of Pine City for their ready assistance during this trying time, as well as many from Rush City, who came up during the night by train. More valuable than any one thing sent for the relief of suffering, was the milk furnished by the farmers in the vicinity of Rush City, two thousand gallons of which was sent as fast as the trains could be secured to handle it. It was indeed a God-send to the poor homeless, half famished, half burned and totally despairing creatures.

A staff of volunteer nurses was established at the rink hospital in Pine City, and the work of caring for the injured continued until relief came from St. Paul and Minneapolis, when fresh hands relieved those weary with their arduous work. The most severely burned were taken to the hospitals in St. Paul and Minneapolis.

AN EXCITING TRIP.

"But another light than sunrise
Aroused the sleeping street,
For a cry was heard at midnight
And the rush of trampling feet."

Than these no words can better describe what happened in Rush City last Saturday night, when the news of the awful disaster at Hinckley first reached the town. In the early afternoon it was known that a serious fire threatened the neighboring town, as a request had been received by the fire department for five hundred feet of hose. This request was promptly responded to and the apparatus shipped at once, though it never reached its destination. As nothing further was heard during the afternoon and evening, the fears of the citizens were allayed, and every one was satisfied that Hinckley was safe.

Shortly before midnight, Miss Brown, the lady operator here, was sitting in the depot, when suddenly a message came from Pine City, giving in brief the dreadful tidings of the burning of Hinckley, and asking for rescue and relief for the suffering. Realizing the situation at once, Miss Brown hurried out to give the alarm, and in a few moments the shrill sounds of the mill whistle called the citizens together, while the telegraphic summons for help was sounded along the line. The message called for doctors and supplies, and before the fire alarm had ceased Doctors Stowe and Gemmel were at the depot already equipped. A few moments later they, with a few chosen assistants, were in the cab of an engine speeding rapidly to the scene of the disaster.

Those who remained were formed into an impromptu relief committee and busied themselves in preparing provisions, clothing and supplies of all kinds in readiness for the "special" coming from St. Paul. Nearly all the ladies in town proffered their services, and the scene at the depot during the night was one of activity personified. In the absence of definite news from the scene of the disaster the greatest anxiety prevailed, for there were many who had friends and relatives in the burned district, and it would be safe to say that not an eye was closed in Rush City during the night.

In the meantime the "Advance Guard," as it might be called, were speeding towards Pine City. Drs. Stowe and Gemmel with Messrs. J. D. Markham, S. C. Johnson, C. E. Elmquist, Howard Folsom and others were in the cab of the engine and though the

FOREMAN POWELL.

MAYOR JOHNSON, RUSH CITY.

DR. STOWE.

C. C. FREEMAN.

ride was rough, the pace was none too fast for them. The engineer and fireman shared the anxiety and Pine City was speedily reached.

Here a vexatious, though perhaps necessary, delay occurred. A relief train had been sent to Hinckley and was expected to return any moment, and it was therefore not thought safe to send another train out through the fire and smoke at that time. While waiting the two physicians attended to the injuries of some half dozen people who had been brought down from Hinckley and Mission Creek, and while they were performing this duty the special arrived, bringing with it not only the necessary supplies, but Dr. Krogstadt, of North Branch, Dr. Tictin, of Harris, many of the Rush City citizens and several hand cars. The latter were at once put into service and the relief party started on a wild ride to Hinckley. The first car contained Drs. Stowe, Gemmel, Krogstadt and Messrs. S. C. Johnson, C. F. Jackson, G. Smith, W. S. Chapin, Gust Lindgren, Robert O'Leary and C. E. Elmquist. The second car had J. D. Markham, L. M. Gale, W. G. Hopps, H. Squires, Peter Engel, Jos. Schmitz, Fidel Schmitz, Dr. Tictin and others of the Rush City Relief Committee.

Then commenced the most exciting part of the journey made by the vanguard of the Rush City Relief Corps. After crossing Snake river there was nothing to relieve the monotony of darkness but the fitful lights of the lanterns on the car and the occasional glare of a burning stump or a telegraph pole. The way was full of danger, for the relief train from Hinckley might be expected any moment; the fire had been raging on all sides for many hours and none knew but that the track might have been destroyed. But knowing of the suffering before then, there was no thought of danger amongst the willing workers who manned the handcars, and they plunged into the inky blackness of the night, through mingled fire and smoke, intent only on giving relief to their fellow beings.

The scene, had there been time to notice it, was one of incomparable grandeur. The night was intensely dark; the smoke from the forest fires, which had been raging for days, was almost thick enough to cut with a knife, and the lanterns on the cars only served to light for a short distance ahead "the straight and narrow way" over which the pioneers were traveling. It was too dark to distinguish the forest on either side of the track, but with every rod traveled could be seen in the distance "as through a glass dimly" the light of a burning pine tree. Very often the fire would be seen suspicously close to the track, and, to the anxious eyes of those who were in advance, appeared to be the red light of an approaching train. Then the speed would slacken and a flagman sent ahead to investigate. There were many false alarms but in spite of them Mission Creek ten miles from Pine City, was reached in an incredibly short space of time. Here an unlucky accident to one of the occupants of the first handcar furnished the only ludicrous oasis in a wide desert of misery.

Soon after leaving Mission Creek, the first relief train was met returning from Hinckley bringing down most of the survivors from that place. Many of these were burned more or less severely and everyone presented a most terribly destitute and woe-be-gone appearance. After a hasty examination of the sufferers by the medical men it was decided to return to Pine City, Drs. Stowe and Krogstadt going back with the train, while Drs. Gemmel and Tietin pushed on with the handcar to Hinckley where there were several still awaiting help. On this handcar were also Messrs. C. F. Jackson, W. G. Hopps, R. O'Leary, Gust Lindgren and others from Rush City.

On returning to Pine City the relieving party found the citizens ready to receive them, and lost no time in administering to the wants of the sufferers. A hospital was hastily improvised in the skating rink for the more seriously burned, and here the medical men were kept busy for hours dressing the injuries. The town hall was thrown open to the other fugitives and their wants in the way of clothing and food promptly attended to. The relief train for Rush City had brought up not only many ladies to assist in the work, but a vast amount of clothing and provisions. Among the latter were several hundred gallons of fresh milk, and this particularly was a perfect boon to the sufferers.

Meanwhile the handcar with the two physicians and others had reached the ruins of Hinckley. Here in the round house of the Eastern Minnesota, the only building left standing in the place, were eight or ten people all more or less suffering from the effects of the fire. The principal trouble with them, however, was the effect of the smoke and fire on their eyes, and this was relieved as well as possible by the doctors.

The early morning light was just appearing when the doctors finished their work amongst the sufferers in the round house, and as they stepped out to view the ruins of Hinckley, the scene was one of magnified horror and wide spread desolation. The coal in the sheds where the depot once stood was blazing fiercely, while on the other side of the track and close to the bridge, piles upon piles of lumber were burning. Thick, dense clouds of black smoke filled the air and myriads of sparks were borne northward on the morning wind. Looking northeast from the Eastern Minnesota round house, not a vestige could be seen of what was, a day before, a fair and flourishing town. Nothing but ashes, smoke and flame met the eye. Even the very dust in the streets was burnt by that terrible fire. The horror deepend on closer inspection. At almost every step through the place one would see some sight evidencing the awful fatality. The bodies of men, women and children were found on every side, mingled often in a confused mass with dead animals. The sight was one utterly impossible to describe or imagine, and one which, once seen, could never be forgotten.

Soon after daylight the relief train again arrived from Pine City, bringing many Rush City citizens, plenty of food, milk and other necessities. Messrs. J. C. Carlson and S. Abraham had charge of the commissariat, and among others who rendered valuable assistance were David Bloom and W. F. Anderson, all of Rush City. Drs. Clark and Francis, of White Bear, accompanied the train, and with the two doctors already on the spot, were in time to meet the injured passengers who had been on the destroyed limited. These had been brought in from Skunk lake on hand cars and were speedily transferred to the train. The latter then started back to Pine City and while the surgeons were dressing the wounds of the injured, the laymen were supplying the poor unfortunates with food and other necessaries.

The arrival of the survivors was another saddening sight. Men, women and children had spent the night in the dismal swamp, shivering with cold and shuddering with horror at the scene they had passed through. Never were people more gladly welcomed than were the relief party that reached there in the early morning, and warmly did they welcome the prospect of a speedy rescue from their desperate condition. A relief train from Duluth arrived almost at the same time and while some of the ill fated passengers elected to return to the Zenith City, others were placed on hand cars and, as stated above, brought to the relief train at Hinckley.

By the time this latter train reached Pine City the wants of the sufferers had been fairly well attended to, and they all presented a more cheerful appearance. The more severely hurt were taken to the improvised hospital, while the others continued their journey to other points along the line.

J. E. GEMMEL, M. D. CM.

RT. REV. M. N. GILBERT, D. D.

Any seeming contradictions between the subjoined account and the narrations of the calamity visited upon other portions of the fire burned districts, will be made perspicuous in the light of this explanation, namely:

Pine City is the nearest town to Hinckley, Brown's Hill lying between Pine City and Hinckley. On September first, 1894, there was a fire raging at Brown's Hill—entirely independent of the Hinckley fire.

The officials of the St. Paul and Duluth Railway thought the fire at Brown's Hill had burned down the telegraph line, destroying communication with Hinckley, therefore felt no anxiety relative to the latter place.

On the Eastern division of the Great Northern railway a fire was burning at Quamba, which is between Mora and Hinckley. The train crews were all at work the entire afternoon, endeavoring to save the culverts for the passage of trains at Brown's Hill, on the supposition that Hinckley was safe, as stated. And at Brown's Hill it was not known that Hinckley was burned until Saturday night, when a telegram was received from Miss Olive Brown, of Rush City, announcing the calamity.

At Rush City word was received by wire by Miss Olive Brown, day operator at the depot (who had remained steadily at her post all day, refusing to leave at night, knowing that the country at the north was in flames, but could get no facts), that Hinckley and Mission Creek were wiped out. It was then nearly twelve o'clock midnight. The message asked for doctors, nurses and relief generally. Instantly Miss Brown ran to Dr. A. J. Stowe, (railroad surgeon at Rush City) and to Dr. J. E. Gemmel; then, with Mrs. A. J. Stowe, hurried from house to house and summoned the people to the rescue. In an incredibly brief time, the physicians above mentioned, the mayor, S. C. Johnson, Attorney J. D. Markham, Editor Charles Elmquist of the Rush City Post, Prof. L. M. Gale of the Rush City schools and Howard Folsom (now one of the editors of the Courier at Sandstone) with medical supplies and bolts of cloth for bandages, etc., at just about midnight, left on an engine, as swiftly as steam could carry them, for the scene of distress, having first arranged for a special train of helpers, provided with tools, food, clothing and all needful supplies for the stricken ones to follow. The bells were ringing, and the whistles blowing signals of distress.

As this engine party started out, through dense smoke and burning ties, railroad men were heard to say: "Those men are taking their lives in their hands," as, of course, they could not know where they might encounter a burned culvert or twisted rail, be ditched and meet with sure death, owing to the speed necessary to make in order to reach the sufferers. They were enjoined to stay on the engine and not on the tender, and they bound themselves together with arms interwoven, standing in the small space usually occupied by the fireman, while the latter industriously piled the coal into the furnace.

They reached Pine City, ten miles distant from Rush City, in a very few minutes. From that point they were obliged to resort to handcars, which were soon manned. The physicians and most of the others in the party, were soon off. J. D. Markham remained at Pine City, helping in preparation for a hospital, and receptacle for supplies, which promptly arrived from Rush City. The special train brought hand car tools, lanterns, blankets, bedding, and food,—comprising all the stock of supplies from every hotel, bakery, meat market, most of the private houses, and included a car of milk and ice.

It was loaded with an army of determined helpers for any work; among whom were John C. Carlson, cashier of Rush City Bank; Grant L. Smith, chief of the fire department; R. G. Rumsberg, merchant, Col. R. H. Grant, of the Grant House; C. F. Jackson, railroad agent, T. W. Wadlow, secretary of brick company; George B. Knight, city marshal; F. Redlech, of Rush City Hotel; J. F. Sommers, merchant; J. L. Murphy, of broom factory; W. G. Hopps, photographer; S. Abraham, merchant; H. Squires, meat market; W. S. Chapin, G. Lundgren. P. Schroeder, W. Anderson, P. Engel, Albert Larson, F. Schmitz, P. Stenger, J. Schmitz, and C. Woods.

These men all went manfully to work, either on hand cars, unloading supplies, or in other preparation for receiving sufferers so soon as they should arrive.'

The afternoon's work of the section crews of Rush City demands the highest commendation, as well as their evening labors as advanced guards, under the able management of Passenger Conductor John Buckley, of St. Paul & Duluth Limited Train No. 3, going north, who left his train at Pine City, and, with an engine and caboose, and Section Foreman John Powell, of Rush City, with his crew, James Earhardt, G. Ruhle and others, accomplished great work in getting to the burned people and conveying them to a place of safety.

It was Conductor Buckley who took the first load of rescued to Pine City, with J. Y. Breckenridge in charge, where they were received by the Pine City and Rush City contingent and carefully con-

veyed—some on foot, others by teams—to the improvised hospital.
To Dr. A. J. Stowe, Dr. J. E. Gemmel, S. C. Johnson and J. D.
Markham belongs unstinted praise for the tender care and attention
given the unfortunates in the hospital, in assisting in dressing the
wounds of these people during that dreadful night. Dr. Stowe and
Mayor Johnson remained true to the last. Later, both went to
Hinckley to render additional service.

At this time another resident of Rush City—George H. Markham
—was surrounded by fire near Mora, but succeeded in reaching that
place, and assisted in receiving and caring for the people of Pokegama (Brook Park) as they were brought in, going early to Mora in
order to do all he could for the unfortunates. He is largely interested
in that place.

Rush City and all the railroad people are justly proud of the noble
work of their day operator, Miss Brown (whose portrait is here represented), as she was first to communicate the news to the physicians
and other residents. She remained at the instrument the entire night
of the 1st of September, besides a part of the previous night, having
temporarily assumed the night man's duties in addition to her own,
to allow him a couple days' vacation. She continued at her place all
day Monday, until finally absolutely dragged by the citizens from her
post and sent to take much needed rest. This she tried toward evening on Monday, but sleep was nothing to her, and after a brief rest,
she resumed her position at the key, remaining until, some time during the following night, when she was forced to leave for rest and
sleep. Through it all she thought of but one thing—relief for the
poor victims of the fire, sending all the words of comfort or sad
news obtainable.

In addition to all this, there were two and three heavily loaded passenger trains at the depot for from 48 to 60 hours, with passengers
sending and receiving messages to and from all parts of the world,
all of which work she performed, with never a frown or unkind remark. Many a passenger will remember her, while reading these
lines. Some of the noble heroes of the fire have been lionized, and
made recipients of medals and various testimonials. This heroine
worked bravely in the performance of her whole duty, modestly and
gladly, with no thought of reward: yet who is more highly deserving
of recognition than she? On whom could a testimonial be more ap-
propriately bestowed?

At a meeting of the council and citizens of Rush City on Monday
forenoon, a relief committee was appointed, composed of Hon. F. S.

P. B. WINSTON.

Christensen, J. D. Markham and R. H. Grant. Two hundred and fifty dollars were immediately voted by the council and the committee, and turned over to the relief committee at Pine City. Besides this, a car load of milk was sent daily for several days.

Mr. Robert Nessel, a farmer adjoining Rush City, hauled a load of sheep and calves to Pine City as food for the sufferers, mention of which has not heretofore been made.

Some of the most laudable contributions were those made by small farmers from the "sand barrens" of Wisconsin—a section in Burnett and Polk counties in that state—lying east of Rush City, where the farmers are all poor, and have been struggling, as new settlers, against drouth and other misfortunes for two or three years. But in their poverty, in this calamity, they hurried across the St. Croix river, with magnanimous contributions to the relief committee of Rush City, of potatoes, wheat, oats, rye, flour, butter, new home knit stockings, pillows, clothing, etc. As these contributions were indeed like the widow's mite, far larger proportionately than those from the great cities, the donors' names should be inscribed on the banner of worthy and perpetual record, although not thought of by themselves. They are:

N. Weyberg, S. Monson, N. Monson, A. S. Freedland, A. Erickson and C. Anderson, of Alstad, Burnett county, Wisconsin; and O. Anderson, Olaf Anderson, G. Olson, K. E. Nordstrom, C. A. Nordstrom, O. Carlson, N. Nelson, L. Norvall, J. Anderson, J. Bayman and P. Martinson, of Sterling, Polk county, Wisconsin, and A. Larson, free ferryage over the St. Croix river. These goods, with suitable acknowledgment, were received and sent by Mayor Johnson to Rev. William Wilkinson, who made distribution, we are informed, among friends of some of these contributors.

J. D. Markham, of Rush City, spent his time almost exclusively for about six weeks in the burned district, in the work of relief, and, at the request of the St. Paul committee, and its representative of the governor—Mr. Harris Richardson, made one of the general relief committee, and member of the finance committee, of which Hon. James Hurley was chairman, and Hon. F. A. Hodge treasurer.

Mr. Markham organized the expedition to Pokegama (Brook Park), where he had interest as one of the owners of the town, and several thousand acres of land, on which the famous hand car trip of the nine men went from Hinckley, where Rev. William Wilkinson, as Mayor Eustis' emissary, was conspicuous by his good works, reference to which is made elsewhere.

Of this band of noble men, it can be truthfully said that no more conscientious, noble thoughts, or better and unselfish purposes ever actuated men to press on to the relief of distressed humanity. They knew not retreat, although at times they seemed vanquished. They all were unused to the average hardships. What think you, then, of them, when I say that these men comprised two ministers,—the Rev. William Wilkinson and the Rev. C. B. Fosbroke, two physicians—Dr. H. B. Allen and Dr. C. W. Higgins, Lawyer J. D. Markham, Banker B. J. Kelsey, Merchant A. Berg; a Brook Park victim of fire, W. W. Brennan, a farmer of the same place (saved, but lost his only son), and Engineer M. Thompson, of New Brighton.

At 3:46 on the afternoon of September 1st, the following Rush City men left that place, with orders to run wild, regardless of Nos. 3 and 4 Limited trains, and take their crews to the fire district:

Section Foreman John Powell (whose portrait appears in this book) with his crew, T. Carroll, J. Earhart and G. Rhodes; Section Foreman B. Farrell, with his sons Ed. and James, and Ed. Fisk, with engine and caboose, Conductor Riley and Engineer Jones, of No. 9. No. 3 followed close behind, under Conductor John Buckley, taking the fire hose of the Rush City fire department, to use, if possible, at Hinckley.

The ladies from Rush City went to Pine City to assist in nursing the sick, the burned, etc., among whom were Mrs. Lou A. White, Mrs. Mary A. Johnson, Mrs. Frank Rogers, and Miss Ellen Lindmark, each of whom rendered good service, especially Mrs. White. They went in charge of Rev. Wilkinson. Several families of Rush City took in and cared for a number of the unfortunates; among them being Martell and Johnson, Dr. Stowe, J. D. Markham, Joseph McLaughlin and Mr. Flynn; while Mesdames Christensen, Carlson, Martell, Johnson, Gemmel, Redlich, Rogers, Stowe, Wadlow and Markham, clothed, sewed for and helped dress not a few. The earnest labors of Drs. Stowe and Gemmel for days,—all free of charge to the relief committee—called forth the highest praise from that body, and special resolutions of thanks.

By reference to the report of the general relief committee, notice will be found of the action of the firm of Kelsey, Markham & Co., who were the owners and proprietors of Brook Park, in giving to each burned out settler, a warranty deed of two acres of land, and extending all payments until November, 1895.

In the burned district were several members of Jasper Lodge, No. 164, A. F. & A. M., of Rush City. Col. John F. Stone, of Pine City, worshipful master, and J. D. Markham, secretary. Through the prompt action of this lodge and the efforts of its worshipful master and secretary, all brothers were helped immediately, whether its members or not; and from among its own people, these brothers and their families received assistance amounting to about six hundred dollars. One member of the order, Mr. Paul Schlans, of Zion Lodge No. 55, of Taylor's Falls, Wisconsin, was burned up.

Judge Calvin L. Brown, of Morris, Minn., most worshipful grand master of the Grand Lodge of Minnesota, in his address at the recent session of the Grand Lodge at St. Paul, said:

"One of the greatest calamities that ever befell the people of Hinckley last summer, the great forest fire which swept over the northern part of our state, and laid waste so much property, and sent so many souls to their final account, is unparalleled in history. It is indescribable, for those who witnessed it tell us that the printed reports but feebly picture its enormity.

"No subordinate lodge was situated at Hinckley, but some members of the fraternity resided there who lost all their property, and barely escaped with their lives. Most of them were members of lodges in this state. They were all in need of assistance, and the members of Jasper Lodge, of Rush City, came promptly to their rescue, and with money and kind hands, relieved them, so far as money and kindness could. * * * Some voluntary contributions were made, and the lodge and brethren of Rush City did the rest. Jasper Lodge is not a wealthy one, but on that occasion the members thereof did their whole duty and work.

"Whether they ask this Grand Lodge to reimburse them or not, they are entitled to its favorable consideration, and I recommend that some action be taken in their behalf."

This lodge declined to ask the Grand Lodge to reimburse it, as above recommended. The following resolution was unanimously adopted:

"Resolved That the thanks of this Grand Lodge are due and are hereby tendered to Jasper Lodge No. 164 of Rush City, for the grand display made by them of the true principles of Masonic charity, during the great forest conflagration which visited this state during the past year; contributing as they did so liberally of their means, to the relief of those who suffered thereby, without expectation of returns or request for reimbursement."

We can only add this, our testimonial, to the joy which fills the hearts of those who know that "it is more blessed to give than to receive."

Great credit is due Superintendent Ed Brown of St. Paul & Duluth Railway Company for assistance to the company in repairs on the railway, etc., with Assistant General Manager L. S. Miller.

DULUTH.

THE first intimation the people of Duluth had of the horrible holocaust impending on the fateful afternoon of September 1st, was by the thickening volumes of smoke whirled through the air by a freshening southwest wind. This smoke became so dense by 4 p. m. that in office buildings lights had to be turned on for the ordinary transaction of business; and when rumors, more or less ominous, began to circulate, due to ill-concealed anxiety in railroad circles, business became suspended; people flocked into the streets, into hotel lobbies, or swarmed about telegraph offices, not knowing and scarcely daring to ask, what was coming next. Later, when a dispatch was received to the effect that the forests around Hinckley were on fire, and that the down "passenger" from Duluth was lost in a sea of flame, the community became fairly wild with excitement. This excitement was "frozen," so to speak, into a sort of terror later on; for as the sun went down, the great whirlwinds of flame, though none nearer than fifty miles, lit up the smoky sky with an effect so strange and awful, that an oppressive feeling of gruesome apprehension took possession of nearly everyone. The sky did not light up from one direction, nor with a bright light, but suddenly, even as one looked, the whole vault of Heaven became a glowing furnace of a dull ruddy color, and with the appearance of the most intense heat. The phenomenon came so suddenly and wore an aspect so threatening, that it was felt as a sort of shock, well calculated to set common intelligence at defiance. If one could have been divested of the notion that life would be impossible under conditions necessary for such an observation, it could readily have been conceived that our planet had suddenly found itself dashed against the atmosphere of a glowing sun, for in every direction the air seemed a vast mass of molten metal, threatening universal destruction.

The message alluded to above was picked from the wires at the St. Paul & Duluth office about 6 p. m. It proved to be from A. L. Thompson, operator at Miller, and was as follows:

RAY LEWIS, MAYOR, DULUTH.

"No. 4" (the down 'passenger' from Duluth) burned up—Sullivan dead—ior God's sake send relief."—After which the instrument became ominously silent. This meant that the wires were down or that the operator had been compelled to flee for his life, and there was too much probability that both had been the case.

Orders were immediately telegraphed to all down trains to be side-tracked, and the "Short Line" arriving at 6:15 was held for the emergency. General Yardmaster D. E. Williams, of the St. Paul & Duluth, made the train up as quickly as possible on its arrival, and with a relief corps, consisting of General Agent C. M. Vance and Doctors Magie, Codding, McCormick and Gilbert, with some representatives of the press, and others, it left the depot at 7:05. Medicines, surgical instruments, blankets, refreshments, and everything that could be thought of and scraped together in so short a time, for the alleviation of such suffering as was anticipated had been hastily provided. Previous to starting, Williams had found a "wayfreight," under Conductor Roper, side-tracked at Willow River, and had "wired" him to take engine, caboose and some box cars, and "flag" his way to the relief of No. 4 passenger. "Hurry for God's sake," the dispatch reads, "Miller reports them burned up." The relief train reached Willow river without incident or impediment worthy of note, except the inconvenience and discomfort of the constantly increasing density of smoke and cinders. There they found Roper. He had made two attempts to reach the wreck of the "passenger," but had not been able to go much beyond Miller, owing to the burned culverts and trestles past that point. He had, however, been so far fortunate that he had been the means of saving some lives,—among them, a woman he had dragged from the water near a burned culvert, beyond Miller. She was holding her baby with outstretched arms to save it from drowning when found, and both finally recovered. He had also been the means of furnishing shelter and the promise of safety to the many refugees who were coming constantly, among whom was Conductor Sullivan, who had escaped, somehow, from the ill-fated train. R. M. Bell, superintendent of the union depot at Duluth, with his fifteen-year-old daughter, was also among these. They had left the train when it was all ablaze and ran along the track, keeping together, until exhausted, then by crawling and running alternately—Bell sometimes carrying the girl—they had somehow escaped the swoop of the flames. But these people

were so completely exhausted by heat, blinded by smoke and un-
nerved by the terrible experiences they had gone through, that they
were entirely unfitted to give any connected account of what had
happened. For instance, Conductor Sullivan was completely blinded by heat and smoke, and was suffering such excrutiating agony
from his eyes, that it was thought he would go insane. Bell, when
asked by Williams what the conditions were at the wreck, could not
give the faintest ray of hope. He said, simply, that "everything was
burned, and everybody dead," and he would advise none to go further, as they "surely would be burned too." But the very hopelessness of the case seems to have stimulated Williams to greater efforts,
for he was determined to go until he found "No. 4." A hurried
consultation was held, with the result that the refugees from Rutledge, Finlayson and Miller, were transferred to the relief train and
sent back to Duluth, in charge of Mr. Vance, and Doctors Mc-
Cormick and Gilbert; while Williams and Doctors Magie and Codding took Roper's train for "the front," that conductor, with Kelly,
the engineer, and crew, being ready and willing, though their locomotive and cars were literally blistered with heat, to dive for the third
time into the maelstrom of smoke, cinders and fire.

Beyond Miller it was impossible to proceed by train, so Williams,
Roper and the two doctors took a hand-car at that place, transferring to it such supplies as it would carry, and pushed forward. They
had literally to feel their way as they proceeded, and where the
woodwork of culverts and bridges had burned away, leaving the
track a skeleton, they had to scramble through on foot, and push the
car along as best they could. To prevent the inhaling of smoke they
had adopted the expedient of tying saturated handkerchiefs over
mouths, nostrils, and as much as possible over the eyes. The glare
of the conflagration through the smoke is described as an awful
sight, and magnificent, when the smoke would lift sufficiently, as it
did at times, to reveal panoramas of blazing forests and groups of
trees, everyone of which was a pillar of fire. But, as may be
imagined, there was but little time or inclination felt by the party
for admiration of the scenic effects; it was only a vivid presentation at best of the horror of the situation, and they were too often
reminded of the ghastly part these vistas of merciless flames had
played in the great tragedy of life. Eighteen dead bodies, all burned
beyond recognition, had been removed from the track, or found beside it, when at midnight the little party reached the smouldering

wreck of the burned train at Skunk Lake. The coaches were simply a mass of smoking debris; the coal in the locomotive tender was still burning quietly, but as no living being put in an appearance, and everything was still as death, the terrible conviction was forced upon them that all their efforts had been in vain; that not a soul was left alive. As Williams puts it in the general railway manner of speech, "We thought all were killed."

Not knowing what to do next, it occurred to them all at once to shout for the benefit of any or everyone that might by some stretch of possibility be left alive and within hearing. It is not worth while to try to express in words the joyful astonishment of our gallant little party of rescuers as a great chorus of voices, from somewhere in the neighborhood, came in quick response to their "Halloos." Amidst exclamations of astonishment and delight, amidst wonder and tears, the marvelous story of heroic men and noble women, and the saving of a train-load of lives by means of an insignificant bog-hole was soon told.

It is impossible to be niggardly in the bestowal of praise on Yard-master David E. Williams, in connection with this first relief expedition, as well as in subsequent efforts for the rescue and relief of the sufferers, while too much cannot be said of Roper and his gallant crew, of Doctors Magie and Codding, who, simply as volunteers, insisted on sharing in every labor as well as danger; it remains to be particularly said of Williams, that in an extremely trying situation he had kept his head remarkably cool and clear, anticipating contingencies and preparing for emergencies, from the dispatching and side-tracking of trains, to the ordering of rations for the hungry. At Skunk Lake he took in the situation rapidly with a view to the necessities of the case, left the two doctors with the supplies to care for the wounded and suffering, while he and Roper took the hand-car back to Miller, promising to have a relief train ready to take them all out by daylight. At Miller he set every available individual to work on the repairs or rebuilding of burned culverts and bridges, not forgetting the while to send such supplies as he could by handcar back to Skunk Lake. It is said of him that he stayed at the front until through connections were made with St. Paul, and that he did not sleep for 70 consecutive hours. Be this as it may, he was certainly the first to relieve the people of Duluth, at least in part, from a continual nightmare of horrors, by sending from Rutledge at about 2 a. m. the following cheerful dispatch:

E. C. GRIDLEY.

"Have been to wreck with handcar—could only get to Miller by train. Wreck is one and one-half miles south of Sandstone and all burned up—passengers all right but exhausted—they are in a marsh —we go with timber to build bridge—tell everyone all are alive and well as can be expected—will arrive in Duluth at 9 a. m."

While this dispatch was being circulated at Duluth and working like magic in awakening her people from a feeling of complete helplessness to a sense of the grave responsibilities suddenly heaped upon them, and serving also to awaken into more intense activity that first great duty of civilized man—the care and protection of the unfortunate; and while Williams and Roper with their noble crew were steadily working their way in heat and smoke from Miller to the wreck, repairing bridges and culverts, Doctors Magie and Codding had applied themselves to the alleviation of such suffering among the survivors at Skunk Lake as their medical stores and skill made possible. The condition of the people found there, under almost any other circumstances would have been called deplorable; but, having escaped as if by a miracle, the most fearful death that human beings are probably ever called upon to face, they considered themselves, as indeed they were, most fortunate. The most that could be done for them was the administering of remedies for smoke and heat strained eyes, and the distributing of such refreshments as had been brought. Some slight surgical operations were performed also, but the instruments brought were of little use—those upon whom they might have been of service being beyond relief.

There seems to be no means of knowing or even approximating the number of passengers and refugees there were at this time at Skunk Lake. The number from Hinckley who had "flagged" the train and who had found safety in its terrific flight from thence, has been variously estimated at from 150 to 200, so that there could not have been less than three hundred, possibly as many as four hundred that had found safety in this marsh of eighteen inches, at best, of muddy water. Some of the dead found between this place and Miller had, no doubt, been passengers who had tried to escape by way of the track but had succumbed to exhaustion or suffocation. O. Rowley, auditor of the Duluth & Winnipeg railroad, was one of these. He had somehow missed the marsh and strayed off into a sort of ditch, where his remains were found afterwards, and only

identified by the laundry mark on his shirt collar. Ex-Senator F.
B. Daugherty and son, and two women, babies in their arms, saved
themselves—the latter by Mr. Daugherty's help, by burrowing in a
potato patch. But they were, it is believed, the only instances where
any were saved outside of the marsh, for all the rest found shelter,
so to speak, in this stagnant pool of stinking, slimy water, by courtesy called a lake. Here, among Duluth's well known citizens was
Mr. W. H. Blades, whose eyes, it was thought, were permanently
injured, A. W. Spyers, who was badly burned in rescuing a little
girl, J. O. Turner and others; and among the prominent St. Paul
people were the Hon. C. D. O'Brien and Mrs. Saunders, the former accompanied by a son and brother, and the latter by her own
children and some young nieces to the number of seven. Mrs. Saunders gives Mr. O'Brien great credit for timely assistance in keeping her little flock together and hurrying them to the marsh. Here
were also the heroic Fireman McGowan, and the great porter,
Blair, the latter even here attending "strictly to business," that is,
to the wants, comforts and safety of his passengers; pouring water
over some, dragging others to places of greater safety, and comforting all with the cheerful prediction that "it would soon be over."
Brave Jim Root, blistered, blinded and wounded by bursting glass,
had been all but carried to the marsh and back again to the cab of
his locomotive by his devoted fireman, and here he was found by
our relief party almost oblivious of things about him from his suffering.

At an early hour in the morning a relief party from the south under Dr. Barnum had worked its way past Hinckley with handcars
and took away St. Paul passengers and refugees to the number of
about 40. Some two hours afterwards Roper's train had worked
its way to the lake, and taken out all the rest. These were subsequently transferred to an emergency train that had been telegraphed
for for the purpose, and arrived in Duluth about noon on that day
—September 2nd.

While these events were transpiring, others of a similar nature, and
almost equal in dramatic intensity, had taken place elsewhere. The
Eastern Minnesota passenger No. 4, Conductor D. H. Powers, with
William Best as engineer, arrived at Hinckley bound north on their
time, 3:25 p. m., Saturday. There Engineer Ed Barry was waiting
for them with a way freight side tracked. After a consultation, an
emergency train of five coaches, one caboose and three box cars,

with the two engines, was made up, and the people packed in as fast as they could be induced to come. Strange to say, many of the citizens had no realizing sense of the danger impending, and were slow to take advantage of the opportunity. By this dilatoriness many lives were lost that might otherwise have been saved. It was 4:25 before Powers would give the signal to leave, and by this time the intensity of the heat was such that human endurance could not have held out longer. Yet another stop was made on the other side of Grindstone bridge, and some 40 additional refugees were picked up. In fact the ties under the track were actually ablaze in some places before the train pulled out again. The first seven miles after this was a ride for life such as only a very few can have experienced and lived. The fire was on both sides of them and roaring like a furnace; the thick smoke made it as black as night; the train was smoking hot and might have burst into flame at any moment; the people were fainting and gasping for air; but the throttle was wide open and the head train was making a mile a minute. Some seven miles from Hinckley it is said the train struck a stratum of cooler air, which revived the almost suffocating people to some extent. At any rate they began to breathe freer; though not by any means out of sight or reach of fire, they had evidently got ahead of it somewhat.

Owing to the density of the smoke there was no possibility of seeing objects very far ahead, and the head lights, although lighted, were of little use, as Barry's locomotive seems to have been ahead of Best's and running backwards. In order to keep a look out for the condition of the bridges, before they came to them, two brakemen were stationed (Beach and the other name not known) at the head on the tank, who, while the train slowed to four miles an hour, would scrutinize as well as possible through the smoke the objects before them. If the result of their observations was satisfactory enough to venture, they would signal the train to go ahead, when a dash would be made to the next bridge and so on. One account makes it that in this way 19 bridges were crossed in about as many miles; some of them already on fire, and all of which were nearly or completely destroyed within a few minutes after the passage of the train. At Sandstone the people had not arrived at a realizing sense of the imminence of the danger impending and many lost their lives because they would not believe and embrace the opportunity that was offered for escape. Near Sandstone the

BISHOP MCGOLLRICK, D. D.

railroad bridge over Kettle River was found to be on fire and the train slowed up before reaching it. The problem was simple enough. If the bridge would not hold them they would go into the river; if they stayed where they were they would be burned. The two watchmen stationed here indicated by signs and gestures that they must make the venture, but no urging was needed, a second of time in which to take in the situation was all that was required. The heavy train moved slowly out upon the burning bridge, quickened its speed and, as if with an abated breath, it was over. Five minutes later what little was left of the structure was a mere skeleton of charred timbers and one of the faithful watchmen who had been so anxious for the safety of the train was unable to reach the bed of the river in time to save himself and perished with his bridge.

In this part of the work it is not expected to do more than simply allude to acts of heroism, and this only in connection with Duluth refugees. It is impossible, however, to review even in the most sketchy way, these details without being struck with the most intense admiration for the men that conducted this train. They could not have been more brave than Root, McGowan, Sullivan or Blair; they did not have quite so much to try their souls, perhaps. Yet in this respect honors must be nearly equal, for, that which one crew did, the other would have done under similar circumstances, is abundantly proved by what was done by either. That Root and his crew came considerably nearer destruction no one will deny, for all corroborative evidence agrees substantially in this, that it was a matter not of minutes but of seconds of time when his train must have enveloped every soul in it in a living furnace of flame. Under such circumstances it is not to be wondered at that strong men were crazed by the unparalleled horror of the situation, and that Root and his fellow heroes could face such a situation at all and retain presence of mind enough to act as intelligently and as coolly as they did, is not only a testimony as to the limit of human endurance, but can only be accounted for upon the theory that they were so much more interested in the lives of those they had in charge as to be entirely oblivious of their own.

On the other hand, Powers, Best, Barry and their associates, though not at any time pushed quite so close to the uttermost brink of destruction, deserve an equal amount of credit, for while a common fate was staring them all in the face, they had moral courage enough to time their actions so well, both in the interest of mercy to some and safety to others, that not a minute could have been spared for the saving of another life. A weaker person than Powers would have stayed until it had been too late, a more timid one would have rushed off too soon and left hundreds of lives to a fearful fate. As it was, if he had owned a time piece from Heaven, he could not have exercised a nicer judgment, or saved another soul without the sacrifice of his train with its cargo of six hundred lives.

The French have a term "D'esprit de corps" for which we have no equivalent in our language, but in America there is now, and is being developed more and more every day, a chivalric spirit animating the "Followers of the Rail," peculiar to themselves. Of this the deeds of the men who saved a thousand lives from the Hinckley fire is only an illustration, but such deeds should be the means at least of creating a term of equal value in English speech.

RELIEF WORK AT DULUTH.

At about 7 p. m. on Saturday, Mayor Lewis was "wired" by the Eastern Minnesota that from five to six hundred fire refugees from Hinckley and Sandstone were on the way to Duluth on an emergency train, and would be in by 9 that night. It did arrive at 9:30 thus bringing the first installment of fire sufferers from the burned district, all of whom were practically in a destitute condition and must be provided with at least temporary help at once. They were met at the depot by Mayor Lewis and a detachment of police, who had instructions to see that all were fed and provided with comfortable quarters for the night.

In the issue of the Duluth Tribune of Sunday morning was published the following:

PROCLAMATION.

MAYOR'S OFFICE, DULUTH, Sept. 3, 1894.

A meeting of the business men and citizens of Duluth will be held at the Council Chamber in the City Hall at 11 o'clock this morning for the purpose of appointing a relief committee to provide ways and means for the care of the people who have been left destitute and homeless by the disastrous fire which has burned so many flourishing neighboring towns. Hundreds of men, women and children were brought to the city list night and are in the armory and lodging houses down town, who have lost their all and are scantily clothed. We must provide food and clothing for them at once. The occasion demands immediate action and I feel assured that there will be a hearty response to this call.

RAY T. LEWIS, Mayor.

Long before the hour of meeting, citizens commenced to congregate in the council chamber, and by 11 o'clock it was filled to overflowing. Mayor Lewis called the meeting to order, and made a brief statement of the object and urgency of the call. He said the situation was a very grave one. Some 500 refugees had been brought in by the Eastern Minnesota the evening before (75 had remained at West Superior. Mr. Vance, of the St. Paul & Duluth, had brought in about 125 from Willow River and Rutledge, and according to the best calculations Williams would bring with him about 400 more from the burned wreck near Hinckley, who were looked for at any moment. In all, over 1,000 people, all more or less destitute. thrown upon our hands without a word of warning or the slightest preparation made to receive them.

On motion, a subscription list was opened forthwith and about $3,000 (this amount was increased during the day to about $4,000) subscribed as fast as the names could be taken down, after which the meeting adjourned. From this hurriedly selected committee which was in fact invested with full control, and by tacit consent empowered to change or extend itself without further reference to public action, grew by degrees the Citizens' Central Relief Committee nearly as it is now constituted, with Col. E. C. Gridley—Hon. J. T. Hale having been unable to serve on account of illness— as chairman.

The refugees who were brought in on Porter's train Saturday at 9:20 as well as those brought later by Mr. Vance, were, in the absence of all organized relief, taken charge of by Mayor Lewis and the police force. The different hotels and restaurants were thrown open to them, and they were quartered afterwards wherever quarters could be found. The "Wolf Building" was furnished with cots by the city, and took in as many as it would hold. The Armory in the Howard Block was thrown open and for the second time made to do duty as a shelter for fire sufferers. The doors of the Bethel were of course wide open, as they always are for every emergency, and many were taken and cared for by private citizens.

The next morning the ladies of the Relief Society were called together by its president, Mrs. Miller, and opened up in one of the basement offices in the Lyceum, to which was brought and un-

SERGT. JOHN KENNA.

SERGT. DANIEL DONOVAN.

packed their stock of clothing and wearing apparel, for both male and female, which that society fortunately had on hand ready for the coming winter's use. It is due to the Ladies' Relief Society to say, that owing to their splendid organization they were really the first in the field, after the city authorities, to afford systematic relief in the way of wearing apparel for both sexes, old as well as young. As soon as it became known that they (the Relief Society) had established headquarters, contributions commenced to pour in, and continued to pour by single garments, by bundles, and by wagon loads, good, bad and indifferent (for the poor were vying with the rich) in a constant stream, until the poor gentlewomen having the place in charge were almost buried in the heaps of donations, and asphixiated by the old-clothes-reek that prevailed. Before the day was over these quarters were found entirely inadequate to their needs, and more commodious ones in the new Duluth Trust Company's Block were donated, into which they moved the following day. Here the ladies of the Relief Society labored constantly for weeks, sometimes as many as thirty or forty at a time, in the distribution of every conceivable kind of wearing apparel, from the brogan of the laborer to the more complicated head dress of the ladies; even flowers for the head gear of the most fastidious were not thought to be out of place in the distribution of necessities, and many a good woman went out of the Ladies' Relief Headquarters rejoicing in a more lovely affair in the shape of a bonnet than she had probably ever owned before. The splendid work of the Ladies' Relief Society will be taken up and summarized later on.

Several of the churches entirely suspended or cut short their services the Sunday morning following the fire, in order that the members might have more time to provide for the refugees already here as well as those who were known to be coming. The services of the Pilgrim Congregational Church were by the pastor, Rev. E. M. Noyes, turned into a business meeting, and the congregation spent the best portion of the day in arranging and fitting up the commodious room in the basement for a temporary home, and by 5 o'clock these were so completely provided, that in fact 98 children had been bathed, fed, clothed and put to bed before 9 o'clock that night. The First Presbyterian Church did likewise, fitting up its capacious basement for a hospital and dormitory. The St. Paul's Episcopal Church secured and fitted up the Berkelman Block for the same purpose, while many other churches or church societies took equally

prompt action. The Odd Fellows prepared their hall and other
vacant portions of the building for the reception and care, not only
of the members of their own order, but for all they could accom-
modate. The Hospitals of St. Mary and St. Luke were making
such extra preparations as were needed. The Maternity Hospital
also made extensive preparations for such cases among the unfortunates as might be brought in need of the care and protection of
such an institution. All these organizations, churches, societies and
institutions commenced the work of relief independently, either Sunday evening or Monday morning, but as soon as the Central Relief
Committee had completed its organization, their operations were
either merged in or conducted under the auspices of the central body.
The Armory and the Bethel were so conducted from the first.
More special mention will be made later on of the labors and the
work accomplished by all these bodies. At present it is enough
to know that the people of Duluth were taking hold of the work
as one being, with a single mind, their only struggle being the noble
one, to see who could do the most good.

While these timely measures were being taken at Duluth, the railroad people were exerting every means at their command to rescue
or relieve the many sufferers, who, it was known or presumed, must
yet be alive in the burned district, from an unpleasant, untenable,
perhaps still a dangerous position. Two thoroughly equipped
relief trains pulled out from Duluth at about the same time, at 4
o'clock Sunday afternoon, one on the St. Paul and Duluth in charge
of Hon. O. D. Kinney, the other on the Eastern Minnesota under
General Manager W. C. Farrington.

Besides a complete outfit of medical stores of every kind, **Mr.**
Kinney had with him Doctors Taylor, Bangs, Weston, Specht, Lyn-
ham, and Weir, also the Misses Trussler, Berisford, Maris and Scott,
all trained nurses from St. Luke's Hospital. A number of experienced woodsmen and "packers" also accompanied Mr. Kinney as
well as a number of volunteers. Among these were ex-Mayor
d'Autremont, Hon. F. C. Gridley, C. E. Shannon, Robert Shannon,
Z. H. Austin, Geo. Dinwoodie and Thomas Walsh. As it was well
known that owing to the burned bridges on the Eastern Minnesota
it had been impossible to reach Sandstone with any relief over that
road, it became the object of ambition with our party to penetrate
the timber to that place, and liberate any of the unfortunates who
might yet be alive and hemmed in there. In order to accomplish

this it was necessary to take a course from the St. Paul and Duluth tracks of some six miles through burned, and, to some extent, yet burning timber. This was only a trifling matter to our gallant woodsmen, however, and in return for their labor they had the immense satisfaction of liberating 247 sufferers from the unpleasant, not to say dangerous, predicament they were in. All these people were guided back to the train by our woodsmen, who at the same time thought it sport to "pack" (carry) out all the little children on their great broad backs. The train returned to Duluth at 7:25, Monday morning.

As before stated Mr. Farrington's train left the Eastern Minnesota depot at the same time as Mr. Kinney's. He was accompanied by Doctors McComb, Salter, Sherwin and Gibson, also Wm. Burgess, B. G. Segog, John Gordon, M. L. Brooks and some 50 woodsmen. Besides a perfect equipment of everything needful this train was provided with two teams and wagons and a boat, the latter to be used as a ferry across Kettle river by the burned bridge, and the former for the carrying of supplies into Sandstone by any route that might be found or made. In fact a detour of several miles, for which a road had to be swamped out, had to be made to find a crossing; meanwhile supplies were sent into Sandstone by "packers." Here it was found that Kinney's party had anticipated them and taken out many people, but in spite of that fact there were some 50 refugees here yet, most of whom were such as had been unable or unwilling to follow that party through the burning timber. Most of these were in a deplorable condition and suffering from burns and bruises, exhaustion, terror and the want of food. All were administered to according to their needs, and taken to the train. Some 62 victims of the fire were buried here by Farrington's party, all of whom had perished in the village of Sandstone. The train arrived in Duluth at 1 p. m. Monday.

About the time the "Kinney" and "Farrington" trains left Duluth, i. e. about 4 o'clock Sunday evening, Yardmaster Williams took out a combined construction and relief train over the St. Paul & Duluth under Conductor Wellman. While Wellman and crew worked all night in repairing damages to tracks and culverts, Williams and another crew conducted a relief party, picking up refugees to the number of 29, who were mainly from Finlayson. At 1 p. m. on Monday the tracks were so far repaired that Williams wired Duluth that communication with St. Paul was open and ready for regular trains. Wellman's train arrived at Duluth at 2:45 p. m. Monday

CHIEF ARMSTRONG, DULUTH.

DETECTIVE THOMAS HAYDEN, DULUTH.

CAPT. S. J. THOMPSON, DULUTH.

DETECTIVE R. A. BENSON, DULUTH.

The same day at 10:30 a. m. Hon. C. A. Towne had, at the request of Mayor Lewis, taken out a fully equipped train for the burned district. The party consisted of Doctor Magie, Ed Patterson, Fred Reynolds and others, and the next day W. T. Bailey took out a party of explorers to scour the woods, but the operations of these parties were mostly confined to the identification of the dead and the burial of the victims. Of this work details are furnished that are heart-rending in the extreme, but as they have been entered into elsewhere they must be entirely omitted here.

As the extent of the calamity became more widely known and appreciated, contributions increased, not only at home but from abroad, not only did the cities in the neighborhood of Duluth and others in the state send goodly sums; but cities in other states, Michigan, Illinois, Iowa and Connecticut sent contributions and one was received from Glasgow, Scotland.

Mr. John D. Rockefeller on hearing of the calamity had caused to be subscribed $500.00 from the funds of the Mesaba Railroad Company, but upon an urgent message from Mr. Megins, of the auditing committee, he withdrew that amount and telegraphed $1,000.00 from his private funds. Mr. A. M. Miller, who never allows an opportunity to pass without doing something pleasant, telegraphed from New York to Treasurer Chapin as follows:

"First National Bank will pay you $500.00 on my account. This is authority for same. If Mike Dunn, my old section foreman, at Hinckley, is among the sufferers, give him and wife $50.00 each, preference on balance to my old railroad employes if in need. Engineer Root knows them."

The banks contributed as high as $250.00 each, and individuals as much as $100.00, the rest ranging from $1.00 to $50.00. At the end of the first week (Sept. 6,) the committee was able to report cash received $10,489.79 and subscribed additionally $2,675.00, besides not less than $9,000.00 in commodities of all kinds, not including railroad transportation, of which no computation was attempted. Of all these contributions, magnificent as some of them were, none was more welcome or more deserving of special mention than the so-called "News Boys' Relief." Eighty-one little fellows, a list of whose names is preserved and treasured by the Relief Committee, made up a sum of $18.18 for the fire sufferers in amounts ranging from $1.00 to three cents, Billie Groosky, the "Newsboys' Mascot," contributing the latter amount, which is probably the smallest contribution to the relief fund of any one individual on record.

The state relief commission, consisting of C. A. Pillsbury, of Minneapolis, Kenneth H. Clarke, of St. Paul, and M. G. Norton, of Winona, C. H. Graves of this city, and Secretary Hart arrived in Duluth on the afternoon "Limited" September 6th, for the purpose of conferring with the Duluth Relief Committee and for the adoption of such measures as the gravity of the situation might suggest. The commission was accompanied by Governor Nelson, Mayor Eustis, of Minneapolis, and other prominent people. A conference was held in the evening at the Spalding Hotel, at which Chairman Gridley and all the heads of committees were present.

By this time the relief work carried on at Duluth had been so systematized by the able and continuous efforts of Chairman Gridley that its operations took on more the character of a business than the temporary labors in a contingency. The accounts of the finance committee had been placed in the hands of an expert accountant and were in a state of absolute perfection. Mr. Wm. Craig had been placed at the head of the purchasing and supply committee and had reduced the important function of buying to first business principles. A supply depot had been established in connection with the Ladies' Relief Society and placed in charge of Messrs. H. L. Shepard and Frank Burke. The issuing of transportation tickets in charge of Mr. W. Buchanan was conducted with perfect satisfaction to the recipients as well as the railroad companies. Rev. Bishop McGolrick, in charge of lumber and building supplies, was indefatigable in his labors, and accomplished wonders. Messrs. Batchelor and Geggie, on the committee on rooms and quarters, Mrs Bangs on the bureau of information, in fact everyone connected with the committee was working steadily, enthusiastically and harmoniously, and in a manner that could call forth no criticism.

The work accomplished by this committee in its various branches up to this time (September 6th) was summed up and laid before the state committee as follows:

The number of persons actually maintained in some way for more or less time, 1,582. Public quarters established for refugees 12 Private quarters where refugees had been or were yet maintained 17.

Total cash and unpaid subscriptions received, $13,103.79.

Value of subscriptions other than cash (estimated), $10,000.00

Number of people at that time under relief committee, 932.

Estimated number remaining in city in need of help, $1,000.

The conference terminated after a very interesting session of some two hours, and in a manner very satisfactory to the committee, after which the distinguished party was put into carriages and conducted to the Bethel, Armory, Berkelman Block and other places, where short addresses were made to the sufferers and words of encouragement and the promise of such assistance as the state could grant, were spoken.

Without going into details the result of the conference was, that Duluth should continue the temporary relief of such refugees as were here until they should be able to take care of themselves, or until means could be provided for them by the state; that John, G Howard and X. J. Miller were to act for Duluth under the relief commission in the rebuilding and furnishing of houses at Hinckley and Sandstone for such as desired to return to those places. The state would gradually assume control of the more permanent relief measures contemplated by the commission, and would at once take charge of the work of taking depositions upon an established plan of its own, and some three hundred of these documents—descriptive lists of families upon which to base applications or administrations of relief—were turned over by the committee on information to Mr. Hart, the secretary of the commission.

As fast as the people could provide for themselves, or be provided for permanently, or were sent away, the more temporary "Harbors of Refuge" were given up and the inmates transferred to the Bethel, the Armory or the Berkelman Block. The hospital cases were of course continued without interruption until the patients were cured, and, if need there were, provided for otherwise.

Thus the Pilgrim Congregational Church, which stands among the foremost in energetic preparations for the emergency, was relieved of its charge by the General Relief Committee on the 7th of September, up to which time 200 people had been clothed, fed and housed. This society has been alluded to elsewhere for exceeding promptness in its preparations so that 98 refugee children had been bathed, fed, and put to bed, in clean night clothes, before 9 o'clock Sunday evening. A professional nurse was put in charge of the sleeping apartments, a physician was engaged, and owing to the foreign parentage of the greater part of the children it was found necessary to have an interpreter. On Monday so many people, (their number must have run into thousands,) kept crowding into the church, some in the hope of finding friends or relatives, others simply to offer help and assistance—that it was found necesary to

C. F. JOHNSON.

THOMAS SULLIVAN.

station guards outside to keep them out. The expedient was also hit upon to keep a bulletin board outside with the names thereon of the families within. These names were, of course, erased as fast, as the families were taken away or sent to friends, thus avoiding much confusion. In the rear of the church the large open space was converted into a play ground for the older children while kindergarten games were provided inside for the little ones.

The First Presbyterian Church was also among the very first to make excellent preparations for the emergency. The basement of this elegant edifice being provided with numerous class rooms, a kitchen, dining room, lavatory, etc., is easily adapted for the purposes of hospital and dormitory, when required. The members spent all of Sunday afternoon in fitting up this basement with cots, beds and bedding, clothing, food and medical supplies, in short with everything needful. The Central Relief Committee were only too glad to avail themselves of such admirable quarters, and as fast as refugees arrived whose condition demanded special care and treatment, they were sent to the Presbyterian Church. While all the members and their friends contributed with enthusiasm and zeal to the work, Mrs. Cleland, Mrs. J. D. Day, Mrs. Laitte and Messrs. Webb and Gorton may be particularly mentioned as leaders in the work. Mrs. Cleland having in her special charge the lavatory, which was not always agreeable, and the latter had the distribution of supplies, clothing, groceries, etc. This work was kept up for something more than a week when the inmates were transferred to the Bethel. During this time nearly 150 people had been cared for, one family contributing quite largely to swell this number, consisting as it did of fourteen members, Mr. and Mrs. O'Neil with 12 children.

Miss Erickson, the eighteen year old postmistress of Sandstone, found refuge here. The brave girl deserves special mention, for while having lost all her own worldy goods, she had managed to save the proceeds of the stamp sale of that town to the amount of some $36.00 in a cigar box. With this box she had fled from the fire to the river, clutching it in her determined hold while forced to dive again and again away from the flames. The money was turned over to the Duluth postmaster and by that official forwarded to Washington while she was here.

The ladies of the St. Paul's Episcopal Church, though their edifice would not admit of the care of any sufferers within the building itself, were among the foremost to provide quarters and devote themselves to the great work of relief. A committee consisting of Mesdames J. F. McLaren, O. K. Kinney, J. E. Bowers, W. R. Stone, H. M. Peyton and Dr. Gurd were at an early hour on Sunday appointed to take active measures. Through the generosity of Mr. Wm. E. Lucas the Berkelman Block, which happened to be vacant, was secured and quickly fitted up with beds and other accessories. The place was opened Monday morning and was intended more to serve the purpose of a hospital for the care of acute cases of suffering than for general purposes. The great need of accommodations, however, compelled the admittance of a large number of all classes, and in eight days a varying number of men, women and children were comfortably housed, fed and furnished with medical attendance. The whole number cared for in this time was 86 men, 32 women and 96 children, a total of 214. At the expiration of this time the Central Relief Committee relieved the ladies and the place was put in charge of Col. J. B. Geggie, of the Central Relief Committee.

The Duluth Woman's Home Society made a speciality of caring for waifs and strays, such as were separated from their families or were mourning the loss of near and dear ones. Many pathetic incidents transpired here. Among the rest, one woman with four little children had been mourning the loss of the husband and father as dead for several days, when, through the bureau of information of the central committee he was at last able to locate them. In the same way a little child, who it was supposed was left entirely alone in the world, was found by her father, and great was the rejoicing over her.

The order of Odd Fellows was, it is supposed, instituted more for the relief of their own members when necessary, than for people generally. But be this as it may, they certainly did not in this instance confine themselves to such narrow limits. On Sunday, the 2nd, some 200 Odd Fellows assembled in their hall on Lake Avenue, and in a few minutes raised $400.00 for relief purposes. A committee was appointed consisting of G. W. Goldsmith, chairman (since deceased), John Douglas, Wm. M. Donaldson, E. L. Sly and McG. McDonald, secretary. Two of their members were the same day dispatched to Hinckley and Sandstone to hunt up or ascertain the fate of their brethren who were known or supposed to be there at the time. Meanwhile their large hall and some vacant rooms in other parts of their building were carefully fitted up for the reception of unfortunates. These quarters were in co-operation with the Central Relief, in constant use for six weeks and for general relief purposes, and all this time the ladies of the order known as the Daughters of Rebecca, administered to the wants of the inmates with great good nature and unwavering patience.

St. Luke's Hospital cared for 12 patients in all. In this case it was not the amount of service for the many, but the great service to the few that claims our admiration. Erick Elstrom, one of the cases treated, (see portrait or picture) owes his life probably, certainly his eyesight and the partial use of his hands, to the skillful medical treatment of Dr. Chase, and the very careful nursing he received. He had suffered from almost criminal neglect elsewhere, and was considered a hopeless case when first brought to the hospital. One Billado, whose life was also despaired of when brought in, recovered entirely, and his hands, that were in a shocking condition, were also saved. This hospital had sent out professional nurses on one of the early relief trains, as mentioned elsewhere, so as to be on hand, so to speak, on the very "field of battle."

St. Mary's Hospital cared for 22 "fire patients" in all, among whom were a number of very interesting cases. Here brave Conductor Sullivan, of the ill-fated St. Paul & Duluth "Limited," was cared for. Sullivan, from the very responsibility of his position, had probably been able to realize more fully than any others the unparalleled horror of the situation and his utter helplessness in the face of it. The strain was too great and his reason gave away. It seemed to be while in the act of saving, as he thought, a child by throwing it out of a car window that his reasoning powers ceased to act; at any rate the impression of this action remained firmly stamped upon his mind until he regained his right senses. In his delirium while at the hospital, it was pitiable to hear him at times pleading as it were for the safety of this child. The incident seems to have taken place at the very moment the train stopped at Skunk Lake, for the child that figured so vividly in his disordered mind was picked up and saved.

Another interesting case under treatment here was that of a poor woman almost in the last stages of, and entirely helpless from, dropsy, but whose life had been saved by the strength, devotion, and courage of a daughter, in whose arms she had been carried a considerable distance to a place of safety. Another patient under treat-

ment in St. Mary's was Father Lawler, the heroic priest, who at the
last extremity, so it could not but seem, had torn his coat into
pieces to serve as shields for others against the flames. The following pathetic and curious incident is related of him.

It seems he was standing among quite a number of people in
some shallow water in which they would crouch as best they could
to escape the sheets of flame as they passed over. During one of
their breathing spells one poor fellow near him asked for confes-
sion. As this was manifestly impossible under the circumstances,
he could not comply, but the incident served to remind him nevertheless of his duties even here, and the good priest pronounced ab-
solution to all around.

At the Maternity Hospital three children were registered as born
to the fire sufferers. The first a boy, a remarkably fine child (see
picture). He was born on the afternoon of the 2nd to Mrs. James
Crocker, of Finlayson, and was named in compliment to the people
of Duluth "James Paul Duluth Crocker." Many pretty things were
sent to him, among the rest a silver spoon with his name engraved
thereon. A girl was born shortly afterwards to Mrs. John Turn-
quest, of Hinckley, she was named "Mary Addie Amerit," in hon-
or of the three nurses from St. Luke's who had officiated at her
birth. Mrs. Julia Stewart, of Sandstone, was delivered of a girl
soon after; she was also named after her three St. Luke's nurses,
"Jessie Francis Maud." Many children were bathed and clothed,
and five sick mothers and seven children were cared for until they
were well. A Mrs. John Anderson with three little children stayed
here over the terrible night of the 2nd. She was wild with grief,
thinking her husband lost, while the little ones were calling all
through the night for "papa." The husband had been equally wild
with fears for their safety, when he found them the next day.

When Mayor Lewis was authorized at a public meeting to appoint a general committee, Dr. C. C. Salter, pastor of the "Bethel,"
offered the use of the entire building for the fire refugees, while
the superintendent, Mr. C. F. Robel, set the building in order to receive refugees, also opened a restaurant to feed the famishing hungry. The good friends of the "Bethel" came to his assistance, sending in cots, clothing, medicines, bandages, etc., for the injured and
destitute. The noble women of the city tendered their services
to administer to the wants of the sufferers, while the Bethel restaurant furnished food in abundance, and plenty of milk and suitable
delicacies for babes and children.

The women and children were taken in charge of by Mrs. J. J. Crowley, of the Ladies' Relief Society, who saw that all received a bath and clean clothing, and were assigned to their proper places in the building.

Dr. H. C. Watson, of Beaver Falls, Pa., who was sojourning temporarily on Minnesota Point, volunteered his services, and was placed in charge of the sick and injured at the Bethel by Supt. C. F. Robel. Many had received burns, others had almost lost their eyesight, and all were in a frantic state of excitement; mothers mourning for the loss of their children, children searching for their parents.

The large assembly hall, gymnasium, and bowling alley were speedily transformed into dormitories, and by 9 o'clock p. m. two hundred men, women and children were resting comfortably on cots and bedding furnished by the good citizens of Duluth, while gentle hands ministered to the sick and injured.

The benevolent face of Dr. Salter loomed up on every hand, giving aid and comfort to those at the Bethel, hospitals, and all places he could be of use. On Wednesday, September 5th, he visited the burnt district and assisted in burying the dead and held religious services over the bodies of the Sherman and Lowell families and a large number of unidentified dead.

On Monday, September 3d, nine hundred meals were served in the restaurant to refugees.

Gospel meetings were held nightly and largely attended by the refugees and much interest manifested. Services were held in Swedish language.

On Friday Sept. 7th, Gov. Nelson, his private secretary, H. H. Hart, secretary of state board of charities, and Mr. C. A. Pillsbury, of Minneapolis, visited the refugees at the Bethel, shaking hands and giving words of encouragement and comfort to those in trouble.

The cloud of gloom that was hanging over the refugees at the Bethel was somewhat dissipated by a romance at noon, Sept. 4th. Miss Minnie Samuelson and John de Rosier, from near Hinckley, were united in the bonds of matrimony by the Rev. Dr. C. C. Salter. The Samuelson family had bidden their friends to the wedding feast on the fateful Saturday preceding the fire. All was going on merrily but just before the ceremony was to be performed the homestead was in ashes and the parties were fighting for their lives in a root house near by. They owe their lives to the fact that

SENATOR F. HODGE, PINE COUNTY.

REPRESENTATIVE ANDERSON, PINE COUNTY.

in this house were a number of pans of milk and with this they kept the wooden door from burning.

At 1 o'clock p. m. to the strains of the wedding march by Mrs. McKinley, the bride and bridegroom entered the hall of the "Bethel" and marched up to where the doctor stood, beaming like the incarnation of benevolence. They were attended by Mrs. J. J. Crowley, who was escorted by Chief of Police H. T. Armstrong. The ladies had provided the bride with a light colored dress that suited her to perfection. In her hand and corsage she wore some beautiful roses presented by Mrs. Judge Stearns. On her head was a wreath of orange flowers surmounted by a lace veil presented by Mrs. Humes, while others had sent and brought fruits, and flowers, and dainties wherewith to set forth the wedding feast. Dr. Salter read the wedding service, gallantly congratulating the bride. After the ceremony, the Samuelson family sat down in several detachments and the simple festivities were prolonged far into the afternoon. Mrs. Dr. Watson took up a collection for the bride among Bethel friends, and a nice little sum was contributed and presented to her by C. F. Robel.

Of nationalities, Norwegians predominated; Swedish next, but few Americans, and only two German families were represented. I found the refugees to be rather above the average in intelligence and moral tone, well behaved and sympathetic. Saw no one intoxicated during their stay at the Bethel.

After the first week many of the places where refugees were provided for were closed, and those remaining were sent to the Bethel, so that this institution was the last to close, which was on Sept. 26th. During this time from Sept. 2nd to 26th, three hundred and sixty people had been taken care of, clothed and fed.

The most important rendezvous for the fire sufferers and really the headquarters of the Central Relief Committee's operations, was the Armory in the Howard Block on Michigan street. As before mentioned this was the second time the drill room of Company "C," was called upon to serve the purpose of refuge for fire sufferers, the first occasion being the Virginia fire on the Iron Range. In this connection it may not be out of place to mention that the patriotic members of Company "C," Third Infantry, not content with turning their headquarters into an asylum for the needy, volunteered their services to the mayor in a body to assist the fire sufferers in any capacity he might see fit. That these services were not called upon seems strange, as they might for the first few days, at least, have rendered very effective assistance.

A. C. Batchelor and Col. Geggie secured the use of the Armory on Sunday noon (Sept. 2nd) and in spite of the fact of business houses being closed on that day, by 6 o'clock 265 refugees had been furnished with a substantial meal, and as many as desired with blankets and mattresses to sleep on. The kitchen of the Armory supplied not only meals for its own inmates, but for those of the Berkelman Block also. Besides this, it was the outfitting point for the various relief expeditions on the 3d, 4th, and 5th. This depot was in active charge of Col. J. B. Geggie, until it closed on the first day of November.

It is impossible to know just how many refugees were entertained here, but it is certain that as many as 1,505 people had been guests for more or less time at this place and at the Berkelman Block together. The greatest number of meals supplied in any one day was 455, and total number of meals furnished while open, 17,912.

In closing this account of the relief work at Duluth, it must be stated that great embarrassment has been experienced mainly on account of the short time allowed in which to gather and collate the materials from a chaotic mass of matter. The greatest difficulty has been from a want of anything like a correct knowledge of the names connected with the most interesting experiences, particularly has this been the case with the more subordinate class of railroad men, the so-called "railroad crews." In the most interesting events mentioned in this narrative, these men were heroes, every one of them, and their names would have been gladly displayed with Root's, Barry's or Best's, with those of Powers, Sullivan, McGowan or Blair if we could only have had them. As it is they must perforce be content to shine by the reflected light of their superiors.

The same may be said of the active relief work at Duluth. Where a whole community turns out as if with a single purpose, it is manifestly impossible to name them all, hence, many good and great workers are thus necessarily left out of the prominence in these details that by right belongs to them. In justice to the compilers, however, it may be mentioned that some names have been left out at the expressed wish of their owners. And then it must be remembered too, that the compilers of this narrative have made it a point to call attention to deeds only upon the principle that when deeds are praiseworthy they praise themselves.

When it comes to the work of Duluth as a whole, however, it is thought that the citizens generally may be held pardonable for the enjoyment of some pride.

The financial statement given above, though quite a remarkable exhibit in itself, does not represent the full value of the relief work done by the people of Duluth.

To say nothing of valuable time taken from business, or other pursuits and freely offered,—for instance, Chairman Gridley must have devoted the best business part of three months to the work of his committee; no account has, properly enough, been made in this statement, of the tons of clothing, wearing apparel and other supplies contributed by our citizens and distributed by the Ladies' Relief Society and at the "Armory," nor have the magnificent donations of lumber through Bishop McGolrick been mentioned. The great supplies of beef, of groceries, of fuel, of telegraph, telephone and gas and water service, of carriage and drayage, the free use of rooms and quarters, all so liberally donated by our citizens, could not, of course, be included in this statement, but these things all represent a cash value and should be taken into account in a general summary. Another item which is necessarily left out is the greatest of all, viz., railroad transportation. The compilers will not attempt a computation of this great donation in dollars and cents, in one sense it cannot be so considered. The opinion is ventured, however, that were all these things taken into account, the Duluth Relief Fund for the fire sufferers would reach a sum nearer $40,000 than $20,000. Then, if the estimate that has been made is correct, viz., that 2,000 people from the burned district have received more or less relief from Duluth, it follows that an average value in money of $20 per capita has been the cost of the outlay.

All this, when, considering the great stringency of money matters and the commercial depression of the times, certainly shows that a genuine spirit of self-sacrifice is always ready whenever the wellsprings of the human heart are deeply touched.

COL. GRAVES, DULUTH.

ST. CLOUD.

ST. CLOUD is one of the places in Minnesota where light and sweetness are said to dwell. It is the seat of a bishop of the Roman Catholic church, has a great normal school, daily newspaper, and a reformatory. It is in direct line with the area devastated by the great fire. From St. Cloud every day trains start to Hinckley, and every day trains come from Hinckley to St. Cloud. A large number of men who work for the Great Northern Railway Company live in this city, and amongst them, officials of the road. All this kept the people informed of fires which were burning for a long time before the fatal day, when so much damage was done and so many lives were destroyed. News had come that there were fires burning in the woods, and the season being so hot, the danger of their spreading had been talked about.

St. Cloud had had experience of ruin caused by a cyclone of wind years before, which took place at Sauk Rapids; now it was to see what a veritable cyclone of fire could do. When the hour came, the people of St. Cloud proved to be equal to the opportunity, and with a zeal which only needs to be known to excite admiration, the willing, wise and sympathetic help given was indeed as a hand of mercy in a time of dire need. The committee went about their work in a business-like way; they sent a competent man to look over the wants of those who were in need, drew up a set of questions, which left nothing to be desired; each and all who had to do with the work did their best. The people of Brook Park; the sufferers in and around Milaca, owe to the mayor of St. Cloud, Mr. D. W. Bruckart, to Mr. Alvah Eastman, to Alderman De Leo, and the other members of the committee, a deep debt of gratitude. And credit must be given to the working men who were sent out from St. Cloud to the fire district. The report shows in part what was done, and how; the whole it cannot tell, because words cannot show all that love can do. Mr. Ponsonby, assistant superintendent on the Great Northern, had a telegraphic apparatus along the line. He tapped the wires as the work of reconstruction proceeded. This telegraphic office in the burnt districts was a blessing, made doubly so by the ever ready kindness of the genial superintendent, who would send any message, free of course, and with such a sweet manner as to endear its memory to many whose griefs were lessened by such consideration.

EXPRESS MESSENGER JOHN SANDERLUIS.

You have requested me to write of my experience and whatever else I know of the Hinckley fire. I will enclose a few photographs which may be of use to you in your book, and also give you all the information I have relating to the fire. I am an express messenger for the Great Northern Express Company, on the St. Cloud and Hinckley branch of the Great Northern Railway line. On the first day of September, 1894, accommodation train No. 45 left St. Cloud for Hinckley with her crew, viz.: E. E. Parr, conductor, William Vogel, engineer, Joseph Laucher, fireman, John Delaney, B. S. Carrier and M. J. Whalen, brakemen, and myself, making seven in all the crew. It was a beautiful clear day, but very warm in the forenoon, and the boys were congratulating themselves on a light day's work.

The trip was uneventful in the forenoon until we reached the vicinity of Brook Park, where we noticed it was very smoky: in fact, it was so bad that the engineer had to slacken speed, and we had to close the doors of the car. We arrived in Hinckley about 2 o'clock p. m.,—about two hours late. The smoke there was now very oppressive and the boys finished their switching as quickly as possible. There was a small fire blazing back of the Great Northern round house, which Agent George Surgeon was fighting with a crew of men. There were no loads in Hinckley for our train, so the engine was coupled to the baggage car and coach, and the air-brake adjusted. We were all feeling good at the idea of having a fast ride through the smoke, our train being very light. When all was ready the conductor called, "Get out of town!" and away we went, little dreaming of the terrible danger we were running into.

About one mile out of Hinckley, we noticed a small fire burning in the timber at the side of the track, then all of a sudden everything was ablaze, as gas ignites when it is brought in contact with fire. The very air seemed to be burning. The train thundered through this about three miles, when it stopped. The engineer saw that the Mission Creek bridge was almost destroyed, but the rails were still

straight, and the plucky engineer pulled the throttle open and started
again. We were taking terrible chances, but we got over the bridge
all right, although it was much sagged, when we went over it, and we
thought we would go through it, but we were not destined to stop
here. On we went, tumbling and rolling, striking dead trees and
crooked rails, until at last the engine, striking a crooked rail, plunged
into the ditch, taking the baggage car with it, leaving the coach on
the dump.

We were now in a desperate condition, expecting the Eastern Minnesota passenger train to crash into us, as we could not flag it because the flames were so bad that it would have been sure death then
to venture outside the coach for one minute. We did not know
how great the fire was. When the train first ditched, the conductor
and myself were in the baggage car, the three brakemen being in the
coach with the passengers, a Mr. Kingsley, an advance agent for the
Wells Theater Company, and an old man named Carver, living at
Brook Park, whither he was then bound.

When the train ditched, we got a very bad shaking up, as well in
body as in mind, and I turned toward the conductor and said, "I
guess we are done for now!" "I guess so," said Ed, quietly. Then
I asked him what we would better do to save ourselves, and he said
that it would be better to dig a hole in the ground and get into it,
which was much easier said than done, as we found out later on. But
I got a couple of shovels, and handing him one of them, we started
to go out, but no sooner had we opened the door than we were
overwhelmed by flames and hot air rushing into the car, and we had
to give up this idea entirely. The conductor then started for the
coach, which he reached in safety, and I started after as quick as I
could. We both burned our hands and faces badly

The wind was now blowing a hurricane and the flames were shoot-
ing in through every crack and crevice on the coach around the
windows and doors. The cushions of the coach then caught fire,
and we had to throw them out to keep the fire from spreading. The
flames were getting much worse and we gave up all hopes of getting
out of there alive. We all laid on the floor to avoid, as much as
possible, the heat that came from the windows, and were trying to
settle our accounts with our Maker while we had time. But fortune
favored us again, when brakeman Whalen thought of the water in the
engine tank, and called for volunteers to help him save the coaches
which were on fire underneath. Of course everybody was glad to

MAYOR BRUCKHART.

do what they could to save themselves, so we got a couple of pails and started at it in a novel but safe way, two going out at a time and throwing a pail or two of water on the fire, then struggling in again, when two more would take their places. After an hour's hard fight, we at last got control of the fire under the cars.

While this hard fight for life was going on, the conductor went to see if the engineer and fireman were alive. He found that they were both alive, lying on the deck of the engine with the water of the tank turned on them.

I wish to give William Vogel all the credit possible, he being a young engineer and running right into the fire to avoid the east-bound passenger train, which would have brought certain destruction, not only to his crew, but the crew of the other passenger train which was expected right behind him. This was a brave and noble deed.

After we had the fire under control, we noticed two men coming down the track, one partially carrying the other. When they came up to the car, we learned that they were Thomas Gorman and his son, section men of the Great Northern Railway. The boy had dragged his father almost a mile through the dense smoke and falling cinders to the train which they expected to be ditched, having been under bridge Eighty-four when we passed over it. The boy after saving the bridge, took his father to the wrecked train and then started right back to see if the rest of the family were all right, a deed which not one in a thousand would have done under the circumstances.

About 5 o'clock that evening, after the fire had subsided a little, we all started for Brook Park, except Mr. Gorman, who could not walk, to find shelter and supper. But on arriving there, we were not only disappointed, but horrified to find the town in ashes, as well as many of the citizens burned to death. Such a scene I hope none of the readers of your book will have to gaze upon.

In a little pool, about twenty-five feet square, we found twenty-three people, men, women and children. They were in a terrible condition, with not sufficient life left in them to get out of it. Their suffering must have been awful, as they were surrounded by fire on all sides. The railroad bridge above them was burning, and the burning timbers fell in amongst them. It seems almost a miracle that they escaped death. Even the clothes were burned off their backs. Besides this bridge burning near them, the pool was surrounded by a saw mill, log camp and section house, and an old dam close by. These were burning intensely on every side and imagine the situation; even the fishes in the pool died from the effects of the heat.

Besides all their physical tortures, these people in the pool were constantly on the watch for our train, which they expected every moment to rush in and destroy, not only them, but our crew also. Happily events turned out differently.

Conductor Parr, seeing the terrible plight these people were in, forgot his own troubles and got them out of the pool, bringing them to our train where they stayed over night, having reached there about 7 o'clock. We made them as comfortable as possible under the circumstances; nevertheless this night will never be forgotten by me or any one there.

The cries of the children, and the moans and groans of the men and women, were something terrible; pen cannot describe it. The smoke and air were suffocating in the extreme and the heat terrible. We placed wet clothes over their faces and in their mouths every five minutes.

That night seemed an age to me, as I could not sleep. About 5 o'clock the day dawned, and the engineer, fireman, conductor, passenger Kingsley and myself started to walk to Hinckley, leaving the three brakemen asleep, and the rest of the people in the coach. The smoke was still suffocating, and we had to fill our mouths with waste which we had to dip in a pail of water. The first thing we found on arriving at Hinckley, was about one hundred and fifty cars of wheat burning, which gave out such a heat that we had to avoid it, by at least two blocks to the south. The Great Northern round house, coal shed and water tank were the only building left in Hinckley. We found some bread and crackers which we ate greedily, being very hungry.

The only living thing we saw from the round house, was a man leading a cow along the railway track toward Pine City. After asking him, he gave Conductor Parr permission to milk the cow, which he did, and sent the milk in one of the pails with the crackers and bread, we had found at the round house, to the sufferers on the track. You most probably know that we saw at Hinckley nothing but death and destruction on every side.

We then took a relief train on the St. Paul & Duluth Railroad, which happened along just then, and were taken to Pine City, where we were well fed and cared for by the kind people of that town.

On our arrival at Pine City, we at once sent relief to Brook Park and the sufferers on our train. That afternoon we went to St. Paul, and from there home to St. Cloud, thanking God that we were alive and on earth. We must not forget to mention Peter Clarity, assistant road master, who worked a crew of men at Brook Park, fixing up the track, for almost a month, enduring many hardships. We might mention M. E. Cantillon as being instrumental in saving many lives and considerable property, as he ran a water train between Milaca and Mora, and carried many people from the scene of fire to a place of safety, and also fought fire along the line for about three weeks after the Hinckley holocaust.

It is very hard for me to write stories as they ought to be written, and especially about this Hinckley fire, which ordinary words cannot express, so please put this information in your own words, and if you wish to learn anything more and I can help you, I will gladly do so.

RELIEF WORK.

The people of St. Cloud deserve very great credit for the part they took in relief work. Being on the Great Northern Railroad they had easy access to all the places between their city and Hinckley. From the time the first news of the fire reached them, to the close of their work, the interest in the sufferers never failed, and all their work was done in a way which calls for high praise. The official report to the state committee is to be seen in the state report. The mayor of St. Cloud, D. W. Bruckart; Mr. Alvah Eastman and Alderman DeLeo, as well as other members of the committee, worked with an enthusiasm and a thoroughness which left nothing to be desired.

It was Saturday afternoon, September first, when news came to St. Cloud that the villages of Foreston and Milaca, on the St. Cloud and Hinckley branch of the Great Northern Road, were in danger of destruction by fire. Immediately a train, consisting principally of water cars, was sent to their relief, with Division Superintendent Ponsonby in charge. The train proceeded as far as Foreston, where the railroad bridge was found to be on fire. This was saved after a hard fight, but it was found impracticable to proceed further.

Leaving a part of the crew to protect the bridge from fires, which were still burning near, the train returned to St. Cloud for reinforcements, and soon another train was sent out, containing a number of bridge builders to replace the bridges known to have been burned. On Saturday, this train succeeded in getting as far as Brook Park,

JOHN F. BRADFORD.

ALVAH EASTMAN.

JOHN CHOATES.

H. J. ANDERSON.

and there for the first time learned of the fearful terrors of the fires. The train men did heroic work and brought the Brook Park sufferers to Mora, where an improvised hospital had been made of the Methodist Episcopal Church, and they were given the best care possible.

The village of Milaca had been saved by hard work, but the farmers surrounding it met with severe losses, many of their homes being destroyed, as well as their year's work, consisting of logs and ties and all their crops.

All Sunday the people of St. Cloud were vainly endeavoring to learn the extent of the fire. Efforts were made to reach Milaca and other places nearest the fire, but without avail, because the telegraph poles and wires were burned down. St. Paul was tried, nothing definite was learned except that a relief train was being sent out.

Vague rumors were received of the destruction of Hinckley, with great loss of life. It was generally believed that so great a holocaust was impossible. The reality, however, was much worse than the first reports. Enough had been learned to warrant prompt action for measures of relief.

Mayor Bruckart, Sunday afternoon, called a meeting of citizens at the Grand Central Hotel, which was largely attended. It was then decided to send a special train to Brook Park as soon as possible.

At 7:30 the next morning, Monday, a special meeting of the city council was held, and committees appointed to purchase food, cots and clothing; it was also decided to send physicians and trained nurses. At 12:45, the train pulled out on its errand of mercy. On board were Aldermen Anderson, Atwood, DeLeo, Donohue, Thursdale, and Stewart, City Clerk James A. Martin, Street Commissioner Lorenser with a crew of men, Dr. Junk and Dr. Boehm and two nurses. The mayor distributed all over the city, by his policemen, the following appeal, which also appeared in the evening papers:

MAYOR'S OFFICE, ST. CLOUD, MINN., Sept. 3, 1894.

There is much suffering, the result of forest fires that have lately swept over the country round about Hinckley. We this day sent a car load of provisions to Brook Park. They need clothing and bedding. We will send teams to your doors at about 5 o'clock this afternoon to receive such contributions as you feel able to make. Have them ready. D. W. BRUCKART,

The people of St. Cloud responded generously, and Tuesday morning another car load of food and clothing was sent to the afflicted people at Brook Park. The following day, Wednesday, September fifth, the city council held another special meeting and decided to appoint a relief committee to receive contributions and take charge of the work of relief on behalf of the citizens of St. Cloud. Aldermen H. J. Anderson, John DeLeo, J. F. Bradford, and Messrs. John Coats and Alvah Eastman were appointed such committee. That same evening these gentlemen met and organized, with Alderman Anderson as chairman, and Alvah Eastman secretary. The following appeal was then issued.

The undersigned committee has been designated by the common council to take charge of all matters pertaining to collecting and distributing money, provisions and other property to the unfortunate people who suffered severe losses in the recent forest fires between Bridgman and Hinckley, and particularly at Pokegama. There are twenty-seven families at the latter place, comprising 117 souls, who have lost everything but their lives, none of them having saved sufficient clothing to afford necessary protection against the elements. At this writing twenty-five of their neighbors and friends have been found charred corpses, and a few are yet missing. A number of families, estimated at about twenty, who resided in the vicinity of Bridgman and Milaca, have lost their homes and are in need of assistance. This committee will co-operate with similar committees from St. Paul, Minneapolis and Duluth with a view to doing the greatest possible amount of good with the money and other contributions placed at the disposal of the committee.

Cash contributions can be handed to any member of the committee, and a complete list will be published daily. Clothing, bedding, household goods and provisions will be received daily at the McCormick warehouse, or will be called for, if request is made to a member of this committee or at the office of John Coates.

We trust that this community will respond with such liberality as will show that it has not forgotten the generous aid extended to it, at the time of the cyclone of 1886.

> H. J. ANDERSEN, Chairman.
> J. F. BRADFORD,
> JOHN DE LEO,
> JOHN COATES,
> ALVAH EASTMAN, Secretary."

From that moment everything moved as by clockwork. The care

of the fire sufferers in Milaca and vicinity was given into the hands of the St. Cloud committee exclusively, by the state committee, and the work was set about in a way which would ensure two things at once,—full knowledge of the losses and needs of the sufferers, and an adequate amount of relief. The following form prepared by the committees will show how the whole purpose was covered. It may be safely said that those who were most interested,—people burned out of their homes, the persons who subscribed the funds, and the state committee, were all satisfied with the result. That the St. Cloud people might see how complete was the destruction in the burned district, the committee arranged an excursion, and the money made was given to the fire sufferers, as will be seen from the list of subscriptions in cash, here printed. In addition to this there were large gifts of all kinds of food, clothing and goods.

SUBSCRIPTIONS AND EXCURSIONS RECEIPTS.

Proceeds from the Hinckley excursion, $457.28; employes of Great Northern shops, $155.25; Foley Bros., $100; George Tileston, $50; First National Bank, $50; students and teachers of State Normal School, St. Cloud, $31.50; A. Barto, $25; Knights of Pythias Lodge, $25; Merchants' National Bank, $25; pupils of the Immaculate Conception school, $22.50; the City School teachers, $21.75; the pupils of the Pro-Cathedral school, $20.26; Catholic Order of Foresters, $15; Sisters of the Order of St. Benedict, St. Joseph, Minn., $15; citizens of Maine Prairie, $13.07; St. Stephen's Ladies' Aid Society, of New Paynesville, $10; J. W. Metzroth, $10; Mathias Weirens, $10; Journal-Press Company, $10; Daily Times, $10; John M. Schwartz, cashier, $10; Henry Munsinger, $10; C. F. Powell, $10; W. B. Mitchell, $10; James F. Bradford, $10; M. Majerous, $10; Royal Arcanum Lodge, $10; Mrs. Catharine Eiche, $5; John G. Mihemitch, $5; Jesse A. Chase, $5; a "Friend," Racine, Wis., $5; A. D. Deane, $4; Earl C. Scott, $2; cash donation, $1; Mrs. J. B. Getchell, $1.

H. H. HART, SECRETARY STATE COMMISSION.

MORA

MORA is the town nearest Quamba, where the fire that destroyed Brook Park started, and was itself in fear of being burned. The people here knew many of the dead; had had business with them, and so there was a oneness of interest and of feeling. Being settlers in a comparatively new country, they knew just how to commiserate the afflictions of those who had lost their homes and friends, and they proved their knowledge by their deeds. The people of Brook Park have a warm place in their hearts for the men and women of Mora.

What the "Times" says:

"What a transformation! What desolation can be wrought in the short space of a day. What a devilish incarnate fiend a fire can be when driven forward by a tornado. Last Saturday was a dreadful day in the history of Minnesota. The lively, hustling town of Hinckley, containing upwards of twelve hundred souls, was completely wiped off the face of the earth, and six hundred of her people perished by smoke and flames. Their charred and ghastly remains strewn on the streets, by the door-ways, in the pools and along the railroad tracks, told a tale of suffering that brought tears from the stoutest hearted and grief to many a family. Many of the survivors of that holocaust are maimed for life and will carry scars to their graves. Whole families perished. Some families were partly destroyed and mothers and fathers were crazed with grief for the loss of their children, while many children were orphaned.

Hinckley was an industry within itself, kept up mainly by the big saw mill owned by the Brennan Lumber Company. That, together with the railroad business, kept a good many people employed, but the million dollars' worth of property has disappeared.

The fires came from the southeast and with such a sudden, fierce velocity that the citizens were completely terrified. It struck the town about 2:30 p. m., when the Eastern Minnesota train, with Conductor Powers, was just ready to pull out. The citizens massed on to his train and implored him to save them. He coupled on some box cars and pulled out nearly five hundred souls to Duluth. The St. Paul & Duluth limited, which dashed into the flames pulled out a large number to Skunk Lake. Arriving there, the train was abandoned to the fire, and the passengers, who were not too much exhausted, managed to save themselves by getting into the lake.

Those left at Hinckley were driven into a pond at the gravel pit and the river near by, where some survived, while others were tramped to death by cattle, horses and other animals. When the fire had spent its force, some of those who were able struck out for Pine City for relief, which came on the next morning and took the survivors to Pine City.

The first news of the terrible disaster was brought to Mora by Anton Smith from Pine City. His report seemed almost incredible, but later reports increased the calamity ten-fold. Mora was cut off from communication with Hinckley, the bridges and a great extent of railroad track and the telegraph wires had been consumed, hence it was impossible to get any early information over that line.

Ole Nelson, section foreman, with his crew, started promptly for Brook Park, and arrived there early Sunday morning. When they got to the station they found everything in ashes, and about sixty people homeless, many of them suffering with blistered hands and feet, and surrounded by smoke. They were undoubtedly the first persons on the scene after the disaster. They divided their dinners among the sufferers, who had been without anything to eat from the previous day, and then returned to Mora, bringing with them on the hand car Joseph Gonyea, William Thompson, and Frank Littengarver. Joseph Gonyea, who was badly burned about the hands and feet, was placed in the town hall and well cared for until the church could be got ready. William Thompson and Frank Littengarver, being uninjured, were sent to Minneapolis at their own request, their fares being paid by the Mora relief committee.

A relief party was made up immediately and dispatched with provisions, two hand cars and a push car, to the scene of disaster. Dr. Cowan preceded them on a velocipede with medicine and bandages for the sufferers. Right behind them came the work train from St. Cloud, which proceeded as far as it could, and that night the families of Wright, Kelsey, Hans Nelson and Mrs. Fream and children were brought in, the others remaining there to be attended on the morrow.

The church was thrown open by the Rev. Thompson as a hospital. Bedding, blankets and clothing were contributed by our citizens, also provisions; and the ladies of the town were out en masse to render all the assistance in their power to the sufferers.

Monday morning the village council convened and took action. A relief committee was appointed and fifty dollars was appropriated from the treasury to meet the immediate needs. The committee appointed were: Rev. J. Thompson, T. B. Vickery and Andrew Larson.

Mayor Smith, of St. Paul, was notified of the calamity, and aid solicited for the sufferers. A relief train came on from St. Cloud on Monday afternoon, loaded with everything necessary to make the people comfortable, and lumber to make coffins for the dead, and to construct houses for the survivors. Dr. Boehm, of St. Cloud, and Rev. Barnes, of Milaca, came with the train; also two trained nurses. Dr. Kelsey's family were brought to Mora, and with the family of Wright Kelsey, went to St. Paul.

Aid was offered the Russian sufferers at Brook Park, thirty-two in number; but they objected to remaining longer in that place, and through the intercession of Rev. Thompson, were permitted to proceed to Mora, thence to St. Paul, to which place the Great Northern transported them free of charge.

THE VICTIMS OF BROOK PARK.

The following is a list of the dead found up to date:

Thomas Raymond, wife, and three children.

Charles Anderson, wife, and three children, and Mrs. Anderson's brother and sister.

Fred Molander, wife, and three children, and Miss Olson, sister of Mrs. Molander.

Oscar Larson and sister.

David Goodsell, Charles Whitney, James Barnes, and J. Brennan.

Eleven of these bodies were found on Tuesday in a tamarack swamp by the searching party, and were supposed to be Mrs. Anderson and her three children, her brother and sister, T. Raymond, wife and three children. The Molander family was found close by their home burned to cinders. J. Breman's body was identified by a new pair of boots. Mr. Barnes, who perished, belonged to St. Paul, to which place his remains were carried on Tuesday, accompanied by his sister, who had come to take charge of them.

BISHOP WHIPPLE, D. D., L. L. D.

The injured are: Dr. Kelsey, hands and eyes burned; Joseph Gonyea, hands and feet burned; Wright Kelsey, blinded by the smoke; two Rosenberger children, burned feet and eyes, and many others blinded by heat and smoke.

Among those in the relief party from St. Cloud was Dr. J. C. Boehm. Rev. Thompson is authority for the statement that no one could watch the doctor as he moved among the sick and wounded, without being impressed with the fact that he was in deep sympathy with the afflicted, and that he was a skillful, experienced physician. The burial of the dead who are interred as fast as found, is in charge of Rev. William Wilkinson, of Minneapolis.

The Fream family's escape was almost miraculous. They were out picking berries, and the fire coming on them suddenly, sought shelter in a ditch, where they found water sufficient to wet cloths and hold to their mouths while lying flat on the ground, and the fire passed over them without doing any serious injury.

Some sought refuge in wells, and others went into the Pokegama creek, where they were saved by diving and splashing water on themselves. To give all the incidents connected with this awful calamity is not within our ability, time or space. The tales of suffering and escape will be told by the survivors for years to come.

Messrs. Kelsey & Markham and all the others are loud in their praises of the citizens of Mora for the deep interest manifested for the victims of Brook Park; while Rev. Thompson for his genuine sympathy and untiring work in the relief of the sufferers, has been praised on all sides. He is doing heroic service and has a true conception of his noble profession.

The thanks of the sufferers are also extended to all the good people of the surrounding cities, who have heartily responded with a practical sympathy that should come in a time like this. The relief committee extend special thanks to the following gentlemen for cash subscriptions so far:

Hon. R. C. Dunn, Princeton $25.00
Mattson & Blakely, Lawrence 10.00
Clarence Vinton, Lawrence 4.00
Joseph Carter, Lawrence 1.00

Brook Park (Pokegama Station) was a new town, not much over a year old. There had already been erected a saw mill which had on hand three hundred thousand feet of lumber, a hotel, a store, post office, and a handsome two-story school house, besides some family dwellings; and the country was being developed by a hard working class of citizens. This property with the homes of twenty-five farmers, twenty head of horses, thirty head of cattle and five hundred tons of hay, was totally destroyed and not one cent of insurance on any of it.

The Great Northern Railroad Company's loss is extensive. Almost every bridge from Mud Creek to the other side of Kettle River was destroyed. The ties for a long distance between Brook Park and Hinckley will have to be replaced by new ones, and many miles of rail will have to be replaced.

Besides the destruction of Hinckley and Brook Park, were the towns of Sandstone and Mission Creek; Milaca was scorched, and about twenty-five settlers in that vicinity rendered homeless. The relief train sent from Princeton to Mora in charge of Hon. R. C. Dunn and C. T. Johnson was ordered back to Milaca to feed and clothe the sufferers, it having been found that it was most needed there.

The work of reconstruction is going ahead at a rapid rate. The Great Northern has a work train at the front, with upwards of one hundred men, and timbers, ties and rails are being put in place as fast as the men can handle them. Assistant Superintendent Ponsonby has charge of the reconstruction. Kelsey & Markham made the statement that Brook Park will be rebuilt, as it is backed up by large wealth and too much has already been invested there to be deserted by any calamity.

The family of John Currie and Dr. E. L. Stephan were carried out to Duluth on the Eastern Minnesota train. They have since returned to Pine City, where Mrs. Currie lies in a critical condition at the home of A. Pennington. They lost everything they had excepting a cow, which for some reason passed through the fire without much harm.

Dr. Cowan was a heavy loser. He lost his library, surgical instruments, office fixtures, clothing, a large interest in the Currie drug store, and his residence.

Angus Hay's newspaper plant, the Enterprise, was wiped out. The Enterprise will be missed by a host of readers, and particularly by its exchanges. Mr. Hay had a narrow escape from death.

Hans Nelson, the section foreman at Book Park, lost, besides his other property, one hundred and seventy-five dollars in money which he had in a trunk. He tried to save the trunk, but had to drop it to save his life.

George W. Marchant and Mr. Geesaman, members of the state relief committee, are here today looking after the needs of the sufferers.

Among the victims of the late fire at Hinckley were the two daughters of Swan P. Hanson, of Rice Lake, and Maggie Nyberg, of Brunswick.

P. R. Gray returned home from his trip to Sandstone last Saturday, accompanied by Carl Staples and family, who were losers in the Sandstone fire. The family was well provided with clothing by the Mora relief committee.

Eric Ericson, one of the heaviest farmers in the town of Comfort, lost his house and barn and eighty tons of hay by forest fires on Wednesday. His lost is estimated about thirty thousand five hundred dollars. He carried an insurance of about two thousand dollars. Comfort is a town only a few miles from Mora.

Joseph Genvea, one of the Brook Park sufferers, was taken to St. Cloud by Rev. Thompson last Friday and placed in St. Raphael's hospital.

John Currie, one of the recent sufferers at Hinckley, brought his family to Mora last Saturday. Mr. Currie said he and Dr. Cowan had an insurance of eighteen hundred dollars on their property. He still retains faith in a bright future for Hinckley, and will rebuild there at once.

In our review of the Hinckley and Brook Park fires last week, we overlooked our local physician, Dr. J. A. Lewis. The doctor did noble service in relieving the sufferings of the injured ones, and in fact did about all that was done in that line for them, for which he deserves great credit.

Last Sunday afternoon, September ninth, was an exciting time in Mora. The wind blew a gale from the southwest and the whole country seemed to be on fire. Many of the citizens went onto the island in Lake Mora, while others were prepared to leave for a place of safety at any moment. The wind changed to the northwest about 4 o'clock and sent the smoke scudding in another direction, and all signs of danger disappeared. There were no fires within six miles of Mora. The fires were bad at Ground House and in the town of Hillman, and the women and children were all brought up to Mora. But up to the present writing (Thursday) we have heard of but two

REV. FATHER BEJEC, PINE CITY.

houses having burned from forest fires in the entire country adjacent. Large quantities of hay, several camps and some stock have been destroyed in different localities.

From the Minneapolis Times of the tenth instant, we clip the following, which is a part of a report made by the state relief committee, who were sent here last Friday:

"George W. Marchant and Ed Geesaman returned this morning from their visit to Mora and Brook Park, whither they were sent by the direction of the local relief association, to ascertain what was being done to aid the fire sufferers. They were pleased to find that relief had come from the west as promptly as from the other sides. The dead were buried, the injured removed to a place where they could be made comfortable, and other survivors were well taken care of. At Mora an active relief committee, composed of Rev. James Thompson, Andrew Larson and T. B. Vickery, had been indefatigable in their efforts to render assistance, and with supplies of clothing and provisions sent from St. Cloud, had housed and fed the homeless from Brook Park. At the latter place, which was almost wiped out, there was found a box car in which a colony of nine destitute people were sheltering themselves. Three of these were sent to Hinckley by the Minneapolis relief committee, and those who preferred to remain were fully provided for. A resident of Brook Park named Gonyea, who had been very badly burned, was sent over to St. Cloud, where he will be turned over to one of the hospitals. It was found that the Mora relief committee had sent search parties all through the burned districts from Mora to Hinckley, and that everybody had been found and all of the refugees cared for. Having seen everything in good working order, Messrs. Marchant and Geesaman proceeded to Hinckley, where they joined the state relief committee.

The local relief committee, which consisted of W. Y. D. Long, Ole Nelson and section crew, Dr. Cowan, Henry Renes, now county auditor, Victor Molander, Jas. Golden, Thomas Dowds, and Chas. Olson, was in charge of W. Y. D. Long, depot agent, Mora. They took with them provisions to last the sufferers two days and arrived at Pokegama Sunday afternoon. They found and temporarily covered a number of dead bodies, their first thought being for the living. Among the living was found Dr. Kelsey and family, Mr. and Mrs. R. W. Kelsey and family, Mr. and Mrs. Fream and family, Mr. and

Mrs. Ward and sons, and thirty-two Polish Jews who were sheltered in a box car. The expedition proceeded one mile and a half down the railway track to the place where the Great Northern train was lying and found there Hans. Nelson, section foreman, and family, and Mr. and Mrs. Braman. Mr. and Mrs. Braman were sent to Pine City. The relief party then started to return to Mora, bringing with them Mr. and Mrs. R. W. Kelsey and family, Mr. and Mrs. Fream and four children, Mr. and Mrs. Hans Nelson and family, and Jacob Greenberg. When four miles from Mora they were met by the St. Cloud work train, which had proceeded as far as it could. The expedition was taken on board and brought to Mora, where they arrived about 9 o'clock p. m., the whole party of the sufferers were placed in the church and well cared for, medical assistance being given by Dr. J. A. Lewis, local physician.

No help whatever was accepted from this relief train from St. Cloud by the Mora relief committee, except that two nurses,—Mrs. Margaret Mitchell and Mrs. Marshall—were retained to nurse the sufferers.

A car load of clothing arrived at Mora from St. Cloud on Tuesday morning about 10 o'clock. This clothing was distributed by Rev. Thompson on Tuesday afternoon among the sufferers who were at Mora, and among the sufferers at Brook Park on Tuesday evening. Two barrels of clothing were also received from the Woman's Home Missionary Society of Wesley M. E. Church, Minneapolis. Also one box of clothing from Rev. George H. Wareham, pastor of M. E. Church at Jonesville. Help in provisions and clothing was also offered by Rev. H. C. Jonnenys, D. D., pastor of M. E. Church, Red Wing, Minn., but was declined.

The thirty-two Russian sufferers were removed by James Suydam from Minnesota Home to 249 East Fairfield avenue, St. Paul.

The body of Mr. James Barnes was brought to Mora, accompanied by his two sisters Mary and Elizabeth, and the father, Robert Barnes. They remained at Mora until the following afternoon and then went to St. Paul, their expenses, railway fees, etc., being paid by the Mora relief committee.

The twenty-five dollars received from Hon. R. C. Dunn, of Princeton, was declined by the Mora relief committee as they determined to take care of the sufferers themselves.

The families from Hillman and Ground House were well cared for by Mora and were sheltered and fed in the church. The families from Hillman remained in the church over a week. In all about one hundred people were cared for, sheltered, fed and partly clothed by the people of Mora during the three weeks preceeding September first.

MAYOR STARKWEATHER, SUPERIOR, 1895.

MAYOR WOODWARD, SUPERIOR, 1894.

SUPERIOR.

SUPERIOR is in Douglas county, in the state of Wisconsin, and is on the banks of Lake Superior. The eastern division of the Great Northern Railway, from Duluth, crosses the bay, and enters Superior, and goes forward till it reaches Carleton county, Minnesota. From this it is clear that the refugees from the fire district on the Eastern line, had to be taken to Superior before reaching Duluth, but as Duluth is the largest city in Northern Minnesota, and as the fires in Pine county were in Minnesota, it was right and proper that the sufferers, as a whole, should be taken to that city. This accounts for the work done in Duluth being greater than that done at Superior, but it does not lessen the credit due to the generous people of Superior, who well deserve the fame their city is attaining in the Northwest. With water ways to the sea, being on level ground, having the shops of the railway, and also being near the great iron ranges so rich in mineral wealth, and on the opposite side of the bay from its neighbor, it has a right to expect a future which will eclipse the present glory it has attained as far as sunlight surpasses moonlight.

I have put in this book every word of report sent to me from Superior, and to that must be added the fact, that many of the men who served through the fire are not only superior men, but they are men who live at Superior. Such men as Thorne, railway superintendent, Whyte, master mechanic, Finlayson, master carpenter, Van Pelt, Best, Ford, Freeman, McLaughlin, Gilham and many others. The people of Minnesota will not forget the kindness of the people of Superior in September, 1894, shown to so many of our citizens, nor will it forget the good work of the Superior newspapers, or their zeal in gathering news. The staff of the Evening Telegram deserves special mention, and I acknowledge my obligations to Mr. Kirby Thomas.

The mayor of Superior was in New York at the time of the disaster, but he did not forget the fire sufferers. Acting Mayor C. J. Norquist filled his place, and Rev. Mr. Starkweather, with a band of ready helpers came to his assistance. The names of the committee are in the report.

When the fire occurred at Philips, Wis., the city of Superior was the first to furnish relief.

In response to the telegram of Mr. Davis, the Hon. F. A. Woodward, mayor of Superior, called a mass meeting at the city hall, and in a few hours a car loaded with food and supplies of all kinds was on its way to Philips, under the charge of Rev. J. H. Nasson. After the first assistance had been given, about $150 remained in the hands of the city clerk, which was, by request of the chairman of the Philips committee sent to him by New York draft.

In this matter the citizens of all classes and wards acted with the greatest harmony and promptness. No charge was made by Mr. Nasson or any one else for services.

When the terrible conflagrations in the vicinity of Hinckley were wired to Superior, a temporary organization was immediately formed by Acting Mayor C. J. Norquist, assisted by Aldermen Harry Rogers and James H. Agen. A relief train was sent out with Dr. Collins in charge, and many volunteer assistants. Some sufferers were rescued and many buried. A second train, also under Dr. Collins, was sent later. For his hard labor and professional services Dr. Collins never made any charge. The first trainload of Minnesota sufferers reached Superior shortly after midnight, September 2nd. Carriages were ready to convey the burned to the hospital, and the half-naked women and children were wrapped in blankets and taken to the city hall, where women were ready with clothing to dress them comfortably. All were provided with comfortable board in the different hotels and boarding houses. Many had friends who provided for them without expense to the committee, and of such relief no record has been made. After some time the Duluth committee sent for the Minnesota fire sufferers, but most of them returned here, after registering in Duluth.

Before they were taken to Duluth they were addressed by Acting Mayor Norquist, who invited them to stay or to register in Duluth and then return to Superior.

When the fires destroyed Hinckley, Sandstone and other Minnesota towns, the woods of Wisconsin were burning in many places. These fires caused but little loss of life, and the great excitement which the terrible loss in the Minnesota towns produced prevented the public generally from appreciating the great financial loss in Northern Wisconsin. The fire burned steadily in all directions, destroying the timber, burning the grass roots, and in some cases calcining the soil, so that grass seed will not germinate. Settlers, who had with great labor gathered hay from the creek bottoms to keep their cows through the winter, were deprived not only of the timber, ties, posts and bark, by the sale of which they expected to support their families through the winter, but of all food for their stock, and it was only by the most prompt and efficient action of the Superior Relief Committee that hundreds of cows and other stock were saved from being slaughtered to keep them from starvation. Two instances will show how complete was the destruction a few miles south of Superior, and how little attention was first given to it. The committee decided to rebuild two log houses which had been burned a few miles south from here, but investigation showed that while the houses had been in the middle of the timber, yet there were then no unburned logs with which to rebuild nearer than five miles.

Theophile Bedard, a tie cutter, lived with his wife on their homestead near Boyleston, seven miles south of Superior. Their nearest neighbor was a half mile from there. He was named Williams. Williams and Bedard were cutting ties some miles away with several other men. On September 2nd Mrs. Bedard escaped from her burning house, and finding Mrs. Williams, the two women searched for their husbands for two days but could not even find the camp where they and several others had been working. The women finally walked to St. Louis, where they took a train to St. Paul, hoping the men had escaped in that direction, but no trace of any of these men has been found. Mrs. Williams remained with friends in St. Paul.

Mrs. Bedard was transferred from St. Paul to Duluth, Sept. 18th, and from Duluth to Superior Sept. 21st. She is still in this city. Till she reached here, it was not known that any lives had been lost in Douglas county.

As soon as it became known that help of all kinds was needed for people in Douglas and Bayfield counties, and that much relief work would have to be done for months, a permanent organization was effected by a mass meeting at the city hall. Mr. Frank Ostrander was elected president. Mr. P. J. Ekstrand (the treasurer of the city), elected treasurer, and the city clerk appointed secretary. Committees of two men from each ward were selected to solicit mon-

Rev. J. H. Nason.

ey for the relief fund, and a special committee chosen to raise money from the banks and corporations.

The committeemen from the 1st and 2nd wards did not turn in the funds to the treasurer, but a seperate organization was made in the Eastern wards of the city, and the work done by that organization is not included in this report.

Some misunderstanding arose from this division and from the fact that Mayor Woodward, who was in New York when Hinckley was destroyed, was offered help by Eastern parties. The state officials considered no assistance outside of Wisconsin to be necessary, although when it was freely tendered by Chicago merchants and churches, it was gratefully accepted. Many conferences and meetings were held, and after a visit to Milwaukee by the secretary, who laid the whole condition of this section of the state before Colonel W. J. Boyle, treasurer of the state relief, no further trouble arose and the state promptly and generously filled all requisitions and furnished all the feed, hay, provisions and bedding which was asked for or needed. Too much praise cannot be accorded to Col. Boyle's management of the state relief work.

On the executive committee fell most of the work. That committee consisted of Acting Mayor Norquist, Rev. J. H. Nasson, Rev. A. P. Morten, Mr. Chas. Stewart, Capt. Jarvis White, Wm. E. Pickering and the treasurer and secretary. Afterwards changes were made in the committee, and Mayor Woodward on his return took an active part in the work.

Neither the president, treasurer or secretary have asked or received any compensation for their services or expenses, or has any expense for clerical work been incurred.

The committee to raise funds from the corporations reported about $1,500, but this was used as a guaranty fund and only about $60 of it was called on. Outside of the corporations and the money sent by non-residents, about $2,000 was raised by the committees in the seven wards. In this work Alderman Lund was very active and successful.

The Rev. J. H. Nasson, who superintended quite largely the distribution of supplies for the fire sufferers, reports the following points of the special methods employed:

First, I note the promptness with which the city of Superior answered the calls of distress from Phillips, and the fire of September 1st at Hinckley, Partridge, Sandstone, etc. Immediately upon re-

ceiving the telegram reporting the Phillips fire, the mayor of the
city called a meeting of the citizens in the city hall; committees were
appointed, money and provisions were solicited the same afternoon,
and at evening were forwarded to Phillips, reaching there about midnight, and handed over the relief committee in that city the next
morning.   The same promptness was manifested in responding to
the fire sufferers at Hinckley.

The second point would be this: In common with the citizens
of Duluth and other parts of the country, no regard was paid to
state lines, but the people of Superior desired to be useful to the
needy in Minnesota as well as in Wisconsin, because of our proximity to the suffering in Eastern Minnesota, and we felt that we
ought to share with Duluth the care of the first trains of sufferers
that arrived; so that private houses and hotels of our city were
thrown wide open for receiving the sufferers, and after Minnesota
asked the privilege of taking care of her own citizens, still, because
many of them preferred to remain in Superior, we still continued to
furnish them with supplies.

The third point would be: That great pains were taken to explore the woods where many of the settlers were to be found on
their claims, many miles away from the railroad towns, and in that
way numerous destitute cases were found that otherwise would never
have been known to the general public.

The fourth point would be: That careful discrimination was exercised, so that those who suffered most in the loss of property,
houses and gardens, were aided proportionately to their losses.   That
while few lives were lost, aside from the loss at Phillips, in Northern Wisconsin, there were really great losses of property, of the
comforts of life, the gardens and the hay fields of the settlers, and
immense quantities of wood, cedar posts, railroad ties and other
property that the settlers depended on for their living.   The committee who investigated the condition of these sufferers found a
large number of Finlanders, and other nationalities, who had set-
tled within the fire swept territory, and like all new settlers had endured great suffering and privation in order to improve their lands,
and in consequence of the two years of hard times through which
they had passed, and the double scourge of drought and grasshop-
pers which they had experienced that year, before the fire came.

Fifthly, in the judgment of the relief committee it was thought
best to ask the state of Wisconsin to furnish a store room of sup-

plies against the needs of the coming winter, and this afforded distribution during the autumn at the various points where destitution had occurred. It was found to have been a very wise precaution to have that store of supplies, and it was visited by great numbers of the suffering during the greater part of the winter.

Superintendent Thorne, J. N. Hill, Conductor Ed. Gilboy, M. J. Devany, roadmaster, and myself took a handcar and started ahead to ascertain what damage was done, and found every bridge, building and culvert burned out between that point and Hinckley.

At Sandstone we found Kettle river bridge burned, the steel span alone standing, and the oak ties and guard rails burning from each end.

We had all bridges from No. 105 to 113 rebuilt by September sixth. On September seventh we commenced framing Kettle river bridge, and at twelve o'clock, midnight of September sixteenth, the first train passed over it; which I think a very good record for a bridge eight hundred and fifty feet long, and one hundred and thirty-two feet high, and not a man was injured.

JOHN FINLAYSON,

Master Carpenter.

LORD MOUNT-STEPHEN, LONDON.

WHAT DULUTH PEOPLE DID.

DULUTH is the greatest city in the northern part of Minnesota and its people are characterized by very great energy and enthusiasm. All the transport business to and from the northern part of the state centers here. The interests of this city are very closely allied to those of the residents in Pine County; trains go through it daily. Every one who has ever visited Duluth has gone through the burnt district. All this made the people of the city at the head of the Great Lakes take a personal interest in the fire sufferers. It was from the St. Paul and Duluth depot in Duluth that the ill-fated train, which had Conductor Sullivan and Engineer J. Root on board, with many citizens known to large numbers of the people, started. All this stimulated deep concern, besides the men and women who took a part in the fire relief work were actuated by a Christian sympathy which had manifested itself often before. The Ladies' Relief Society had for years been widely known for its work for unfortunate people. The Rev. E. M. Noyes, the pastor of the Pilgrim Congregational Church, was known in all the region round for his wide sympathies. The Roman Catholic bishop, James McGolrick, had, before he was a bishop, when a priest at the Church of the Immaculate Conception, Minneapolis, for more than twenty years stood a friend of thousands in trouble, sorrow, need and all kinds of distress; a man of active, tireless energy, who had copied after the late Cardinal Manning, probably.

The Rev. C. C. Salter is said be a man in ten thousand. A very rough man said to the writer, "If ever there was a man who followed Jesus Christ, a saint on earth, I believe it is Mr. Salter." Every tramp, every man who needs a friend at Duluth, knows the pastor of the Bethel. The mayor, Mr. Lewis, is a quiet man with a clear head and a warm heart. He threw all the energy of his soul into the work of relief.

The physicians of Duluth should be honored for the brave and faithful manner in which their professional duties were discharged during these trying days. They were: Doctors Salter, McComb, Retchie, Sherwin, Gibson, McCormick, Gilbert, Magie, Weston, Lyman and Codding.

On the afternoon of September first the citizens of Duluth were at first surprised, then alarmed by the peculiar effects in the sky which could only be compared to descriptions of simoons in that gradual and at last almost total darkness that succeeded an otherwise brilliant day as early as noon. At four o'clock in the afternoon it became so dark that lamps had to be lighted, and a short time afterwards the streets were almost in total darkness. People began to wonder and to look into each other's faces, as if inquiring whether the end of the world, which had been prophecied by certain religious sects, was about to be fulfilled. Later it became rumored that the fires had reached Hinckley on the St. Paul and Duluth road, and while the information was vague in the extreme, it was not lessened by the reports which succeeded each other in rapid succession. Between five and six o'clock in the afternoon, it was stated that the limited train on the St. Paul and Duluth road had been detained on account of the fires, and numerous sensational reports were started, evidently originating from those who had friends detained by the unusual occurrence; but later in the evening it became apparent that some unusual event had happened for the reason that the limited St. Paul and Duluth train, usually on time, did not arrive; and when messages came over the wires of the Eastern Minnesota Company indicating that Hinckley had burned and that the St. Paul and Duluth south bound limited had been obliged to turn back, the first evidence of the worst fears began to be realized. These fears were abundantly corroborated when the Eastern Minnesota train, which left Duluth at one p. m., returned from Hinckley, bringing in addition to its south bound passengers, four hundred and seventy-six residents of Hinckley who had been obliged to desert that village on account of the fires.

As the wires brought no news concerning the condition of the St. Paul and Duluth train up to eleven p. m., the rumors which had been current were thought to be true, and the citizens of Duluth began to show their interest in the probable distress of the passengers of that train by numerous inquiries at the local offices of the company. The dispatcher's office of the St. Paul and Duluth road was filled during the night with persons whose anxious inquiries showed the public interest in the fate of that train.

At about two o'clock Sunday morning a number of gentlemen who had made repeated visits to the dispatcher's office of the St. Paul and Duluth road, being anxious as to the welfare of certain friends on the south bound limited train (Mrs. E. N. Saunders and family), began to feel desperate, when the wire at last ticked off, in an almost unintelligible manner, a message indicating that R. N. Bell and daughter and Mrs. E. N. Saunders and family were safe; the relief shown in the expression of their faces plainly indicated the anxiety which they had felt before.

Upon returning to the Spalding Hotel and after some little conversation Mr. J. L. Greatsinger, president and general manager of the Duluth and Iron Railway, turned to one of the party and said, "It does not seem right that no effort is being made to reach the women and children at the point where the limited train burned. If we were in the same place, it would cheer us to think that our friends were making an endeavor to reach us. If you will go with me I will get an engine and car and we will start tonight." The person addressed was of the same opinion and readily assented. Both gentlemen started for the dispatcher's office of the St. Paul and Duluth in order to ascertain whether they could get the rights of the road at that time and start out. The officials seemed anxious to further any effort to aid those in distress, and promptly called a crew of their men to get ready to take the party out. It was four o'clock in the morning before everything was in readiness to start, and by that time the Union Station was filled with citizens who were only too anxious and willing to volunteer their services in rendering assistance to the needy. The train started, but owing to the fact that the condition of the road at that time was not known, as to whether bridges were intact, or had been destroyed by the fires, it took until ten o'clock Sunday morning for this relief party to reach Rutledge, a short distance north of where the limited train was burned. At that station the St. Paul and Duluth train, which had been sent out early in the evening, returned, bringing forty or fifty, of the survivors, who were taken care of by the train, practically in charge of Mr. Greatsinger, and of course operated by the St. Paul and Duluth road. Mr. Greatsinger's private car was given to the injured, and the doctors who had been invited and had most readily consented to accompany the party at once made themselves busy, endeavoring to relieve the sufferings of those who had been burned. It was learned from the St. Paul and Duluth work train that all of the passengers

MRS. E. M. BANGS.

of the St. Paul and Duluth limited who had not reported at Rutledge had started south on hand cars to reach Pine City.

Mr. O'Brien and Mrs. Saunders and her family were reported in first rate condition, considering the awful distress they had gone through, and consequently the train started with the forty or fifty rescued toward Duluth and arrived safely, late in the afternoon. The sufferers were immediately taken in hand by the citizens' relief committee and the Ladies' Aid Society, and given every comfort which was possible to tender them at that period of their distress.

Mr. Farrington, general manager of the Eastern Minnesota Railway, did all in his power to help the work of relief and reconstruction.

Sunday, the second of September, was a busy day in Duluth, in that all of its citizens seemed to respond as one man to the call made upon them in the daily press, for means of relief to offer to the stricken district.

The Ladies' Aid Society established headquarters in the basement of the Lyceum Building, generously tendered by Mrs. A. M. Miller, and all of that day relief of every kind, money, clothing and provisions poured into the headquarters in such quantities that everyone received an abundant supply.

About six o'clock in the evening, the Eastern Minnesota road was waited upon by a committee, stating that they understood that some four hundred people were in the Sandstone river bottoms, desolate and without any means of subsistence, and asking if the Eastern would furnish transportation to parties desiring to go their to afford them relief. The officials of the road had not received any advice up to that time that the fire had burned any other towns than Hinckley, and considered that the reason for their not receiving further advices was that the wires through the town of Hinckley had been burned and therefore had cut off the circuit. A train was heartily tendered to the citizens of Duluth, and any other assistance which the company could offer in equipment or money. After receiving this answer the committee began to get together supplies of food, medical necessaries, etc., and selected volunteers to go with the train, which by request was to start from Duluth about twelve o'clock Sunday night. The train was made up, consisting of an engine, two flat cars, two freight box cars, two day coaches and a private car, which left Duluth between three and four o'clock in the morning. The train was provided with lumber to make coffins,

four wagons and teams, provisions, and supplies to be distributed
to the needy, six doctors, and forty-five of Duluth's most prominent
citizens.   Up to midnight the reports indicated that many people
had been burned; consequently knowing that quick action in such
cases is required, each man was equipped with a shovel for the purpose of lending his energy to bury the dead.   The train proceeded
on its way until Mansfield station, fifteen miles north of Sandstone,
was reached.   After that point was passed frequent stops were made
at every lumber camp between that point and to Sandstone, in order to enable certain ones from the relief train to get off, and investigate as to whether all parties living there were safe.   Everything
was found to be in good condition until Partridge was reached,
and at that station a dissolution began to be apparent, from the fact
that not a board was left in the town to indicate that a settlement
had existed there prior to the first of September.   At this place,
owing to the intensity of the heat, the train could not proceed further
for the reason that between Partridge and Sandstone—a distance of
seven miles—the entire roadway of the Eastern Minnesota had been
burned to such an extent that the steel in the track was warped and
crimped to a degree rendering it impossible for even hand cars to
proceed beyond that station.   The relief party disembarked from
the train, and under the direction of Mr. Seagog, of Duluth, were
divided into two parties, one to proceed by wagon in a direction
slightly deviating from the path of the railroad, in order to reach
what was known as the Sandstone quarries of the St. Paul and
Duluth road, and rescue any persons who might be suffering at that
place; the other party started on hand cars to go as far as they could,
and the balance of the distance walked to Kettle river, running one-
fourth mile north of Sandstone.   Each member of the party was
equipped with a knapsack, containing a large quantity of sandwiches
and other food supplies which might be found necessary to be used
en route, and also carried axes and shovels, and as much lumber as
they possibly could.   The walk of seven miles between Partridge
and Sandstone was something that will be remembered to the last
day of every member of the party.   The fires had passed over, but
had left quietly burning vegetation, and the air full of smoke and
ashes, making breathing almost unbearable, and the heat was so
intense that every one suffered to a greater or less degree.

   Upon arriving at Kettle River, seven miles from Sandstone, they
walked down the rocky bluffs where no roadway existed, one hun-

dred and thirty-five feet, reaching the river. After hailing one of the survivors in the quarries, he succeeded in ferrying across the river in a flat bottom boat, twelve feet long and two and a half feet wide, and the party took turns in this cranky skiff. Upon reaching the other side it was found that but one building was left in the town of Sandstone, where before had lived a population of seven hundred people. This building was the office of the Sandstone Quarry Company, located on the bank of the river where the relief party crossed the stream. The building was probably fifteen by twenty feet and consisted of two rooms down stairs and as many above. There were twenty-eight people in this building frightfully burned, and suffering untold agonies; the floors of the lower rooms were covered with the prostrate forms of the poor sufferers, whose agony had put them into that state where they could not realize or appreciate their condition. The faces of all were frightfully swollen and distorted, and some were suffering such agonies as were impossible to depict.

The doctors of the party at once began their humane work, assisted by as many as could conveniently work with them. The other members of the relief party started to the place where the town of Sandstone had existed, each one carrying on his shoulder a long handled shovel for the purpose of interring the dead. Not a particle of timber or a board was left where the town had once flourished, and upon ascending the road leading up through a ravine to the townsite, they were at once brought into full view of the ghastly devastation which had been wrought by this fearful work of the elements. No evidence remained that anyone had ever existed in this place, excepting only by the groups of bodies, indicating the families where dwellings had once stood. But two cellars were shown in the town, otherwise it would have appeared as though there had been no habitation. From the position of the remains of the people who had been burned, it would seem that they had not actually suffered, and this idea is borne out in the fact that the air was so charged with gaseous flame that their lungs must have collapsed immediately after it was inhaled. Wherever the bodies were found indications that the villagers appreciated the frightful fate that was in store for them were apparent, for nearly all laid on their faces, with their arms covering their eyes. Mothers were found lying on top of their babies as if in the endeavor to shelter them from the frightful heat, which followed this awful holocaust.

G. A. LELAND.

GEO. E. NEVERS.
Kept Eating House at Hinckley for State Commission.

In nearly every instance the bodies were found relieved of all clothing, the intensity of the fire having scorched the fabrics so that they were either destroyed or blown away by the cyclone following, and all lay on the ground in a position indicating rapid motion, or an endeavor to run away from the intensity of the fire.

The relief party, during that sad Monday's experience the third day of September, buried sixty-one people in the town of Sandstone. The burial was of necessity of the rudest form. The bodies were in no condition to remain exposed to the heat of the atmosphere, and as no official relief from the coroner could be expected at that time, they were simply laid in trenches not over two feet deep, to await the arrival of the county officials. Each grave was carefully marked so that later on the various bodies could be identified. Upon returning at about seven o'clock in the evening to the river bottom, it was found that those left in charge had succeeded in relieving as much as possible the suffering of the people sheltered in the only building at Sandstone, and while some had died in the meantime and were duly cared for, preparations had been made to remove the others to West Superior or Duluth in the most comfortable manner possible. The bed spring which had been relieved of its wooden frame by the fire, was rigged up into a stretcher, and a piece of canvas brought down by the relief committee was improvised into another. Upon these the unconscious were laid and carefully carried to the river. The only means of crossing was the same cranky flat-bottom skiff, which had to be operated so carefully. The rescued were laid, one at a time, in the bottom of this boat and two of the relief party, one in each end of the skiff, propelled it across to the other bank, where it was received, and its freight carefully taken care of by those on the other shore. After all had had been carried over they had to be taken off by main strength, and carried up the rugged cliffs one hundred and thirty-five feet, with no path, to the point where the railroad track had been.

One of the most active participants of this relief work was Mr. J. N. Hill, son of Mr. J. J. Hill, who seemed to be tireless in his endeavors to relieve the needy, and to help even those who were competent to take care of themselves. In order to make the journey of the burned more comfortable, from the point where they were carried by the relief party at the top of the bluffs of Kettle river to Partridge, seven miles, he had made two or three trips for the purpose of getting such necessary conveniences as could be strung between two hand cars, and thereby make slings in which to lay the almost lifeless bodies of the rescued.   Late in the evening, after discomforts which can only be realized by those who were active participants, they, with their unhappy charges, arrived at Partridge where all were transferred to the train there in waiting, and were afforded such comforts and facilities as the skilled practitioners who were with the party and others could give them.

The train started for West Superior sometime between eight and nine o'clock in the evening and arrived there about midnight.   Communications had been passing by wire between that city and the members of the party, so that upon the arrival of the train quarters had been provided for a large number of the sufferers, and the injured were taken to the hospitals.

Immediately the news was known in St. Paul on Saturday night, that the fire had created such damage, President Samuel Hill, of the Eastern Minnesota road, Mr. R. I. Farrington, comptroller, and others, started Sunday morning, September second, on the St. Paul & Duluth road, got off at Finlayson, and walked across, several miles, to Sandstone, then returned to St. Paul; and on the following day President Samuel Hill again, in order to see if he could do anything to help the sufferers, came to Hinckley on the St. Paul & Duluth, and walked from Hinckley to Sandstone, ten miles, where he met the relief train party above mentioned, which was then engaged in their work at Sandstone.

President J. J. Hill, at the time of the fire, was in Helena, Mont., and upon receiving advices from Duluth of the extent and damage of the fire, it is pleasant to remember, that not considering for a moment his loss or the loss of the railroad company, his first thought was for the distressed people who had been burned out, and he immediately wired authority to make liberal donations of money on his account, and to give instructions to do everything possible for the sufferers.

On Sunday morning following the fire, Superintendent W. V. S. Thorne, Mr. J. J. Hill, Road Master Deviny, and others, started on a special work train for the scene of the fire, in order to ascertain the extent of the damage, no one realizing at that time that the road had suffered so severely.   The party reached Partridge and then walked to Sandstone, taking in the situation, and returning to West Superior in order to make proper reports of the incidents surrounding the disaster.

Mr. Farrington, general manager of the Eastern Railway, also did all in his power to help in the work of mercy and reconstruction.

The second St. Paul & Duluth relief train, which, under the direction of Major Kinney, left Duluth about 4 o'clock p. m., Sunday, September 2nd, carried a liberal supply of all that might be needed in the work of caring for the victims. There were baskets of food, gallons of coffee, ice, liquors, clothing, etc., and among the relief party were several surgeons, two trained nurses and two representatives of the Evening Telegram, Le Roy Thomas and L. E. Wharton.

Near the place where the Hinckley train burned, at Skunk Lake, the party alighted and began a search in the darkness, soon coming upon ten bodies which had been gathered from the neighborhood, and further on were eight more. In a short time a figure was seen coming through the darkness, attracted by the lights of the train. He was ragged, weary and disheartened after a tramp of miles through the desolate woods, and after being fed, told his story of escape from the flames near Hell Gate, and gave the first report of the total destruction of Sandstone. From the bodies he saw in his walk over the town site, he judged the mortality great, and a party was immediately formed to visit the scene, and hastily gathering such necessaries as could be carried, started under guidance of the informant. A walk of three miles through inky darkness, lighted by flickering lanterns, brought them to the government road.

As the first of the party marched along, his swinging lantern struck something at the roadside, which a glance showed to be the body of a young woman, whose arms, stretched upward in the agony of death, had caught the lantern.

It was but the first of many frightful scenes. Upon the whole site there was no sign of life; but descending to the quarry along the river, the party found a few survivors cowering among the rocks and in the little quarry office building, which alone escaped the flames, were gathered the sick and injured, crowded thick upon the floor. It was useless to attempt their removal to the train that night, so after affording all relief possible, the party started on its return, expecting to remove the sufferers in the morning. The newspaper men concluded to remain and spend the night wandering about the quarry; coming upon many ghastly evidences of the fearful flames, and as soon as daylight came, started to investigate the site above, and in a walk of an hour, counted thirty-seven half burned bodies where their homes had stood. The unnatural heat of the preceding day

LIEUT. WALTER McLEAN.

J. F. JACKSON.

made it imperative that the decaying bodies should be buried at once; and so, organizing a force, the work was prosecuted, reinforced later by those who came on the Eastern Minnesota train about noon. Sixty-two bodies were hastily covered in rude graves, marked with such surmise as to their identity as could be made, and the party returned, taking with it such survivors as could be moved.

THE BAILEY EXPEDITION.

Among the many relief expeditions which left Duluth for the relief of the fire sufferers, was that which left over the Eastern Minnesota thoroughly to explore the farms and environs of Sandstone, and discover and minister to the injured and bury the dead. The company was under the efficient direction of Mr. William T. Bailey, an experienced lumberman, and Mr. George E. Ash, surveyor general. There were in the party about thirty skilled woodmen, who were especially valuable in making a thorough examination of the country, and three clergymen, the Rev. Prof. C. A. Pool, of Faribault, and J. H. Sheridan and Albert W. Ryan, of Duluth. The train left Duluth about 3 a. m., Tuesday, September 4th, and arrived at Partridge about 6 a. m. Partridge was the temporary terminus of the railroad, the rest of the track being destroyed by the fire, and was about six miles from Sandstone. The remainder of the journey was made on foot through a black forest burdened with an ominous silence. No sound of beast or bird or insect was to be heard, but on every side were dead bodies of animals and the trees were black and stripped to their utmost boughs by the all devouring flames. The peat was still burning below the surface and the heavy rails had been seriously bent by the furious heat. At Kettle River, the party found the wooden approaches to the bridges entirely consumed, but the wires and bars of iron stood firm and uninjured and gracefully light, one hundred and forty feet high. A pon boat was found and all were ferried over to the town, where nothing was left of the houses of more than six hundred inhabitants except one wretched office and a tool house. Here were gathered the few remaining survivors of the holocaust of the previous Saturday. Clothes and food in plenty were provided for them, and the company broke up into exploring parties, who set out in every direction where any were reported to be missing. Houses, fences, crops, were all burned with the sole exception of the potatoes which seemed mostly uninjured. Often in walking, the feet would break through the surface, and rest on the red hot coals underneath. One party at length reached a farm where a girl was reported lost. She had been safely lying under a wet blanket with her mother and the other children when she decided that she would seek another blanket for herself. Her mother remonstrated, but she persisted. After her departure the mother lifted her blanket and saw a vast flame, fifty feet high, sweep over and engulf her child. The woodmen found her poor body where she had dropped after running wildly about four hundred feet, the last twenty-five of which she had probably run without a stich of clothing on her. A poor box was speedily constructed, a grave dug, and all that was mortal of her body was laid away, while the last offices of the church were being said.

Another party, was not so fortunate in discovering the missing —the bodies being evidently reduced to ashes.

On their return to Partridge that evening the clergy found that some woodmen had discovered the body of a man who had been burned, and they buried it as decently as might be but a little distance from the scene of his death.

Last Tuesday a ghastly find was made in Sandstone. A well had been dug, but proving dry, it was fitted out as a root house. It was reported that there were some bodies here.

A little of the surface dirt was thrown out and a body discovered, but the heat was so intense that further work was postponed until the morrow. On Wednesday, the well was opened and eighteen bodies were discovered, decapitated, dismembered, fairly cooked in the vapors from their own bodies. Little children, men and women, were fairly jammed into a space about six by six feet. It was as ghastly and revolting a sight as imagination could well picture. The bodies were carefully examined, placed in boxes, and carried to the cemetery, where graves were dug. Then amid the stillness of that scene of destruction, the men standing with heads reverently uncovered, the offices of the church were said, and whole families rested in a common tomb. A total of twenty-three bodies were discovered and decently buried. The party returned to Duluth, Wednesday night near mid-night.

The following were in the expedition: Robert Londew, Tim Sheean, James Lynn, Thomas Grady, R. J. Ryan, Sim Lawler, Charles Palmer, William McDonald, James E. Drouillard, Charles Caughill, James Neff, Lea Goodell, William Wardell, Andy Morris, William D. McLaren, Dan Husgy, James McKay, J. B. Michell, D. Hannon,

William Hanley, Thomas Gagnon, James Robinson, J. O'Hara, Allen McDonald, William Shear, J. W. Schmidt, William P. McDonald, W. R. McDougall.

The reader will form some conception of the disagreeableness of the work these earnest men did, when it is stated that of the eighteen bodies taken out of the root house, only three had their heads on. All were in a state of decomposition. These men, in this expedition, had been chosen by Mr. Bailey for their fitness, there was not one who could not have found his way in any forest with a compass in his hand. All were intent on their duty, and each strove to do his full duty, and did it in a way which is a credit to human nature. When some weeks after I met a number of them at the Spaulding Hotel in Duluth, and asked them to send me a photograph of themselves in a group, they spoke of all they had done as being little indeed. Mr. Bailey said: "We did only what any men would have done, if they had been in our places. We never expected fame, and we do not want our names mentioned in the matter."

"Did not you help the living in every possible way, and remove eighteen dead from one place?"

"Yes; it was only our duty."

Such men glorify humanity, and build much better than they know. They are, as Lowell says:

> "The bravely dumb that did their deed
>   And scorned to blot it with a name,
> Men of plain heroic breed
>   That love heaven's silence more than fame.
>
> The den they enter grows a shrine,
>   The grimy sash an oriel burns,
> Their cup of water warms like wine,
>   Their speech is filled from heavenly urns."

These woodsmen proved this September day what true and high qualities are in the souls of many men, whose hands are hard and backs are bent with earnest work, and I have placed these names in this roll of honor, that all men who care may read this story of their service.

MRS. DAVID BUCHMAN.

Rev. William Wilkinson, Dear Sir:

I have been requested by the committee who compiled the enclosed account of the work of the Ladies' Relief Society for the sufferers

MRS. A. M. MILLER.

from the Hinckley fire, to state to you that this account is correct
and that they would prefer that it should be published in this form.

THE LADIES' RELIEF SOCIETY.

It was no small task for Duluth to take in, house, clothe and feed
the 1,200 refugees who came here from the Hinckley fire; yet all
these people were made comfortable and were well provided for from
the very outset. The Ladies' Relief Society was a most conspicuous
and most efficient means of meeting the emergency. Their previous
training in city relief work, well prepared them for the occasion, and
their zeal and effective work never failed during the trying days
which followed, each with its own peculiar kind of need to be met.

When the fire relief train arrived on Saturday night, two of the
ladies met the mayor and proffered the assistance of the society, but
on his assurance that all preparation had been made for their care
that night by the city, under the direction of Chief of Police Armstrong, nothing was done until the next morning, when at 6 o'clock
the headquarters of the Ladies' Relief Society in the Lyceum Building were opened. To these rooms were brought and donated the
600 new garments made by the society and in hand. At 9 a. m. fifty
workers were busy distributing clothing to those previously arrived,
which generous citizens had contributed in sufficient quantities almost to fill the room.

During the morning a committee from the Ladies' Relief Headquarters was sent to the union station to distribute the refugees
among the different families who had offered to care for them, in order to make room for the incoming trains.

The ladies sent by the relief train which left during the night, forty-
seven sacks of clothing, together with fifty pair of blankets, disin-
fectants, medicines, chemicals and bandages, to the scene of the fire,
that the bodies of the dead might be suitably cared for before inter-
ment, and all necessary care given to the living. The work was
conducted at four different points, the Lyceum, Armory, Bethel and
the Glass Block. After eight days the room in the Lyceum proving
too small, the headquarters were transferred to the Mann Block,
where the work continued until the state committee took charge.

Some idea of the onerous duties there accomplished may be gathered, when it is realized that much of the time sixty-eight ladies were
constantly at work, and no less than twenty-two thousand five hundred and ninety-one garments were given out, together with fifteen

hundred pairs of shoes, many hundred yards of new material and household goods, not including furniture which was furnished by the Central Committee.

The relief train which arrived at noon on Sunday brought in three hundred men, women and children, who were immediately sent to the Bethel, where they were fed, bathed and clothed under the direction of the Ladies' Relief Society. This work at the Bethel was continued for nearly a month, the places of those leaving the city being filled by others stopping at various homes and churches. Many of the men, returning to rebuild homes, left their families in charge of the committee at this point.

The Glass Block was another center of activity and no less than one hundred and twenty-five were clothed and given comfortable beds.

The Armory in the Howard Block furnished meals to all the refugees who were not elsewhere entertained. Hundreds were fed each day on excellent food which was bountifully provided, and many of the ladies of the city, unused to such labors, willingly acted as Relief Society in charge at this point. All those not provided with clothing at other places were supplied by the society at the Armory. Some of the refugees were also cared for by the Congregational, Presbyterian and Episcopal churches. Clothing was furnished to each of these churches when needed, from the Ladies' Relief Headquarters. Here and there throughout the city, ladies who were not otherwise occupied, were busy cutting out and making or repairing garments for which the Ladies' Relief Society had need. Not only the present needs of every refugee were looked after, but two additional suits of winter clothing were provided, thus preparing them for the reasonable demands of the future.

Refugees, being cared for by families throughout the city also received their full quota from the Ladies' Relief Headquarters.

MRS. DAVID BUCHMAN, Secretary Ladies' Relief Society.

Together with other generous relief work done in Duluth, during the extreme want which followed the great Hinckley fire, that done by the ladies of the Episcopal Church should not be forgotten. The demand for dormitory accommodations increased constantly all day Sunday. By Monday, the ladies of St. Paul's Church, who were not otherwise occupied with the Ladies' Relief Society work, secured what is known as the Berkleman Block, generously offered by Mr.

W. E. Lucas. Here beds were speedily provided and fire sufferers immediately accommodated. Meals were supplied at the Armory, about two blocks distant, by the city authorities and the Ladies' Relief Society.

For eight days, a varying number of men, women, and children were comfortably housed, and even furnished with medical attendance, when that was necessary. The largest number cared for was eighty-six men, thirty-two women, and ninety-six children, making a total of two hundred and fourteen. Later, all the women and children were taken to the Bethel, but the men were housed for ten days more.

J. J. HILL.

TWO HARBORS.

THROUGH all the reports in the press at the time of the fire, Two Harbors received little, if any attention. The readers of the report of what was done by the hardy sons of toil who live here must keep in mind that this is a new place, and the people have had all the expense attendant upon moving to a distant locality, and are engaged in seeking prosperity, which in part they have found, and the fullness of which they deserve to obtain. This was the second time they had been called upon to help fire sufferers in one summer, and the whole-souled way in which they responded, shows the kind of people who live in Two Harbors. It has been said they gave more per head than any place outside of Pine and Chisago counties. What by way of moral achievements may not be expected from such a people as those who are laying the foundations of this northern town.

CITIZENS' RELIEF MASS MEETING.

"At noon Saturday a brisk southwest wind, hot as the breath of a furnace, was blowing, the atmosphere being very hazy. At 3 o'clock the heavens were shrouded with a sulphurous hue, suggesting an approaching storm. Two hours later the atmosphere was filled with smoke, cinders and ashes. It had become dark as night and lamps were lighted. A red flush covering the entire heavens gave to it the semblance of the canopy of hades, and the average sinners felt that the forerunner of the wrath to come was with them. Kerosene lamps burned with a flare as blue and clear as an arc light, a singlar phenomenon of the atmospheric conditions resultant from the great fires, which obliterated Hinckley and other prosperous towns, and devastated the surrounding country. All night long and part of Sunday the ashes fell, their silent and peaceful settling back to earth little indicating the roar of the breakers of flame, and tortured shrieks which preceded their long flight.

Sunday morning meager reports of the frightful calamity reached here. Monday, when the first tangible intelligence of the extent of the calamity was received, measures were taken to contribute relief. Monday afternoon packages of clothing hastily gathered, and a box of socks and shirts contributed by the Bankrupt Store, were forwarded to the relief committee at Duluth. Monday evening a mass meeting was held at the court house. The secretary's report, published below, indicates that those present were there for business.

TWO HARBORS, MINN., Sept. 3, 1894.

A mass meeting of the citizens of Two Harbors, held in the court house on Monday, September third, at which William Moulton was chosen chairman and Theo. Hannon secretary, it was decided to draw up a set of resolutions, asking the governor of the state of Minnesota to take action looking to the immediate relief of the sufferers in the great fire at Hinckley and adjacent country. The following resolutions were presented by Theo. Hannon and unanimously adopted by a vote of the meeting:

"Whereas, We deeply deplore the terrible calamity which has befallen our unfortunate neighbors in the burned district of Hinckley and adjacent territory; and,

"Whereas, We highly appreciate the inefficiency of individual effort to adequately care for those poor sufferers and provide food, clothing and shelter therefor during the approaching inclement winter; now, therefore, be it

"Resolved, That we, the citizens of Lake county in mass meeting assembled, respectfully petition the governor, the Honorable Knute Nelson, of the State of Minnesota, to adopt such measures as to him shall seem advisable for the appropriating of money from the abundance of the state treasury of the State of Minnesota, for the purpose of rebuilding the homes of the survivors of that most terrible catastrophe.

"Resolved, That a copy of these resolutions duly signed by the chairman and attested by the secretary of this meeting be forwarded by early mail to his excellency, the governor of the State of Minnesota."

On motion of Mr. Coggswell, a committee of ten ladies and five gentlemen which was afterwards changed to eight gentlemen, was appointed to solicit food, clothing and money for the relief of the fire sufferers. The committee were as follows:

Mesdames Coggswell, Budd, Rose, Therrien, Hanna, Gufert, Floathe, Cotter, Tracy.

Messrs. Moulton, Bury, Rock, Hannon, Falk, Munford, W. A. Doerr.

A letter was handed in containing twenty dollars and fifty cents as a donation from the crew on the steamer Washburn. On motion of John Brown a vote of thanks was tendered the crew of the steamer Washburn for their generosity.

On motion the corner store in Brick Block was selected as headquarters for the relief committee. On motion George Munford was elected as chairman of committee to receive and pack goods.

On a call being made for financial contribution names were given with amounts opposite, making a total on the night of meeting, including the steamer Washburn, of $363.50.

The committees were at work early Tuesday morning and the result of their efforts was soon manifest. Clothing began to come in lively, and many who had but recently sent all spare garments to Phillips, contributed cash. Nearly every family in the village contributed something, those without money dividing their supply of clothing. There were contributions of goods from the stores. H. Hanson sent up a good sized box of shoes, and H. Silberstein & Co. gave five dollars in clothing from stock. George Munford, who had charge of the packing, shipped several large boxes Wednesday, their contents being estimated to be five hundred dollars in value.

Tuesday, Foreman Headly made a canvass of the car shops for cash contributions, and collected one hundred and fifteen dollars in a very short time.

The Ellsburg employes, engaged in sloping and filling north of Dock No. 1, made up a purse of forty-nine dollars and fifty cents. John Runquist, John Elsberg, P. J. Anderson and Alex Carlson each gave five dollars, and the remainder was in amounts from twenty-five cents to one dollar. The boys did well.

The aggregate of all cash subscriptions is the magnificent sum of nine hundred and forty-three dollars and ninety-five cents, which has been forwarded to the relief committee at Duluth for disposal. Add the other contributions, and Two Harbors' offering is in the vicinity of fifteen hundred dollars. President Moulton informed the Duluth committee, while in that city Monday, that in Two Harbors was more benevolence to the square inch than in any town in the universe. The people have emphasized his statement.

Duluth Division, Order of Railway Conductors, at their meeting Sunday, appropriated twenty-five dollars from the lodge funds for the relief of the sufferers from the great forest fires.

Two Harbors Lodge, Independent Order of Odd Fellows, notified the grand officers Wednesday morning, to draw on their lodge for twenty-five dollars for the relief of any brethren rendered destitute by the Hinckley fire.

Misses Hitchcock, Marble and Booth, while en route to Two Harbors, Saturday, to enter on their duties as teachers in the village schools, passed through Hinckley about one hour preceding the destruction of that village. At that time fires were burning along the tracks, and the smoke and heat rendered the trip disagreeable, and caused much uneasiness among passengers.

Whenever there's a treasurer of a charitable fund to elect, Dean Burk makes a winning. Tuesday he was the hardest worked man in town, entering deposits in the fire fund. This is one of the delights of being a banker.

REPORT OF ST. PAUL RELIEF COMMITTEE.

M INUTES of the proceedings of the executive committee of the General Relief Committee of St. Paul, organized for the aid of the sufferers by the fires at Hinckley and other points on September 3rd, 1894, at the Chamber of Commerce building.

This Executive Committee appointed by the General Relief Committee, consists of the following persons: E. W. Peet, C. W. Hackett, J. J. McCardy, George Benz, Thomas Cochran, W. J. Footner and W. H. Lightner. The first meeting of the committee was held at the Chamber of Commerce building on September 3rd, 1894, at 12:30. Mr. Peet was elected chairman, and Mr. Lightner elected secretary.

On motion it was resolved that there be appointed a finance committee of five members; said committee having power and authority to solicit and receive subscriptions and report the same to this executive committee. All subscriptions to be turned over to the treasurer, W. B. Bend, and said committee on finance to have power to appoint subcommittees to aid them in their work.

On motion the following was chosen as such finance committee: W. B. Bend, chairman, W. H. Lindeke, E. J. Hodgson, H. C. McNair and Richards Gordon.

On motion a committee on supplies office was created, to have power to solicit and receive all contributions other than cash, to have charge of the depot of supplies and to appoint subcommittees to aid in their work, said committee to report to this executive committee.

On motion the following were appointed a committee on supplies: W. L. Wilson, chairman, M. L. Hutchins, M. J. O'Connor, E. Yanish and James F. Jackson.

The committee then arose to report their action to the General Relief Committee; said action being reported to the General Relief Committee was ratified and approved.

It was then unanimously agreed by the committee that the committee should meet each day at 12 o'clock at the Commercial Club

MAYOR SMITH.

rooms, the use of which were kindly tendered by the president, W. J. Footner.

The meeting then adjourned to 8 o'clock p. m., at the Commercial Club.

W. H. LIGHTNER,
Secretary.

Meeting of the executive committee held at 8 p. m., September 3rd, 1894. Present Messrs. Peet, Hackett, McCardy, Cochran, Footner, Benz and Lightner.

Mr. Kingsbury, on behalf of the Opera House and the company now presenting the play the "Devil's Auction," were present, and offered as a donation all of the receipts for the Friday night, September seventh, entertainment over one-half of the receipts based upon the usual prices; Mr. Kingsbury explained by this it meant that if the committee saw fit to sell tickets at a higher price than the usual rates the opera house would only retain one-half of the usual price of such tickets, the committee thus receiving the entire benefits of the increased price. On motion the offer was accepted and it was ordered that the secretary communicate the offer to the finance committee with the request that they act upon it and communicate with Mr. Kingsbury.

Mr. Tams Bixby being present read telegrams from Duluth, Pine City and other points. Mr. Hackett addressed the committee on the necessity of careful action in the distribution of funds in order that they be properly applied.

On motion of Mr. Cochran the following resolution was adopted: Resolved that Gov. Nelson appoint a state commission authorized to receive contributions of money and supplies for the relief of the sufferers by the forest fires and expend and distribute the same.

Mr. Hackett moved that the committee on supplies be requsted to forward to Pine City at once all hospital supplies, and that Mr. James F. Jackson be requested to proceed to Pine City to direct the distribution of the same and to advise this committee as to the necessities of action.

At the request of Mr. Bixby this committee considered the name of some person to represent St. Paul in the state commission and by unanimous vote instructed the secretary to recommend Mr. Kenneth Clark for such position.

W. H. LIGHTNER, Secretary.

Meeting of the executive committee held September 4th, 1894, at

12 m. All members of the committee being present. Mr. Peet in the chair.

A committee of gentlemen representing the society of Ancient Order of United Workmen offered a donation of one thousand dollars. On motion this was accepted with thanks and a request made that they pay the same to W. B. Bend, treasurer.

Mr. George R. Finch presented to the committee a communication from W. R. Bourne in regard to the suffering of people at Cumberland and Shell Lake, Wisconsin, and in the vicinity. (Exhibit 1.)

A report was received from the treasurer of contributions received by him since the meeting of yesterday morning, amounting to five hundred and forty-seven dollars.

The secretary was instructed to request that the chairmen of the committees on finance and supplies attend the noon meetings of this committee.

On motion of Mr. Hackett it was resolved that the committee on supplies be requested to send to the relief committees at Cumberland and Shell Lake, Wisconsin, such supplies as may be deemed necessary.

On motion of Mr. Lightner it was resolved that the treasurer be instructed to pay to W. L. Wilson, chairman of the committee on supplies, the sum of one hundred dollars, to be expended and accounted for by said committee on supplies.

Bishop Gilbert, who at the request of the general committee, visited Pine City and returned this morning, made a verbal report to the committee of the situation at Pine City and in the vicinity. Among other things he stated that F. A. Hodge, of Pine City, is treasurer of the relief committee at that point, that it was determined at Pine City to request that no further supplies or money be sent except upon requisition from the committee at Pine City. Bishop Gilbert stated that the estimate last night at the scene was that out of a population of sixteen hundred at Hinckley and three adjoining towns the dead numbered four hundred, the homeless twelve hundred, of which eight hundred were destitute.

Col. Bunker (C. S.) also reported on the situation at Hinckley.

A telegraphic report from Mr. Jackson, who had proceeded to Pine City as instructed at the last meeting, was then presented and read. (Exhibit 3.)

On motion of Mr. Benz it was resolved that the treasurer send

$500 to F. A. Hodge, treasurer of the relief committee at Pine City, to be used for pressing necessities.

On motion of Mr. Lightner it was resolved that a committee of three on transportation be appointed; said committee to have charge of transportation matters, including the obtaining of free transportation for the fire sufferers and for other purposes; said committee to report to the executive committee. On motion the following were appointed as said committee: George R. Finch, chairman, Walter A. Scott and George Benz.

A party from the fire district desiring transportation, who was present at the meeting, was referred to this committee.

Mr. Gregg, of the firm of Nichols & Dean, briefly presented to the committee the necessities of the people in the vicinity of Milaca.

On motion the meeting adjourned.

W. H. LIGHTNER, Secretary.

Meeting of the executive committee held September 5th, 1894, at 12 m. Present the entire committee, Mr. Peet in the chair.

Th chairman presented communications as follows:

1. Letter from James F. Jackson, at Pine City. (Exhibit 4.)
2. Later dispatch from James F. Jackson. (Exhibit 5.)
3. Dispatch from Thomas Cochran, at Milwaukee. (Exhibit 6.)

The chairman stated that he had communicated the contents of the telegram to Gov. Nelson.

4. Letter from the secretary of Mayor Smith communicating the offer of Dr. O'Brien to furnish nurses.
5. Letter from Mayor Smith enclosing letter from N. H. Danforth, president of village of Mora.
6. Verbal report to the effect that twenty-five refugees from the village of Mora had arrived and had been taken charge of by Capt. Hart and Gen. Bunker, and placed in the Minnesota Home in St. Paul, and that Dr. Ancker had taken charge of the sick and injured among them. Supplies and clothing ordered to be sent them. Mr. Wilson, chairman of committee on supplies, being present, reported that he had charge of these refugees.

Mr. Finch reported that he had accompanied the supplies to Cumberland and Shell Lake last evening and he had personally superintended their delivery.

On motion of Mr. Benz, Mr. Finch was added as a member of the executive committee.

GEO. BENZ.

W. H. LIGHTNER.

Gen. W. B. Bend made a verbal report of the committee on finance, stating that the subcommittees on collections had been appointed and started out on their work; that he had received in cash since yesterday's report from new subscriptions, nineteen hundred and forty-three dollars and forty-five cents, also a check from the Austin-Corben Banking Company, of New York, for five hundred dollars; also from the New York Life Insurance Company one thousand dollars, being five hundred dollars formerly subscribed and five hundred additional; also that he had received subscriptions of Smith & Parker, twenty-five dollars. The treasurer also reported that he had disbursed five hundred dollars to F. A. Hodge, treasurer at Pine City, and one hundred dollars to Mr. Wilson, chairman of committee on supplies, as directed by the committee yesterday.

Resolved that all applications for temporary relief in St. Paul be referred to the committee on supplies for investigation and action.

It was also resolved that the secretary cause notices to be given to the public through the public press requesting that applications made in St. Paul by parties for relief be referred to the committee on supplies, and asking the public to contribute furniture and household goods. And also announcing that nurses and laborers were not needed at the scene of the fire. Mr. H. H. Hart being present, made a verbal report of the situation at Pine City.

On behalf of the Amateur Base Ball Clubs of St. Paul and Minneapolis, it was stated that a base ball game would be held at Minneapolis on Saturday of this week for the benefit of the fire sufferers, half of the proceeds to be turned over to the relief committee of Minneapolis and half to the relief committee of St. Paul.

On motion this offer was accepted with thanks and it was directed that the proceeds be paid to the treasurer of the committee.

Mr. Benz, on behalf of the Beethoven String Quartet, tendered to the committee the proceeds of a concert to be given by that organization at Ford's Hall on Friday evening of this week.

On motion the offer was accepted with thanks and the proceeds directed to be turned over to the treasurer.

On motion the meeting adjourn

W. H. LIGHTNER, Secretary.

Meeting of executive committee held September 6th, 1894, at 12 m. Present the entire committee, except Mr. Cochran. Mr. Peet in the chair.

Mr. Peet presented a letter from Mr. Cochran.

Mr. Peet presented the offer of Mrs. H. E. Pond to act as nurse. The secretary was instructed to acknowledge the same.

The treasurer presented a report of subscriptions and cash received. (Exhibit 11.) The substance of which was as follows: Cash received since last report, two thousand and four dollars and fifty cents. Prior cash subscriptions paid, six thousand five hundred and seven dollars and forty-five cents. Total cash received, eight thousand five hundred and eleven dollars and ninety-five cents. Disbursed on order of executive committee, six hundred dollars. In addition to the above the unpaid subscriptions amount to eleven hundred and fifty-five dollars.

A committee at Shakopee reported they had clothing and other articles ready to ship, and offered to turn them over to our committee on supplies. The offer was accepted. The committee further offered on behalf of the city of Shakopee to send supplies to the amount of four hundred dollars as ordered. On motion this offer was accepted. It was stated that Jacob Reis, Sr., is chairman of the Skakopee committee.

A telegram was received from Mr. Jackson, at Pine City, making requisition for certain supplies and provisions. On motion it was referred to the committee on supplies with instructions to fill the requisition purchasing such supplies called for and not on hand.

On motion Mr. F. A. Abbott was added to the committee on supplies.

On motion Mr. Hackett was chosen vice chairman of this committee.

Mr. La Grave presented an offer to the committee to give a stereoptican entertainment, of which seventy-five per cent of the gross proceeds should be paid to the relief committee for the sufferers. On motion this offer was accepted and the matter referred to the finance committee.   W. H. LIGHTNER, Secretary.

Meeting of the executive committee held September 15th, 1894. Present, Messrs. Peet, McCardy, Cochran and Footner. Mr. Footner was chosen to act as secretary pro tem.

On motion of Mr. Cochran it was resolved that James F. Jackson be paid for one-half of September at the rate of one hundred dollars per month and actual expenses, and that the treasurer be authorized to settle with him accordingly. Also that the act of the chairman in transferring the services of Mr. Jackson to the state commission be approved

A report of the treasurer (Exhibit 20), showing the total receipts to date of nineteen thousand one hundred and eighty-four dollars and ninety-nine cents was presented.

A donation of twenty dollars from Rachel and Gertrude Hill and their young friends, was turned in and directed to be sent to the treasurer.

A communication from M. L. Hutchins, secretary for the relief of the poor, concerning the fire sufferers at Otter Tail county, was read and referred to the state commission for further investigation and such action as they deem proper.

Meeting of the executive committee held September 18th, 1894.

Mr. Wilson reported the case of William Holm burned at Cromwell, who lost his mill and house. Also on a case of a woman with six children, whose husband was burned at Hinckley.

On motion it was resolved that all cases requiring permanent relief be referred to the state commission, and that the state commission be informed of this action and also be advised that this committee will aid the state commission in furnishing persons who will aid them in attending to such cases.

W. H. LIGHTNER, Secretary.

Meeting of the executive committee held September 24th, 1894, at 12 o'clock, at Commercial Club rooms.

The secretary reported an interview with Mr. Kenneth Clark, treasurer of the state commission, stating that Minneapolis had placed at the disposal of the state commission twenty thousand dollars, and would pay five thousand dollars a week, commencing this week.

The treasurer, Gen. Bend, presented his report, showing cash receipts to date twenty thousand eight hundred and twenty-nine dollars and ninety-two cents; disbursements, by order of this committee, one thousand eight hundred and thirty-seven dollars and forty-eight cents, leaving on hand eighteen thousand nine hundred and ninety-two dollars and forty-four cents.

Mr. McCardy moved that the treasurer pay to the state commission five thousand dollars, and also five thousand dollars next week, and five thousand dollars the following week. This motion was seconded. Mr. Cochran moved as a substitute that the treasurer pay to the state commission treasurer five thousand dollars. The original motion being withdrawn, Mr. Cochran's motion was carried.

An invitation from the Commercial Club to attend a meeting of

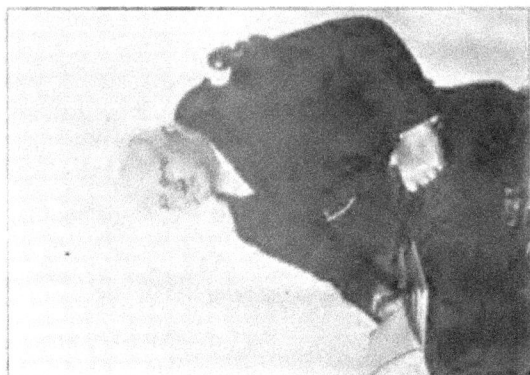

E. W. PEET.

P. H. KELLY.

various bodies to devise if possible some practicable means to cope with the annual recurring forest fires, was presented and on motion accepted.

W. H. LIGHTNER, Secretary.

Meeting of executive committee held September 26th, 1894.

"Resolved, That when we adjourn, that it shall be to meet on call of the president or secretary." Resolution adopted.

"Resolved, That the treasurer call upon Messrs. Griggs, Cooper & Co. for the amount of their subscription, and credit same with the amount they have delivered in provisions."

"Resolved, That Capt. C. W| Hackett be requested to communicate with his correspondents in the southern part of the state, who have communicated with him in regard to the cyclone sufferers, and recommend them to correspond with Gov. Nelson about needed relief, and,

"Resolved, That it is the sense of the committee that the scope of the state commission may be properly enlarged to afford relief to the cyclone sufferers.

J. J. McCARDY, Secretary pro tem.

Meeting of executive committee held October 4th, 1894, at Commercial Club rooms at twelve o'clock, at the call of the chairman.

The secretary presented a bill from Griggs, Cooper & Co. for one hundred and sixteen dollars and firty-three cents for groceries sent to Shell Lake, Wisconsin. Messrs. Griggs, Cooper & Co. having made a subscription payable in groceries, on motion it was ordered that the treasurer settle the same by application of the amount thereof upon the subscription of Griggs, Cooper & Co.

The treasurer presented his report (Exhibit 24), showing total receipts to date twenty-one thousand six hundred and thirty-nine dollars and seventy-four cents; disbursements, six thousand nine hundred and thirty-seven dollars and forty-eight cents, leaving balance of fourteen thousand seven hundred and two dollars and twenty-six cents.

On motion it was resolved that the treasurer pay to the state commission five thousand dollars, including therein credits for moneys which had been disbursed for state sufferers by fire.

W. H. LIGHTNER, Secretary.

Meeting of the executive committee held October 16th, 1894, at 12 ' m., at the Commercial Club rooms.

The treasurer presented his report (Exhibit 25), showing total receipts to date twenty-five thousand and ninety-eight dollars and twenty-eight cents; total disbursements, twelve thousand and fifty-four dollars and one cent, leaving a balance on hand of thirteen thousand and forty-four dollars and twenty-seven cents.

The treasurer also reported that he had paid five thousand dollars to the state commission in accordance with the resolution adopted at the meeting of October fourth; that this payment was all in cash and did not include credits for moneys which had been disbursed for state sufferers by fire. On motion the treasurer's action was ratified.

On motion it was resolved that the treasurer pay to the state commission ten thousand dollars addition, including, however, in such ten thousand dollars, credits for moneys which had been disbursed for the sufferers by fire.

W. H. LIGHTNER, Secretary.

Meeting of the executive relief committee held October 29th, 1894, at the Commercial Club rooms.

Mr. Hackett offered the following resolution which was adopted:

"Resolved, That Treasurer Bend be authorized and directed to pay over to Kenneth Clark, of the state commission, the sum of four thousand dollars.

The following resolution was also adopted:

"Resolved, That the treasurer, secretary, and chairman of the committee on finance, and chairman of the committee on supplies, be requested to make full and detailed statements of all matters in their respective departments at the next meeting of this committee.

On motion meeting adjourned to November 5th, 1894, at 12 o'clock noon, at the Commercial Club rooms.

J. J. McCARDY, Secretary pro tem.

Meeting of the executive relief committee held November 8th, 1894. Present, Messrs. Footner, Hackett, Benz and Lightner.

Mr. Benz reported that German Societies in Chicago were about to hold meetings and entertainments for the purpose of raising funds. On motion the chairman was directed to send a letter of thanks for this action.

On motion the meeting adjourned.

W. H. LIGHTNER, Secretary.

Meeting of the executive relief committee held November 12th,

1894. Present, Messrs. Peet, Hackett, McCardy, Benz and Lightner.

The chairman reported that he had sent a letter to the German societies, as directed at the last meeting.

Mr. W. L. Wilson, chairman of the committee on supplies, presented his report in detail, which was accepted with thanks of the committee for his efficient management and satisfactory report.

Gen. Bend presented his report as treasurer, which was on motion accepted; and together with the report he presented to the committee, his book showing in detail the collections made; he also offered to the committee his checks, receipts, etc., which were declined with thanks.

On motion the secretary was instructed to prepare a final report for the general committee of the actions of this executive committee.

On motion the meeting adjourned.

W. H. LIGHTNER, Secretary.

Report of the executive committee appointed on September 3rd, 1894, by the general committee for the sufferers by fires at Hinckley and other points.

Your executive committee organized immediately upon its appointment, made its headquarters at the Commercial Club rooms, the use of which were kindly tendered by that club, and held daily meetings for the transaction of business for some weeks after their appointment, and have met frequently since that time until their work was completed. A record has been kept of all the formal actions of the committee and most of such actions have been duly reported in the daily press. Your committee appointed several subcommittees, including a committee on supplies which had charge of the depot of supplies and the distribution to the needy sufferers. Also a committee on transportation and various other special committees from time to time. The committee on finance has reported its collections to the treasurer, Gen. W. B. Bend, who has made from time to time frequent reports to the executive committee, and has made his final report.

Accompanying this report your committee submits a very complete and detailed report of the committee on supplies prepared by the chairman, Mr. W. L. Wilson. Also the treasurer's report, which shows that the total amount received and disbursed is the sum of $.........., the greater portion of which, as appears from the re-

KENNETH CLARK.

port, was paid to the state commission. Our committee on transportation took a very active part in furnishing transportation for the fire sufferers and acted mainly in connection with the state commission, to which they furnished a detailed report. In addition to the cash received a large amount of supplies were received, the value of which it is impossible to state, but it is variously estimated at from five to ten thousand dollars. To the cash received and disbursed as stated above the amount of cash does not include the five thousand dollars contributed by Mr. James J. Hill, of this city, which was contributed directly to the state commission.

The records of this committee and the reports mentioned above have been preserved in a book, and by direction of the executive committee with the approval of your body, these records will be deposited for future reference with the Historical Society of Minnesota.

Respectfully submitted on behalf of the executive committee.

W. H. LIGHTNER, Secretary.

MINNEAPOLIS SENDS RELIEF.

It was noon of Sept. 2nd before the mayor of the city had a telegram that the fire in Pine and adjacent counties was of so serious a nature as to call for help from all parts of the state. In all the west no such telegram could have been placed in the hands of a man who would act with more warm heartedness and enthusiasm; his whole administration had been marked by a care for the poor, which had been taken note of all through the state, and far outside its borders. Mayor Eustis' soup kitchen, opened in the winter to serve the needy, had been the subject of discussion in press, pulpit, and on platform. The moment news was spread that Hinckley was a desolation and its people lay dead, he set out to make the facts known and took prompt measures to send help.

No train could be sent direct from Minneapolis nor was it essential, as there was one going from St. Paul. On this Mr. J. T. Mannix left to represent the city and the mayor, who stayed here and knowing that it is lawful to do good on Sunday, he set out to find such men as Geo. R. Newell, Anthony Kelley and other wholesale men and told them of his plan to send a relief train early in the morning. Very late it was that night before the mayor had done his work and at twelve o'clock was going the rounds of the newspaper offices to hear the latest news. Bright and early on Monday, before most men had awakened out of sleep, he was out gathering together all he could to send to Pine City. Every one to whom he spoke entered into his zeal and at eight a. m. a car load of useful things—eatable and wearable—was ready to be sent to the committee at Pine City. Over the St. Paul and Duluth line it was taken. Mr. Ryan sat on a barrel of pork, and Wm. Wilkinson on a box of clothes. At every station on the line the train stopped and into the cars were placed all sorts of things. The people had gathered in throngs at the stations all anxious to hear any scrap of news or see any train going to take help. Women in tears, children of all sizes and conditions, men from the woods, men from offices and mills, and farms, each and all intent on knowing what was being done; many on sending help. As the train passed White Bear men said "Good luck! Send back all the news you can. How many are dead? When do you expect to come back? Will you take us along?" and the like. At Stacey there was a large supply of goods on the platform ready to be sent; and at North Branch yet more; it looked as if the whole county was intent on helping. Here Rev. Mr. Fostroke joined the train, which reached Pine City in due course. All the business men in Minneapolis that day, Monday, knew what had happened and that they would have an opportunity of helping. The papers told the details as far as known. The Tribune and The Times are published in the morning. The Journal and Penny Press are evening papers. All had special editions, which had very large sales. The public interest was very great indeed and soon all was arranged to have the help given conducted in a systematic way. The names of the citizens' committee shows that the men who were upon it represent all that is best in the city.

It was decided to divide the work and classify it. This was done, so the lumbermen, the bankers, the dry goods men and so on were seen as classes, or rather as individuals in those classes. Nothing was left to chance. The finance committee knew what it wanted to do and how to do it. This committee sat daily and gave to every detail of its work a wise and thorough oversight. Every member of it deserves the gratitude of the fire sufferers and all in this state who honor men who do good work for the children of sorrow. Mr. Harvey W. Brown, president of the Gas Light Co., a man who is known well for his generous deeds and interest in the needy, superintended much of the work of collection, especially that in offices. He sent out two gentlemen engaged in their offices—Geo.

N. DeMill and Lawrence S. Shuler, Jr. All the committees did
well and the general committee never slackened its efforts till the
work was ended. The churches led by their pastors, the musicians,
the theater proprietors, men in work shops, and the young ladies
employed in stores each and all assisted. The hospitals took care
of the burned and public bodies as the Odd Fellows, the Knights of
Pythias, the Masons all joined the army of helpers and all deserve
credit alike. It is certain that Minneapolis is never behind in its
readiness to give to any worthy cause in the state. This is its
pleasure and duty. The reports show in detail much that was done.

FIRST RELIEF TRAIN.

It was Sunday, September second, a bright and pleasant day—
one of those delightful days in early autumn which are peculiar to
the Northwest—when the hearts of Minneapolitans were saddened
by the startling information that forest fires had destroyed several
peaceful communities and killed hundreds of human beings. The
wires were in such bad shape during the night that only very meager
reports of the holocaust were presented in the papers the morning
after the visitation. The newspapers published fragmentary statements and in the absence of very definite and positive accounts
the people naturally believed the story to be exaggerated, so far
as the tremendous loss of life was concerned. The community,
with its ever quickened impulses for well doing, was in a fever heat
of excitement, extremely desirous of learning the exact facts in the
case.

Mayor W. H. Eustis, acting with that promptness which is one
of the marked characteristics of the man, made every effort to ascertain, and at an early hour, the true situation of affairs. In response to his telegrams there came to the city hall the most dis-
tressing information, that at least three hundred lives were lost.
His honor, appreciating that the homeless would require immediate
succor, quickly conferred with some of the flour millers and other
prominent citizens, and all were of course ready and anxious to do
everything to relieve the unfortunate people as far as human agencies could relieve, under such terrible conditions. It was the ambition of Mayor Eustis to have the city of which he was the executive represented among the very first contributions shipped to the
grief stricken communities. But it was impossible under the demoralized conditions which existed with the railroads running into
the fire district to get transportaton facilities that day.

Mayor Eustis, appreciating the necessity of having full particulars of the horror, at once sent his private secretary, J. T. Mannix, to the fire section. Mr. Mannix was fortunate in reaching St. Paul in time to take a special train which had been made up by the St. Paul and Duluth railroad people. This train bore a number of newspaper reporters, a squad of militia men, Secretary Richardson, representing the governor, Secretary H. H. Hart, P. H. Kelly and other gentlemen, all alive to the horror of the disaster, and anxious to reach the stricken communities at the earliest possible moment, that they might care for the injured, feed the hungry and console, if possible, the hundreds of bereaved ones. The train also bore a considerable quantity of groceries, the liberal contribution of the Kelly Mercantile Company.

At all the stations along the line there were people who were delighted beyond the power of human beings to express when they saw that swift going relief train. At a number of points, particularly White Bear, the thoughtful people had hurriedly gathered food and clothing, and these were added to the stock taken from St. Paul. Rev. Father Burke joined the relief party at White Bear. He was a welcome and very valuable worker in the fire section.

It was nearly evening when the relief train reached Pine City. The people of that hospitable community had anticipated the relief train, and the local committee and other prominent citizens were on hand to communicate the sad facts in the case. It was a time when work had to be done, and done with the greatest possible expedition. The local committee, with Thomas Hurley as chairman, met with those on the relief train, who had come up to assist in the great relief work. The meeting was held in one of the passenger coaches. After an hour's discussion of the situation, the local committee was strengthened by making Secretary Hart, of St. Paul, Judge Nethaway, of Stillwater, Daniel Moon, of Duluth and J. T. Mannix, of Minneapolis, members. An hour later this enlarged committee met in one of the halls of the city and proceeded at once with the great work, which for two weeks was conducted in a manner that elicited much praise. Mr. Hurley was very properly continued in the chairmanship. The general committee was divided into sub-committees on burial of dead, commissary, transportation, etc. The committee met every morning at nine o'clock, and the work was done with the greatest possible system consistent with such demoralized conditions as existed at the time.

When the relief train reached Pine City and the extent of the calamity became known, the bare facts were telegraphed Mayor Eustis. The immediate needs of the afflicted section were indicated, and some suggestions in regard to clothing, etc., were made. The next morning there came to Pine City a car load of groceries, bedding, general clothing, etc., the first installment of Minneapolis' noble contribution. The committee quickly disposed of these goods, and then telegraphed the good people of the Twin Cities just what was needed.

This is but a general statement of the first relief work. The general local committee, as the Pine City committee was called, got things in good shape for the State Relief Commission, which succeeded to the great and humane work. The splendid work of the local committee, and particularly of the Pine City members of that committee, is certainly deserving of every praise. Amid the horror and gloom of that most terrible visitation, the members of that committee worked manfully and incessantly and brought something like order out of the chaos and confusion that prevailed in the fire district.

MINNEAPOLIS RELIEF COMMITTEE.

First meeting of the Citizens' Relief Committee, held Monday, September 3rd, 1894, at Commercial Club Rooms.

Meeting called to order by Mayor W. H. Eustis, who stated why the meeting was called. On motion by the mayor Mr. C. A. Pillsbury was called to the chair. The chairman stated that the first business would be the election of a secretary, and on motion adopted, Mr. W. H. Rendell was chosen.

Mr. Pillsbury made a few remarks on the importance of immediate action and called on those present for their opinions as to the best method of proceedure. After considerable discussion Mr. P. B. Winston offered the following resolution:

Whereas, Terrible and destructive forest fires have visited the Northern part of our state causing great loss of life, and rendering homeless hundreds of our fellow citizens,

Resolved, That the chairman of this meeting is authorized to appoint a committee of twenty-one, for the purpose of securing immediate relief for the sufferers, and that the committee is empowered to increase this committee and to appoint other committees with full power to act;

Resolved, Further, that the Mayor of this city is requested to call

MAYOR W. H. EUSTIS.

a special meeting of the city council tonight, to take such action as is in their power for the relief of the fire sufferers.

The chairman appointed as this committee C. A. Pillsbury, chairman; P. B. Winston, W. H. Eustis, Rev. Dr. Hoyt, Geo. W. Marchant, O. B. Clark, C. M. Loring, W. H. Rendell, J H Sullivan, Senator Washburn, Geo. R. Newell, W. J. Dean, Dr. Higbee, Senator F. F. McMillan, R. B. Squires, Geo. A. Brackett, A. C. Haugan, Rev. J. M. Cleary, W. H. Warrington, J. C. Haynes, and B. F. Nelson.

Mr. O. B. Clark, agent Adams' Express Co., offered to carry free anything for the relief of the fire sufferers. His offer was accepted. Mr. Theo. Hayes offered to give a benefit at the Bijou Theater, Saturday evening. On motion adopted the offer was accepted.

Misses Salisbury and Satterlee to give two cots; offer accepted.

Mr. O. B. Clark was apointed to secure special train to start for the scene of the fire as soon as possible.

A motion by Mr. R. J. Anderson, that a committee consisting of Eugene Hay, Rev. Dr. Hoyt, R. J. Anderson and Senator Washburn to draw up a memorial to be sent to Engineer J. M. Root for his bravery in saving so many lives, was adopted. Meeting adjourned   W. H. RENDELL.

FIRST MEETING OF EXECUTIVE COMMITTEE.

Meeting was called to order by Chairman C. A. Pillsbury.

On motion adopted. J. H. Sullivan was elected secretary and P. B. Winston treasurer.

On motion by Senator Washburn, F. G. Winston, W. J. Dean, Nelson Williams, J. T. Wyman and H. W. Brown were appointed committee on finance; and P. B. Winston, C. M. Loring, A. E. Higbee, Rev. Dr. Hoyt and Geo. W. Marchant, committee to start for the scene of the fire at once and report to the meeting on Tuesday at three o'clock p. m. Dr. Higbee was empowered to purchase anything necessary for immediate use.

A motion by Mr. Pillsbury was adopted to send out an appeal through the papers to associations and churches next Sunday, to raise subscriptions as soon as possible for the fire sufferers, for which work Dr. Hoyt and Mayor Eustis were appointed.

Mr. Dean made a motion which carried, that a sub-executive committee be appointed, composed of Messrs. C. A. Pillsbury, Mayor Eustis, Geo. R. Newell, P. B. Winston and H. W. Brown.

Report of adjourned meeting of the Executive Committee of the Citizens' Relief Association held at the rooms of the Jobbers' & Manufacturers' Association September fourth, 1894, 3 o'clock p. m.

The meeting was called to order by Chairman Pillsbury, who stated that its purpose was to hear the report of the committee of visitation and inquiry, and to decide on what action to take for the permanent needs of the fire sufferers. Rev. Wayland Hoyt read the report, which was accepted. Mr. F. G. Winston reported for the finance committee that the chairman was meeting with much success and was well received everywhere. Mayor Eustis stated that Gov. Nelson had issued a proclamation, asking the different towns and cities to aid the sufferers, and had appointed an executive committee consisting of C. A. Pillsbury of Minneapolis, Kenneth Clark, of St. Paul, Mr. Graves, of Duluth, Mr. Norton, of Winona, and Mr. Hart of the state board of Correction and Charities, to look after the needs of the fire sufferers. Mayor Lewis, of Duluth, who was present, made a few remarks on the condition of things on the Duluth side of the fire. Mr. W. C. Gregy, who had just returned from Milaca, stated that about 30 families had been completely burned out at that place and had lost everything. On motion adopted, Mr. F. B. Nelson, Geo. R. Newell and J. H. Sullivan were appointed auditing committee to audit all bills before the same were paid. On motion by Mr. Pillsbury, Mr. H. W. Brown was elected vice president. A gentleman from the Musicians' Association was present and stated that they would like to give a sacred concert at the Exposition building, Sunday afternoon, and turn into the treasury the receipts. On motion adopted the meeting adjourned. J. H. SULLIVAN, Secretary.

To Citizens' Relief Committee: Gentlemen:—Acting under the instructions of the committee, and asking Doctors Norton and McDonald to assist in the work, I visited Pine City to look after the wounded and sick there, who were victims of the fire. At the depot we were joined by Doctors J. T. Moore and S. S. Kilvington and Mulberg, of Minneapolis, Foster, of St. Paul, Perkins, of Excelsior, and Mitchell, of Shakopee. Upon arriving at Pine City we found the seriously burned gathered together in an old warehouse, and sadly in need of medical attendance. This was given as rapidly as possible and as efficiently as the surroundings would allow. All the medical men joined in the opinion that it was impossible to give the injured the care required, as they were situated, and in consultation with Mr. C. M. Loring and the committee from Minneapolis, acting with the local committee, it was decided to remove the most seriously injured to this city, and place them in the hospitals here. Accordingly at noon Tuesday, the 4th day of September, ten adults by train offered us by Superintendent Miller of the St. Paul and Duluth Railroad were brought to this city and sent to the following hospitals:

At Asbury, Mrs. Otto Olson, aged 35 years (lost husband and three children), burned on head and face, respiratory organs injured by inhaling hot air and smoke, will recover. Mr. Nels Friske, age 42 years, right eye bruised and burned, both hands and wrists burned, and lungs inflamed; will recover. At Northwestern Hospital, Mrs. May Olson, 31 years of age, burned on face and head, respiratory organs injured. Ella Olson, 2 years old; not burned. Gurt Olson, 4 years old; burned on face. These are children of Mrs. Olson. Mrs. Olson will recover. Mrs. Agusta Will, age 31 years; burned on face and hands, inflammation of lungs caused by smoke and hot air; will recover. Mrs. Hilda Benton, age 18 years, daughter of Mrs. Will. These two women report no friends and no place of shelter. Dr. Norton carefully investigated the case of Mrs. Benton and reports her worthy of aid. At Homeopathic Hospital, Mr. M. E. Greenfield, age 50 years; eyes very badly burned, had pneumonia, will recover. Mrs. M. E. Greenfield, age 27 years, terribly burned on chest, abdomen, back, arms and legs; recovery very doubtful, or if she does will be a matter of months. Chas. Greenfield, son of M. E. Greenfield, age 10 years, only slight burns. Mrs. and Mr. Greenfield lost five children and everything they possessed, did not have an article of clothing. They are reported very worthy; the boy was brought with his parents. Betty Westerland, age 35 years, face badly burned, pneumonia and prostration; was in water eight hours; worthy and will recover. At St. Mary's Hospital, Emma Hammond, age 48 years, burned on nearly every portion of her body; recovery very doubtful. Do not think this case demands the charity of the committee only so far as medical attendance is required. John Larson, age 36, burned on hands, face and slightly on body; worthy and will recover.

These hospital cases require much care and attention; some of them a great deal of care and expensive dressings, and I would strongly recommend that the hospitals caring for them be allowed a dollar a day for each adult; this to cover all charges of every kind.

ALBERT E. HIGBEE, M. D.

Your committee of visitation and inquiry started for the scene of suffering and of help yesterday afternoon. While waiting change of train at White Bear, they organized. Hon. C. M. Loring was made president and Mr. George N. Marchant secretary. By resolution of the committee, Dr. Higbee was made general medical director.

Dr. Higbee had requested Doctors Norton and Macdonald to accompany him; and at the suggestion of his honor, the mayor, and by glad volunteering, these additional physicians, Doctors Moore Nippert, Kilvington, Muldberg and Fitzgerald, of Minneapolis, and Dr. Mitchell, of Shakopee, and Dr. Perkins, of Excelsior, were accompanying; and at once at the suggestion of your committee most cheerfully put themselves under the general direction of Dr. Higbee, that all medical ministry might be speedily apportioned and accomplished.

Mr. Sapendtier, of Minneapolis, was also requested to act as druggist.

The other members of your committee held themselves ready to do whatever service might be set for them; especially were they to gather all possible facts as to the general condition of affairs, that they might present to you the direct and most accurate account just then obtainable.

On arriving at Pine City, part of the committee stopped there, that point being, for our side of the fire, the base of operations, and the place to which most of the injured on our side have been and are being carried; and is also the place where, from our side, most of the burned-out people have been and are gathering. Mr. O. P. Clark and Dr. Kilvington went out at once to Hinckley, to see if any service of any sort could be rendered by your committee there. On their return they reported that nothing whatever could be done at Hinckley, that everything that could be done was either already accomplished, or was being done by most efficient hands at that place.

Meanwhile the members of our committee at Pine City set themselves to work there. The medical stores were unloaded, taken to the rink, which serves as a hospital at that point, and the physicians at once applied themselves to the dressing of the burns and wounds of the injured, and making them as comfortable as possible. The other members sought at once to gain as clear an undertaking as they could of the condition of affairs.

It may be as well stated here as anywhere, that one member of the committee, Mr. Marchant, remained upon the ground to visit more thoroughly the burned district, and to discover additional facts, and to present to you a supplemental report, should such report be found necessary.

The town of Hinckley, numbering alone one thousand inhabitants —some say fifteen hundred or even more; Sandstone, numbering about three hundred; Mission Creek, about one hundred; Brook Park (or Pokegama), about one hundred, and Partridge, about one hundred, have been devastated, and all, save Partridge, totally destroyed by the fire. This makes, in round numbers, about two thousand people who have been burned out. From this two thousand about four hundred—it may be more, it may be less—are to be deducted, who are dead. Thus sixteen hundred people are left destitute. From this is to be deducted about one hundred and fifty operatives, who will probably never return, but drift variously away. This leaves about fourteen hundred and fifty people who will need care, food, clothing and various assistance.

The fire was so terrific and so awfully swift in its destructive energy, that there are, considering the number of dead, comparatively few injured people. In the hospital at Pine City, nine were lying severely, and some dangerously burned. There was also quite a large number of persons, whose burns having been dressed by the physicians, have gone from their care, exactly how many, it is as yet impossible to find out. It is estimated that at least ninety-five per cent. of the burned-out are nearly or entirely destitute. As nearly as can be estimated, about eight or nine hundred destitute people have been and will be dependent upon the depot of supplies and service at Pine City. Some of these are single men and operatives, who will have to be fed for a time, supplied with clothing, and given transportation to some other points. There are no sufferers now known to be at any of the places struck by the fire. All have been removed to Pine City, to Superior or to Duluth.

It is possible that the searching parties, who today are scouring thoroughly the entire neighborhood of the places smitten by the fire, may discover other sufferers not dead, but injured. It is probable that other dead bodies will be thus discovered. We find the organization at Pine City well in hand, and most efficiently working.

MRS. JESSIE SMITH, STENOGRAPHER TO MR. PILLSBURY.

ANNA M. KRIEDT, MAYOR'S STENOGRAPHER.

Indeed, too much praise cannot be bestowed upon the way in which the organization at Pine City has grasped this great calamity, to manage it, to help and soothe the sufferers. This organization is as follows: There is a general relief committee composed of citizens of Pine City, Minneapolis, St. Paul, and Stillwater. Under this general committee are, thoroughly equipped and in complete order, the following subcommittees:

First. An executive committee composed of Mr. James Hurley, a prominent merchant; Mr. Hodge, county auditor, and Mr. Breckinridge, the secretary of this committee, all of Pine City.

Second. A committee on registration, of which Mr. H. H. Hart, the president of corrections and charities of the state, is the efficient chairman. Mr. Hart has had cards printed on which, filling out the approximate blanks, is accurately registered, everything about each applicant, and thus fraudulent applications are abundantly guarded against.

Third. A committee on burials composed of Mr. J. G. Lonnely of St. Paul, Mr. H. I. Davis of Hinckley, Messrs. A. G. Perkins, John W. Hunt, and Frank Webber of Pine City. This committee is carefully and swiftly attending to the burial of the dead, and have already nearly completed their sad task.

Fourth. A commissary committee of which Mr. F. A. Hodge of Pine City is chairman. This commissary committee is feeding the persons to whom meal tickets are issued by the registration committee, drawing its supplies on requisition from the warehouse of supplies—a church, the use of which was tendered for the purpose. In this warehouse all supplies which have as yet been sent, have been deposited, and accurate account is taken and kept of them.

Fifth. A committee on care of the sick, in whose charge is the hospital.

Sixth. A financial committee, of which Mr. Albert Pennington, a well known merchant of Pine City, is chairman. This committee consists of five, including Mr. Mannix, as representing Minneapolis, and Mr. Dan H. Moore, as representing St. Paul. The duty of this committee is to audit all bills and to order the payment of the same by the treasurer.

Seventh. A general treasurer, Mr. Fred Hodge, a gentleman of wealth and position in Pine City. To Mr. Hodge all money contributions should be sent. It is to be said that his appointment to this position may, and probably will, cause his withdrawal from serv-

ice on other committees. On the whole, and considering the extent
and suddenness of the calamity, the organization set up at Pine City
is marvelously strong, accurate and in splendid running order.

Eighty tents have been supplied by the state for the use of the
burned-out families and single persons. Fifty of them are pitched
at Pine City, and twenty at Hinckley, for the shelter of those engaged
in burying the dead. Ten we held in reserve to be pitched where
and when they may be needed. These tents we find abundantly
supplied with cots, bedding, blankets, etc. There is immediately
needed, however, a lot of lumber for flooring to the tents. We also
find that Gen. Merrit has sent fifty regulars from Fort Snelling to do
any service which may be needful, and also a hospital steward with
hospital supplies. At the suggestion of Dr. Higbee and other physicians, your committee telegraphed His Honor, Mayor Eustis, to
send for hospital service in Pine City three trained women nurses.
These nurses, together with Dr. Martha Ripley, left for Pine City on
the 10:10 train last night. After the telegram was sent and after
Dr. Ripley and the nurses had started, it was thought on further examination of Dr. Higbee and other physicians, that since some eight
or possibly nine of the sufferers were so badly burned as to need long
and constant attention, and since, in order to recover, they could
be vastly better cared for should they be taken from the extempor-
ized hospital at Pine City to the permanent and thoroughly furnished
hospitals of Minneapolis, therefore they suggested that these sufferers
be removed to Minneapolis. Your committee sanctioned such removal. Dr. Ripley and the nurses were of great value last night
in relieving wearied attendants upon the sufferers, and will be of
indispensable service today, as these sufferers are transported to their
destination.

It was found that, for the present, there are abundant supplies of
every sort at Pine City. In view of all the above, the following
suggestions seem wise:

First. That no further supplies of perishable sort be sent, at least
until there should be direct call for them by the committees at Pine
City.

Second. That in all our future endeavors we co-operate with the
efficient organization already working at Pine City.

Third. That whatever money and supplies may be contributed
hereafter by Minneapolis, be not immediately sent to Pine City or
elsewhere, but be held by the proper persons here in treasury depot,

to be sent as the committee in Pine City may make requisition for them.

Fourth. That inasmuch as the surviving sufferers, both injured and uninjured, have lost in almost every case, their entire clothing, stores, bedding, etc., the citizens of Minneapolis be asked to contribute such articles, which shall be sent for depot to Mr. Holt, of the Associated Charities of Minneapolis, who shall be requested to sort, and, if need be, repair them; and that the committee at Pine City draw on Mr. Holt for such articles. Here everything in the shape of clothing will be of use, underwear, outerwear, stockings, shoes, etc., for men, women and children; also bedding of every sort. It is to be remembered that the season for summer wear has nearly passed, and at the suggestion of Mr. Marchant, whose efficient service in the helping of the St. Cloud sufferers has made his experience so valuable in the present case, we think it a good idea for the good people of Minneapolis to mingle with their gifts of clothing, some dolls and toys for the burned-out children. Such gifts will help the children and the wearied mothers also.

Fifth. Let it be remembered that the burned-out sufferers have lost everything in the shape of stores, kitchen utensils and house furnishings of all kinds; consequently such things as these will be greatly needed, and we would suggest the appointment of a special committee, who shall make depot for such articles and have charge of them, and keep themselves informed as to special need for these things, in correspondence with the secretary of the general relief committee of Pine City, Mr. J. G. Loring of Pine City.

Sixth. That all the churches and other organizations in Minneapolis be asked to make offerings for the sufferers next Sunday, or as near that date as possible. That these offerings be all sent to Mr. F. G. Winston, the treasurer of the general committee of Minneapolis, to be disbursed by him at the call of the committees in Pine City. It is to be remembered that a very large proportion of the sufferers have lost everything; that they need to be assisted to get upon their feet again, and that it is essentially necessary that there be in Minneapolis a sum of money in hand, which can be drawn upon as the committees in Pine City shall investigate each case, and indicate the amount of money to be disbursed for the same. It should be and is, most gladly said by your committee, that we found the St. Paul & Duluth Railroad Company as accommodating as possible. No least suggestion or request was made by us which was

WAYLAND HOYT, D. D.

FALK M. GJERTSEN, M. A.

not instantly seconded and met by the railroad officials at the earliest minute possible.

CITIZENS' RELIEF ASSOCIATION.

Called to order by Chairman C. A. Pillsbury at 3:30 o'clock p. m. Mr. Pillsbury stated that he was going away soon and if it were the desire of the other members, it would be well to close up matters, and it was so ordered.

The bills from the Northwestern, St. Mary's, and Homeopathic hospitals were allowed and ordered paid.

On motion by Mr. O. B. Clark, that the funds in the hands of the treasurer be turned over to the state commission, it was so ordered.

It was the sense of the meeting that a supplementary list of contributors be published.

On motion by Mr. P. B. Winston, Mr. Pillsbury was given a hearty vote of thanks for the very efficient manner in which he performed his duties as chairman.

On motion by Nelson Williams, a medal and a resolution were ordered sent to the fireman on Engineer Root's train. Adjourned.

At a regular meeting of the Citizens' Relief Association of Minneapolis, held October 22nd, 1894, the following resolution was unanimously passed:

Resolved, That this committee now, at the ending of its service and final report, tender to the St. Paul & Duluth Railway Company their heartfelt thanks for many favors and kindnesses shown, and especially do we thank General Manager Mr. A. B. Plough, and Assistant General Manager Mr. L. S. Miller, for their untiring efforts in getting the special committees and physicians appointed by the citizens' committee, to Hinckley, there and return; and for their free transportation of fire sufferers to this city; and the sending of supplies to Pine City, Minnesota; and that a copy of this resolution be sent to Manager Plough and Assistant General Manager Miller, and that it be printed in our daily papers.

STATEMENT.

Source.	Book No.	Cash.	Mdse.	Total.
Attorneys	10	$561.00	....	$561.00
Wholesale dealers	2	2,666.52	$160.00	2,826.52
Banks, bankers, etc	3	5,763.87	520.00	6,283.87
Chamber of Commerce	4	2,453.00	....	2,453.00
Lumbermen	5	530.00	2,650.00	3,180.00

Source.	Book No.	Cash.	Mdse.	Total.
Commercial Club	6	12.00	....	12.00
Commission dealers	9	150.00	....	150.00
Ag'l implement dealers	12	570.50	25.00	595.50
General subscriptions..1 and	8	314.35	....	314.35
Mayor's office	.	3,721.68	3,740.73	7,462.41
Outside subscriptions	7	1,288.52	150.00	150.00
Office subscriptions	13	4,699.49	....	5,988.01
Totals		$22,730.93	$3,505.00	$29,976.66
			3,740.73	

Cash $22,730.93
Merchandise 3,505.00
Due from mayor........ 3,740.73—uncollected.

Total $29,976.66

George D. Holt, the secretary of the Associated Charities of Minneapolis since its organization in 1885, was secured by the commission to represent it and conduct its work of registration and permanent relief at Duluth.

He accompanied the commission and Mayor W. H. Eustis on their first visit to that city on September seventh, and together with them looked over the field and remained in charge of the work at that place until he had named his successor, and was placed by the commission permanently in charge of the relief work at Hinckley and vicinity.

Mr. Holt's experience in the conduct and management of the fire relief work connected with the extensive Northeast Minneapolis fire, occuring in August, 1893, at which one hundred and seventy-five poor families were rendered homeless in a night, the better fitted him for the painstaking, arduous and often thankless task of rendering immediate temporary aid to bonafide and deserving fire sufferers only, and still help them without fostering dependency to permanent relief, and final disposition.

THE HOMŒOPATHIC HOSPITAL.

The authorities of this institution took great care of Mrs. Greenfield. It was a wonder to many who knew the seriousness of the injuries she had sustained, when it was told that she was recovering. Only great skill and the most faithful nursing could have brought this about. She was, all through her illness, oppressed with the memory of the sad end of her five dear children, who died before her eyes, and also with the knowledge of the fact that her faithful and hard working husband had to begin live anew, having lost his all. It is a providence to him that his wife is spared to help him in the future, as in the past.

Mr. Greenfield's conduct all through the eight months' work of the state commission commended him to it.

Mrs. Greenfield, a victim of the fire north of Hinckley, was brought to Minneapolis and assigned to the Homeopathic hospital September 4th, 1894. Upon examination of her injuries, it was found that the burns and wounds covered two-thirds of her entire body, and were of so serious a nature that the physicians entertained little hope of saving her life. For five long months she lay unable to help herself in any way. The burns were so deep and severe that any attempt to move aggravated the pain and caused bleeding from the large raw surfaces.

Special care was given her day and night, and at first it was necessary to dress the wounds every four hours with cerates and antiseptics. As she improved, the dressing, of course, was done less frequently; much patience was requisite in caring for her, as such extreme suffering of so long standing causes irritability, for which a patient should not be held responsible.

As recovery advanced she manifested by the many kind things she said, her gratitude for what had been done in her behalf, and realized that she had been saved from the very jaws of death.

Dr. Matchen deserves great credit for his skill displayed in the treatment of this case, as well as for his kindly attendance, for Mrs. Greenfield was not only the worst burned of all the victims who recovered, but naturally the case was of long continuance. It was nearly seven months from the date of her entering this hospital before she was able to leave it. The care given was of the best, and nothing was spared which could benefit her.

Mrs. Greenfield, in addition to her physical suffering, had the grief to bear of the loss of five children by the fire; four daughters and one son.

MINNEAPOLIS, MINN., April 26, 1895.

In answer to your letter, we shall say that two cases of the fire sufferers were sent to St. Mary's Hospital, Minneapolis. Mr. Larson

got well enough to leave the hospital in two weeks. Mrs. Hammond was taken with pneumonia, besides being burned very severely
all over; she is now just able to take care of herself, but not to work.

Yours respectfully,

SISTER JANE FRANCES.

Fully 2,500 people paid admission to hear the concert given by the
Minneapolis Musicians' Association in the Exposition hall yesterday
afternoon, in behalf of the fire sufferers. Long before the doors
opened a large crowd was gathered at the entrance and was waiting
for the first chance to get the best seats, but on account of the size
of the hall those who came late even were not disappointed in regard
to seats. The crowd was enthusiastic and showed its appreciation by
generous applause, number after number being encored, and the
speeches which were interspersed through the program were listened
to with rapt attention, and very often the speaker touched a responsive chord in the hearts of his audience, and then the applause
was great. The hall was prettily decorated with ferns, the gift of
some of Minneapolis' florists, and everything about the entertainment
was donated by generous Minneapolis people, and apt was the remark which Mayor Eustis made in the course of his remarks, namely,
that he was well pleased with the flavor of Minneapolis giving.

The program from the musical standpoint was one of the finest
which had been given in this city, and the Musicians' Association
may well feel proud of this effort in behalf of charity. The band
was composed of fifty-two pieces, and the selections which it rendered
were of first-class quality; the musicians seemed to be in sympathy
with their work. Rossini's "William Tell" was played with wonderful effect, and the applause which followed showed that the audience
appreciated the effort. The selection from Donizetti's "Lucia" by the
grand opera quartet received a merited recall, and the popular Masonic quartet's selection also was well received. Mr. Laird's cornet
solo and Frank Danz, Jr.'s, violin solo were features of the program.

Mayor Eustis, in his address, was at his best, and as he related
incidents that occurred in his efforts in behalf of the sufferers, his
hearers were moved to tears; as he told of the deeds of heroism and
of self-sacrifice which have characterized the people in the fire-ridden
district he was interrupted often by the plaudits of the people who
admired bravery. The address of Rev. Father Cleary was along
the line of congratulating the citizens of Minneapolis on their whole-
hearted generosity. Rev. W. H. Geisweit closed the program by

thanking those who rendered their services gratis and thus made the concert yesterday afternoon possible.

The receipts from the concert will foot up to about $1,200, as there were about 5,000 tickets sold.

During the week, Prof. J. A. Walker, with 200 of his pupils, will give his "Pageant of Nations," which was so popular at Lake Harriet this summer, in the Exposition hall. A number of new dances will be presented, and the proceeds from the entertainments will be devoted exclusively to the fire sufferers. Jim Root, the brave engineer, will tell his experience tomorrow night.

Detailed statement of subscriptions to fire relief fund turned over to Chairman Winston, of the finance committee, up to this noon, September 15th; this will undoubtedly be augmented by other returns, such as baseball, theatrical and musical entertainments that are waiting for complete returns from sale of tickets, etc., before reporting. Benefit sales of merchants, etc., will be reported when heard from. Same as to churches and societies not yet heard from.

So far reported from Bijou Theater, $1,400; People's Theater, $979.50.

Arcade Investment Company, $25; Altman, Taylor Machine Company, $25; Ally, A. J., $5; Aultman, C. & Co., $5; Aultman, Miller & Co., $25; Appleton Manufacturing Company, $5; Advance Thresher Company, $25; Arnott & Corbett, $10; Ames, E. B., $5; Ancient Order Hibernians, Division No. 1, $50; Andrew Presbyterian Church, $22.40; American Loan Association (officials), $63; Amsden, C. M., $20; Austin, Horace, $10; Allen, J. S. & Co., $10; Advent Church, $14; Atwater, J. B., $50; Anderson, Dr. J. D., $50; Allen, J. S., $1; Ainsworth, C. F., $1; Ankeny, John J., $1; Allen, A. E., $1; Alexander, J. B., $1; Adler, Max & Co., $5; All Saints' Church, $6; Abbott, J. H. & Co., $5; Adams, J. Q. & Co., $25; Andrews & Gage, $10; American Express Company (employes), $10.50; Ainsworth, G. A., $1; Altman & Co. (clothing), $100; Averill, H. S., $1; Arcana Chapter, O. E. S., $5.

Brown, H. W., $250; Bank of Minneapolis, $125; Beall, George S., & Co., $10; Bell, D. C., Investment Company, $25; Bauman, J., $5; Brown, Haywood Co., $25; Bradbury, George B., & Co., $10; Bass, G. W., $5; Bemis Bros. Bag Company, $100; Butters, William, $5; Budd, O. P., Kasota, Minn., $10; Babcock, C. W., Kasota,

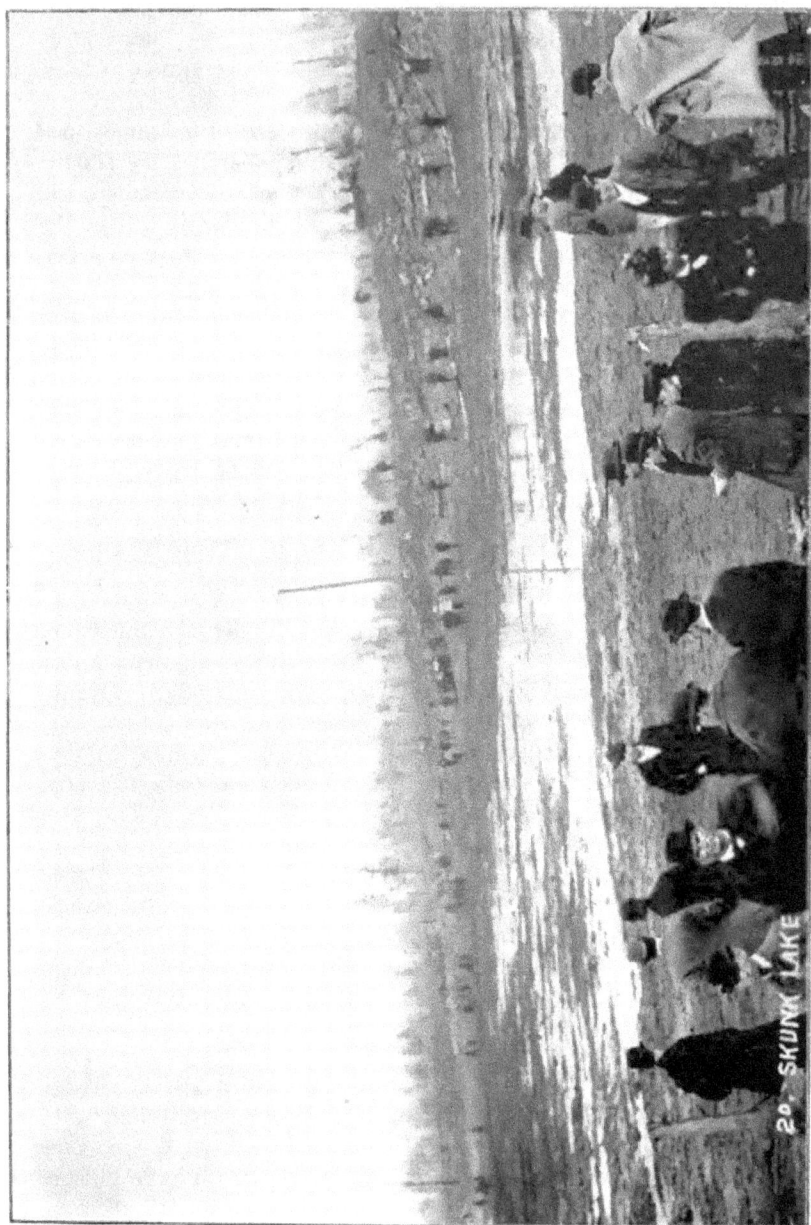

2b. SKUNK LAKE

Minn., $25; Babcock, Mary E., Kasota, Minn., $5; Baily, F. B., $5; Black, Rev. George D., $5; Brick Layer's Union, by Gus Bloom, $10; Barton, A. B., $5; Bismarck Grove, No. 32, U. A. O. D., $10; Blodgett, ——, $2; Benton, R. C., $10; Barnes, H. E., Jr., $5; Booth, Wilbur F., $5; Brown, Jalew, 50 cents; Bram, J. A., $5; Best, E. D., 50 cents; Bladon, James, & Co., $5; B. &. P., $2; Brown, Dan C., $2; Bogerth, G., $1; Bovey, DeLaittre Lumber Company, $200; Brown, H. F., $200; Bassett, J. B., & Co., $100; Backus, E. W., & Co., $100; Bailey, L. J., $5; Bison, J. M., $2; Bealls, W. R., $5; Bucheler, A., $10; Bradney, Joseph, $5; Boys, $6; Barber, D. R. & Son, $20; Brown, W. P., $5; Brooks, Griffith & Co., $25; Bagley, George C., Elevator Company, $25; Berger Commission Company, $10; Benton, W. S., $20; Beltz Bros., $10; Bowen, E. D., $5; Barnes, G. S., & Co., $10; Brundage, Miss Addie, $10; Browning, King & Co. (clothing), $50; Brown, Jonas (liquors), $25; Bosquit & Co. (beef), $10; Bradley, David, & Co., $25; Baptist Church, Garden City, Minn., $11; Busch, H. F. W., $15.

Columbian National Bank, $100; City Bank, $125; Carpenter, H. M., $100; Casey, T. B., $50; Cooley, C. R., $10; Conroy, Ed., $5; Carter, Rittenberg & Hainlin Company, $35; Cleveland Rubber Works, $10; Collom, George H., $10; Countryman, L. N., $10; Cade, E. O., $5; Castle, G. A., $10; Crosby, John, $25; Crosby, Emma, $25; Church of Ascension (Catholic), $40; Clark, J. H., $50; Chadbourne, C. H., $10; Collins, P. V., $2; cash, from Guaranty Loan Building, $41.50; cash, F. D. U., $25; Choate & Merrill, $5; Cohen, Emanuel, $25; Cobb & Wheelwright, $10; Cross, W. M., $1; Chase, S. A., $5; Chase, C. W., $5; Crawford, F. H., 25 cents; Crickler, C. H., $1; Cash, S. M. Company, $5; C. C. Company, $5; C. (W. N.), $1; Chandler, W. B., $2; Chapman, R. M., $5; Cash, B. C. B., $10; Collins, W., $1; Cappellen, F. W., $5; Clarke, N. P., & Co., $100; Cash, A., $15; Chief of Police (office), $12; Cudahy Packing Company, $25; Commons, Bassett & Co., $25; Christian, L., & Co., $15; Cargill, S. D., $25; Chambers, A. G., $10; Central Elevator Company, The, $25; Christian, George H., $20; Crosby, C. F., $5; Columbia Elevator Company, $10; Company "B," First Regiment, $50; Church & Co., New York City (through G. R. Newell & Co.), $125; Columbian Meat Market (beef), $20; City Meat Market (beef), $20; Crane & Ordway Company, $10; Chowen, Minn. (citizens of), $15.60; Clarksville, Iowa (citizens of), $22; cash received from various persons, $196.10.

Dyer, W. J., & Bros., $25; Dickey, C. N., $10; Dodson, Fisher, Brockmann Company, $50; Davis, J. M., $5; Davis, A., Sons & Co., Cincinnati, Ohio, (through George R. Newell & Co.), $25; De-Land & Co., Fairport, New York, (through George R. Newell & Co.), $56.52; Dean & Co., $50; Deere & Webber Company, $100; Deering Harvesting Company, $25; Donaldson, William & Co., $200; Diamond Iron Works, $20; De La Barre, William, $10; De-Land & Co., Fairport, New York, (through Anthony Kelly Company), $54.20; Dorn, G. F., $10; Decker, W. F., (from Guaranty Loan Building), $16.50; Decker, W. F., $10; Downs Bros., $10; DeLand & Co., Fairport, New York, (through Winston, Farrington & Co), $40.90; Davis, F. F., $10; Douglass, George P., $5; Day bros., $5; De Mille, N. S., $5; Darelius, A. B., $5; Dodge, F. B., $5; Dorsett, C. W. & M. A., $2; Deschler, H., $5; Dunn, L. A., $1; Deacon, Thomas, $1; Dickey, T. S., $1; Day, J. W., & Co., $200; Davis-Hubbard Company, $10; Davigneaux, G., $5; Dunwoody, May and Ruth, and Ruth Bayless, $2; Dwight, John, & Co., New York, $125.

Eustis, W. H. $100; Ege, J. H., $25; Electrical Engineering Company, $10; Elfelt, C. C., $5; Emerson, Talcott & Co., $20; Elliott, Wyman, $100; Earl Fruit Company, $10; employes of J. W. Thomas, $1; Emerson & Hall, $25; Edwards, E. J., $10; Euste, J. B. & F., $5; Elliot, Albert F., $2; Elliot, J. K. & Co., $5; Ele, A., $5; Elliot, J. P., $1; Earvington, James, $5; Empire Elevator Company, $35; Engineers' Club of Minneapolis, $11; Eintech Lodge, No. 117, A. O. U. W., $10.

Farmers' & Mechanics' Savings Bank, $250; Ferguson, S. T., $5; Fisher, R. G., $9; Fieber, Jordon & Co., $5; First Swedish Methodist Church, $9.30; French, George F., $25; Farm, Stock and Home, $25; Firkins, O. W., $10; Fanning, N. O., $5; Flour Packers' and Nailers' Union, $10; Fletcher, George H., Board of Trade, $5; Firkins, O. W., Jr., Kasota, Minn., $1; friend, $1; friend, $1; Foss M. E. Church, $15; First Baptist Church, $107.70; Fifth Avenue Congregational Church, $8.25; Frankhauser, H. F., 25 cents; First Unitarian Church, $18.61; Fornere, H. D., $3; Flanagan, J. B., $50; friend, 50 cents; Field, J. W., $5; Fisher, R. G., $8.20; Fraser, Austin, $10; Freemire, W. A., & Co., $5; Fletcher, Loren, $100; faculty of University of Minnesota, $31; First M. E. Church, $12.80; First Norwegian Presbyterian Church, $3.50; Father Hennepin Branch, Catholic Knights of America, $12; Frisk-Turner Company (clothing), $50; First Free Baptist Church, $17.76; Fourth Baptist Church, $8.60; Fife, $5.

Germania Bank, $25; German American Bank, $50; Gillette, Herzog Manufacturing Company, $100; Guaranty Loan Barber Shop, $12; Gilmore, D. M., $5; Gluck, F. P., & Co., $10; Gangelhoff, C. H., $10; Gamble-Robinson Commission Company, $5; Goodrich, H. H., $5; Gleason, J. M., $10; Gluck Brewing Company, $100; Gedney, M. A., Pickling Company, $25; Gluck, Mrs. F., $10; German Evangelical Lutheran Church, $7; German Lutheran Church, Kenyon, Minn., $8.75; G. A. R. S., $1; Grosse, Max H., $5; Grosse, Julius, $3; Gilman, Julia A., $2; Gee, C. S., $1; Gull River Lumber Company, $200; Greenleaf & Tenny, $20; Getchell, Daniel, $1; Great Western Elevator Company, $25; German Baptist Church, $11; Gutworth & Drew (beef) $15; Gannon, M., 50 cents; G. (H. M.), $1;

Hennepin County Savings Bank, $50; Herrick Bros., $25; Hennepin County Medical Society, $100; Harrison, Hugh, $50; Howell, R. R., & Co., $5; Hillman Bros., $5; Mooker, Manley Cigar Company, $25; Hall, A. H., $10; Healey & Co., $5; Henry, F. H. Aryshire, Iowa, $5; Hansen, H., $2; Highland Park Church, $5.02; Holy Trinity Episcopal Church, $15.52; Hennepin Council, No. 1234, Royal Arcanum, $10; Holm, W. J., $25; Haynes, J. C., $25; Hale, W. E., $25; Hedderly & McCracken, $5; Haynes, A. E., $2; Hume & Davis, $5; Hulburd & Clare, $3; Higgins, C. W., $1; Hayes, Warren H., $5; Hill, G. S., $1; Hayward, W. W., $3; Harlow, E. B., $1; Hall, P. M., $5; Hill, W. S., $100; Hungarian American Club, $8; Humboldt Mill Company, $25; Hanson, Thomas, $5; Harper, Thayer & Co., $5; Haines, $5; Hennepin M. E. Church, $54; Hewett, S. M., $5; Hitchcuk, D. L., Gorham, N. H., $25.

Irish-American Bank, $50; Itaska Lumber Company, H. C. Ackley Lumber Company, $300; Ideal Literary Society, $5; Inter-State Grain Company, $25; Interior Elevator Company, $25; Immaculate Conception Church, $80.

Journal, Minneapolis, (subscriptions received by), $744.87; Johnson, J. W., $25; Johnson, Albert, $25; Johnson, H. C., $5; Janny, Semple & Co., $300; Joyslin, J. C., $5; Jacobson, E. D., $5; janitors and elevator boys of New York Life Building, $9; Jorguson, Claus, Belgrade, Minn., $1; Journal, Minneapolis, $50; Jamison, W. S., Board of Trade, $10; Jackson, A. B., $50; Janson, M. G., 50 cents;

Jones, Paul, $1; Jones, J. A., $1; Jones, Alice, 50 cents; Johnson, H., $1; Johns, James, & Co., $5; Janny, Semple & Co. (employes), $38.50; Jacobson-Milkolas Company, The, $10; Johnson, W. W. (car lumber), $50; Jacob Schaeffer Post, G. A. R., $5.

Kirkbridge, Palmer & Co., $10; Kelly, Anthony, & Co., $100; Kinsel, Lem, $2; Kaiser Wilhelm Lodge, No. 2, Sons of Herman, $25; Keith, Evans, Thompson & Fairchild, $50; Koon, Whelan & Bennett, $50; King, Cornelia, $5; Kennedy, Elizabeth, $2; King, H. K., & Co., $10; Kensington, Minn. (citizens of), $25; Keller & Roenisch & Co. (beef), $10; Kennedy Bros., $10; Kitchell, S. R., $25.

Lane, J. S., $5; Linton, A. H., $50; Lund, Erick, $5; Lyman, Eliel Drug Co., $200; Le Roy, Minn., Citizens of, $46.33; Linsay Bros., $50; Lewis & Co., $10; Longiellow, L., & Bros., $10; Linton, S. S., & Co., $25; Leonard, Wm. E., $5; Le Roy, Final, New York, $20; Legg, H. F., Jewelry Co., $20; Lydiard, L. A., $1; Loaf, W., $1; Ladies' Aid Soc., Swedish Lutheran Agustana Church, $25.

Metropolitan Bank, $100; Minnesota Loan & Trust Co., $125; Minneapolis Trust Co., $125; Minnesota Fire Insurance Co., $100; Minnetonka Meat and Provision Co., $10; Menzel Foundry Co., $10; McDonald Bros., $30; Minneapolis Iron Store Co., $100; McMillan, Jas., Co., $10; McKusick, Copelin Co., $10; Minneapolis Threshing Machine Co., $25; Milburn & Stoddard Co., $25; Minnesota Moline Plow Co., $50; Minneapolis Plow Works, $20; Morrison & Stowbridge, $5; Moffett, J. B., $5; McMillan & Co., $100; Michener, A. H., $5; Minneapolis Fire Department Relief Association, $1,000; Morrison, Clinton, $100; Minneapolis Fruit Exchange, $100; Minneapolis Brewing Co., $500; Metcalf & Youatt, Kasota, Minn., $5; Maple Plain, Minn., Citizens of, $15; Martindale, Dr. J. H., $25; Moffett, F. L., $5; McGowan, H. S., Board of Trade, $1; Minneapolis Dry Goods Co., $207.15; Milwaukee Harvester Co., of Minneapolis, $25; Montezuma Aztec Council No. 4, $15; Minneapolis Dancing Club, $12; Minnehaha Lodge No. 81, A. O. U. W., $10; McHale, J. J., $2; Moore, J. G., 25 cents; McCarthy, Nathaniel, $2; Mooney & Dassett, $2; Mahoney, Stephen, $5; McAllister, J. C., $1; Moore, H., $1; Moffett, W. Z., $1; Miller, J. H., $5; Municipal Court Officers, $5; Minnehaha Council R. A. No. 1160, $25; Mohler, Wm. B., $5; McEnary, J. H., $1; McCarthy Bros., $10; Martin & Wyman, $20; McCord, T., & Co.,

$10; Marshall, James, $5; Mayer, C. E., $5; Momaw, The Geo. A.,
Co., $10; Moore & Maxfield, $10; Minn. & Western Grain Co., $10;
Morse, Samuel, $15; Minneapolis Union Elevator Co., $10; Met-
calf, T. C., $5; Minnesota Linseed Oil Works, $20; Milwaukee Har-
vester Co., of Minneapolis, $25; Minneapolis, St. Paul Baseball
Game, $749.46; Minneapolis Musicians' Association, $717.50; Moni-
ter Manufacturing Co., $10; Minneapolis Provision Co., beef, $30;
Morison, W. K., & Co., nails, $25; Martin, John, $50; Morrison, D.,
$100; McDougall, Geo. A., $10; Monarch Elevator Co., $25; Merz,
John, Spencerport, N. Y., $2.27; Merion, Mrs. L. O., Emerson &
Hall, $1.

N. W. National Bank, $500; Nicollet National Bank, $250; Na-
tional Bank of Commerce, $250; Northern Trust Co., $50; New
England Furniture & Carpet Co., $100; Northrup, Braslan & Good-
win Co., $50; North Star Woolen Mills, $25; Newell, Geo. R., &
Co., $300; North Star Boot & Shoe Co., $125; Nott, W. S., & Co.,
$50; Nicholas & Shepard Co., $10; Northwestern Implement &
Wagon Co., $20; Northwestern Miller, $50; North Star Barrel Co.,
$25; Nobody, 50 cents; Nagel, T. W., 50 cents; Nelson, Tenny &
Co., $200; Norris, W. H., $15; No. 19 Engine House, $14; National
Beef Co., $30; Nicholas & Taylor, $10; N. W. Elevator Co., $25;
Nye, Jenks & Co., $15; Northwestern Consolidated Milling Co.,
$100; North M. E. Church, Camden Place, $35; New York Biscuit
Co., crackers, $25; North Star Woolen Mill, blankets, $25; Nye,
W. G., $5; Nelson, Chas., $1.

Oswald, J. C., & Co., $100; Olson & Fjellman, $10; Ostrander,
M. A., Kasota, Minn., $5; Oliver Presbyterian Church, $37.12; Owre,
Lars, $1; Ogden, John, $1; Osborn, McMillan Elevator Co., $25;
Osborn, E. F., & Co., $5; Olson, S. E., & Co., $402.40; Orquist,
C. G., $1; Odin Lodge A. O. D., $10.

Plummer, W. A., $5; Peck, O. H., $10; Pond & Hasy Co., $5;
Park Avenue Congregational Church, $38.42; Patterson & Stev-
eson, $50; Preece, J. T., Mercantile Co., $25; Pratt, A. M., & Co.,
$10; Porter Bros. & Co., $10; Potter, E. F., $5; Paris, Murton Co.,
$10; Pillsbury, Mrs. F. C., $25; Pearce, H. C., $2; Perry, J. H., $5;
Pratt, Helen A., $5; Petran, Henry J., $10; Postoffice Employes,
$115; Palace Clothing Co., $25; Pierce, Mrs. Margaret, $5; Phone,
Mr. Chas., $2; Parkhurst, A. G., $3; Powell, Wm., $5; Pope, E. R.,
Board of Trade, $2; Press Club "Old Hoss" Ball Game, $214; Per-

kins, John W., $2; Peck, H. N., $5; Pioneer Fuel Co., $50; Purdy, M. D., $1; Parkhurst, M. I., $1; Perry, J. H., $5; Plummer, J. A., $1; Pilgrim Congregational Church, $9; Porter, A. H., $1; Palmer, Edna, $4.50; Police, Second Precinct, $27; Police, First Precinct, $32.50; Plummer, J. G., $10; Powell, H. C., $10; Police, Third Precinct, $37; Police, Fourth Precinct, $30; Police, Fifth Precinct, $19; Plymouth Lodge No. 79, K. of P., $25; Place, Col. E. B., New York City, $100; Pillsbury, Washburn, Crosby Flour Mills Co., $500; Phoenix Mill Co., $20; Poehler, H., $10; Pertig, H. G., $5; Peacock, J. H., $5; Piper, G. F., $1; Peavey Elevator Co., $25; Peavey, F. H., & Co., $100; Periman, D., $5; Park Avenue Congregational Church, $2; Pettijohn, Eli, Cereal Co., breakfast food, $90; Pratt, Robt., $3.60; Pierson, Willie B., 47 cents; Plymouth Junior Christian Endeavor, $3; Paulle, L., $10.

Quinn, P. G., $1.

Rand, A. T., $125; Rand, A. R., $125; Rees, Julius, $5; Russell, Robt. D., $10; Revere Rubber Co., cashier, $25; Ryan, D. E., & Co., $10; Rinker & Hoff, $20; Regan Bros.' Employes, $25; Rich, W. W., $10; Rea, Hubachek & Healy, $10; Reno, R. C., $10; Robothan, Geo., Board of Trade, $1; Roberts, H. P., $10; Roensch, Jos., $1; Russell, T. C., $1; Reg. Publishing Co., $2.50; Reese, C. B., 50 cents; Redfield, Wm. W., 25 cents; Robue, Rufus, $1; Ryan, McKeown & Co., $5; Russell Coffee House, $25; Rogers, Mrs. W. F., $5.

Security Bank, $500; Swedish American Bank, $100; St. Anthony Falls Bank, $50; Scandia Bank of Minneapolis, $25; Stewart, L. M., $100; Segelbaum, S., $10; Stone, Jacob, $5; St. John's Church, Minnetonka Mills, $6.45; Spink & Keyes, $10; Shea, J. A., & Co., $10; Smith, H. S., & Co., $10; Stacy, E. P., & Sons, $10; Swanson Bros., $5; Snyder, James E., $25; Simmons, H. M., $10; Shattuck & Wood, $20; St. Joseph's Catholic Church, $57.88; St. Boniface Catholic Church, $35; Silver Lake Congregational Church, $14.10; St. Paul's Episcopal Church, $28.40; St. Paul's Episcopal Sunday School, $1.71; Swedish Bros.' Society, $50; Shaw and Gray, $100; Shaw, Frank W., $25; Savage, Ed., $10; Sumner, E. W., $10; Snyder Bros., $3; Smith, H. E., $1; Salfinger, John J., $1; Smith, W. H., 50 cents; Stone, W. M., $1; Stevens, C. B., $2; Sturzel, E. J., $1; Simpson, David, $3; Shevlin Carpenter Co., $200; Smith, C. A., Lumber Co., $100; Smith & Wyman, $50; Steele, Dr., $5; Shadrick, Master Dickey, 40 cents; Simmons, A. G., $5; Security Grain

Co., $10; Sowle, C. T., & Sons, $25; Storms, L. E., $5; Swart, J. G., & Co., $5; Sawyer Grain Co., $5; St. Anthony & Dakota Elevator Co., $25; Strong & Miller, $5; Strong, II., $5; St. Charles Church, $31.20; Supt., Supervisors & Teachers of Public Schools, $335.40; South Side Citizens' Meeting held at Emanual Baptist Church, $95; St. Anthony Falls Masonic Chapter No. 3, $50; Society Dania, $25; Scandinavian Fire Relief Com., $654.87; St. Anthony Turn Veren, $25; Sixth Avenue Evangelical Church, $11.40; Sixth Avenue Evangelical Sunday School, $2.60; St. Benedict Society, $15; Schuler, F., $6.35; Steuben Lodge No. 23, Sons of Herman, $10; St. Louis Park, Citizens of, $56; Smeel, C. A., Mgr., $3; Shick, Fred, $27.

Tunstead & Moore, $10; Tuttle, Rev. J. II., $5; Thompson, W. C., $2; Twin City Hide & Tallow Co., $5; Thomas, A. C., $5; Turner, Howard A., $5; Taussing, S., & Co., $10; Tromanhauser Bros., $20; Thompson, John I., $25; Thayer, Samuel, $25; Tribble, Mrs. M. E., Emerson & Hall, $5; Thame, W. B., $10; Twin City Iron Works, $25; Todd, J. S., & Co., $5; Treadwell Shoe Co., $4; Taylor, W. N., & Co., $5; Trussell, A. N., $3; Taylor, Norman, $1.50; Trade & Labor Council, $10; Third Precinct, $1; Twin City Rapid Transit Co., acc. of benefit, $216.40; Taylor, A. B., & Co., $5; Tomlinson, R. B., & Son, caps, gloves, etc., $25; Times, Minneapolis, $50.

Union National Bank, $100; Unknown, $5; Unknown, $1; Unknown, $1; Unknown, $2; U. (R. L.), $1.

Victoria Elevator Co., $10; Van Dusen, Harrington Co., $25; Verhoff, J. C., $5; Village & Congregation Church of Robbinsdale, $49.07; Vine Congregational Church, $7.30; Vetter, Geo., $5; Von Ende, Aug., $1; Vose, Z. Pope, $5; Van Dusen, G. W., $100.

Washington Bank, $50; Winston Bros., $250; Wyman, Partridge & Co., $750; Winston, Farrington & Co., $250; Winecke & Doerr, $50; Walters & Wagner, $10; Waite, E. F., $5; Williamson, L. B., $5; Wilcox, . S., Kasota, Minn., $5; Wedstrand, C. A., $5; Welles, II. T., $100; Wilkinson, Rev. Wm., collection, $10.21; Willard, Chas. A., $10; Wolsey, D. W., 50 cents; Webster, H. G., $1; Willis & Dunham, $2; Warner, H. L., $1; Whitney, E. D., 50 cents; Wingate, W. S., $2; Wenzin, John, $2; White, M. F., $15; Washburn Crosby Co., $500; Watson & Co., $10; Wilson, Geo. S., $5; Welsh & Son, $5; Wheeler, Carter & Co., $20; Woodworth, E. S., & Co.,

W. S. HINCKLEY. CATHERINE UP BEFORE OYSTERBURG MEET.

$15; Woodward & Co., $25; Whalen & Co., $10; Wagner, D. R.,
& Co., $10; Williams, W., $1; Wyman, Partridge & Co., employes,
$100; Washburn, W. D., $200; Watertown Steam Engine Co., $5;
Wheeler, Geo. E., $5; Wheeler, Mrs. Geo. E., $5; Washburn, Crosby
& A. B. C. S. D. Mill employes, $340; Winter, R. H., $1; Wolver-
ton, J. A., $1; Woodman, J. W., $1; Walker, T. B., $1,000.

Young, Winthrop, $25; Y. M. C. A., $7.50; Yerxa, M. W., $5.

Zonne, A. E. &. F. E., $5.

Total, $27,449.56.

WHITE BEAR.

This is the place in which James Root and Rev. Father Burke
lived. Through White Bear the railways from Minneapolis, St.
Paul and Stillwater, on the St. Paul and Duluth, pass to the burned
district, so the people knew all the news quickly. The report shows
what steps were taken to assist those in need.

As chairman and treasurer of the White Bear Hinckley relief committee, the undersigned has the honor of submitting the following
report of cash received and disbursed:

Cash received		$359.50
Cash paid out	$342.41	
Cash on hand	17.09	359.50

ALBERT E. QUINN.

STILLWATER.

Stillwater took special interest in Hinckley, which had been often
said to be a Stillwater town. Ever since the foundation of Hinckley it had been, in more ways than one, tributary to the city on the
St. Croix, which was itself laid out by Mr. McKusick, who took an
active part in the work of relief, and was very energetic in all that
had to do with collecting help for the men, women and children in
Pine county in their awful calamity. Mr. Isaac Staples knew Hinckley well and had been long interested in business with the burned
district in various ways. Judge Nethaway had been, if not in fasts,
in many a feast at Hinckley, had told the people good stories often,
and roused them to better thinking, and higher living by his elo-
quence; he was a well known man at the Lumber City of Pine county.
When the fire came and laid it waste he was soon on hand to help;
day and night he gave his aid and direction, found the dead and
helped the bereaved, with a tenderness, the recital of which, eight
months after, brought tears to the eyes of many men at a meeting
to open the new town hall.

Stillwater shares the honor of duty nobly done, and no story of work for those who suffered loss by fire in the burnt district would be complete which did not tell of what its citizens and their committee did. The Gazette newspaper furnished the writer the report of what was done, and is the sponsor for its correctness.

Mr. Byron J. Mosier, chairman of the relief committee, and many others, visited Hinckley and the places to which the help was sent often, and have kept an intelligent view of all that was being done and of what needed to be done, from first to last. At the dedication of the new town hall in Hinckley Judge Nethaway was one of the speakers, and the following gentlemen represented Stillwater as delegates: Byron J. Moshier, Hiram T. King, Albert J. Lammers, Nicholas A. Nelson and Judge John C. Nethaway.

J. C. NETHAWAY.

On arriving in St. Paul from the West, Sunday morning, September second, 1894, I first heard of the terrible fire at Hinckley, and immediately made arrangements to go up to the relief of the sufferers. I took the first train to White Bear, where I was in hopes I could get aboard a train going to the relief of the people. This I was unable to do, and did not leave White Bear until the relief train arrived from St. Paul. After experiencing a rather wild ride we arrived at Pine City, where we were met by the local relief committee, who very briefly laid the condition of affairs before the party. I continued on to Hinckley, arriving there about 8:30 Sunday night, and there beheld sights which would make the strongest man shudder. The dead were lying about in heaps; mothers still embracing their babies were burned to a crisp and lying promiscuously about upon the ground.

With the aid of lanterns we immediately set about to find and relieve any who might still be living, but sad to say, not a living thing did we see in our movements about that devastated place. Not a living thing greeted the rays of the lanterns, but upon every side were the dead burned to a crisp; men, women and children; dogs, cats, cows, horses and fowls all lying where the terrible fire struck them down.

On Monday morning, through the kindness of Mr. Miller, of the St. Paul and Duluth Railway Co., I procured a hand car, and loading it with one hundred and fifty loaves of bread, two boxes of canned meat, some tea, coffee, cups and necessary utensils, and ingredients for a good cup of coffee, in company with J. D. Markham, of Rush City. Joseph Muckenhauser, of White Bear, and three other gentlemen whose names I am now unable to recall, started for Sandstone to relieve the people, who, we had been informed, were suffring for the want of food. Our route was north on the St. Paul and Duluth Railway to a station called Miller; thence east to Sandstone over a branch of the St. Paul and Duluth Railway. We experienced difficulty in reaching Miller, being compelled to carry our load and hand car across several burned culverts and bridges, and many places in the track were curved, through the effects of the heat.

When we arrived near Sandstone Junction we met the work train from Duluth and learned that the people at Sandstone had been reached and relieved by a party from Duluth, who had come down the Eastern Minnesota Railroad to a station called Partridge, and walked from there to Sandstone. I then, in company with two others, took a westerly course, carefully examining the country as we proceeded in order to find the dead and living, if any. We had some bologna sausage and crackers with us; also a tin cup. Space will not permit a detailed statement of what occurred on that trip; suffice it to say that we continued on to Grindstone Lake, where we spent our first night.

The country between Sandstone Junction and Grindstone Lake was completely burned over, and along our path we found dead squirrels, rabbits, pleasants, deer and other wild game. The next morning we worked our way southeasterly, reaching Hinckley the next night. As an illustration of some of the sights which met our eyes on that trip, I would speak of one instance in particular. While working our way west to Grindstone Lake, we came upon the ruins of a once happy home, the house being completely destroyed. We immediately set about examining the grounds to find any dead or living, and upon looking into the cellar we saw a sight that brought tears to our eyes. Embraced in each other's arms were, as we afterward learned, husband and wife, and beside them two other female bodies and a little baby, with its outstretched arms, protruding tongue, and agonizing expression, was lying near its mother who, from all indications, had attempted to save it from the flames by the aid of a shawl, which, while burned to a crisp, still retained its character. This is but one of the many horrible sights I saw in those two day

On my return to Hinckley I assisted in the burying of the dead

and went out with parties to bury where found, or bring in those
who had been found, for burial at the cemetery east of Hinckley.
One case in particular was the finding of the body of John Ross,
who resided in St. Paul.

We found his body about three-quarters of a mile east of Finlayson and with the aid of a blanket brought it to Finlayson, there
placed it in a rough box and took it to Hinckley, where it was received by friends, and as I learned afterwards, taken to Eau Claire
for burial. I was also with a party who found Mr. Rowley's body.
I did not know him and afterwards learned that he was the auditor
of the Duluth and Winnipeg Railroad Company.

I spent twelve days at Hinckley and vicinity and while I would be
willing to again help any in distress and suffering, I nevertheless
hope another such mission does not await me.

Many of the people in Stillwater had large interests in and around
Hinckley. For many years Pine City and counties adjacent had
lived settlers from this place and as Stillwater is essentially a lumbering town, the sympathies of our people were deeply stirred when
news of the disaster came and all was done that was possible in
the circumstances to do for the sufferers.

STILLWATER RELIEF COMMITTEE.

The committee of H. T. King, B. J. Mosier, J. T. Barron, J. J.
Robertson and E. W. Durant, appointed to receive and dispense aid
to the sufferers of the terrible forest fires that swept over the northern part of the state about two months ago, gave a Gazette reporter
the following interesting statement of the contributions and their
disposal:

R. W. Turnbull, 3 cars lumber, $275; R. W. Turnbull, horses,
wagon and harness, $325; Charles Conhaim, clothing, $100; A. G.
Schuttinger, merchandise, $50; Isaac Staples, one car flour, $300;
Schulenburg & Boeckeler, boots and shoes, $50; Stillwater Hardware
Co., hardware, $100; Simonet Brothers, merchandise, $50; Elmore
Lowell, bedding, $25; F. Garen, furniture, $50; Standard Clothing
Co., merchandise, $25; Alex Johnson, merchandise, $50; L. Alben-
berg and L. Albenburg & Co., merchandise, $175; R. M. Coles, two
cows, $60; J. O. Holen & Co., groceries, $25; F. W. Schendel, shoes,
$10; Thoe. Jassoy & Sons, blankets, $35; Zeigler Brothers, merchandise, $25. Total, $1,730.

Aside from this the citizens contributed clothing amounting to at least $1,500 in value. This was a generous and spontaneous out-pouring from every part of the city, Oak Park and South Stillwater, and was indeed timely. Added to this, the cash subscriptions, amounting to $2,607.20, makes up the very respectable total of about $5,930, contributed by Stillwater and vicinity. Following is a statement of the cash contributions:

A. T. Jenks, $50; M. H. Bromley, $1; T. Donovan, $10; W. J. Stein, $3; F. W. Durant, $50; Aug. Booth, $3; Otis Staples, $25; Aug. Booren, $10; Peter Jourdain, $5; D. L. Burlingham, $5; J. J. Robertson, $10; Chas. Swanson, $3; Stillwater Mfg. Co., $10; Andrew Severson, $5; Joseph Wolf, $50; Merrill & Clark, $10; Frank Withrow, $5; E. C. Holmes, $5; Jas. G. Foley, $5; F. J. R. Aiple, $25; Samuel Bloomer, $15; McSweeney, $3; Chas. A. Staples, $5; E. Flynn, $5; Jerry Collins, $5; Fred Wolf, $2; A. W. Pattee, $5; Jas. Hanson, $5; First Nat. Bank, $100; Ed. O'Brien, $5; F. B. Yates, $10; J. B. Taft, $5; C. M. McCluer, $25; J. C. Zietler, $2; R. H. Bronson, $10; Adolph Peterson, $1; H. H. Gillen, $5; J. H. Pratt, $1; David Swank, $5; A. C. Haier, $2; John O. Anderson, $10; C. E. Connors, $2; M. Johnson, $5; John Marcusen, $1; Schulenberg & B. L. Co., $50; James Roney, $20; Linder & Erickson, $3; Village of South Stillwater, $50; John Goodrich, $2; C. O. Burnham, $5; E. N. Swanson, $2; J. B. Northey, $2; J. W. Wheeler, $10; W. H. Pratt, M. D., $2; F. W. McGray, $5; John Thornquist, $2; Mrs. F. W. McGray, $2; Levi Thompson, $2; J. F. Burke, $10; J. M. Schafer, $3; L. H. Seymour, $5; Ed. Masterman, $1; D. J. Sullivan, $5; Mart McPheters, $5; Phil. McDermott, $10; Gust Ekblad, $1; A. Marty, $5; Chas. Heitman, $5; Lady from Maine by Mrs. Treat, $2; A. Brocious, $1; Mackinhausen & Lustig, $5; A. G. Tribel, $5; Theo. Jassoy, $10; Hugh McKinsie, $2; East Side L. Co., $150; Alb. Drewke, $1; Bronson & Folsom, $50; D. McDermott, $1; F. W. Gail, $5; Scully & Tracy, $5; Gazette Ptg. Co., $10; Hillskotter & Kelm, $2; J. A. O'Shaughnessy, $5; Fitzgerald & Dyson, $5; C. E. Mosier, $5; J. W. Foley, $5; O. J. Olson, $2; M. L. Murphy, $5; Aug. Loeber, $1; King Bros., $15; Wm. Evans, $1; B. I. Mosier, $15; Geo. Erickson, $1; J. T. Barron, $5; Frank Swanson, $1; J. J. Eichten, $15; Paul Hanson, $2; John McKusick, $100; P. J. Stenstrom, $1; G. W. Smith, $5; B. F. Rice, $1; L. F. Collins, $5; J. P. Hanson, $2; Myron Shepard, $5; C. W. Merry, $5; St. Croix Drug Co., $25; Saul Stein, $1; M. A. Thon, $5; Peter Blad, $1; Mulvey & Carmichael, $100; Wm. Bain, $1; Herman Apman, $1; C. H. Browne,

EDITOR ELMQUIST, RUSH_CITY.

J. THOMPSON, MORA.

B. J. MOSIER.

$5; Ed. Welsch, $1; St. Croix L. Co., $200; Wm. English, $1; Fred
Pennington, $30; Henry Daily, $1; Florence Mill Co., $15; Patrick
Barrett, $1; C. T. Goodrich, $5; Henry Stussi, $1; Jas. Mathews,
$5; George McCharty, $1; R. W. McGarry, $5; A. J. Collins, $5;
H. Koesters. $5; Elis Bergund, $1; F. E. Joy & Co., $5; Aug. Peter-
son, $1; B. B. Smith, $3; John Albin, $1; G. H. Sullivan, $5; Alfred
Johnson, $1; J. C. Nethaway, $5; C. D. Anderson, $1; Tozer, Mc-
Clure & Co., $150; Dr. C. B. Marshall, $25; Maurice Clancy, $5;
T. H. Warren, $10; Mrs. Mary Hefti, $1; Fred Scott, $5; Thos.
J. Welch, $1; F. L. Grace & Co., $5; Thos. Morrisey, $1; H. L.
Foster, $5; John Erig, $1; P. S. Deragisch, $5; E. G. Foster, $1;
F. Pennington & Co., $20; J. M. Kuhn, $5; J. H. Griffin, $1; J.
A. McDermott, $5; H. B. Prince, $2; Minn. Mercantile Co., $150;
J. M. Lupien, $1; Mrs. Jno. Hoy, $5; Hershey Lumber Co., $50;
Rudolph Lehmicke, $3; Jno. Roney, $1; Joseph Schupp, $20; Mrs.
Jno. Roney, $1; H. Heisel & Co., $25; Nat Roney, $1; H. J. Mc-
Kusick, $10; Alfred Roney, $1; Leonard Clark, $10; Herb Roney,
$1; Alex. Richard, $5; Pat Murphy, $5; C. Henningsen, $10; A. H.
Drake, $1; Albert Wilson, $5; J. A. Deragisch, $5; A. M. Phoenix,
$3; Abner Brotherton, $3; John G. Nelson, $15; Wm. H. Hewitt,
$5; D. A. Blakeney, $5; W. L. Prince, $2; W. F. Mackey, $5; Mrs.
P. Lund, $1; Eagle Hardware Co., $5; A. P. Nehring, $1; Fr. Frey-
nieller, $1; R. S. Davis, $5; N. A. McKay, $5; Wm. Sauntry, $200;
P. Laviolett, $1; F. Kirchoff, $3; A. Parson, $1; A. T. Lindholm,
$5; Third Ward Committee, $5; E. Grant, $5; McLaughlin & Kilty,
$5; D. A. Masterman, $1; Geo. A. Lammers, $5; J. Ceaser, $5; John
O'Brien, $25; A. Rhorbach, $15; H. Voligny, $5; E. A. Phinney,
$3; A. J. Holm, $3; Oak Park Citizens, $89.45; Thos. Dunn, $1.50;
C. H. Cannon, $2.50; A. R. Campbell, 50 cents; Wm. Foley, 50
cents; John Wallis, 50 cents; P. C. Peterson, 50 cents; Fritz Gramenz,
50 cents; Richard Doran, 50 cents; James Blay, 50 cents; Arthur
W. Doran, 50 cents; Nels Danelson, 50 cents; John Peterson, 25
cents; Anton Carlson, 30 cents; John Munson, 50 cents; Mrs. Geo.
Hinchy, 35 cents; Mrs. M. Dawson, 50 cents; Mrs. Andrew Kearney,
80 cents; A. E. Howden, 50 cents; F. Holmblad, 10 cents; D. Holmblad, 25 cents; Mrs. McIlree, 50 cents; Scandia by F. J. Lake, $67.20.
Total, $2,697.20.

The committee has sent the following relief: One car flour to
Pine City; five cars of lumber, three to Hinckley, one to North
Branch, and one to Pokegama; one car of provisions, regular lum-

bermen's supplies, to Pine City; one carload of clothing to Pine City; one car of hardware, stoves, etc., for Hinckley and Pokegama; team, harness and wagon to Nels Henry at Hinckley; 55 sacks of flour to Hinckley and Pine City, and $375 in cash to those two places.

The committee still has remaining on hand about $1,300 which will be expended along during the fall and winter to relieve the fire sufferers. Every few days moneys or provisions are sent up and their distribution, superintended by Messrs. Fred Hodge and James Hurley, of Pine City, and Dug Greeley, of Hinckley, brings joy to many a disheartened settler who is trying to rebuild his little home. These three gentlemen just named have the thanks of our local committee for their kind assistance and painstaking efforts to see that only deserving ones, the sufferers themselves, should receive the aid.

Of our local committee and its work too much cannot be said. Messrs. King, Mosier, Barron, Robertson and Durant have devoted a large portion of their time the past seven or eight weeks to this charitable work and paying their own traveling expenses ungrudgingly.

They carried into the work an enthusiasm that was infectious and which had much to do with the very satisfactory success attending their labors.

MANKATO.

THIS town is situated on the Minnesota river and is blessed with many great advantages, which a bountiful God has placed within its reach. It is in the southern part of the state, adjacent to it is one of the best farming countries in the West and one which has felt the hard times in 1893 four and five less, perhaps, than any part of America. Mankato is a great railway center and has a State Normal School and is well supplied with public institutions for the cultivation of man in his higher nature. The annexed report has been sent to me which tells part of what was done. No doubt much was given in other ways, of which no record has been furnished.

On the news of the terrible conflagration in the northern part of the state last summer the sympathy of the Mankatoans was stirred to have a hand in the relief. It was accomplished as follows:

Fully fifty business men met at the Board of Trade in response to a public call of all citizens. Judge Daniel Buck, of the supreme court, was elected chairman, County Attorney Benedict, secretary. The result of the meeting was the appointment of the following committee to canvass the city for funds: Geo. H. Clark, E. M. Pope, Robert Roberts, W. N. Pyymat, Rev. Lee W. Beattie, J. C. Theo, J. F. Fowler, John Klein, Leo Laurn, J. C. Noe, Dr. J. W. Andrews, F. R. Coughlan. The following resolution offered by Senator Barr was passed:

Resolved, That the committee be authorized to solicit aid in money, provisions and other articles, and that the committee have full power to use each subscription in any direction or channel they think proper.

The committee met the next day. Rev. Lee W. Beattie was elected chairman, Geo. H. Clark secretary and treasurer. A general call was issued to all residents of this county and vicinity to make such donations as they could. Various churches were asked to take up a collection. Every church responded with a laudable

LEGISLATIVE COMMITTEE.

contribution. The committee was subdivided into smaller committees to canvass each ward of the city, and the normal and public schools. By this systematic way everyone was given an opportunity to contribute. Through a committee of ladies, an additional amount was raised by an entertainment in the Opera House, under the management of Mesdames L. P. Hunt and W. Craig. The young people from St. Clair township gave a benefit sending in twenty dollars as the proceeds.

The total amount received was as follows:

Church collection and city canvass	$ 866.15
Farmers, cash	8.00
Farmers, wheat sold by committee	17.23
Ladies of St. Clair	20.00
Opera House benefit	120.00
Total	$1,031.38

R. D. Hubbard forty sacks of flour, other parties supplies of lard, flour, clothing, furniture to quite an extent.

The state committee notifying us they needed lumber, pork and flour and all other articles that could be turned into cash were sent to it. The old clothing and furniture was disposed of to the city relief societies, the committee not being able to use them. With some of this a large quantity of pork was procured and shipped to Hinckley. All the amount was four hundred dollars and was sent to the treasurer of the committee. The four hundred dollars was retained for the following purpose: The committee was requested to take an unfortunate widow and two children, whose husband and father had fallen a victim to the flames. They were Mrs. Strum and two children, one four years old and the other two. Mrs. Strum is a Swede and was, with her children, placed by the committee under the charge of a special committee of Robert Roberts and Mesdames Klein and Crowly, who secured a comfortable suite of rooms on Fourth street, where she has been carefully provided for with all the necessaries of life. The committee's idea is to open the way in the spring for Mrs. Strum to become self supporting.

HENRY IRVING.

LEGISLATION.

St. Paul, Minn., April 1, 1895.

Dear Sir:—Hon. Mr. Mallette requested me to give you some information with reference to the legislation for the relief of the fire sufferers.

At the opening of the session a special committee was appointed, consisting of Hon. J. T. Wyman, Hon. F. A. Hodge, Hon. J. Q. Cronkhite, together with Hon. O. O. Holman, H. R. Mallette, Hon. A. J. Anderson, Hon. C. F. Staples.

At the opening of the session Hon. J. T. Wyman introduced a bill into the senate appropriating $20,000 for the purpose of reimbursing the members of the State Relief Commission for $15,000 advanced by them for the further purpose of affording temporary relief until the legislature should decide what, if anything, further should be done. This bill passed both houses of the legislature and was signed by the governor.

The joint committee of both houses visited the burned district on April 2nd, 1895, and upon their return submitted the following report:

REPORTS OF SELECT COMMITTEES.

By unanimous consent Mr. Wyman, from the select committee on fire relief, submitted the following report and recommendations:

To the Senate of the State of Minnesota:

The joint committee of the Senate and the House of Representatives appointed to investigate the condition of the sufferers by forest fires in Pine and adjacent counties and report what further relief, if any, needed, would report as follows:

Your committee finds that the Minnesota State Commission for the relief of fire sufferers has, up to April 2, 1895, received the following contributions, to be expended under its direction:

Cash donations from foreign countries $11,600.00
Cash donations from United States, except
   Minnesota 14,711.19
Cash donations from Minnesota 70,776.45
   Total cash donations ....$97,087.64 $ 97,087.64
Proceeds of sales of building material, etc....   2,027.24
Appropriations by Legislature, drawn Janu-
   uary 28, 1895 ....   20,000.00
   Total cash receipts $119,114.88
Lumber, etc. donated 10,700.00
Clothing donated 25,000.00
Free railroad transportation (estimated) 13,000.00
   Total receipts $167,814.88

The disbursements of the commission up to April 2, 1895, were
as follows:
Allowance to individual fire sufferers .....$ 23,204.61
Cost of 215 buildings erected 35,322.38
Outfittings 22,238.61
Temporary relief 14,848.42
Miscellaneous disbursements 4,073.20
Unclassified disbursements since January 1,
   1895 .... 10,782.86
Administration expenses; salaries of agents
   clerks, storekeepers, warehouse employes,
   and expenses of delivery teams from Sep-
   tember 5, 1894, to April 2, 1895.........   6,411.51
   Total cash disbursements $116,881.59 $116,881.59
Lumber, etc., donated 10,700.00
Clothing donated, handled through ware-
   houses in St. Paul, Hinckley, Sandstone
   and Duluth 25,000.00
Free railroad transportation obtained by
   the commissioners for fire sufferers, estimated 13,000.00
Total relief rendered by the commission.... $165,581.59
April 2, 1895, ... $2,233.29

February 13th, 1895, the Hon. Mr. Ferris introduced a bill for
an act to furnish grass seed for the benefit of the sufferers by forest
fires, and appropriating $15,000 for that purpose. This bill was duly

passed March 14th, 1895, and the seed was furnished in accordance with the provision of the act. The amount appropriated to the several counties was as follows:

Pine	$4,615.00
Morrison	2,754.00
Mille Lacs	1,374.00
Todd	1,383.00
Crow Wing	806.00
Cass	398.00
Aitkin	1,226.00
Carlton	679.00
Becker	180.00
Wadena	347.00
Kanebec	860.00
Otter Tail	300.00
Benton	78.00
Total	$15,000.00

In the general appropriation bill there was included an amount of $10,000 for the further assistance of fire sufferers, for the purchase of seed potatoes, seed corn, and other necessary relief.

Yours truly,

H. H. HART,

Secretary State Commission.

Your committee visited the towns of Sandstone, Hinckley, Pokegama, Mora and Milaca, and so far as possible conferred with the local authorities and relief committees in those towns, and also with many of the fire sufferers, and all seem to unite in the statement that further help is needed for the people in the burned district in the way of farming utensils and seeds for spring sowing, especially potatoes and garden seeds.

By request of the Minnesota State Commission for the relief of fire sufferers your committee edited the commission's accounts and found them correctly kept, and also found that the funds committed to its care had been wisely applied to the needs of the people.

The work of the commission has up to this date been done well. The cost of administration up to April 2, 1895, being only 3 9-10 per cent. of the receipts, which your committee regards as a very small percentage of cost, taking into consideration the amount of work performed covering a period of five months. It will be necessary for

LADY DONALD A. SMITH.

the commission to continue its work until the first of May, and there-after people in the afflicted districts should be left to their own resources.

In view of the work yet to be performed by the commission to relieve the wants of the fire sufferers and to supply seeds for spring sowing, farming utensils, etc., your committee would recommend that a further appropriation of ten thousand dollars ($10,000) be inserted in the general appropriation bill for the relief of the sufferers by forest fires in Pine and adjacent counties, said appropriation to be payable to the order of the chairman of the Minnesota State Commission for the relief of the fire sufferers.

Respectfully submitted,

J. T. WYMAN,
FRED A. HODGE,
J. Q. CRONKHITE,
On the part of the Senate.
O. O. HOLMAN,
H. R. MALLETTE,
AUG. J. ANDERSON,
C. F. STAPLES,
On the part of the House of Representatives.

BILL TO FURNISH GRASS SEED FOR DISTRIBUTION.

Section 1. That the sum of fifteen thousand ($15,000) dollars, be, and the same is hereby appropriated out of any moneys in the state treasury, not otherwise appropriated, for the purpose of this act.

Sec. 2. It is hereby made the duty of the county auditors of the counties afflicted by forest fires, in the state of Minnesota, wherein the grass and meadows were partially or wholly destroyed by forest fires in the year one thousand eight hundred and ninety-four (1894), to give notice before the tenth (10th) day of March, one thousand eight hundred and ninety-five (1895), to the respective town clerks of the several towns in said counties, requiring them to post notices immediately in at least three of the most public places in each town, notifying all persons wishing to avail themselves of the benefits of this act, to meet at the town clerk's office and file with the said town clerk on or before the 25th day of March, one thousand eight hundred and ninety-five (1895), an application duly subscribed and sworn to by the applicant before said town clerk or other officer authorized to administer oath; provided, that in districts not organized into towns, the said county auditor shall cause such notice to be posted in such unorganized district at such places as he shall deem necessary.

And, provided further, that the notice herein provided for shall also be published one week prior to the 25th day of March, 1895, in the official paper of said county.

Sec. 3. The application provided for in the preceding section shall contain a true statement of the number of acres of meadow owned or controlled by such applicant upon which the grass and grass roots were destroyed by said forest fires during the season of 1894; and how many acres of said medow said applicant intends and desires to re-seed during the season of 1895.

Such application shall further state the amount of hay harvested from said meadow annually, prior to the year of 1894, and the amount and kind of grass seed necessary to re-seed said meadow and the amount that said applicant desires to obtain from the state under the provisions of this act, and that said applicant has not procured and is not able to procure the necessary grass to re-seed said meadows so desired to be re-seeded, and that he desires said grass seed for no other purpose whatever, and that he will not sell or otherwise dispose of the same or any part thereof.

Said application shall also contain a full and true description of all real and personal property owned by the applicant and the incumbrances, if any, thereon; and a full description by government subdivisions of the lands upon which the applicant intends to sow said grass seed.

Sec. 4. The town clerk of each town shall, on or before the 25th day of March, 1895, forward all applications made before him to said county auditor of his county, who shall file the same in his office, and all applications by persons residing in any unorganized district shall, on or before the 25th day of March, 1895, file said application in the office of said county auditor.

All applications filed in any county auditor's office, under the provisions of this act, shall be open to public inspection, and no application shall be considered by the board provided for in section five of this act, except such as have been duly made and filed within the time and manner hereinbefore provided for.

Sec. 5. The board of county commissioners of each county where the provisions of this act are applicable shall be and are hereby constituted and appointed a board of examination and adjustment of the applications for grass seed under this act, and it shall be the duty of said board to meet at the county auditor's office on the first Monday in April, 1895, to examine and consider the applications that shall have been filed under the provisions of this act, and to determine who are entitled to the benefits herein provided for and the amount of moneys to which each applicant is entitled. And said board shall, within ten days thereafter, forward to the governor of the state of Minnesota, a statement giving the number of applicants; the name of such applicant; the number of acres of meadow upon which the grass and grass roots were destroyed by said forest fires in the said year 1894; the number of acres said applicant desires to re-seed; and the amount and kind of grass seed necessary to seed the same; and the amount of money necessary to purchase such seed. Such statement shall comprise and include only such applications as have been approved by said board and shall be signed by the chairman of said board of county commissioners and attested by the auditor of said county; provided, no applicant shall be allowed an amount exceeding the sum of fifty ($50) dollars.

Sec. 6. The governor upon receipt of the statement from such counties, who shall file them with him within the time specified in this act, if the same shall not exceed in the aggregate the sum hereby appropriated for such purpose, shall apportion and distribute the amounts called for to the several counties from which applications have been received, but if the amounts applied for shall exceed in the aggregate the amount herein appropriated for such purpose, then the governor shall apportion and distribute the sum to the counties applying pro rata in proportion to the amounts called for by said counties respectively, as shown by said statement of the county auditor thereof, and thereupon the governor shall inform each county auditor of the amount so apportioned to his county, and shall authorize the board of county commissioner to purchase grass seeds of the kinds necessary to the amount so apportioned and cause the same to be distributed to the applicants in said county, who are entitled to receive the same under the provisions of this act.

It shall be a misdemeanor for any county commissioner or other officer charged with any duty under this act, to make any gain or profit from any transaction growing out of or connected with the operation of this act.

Sec. 7. Immediately upon receiving notice from the governor of the amount apportioned to their county, the board of county com-

missioners shall meet at the county auditor's office and re-adjust the
application in their county, if necessary, for the grass seed, and apportion the amount that has been allowed to the county, among
the applicants approved by the said board pro rata in proportion to
the amount required by each, if there shall not be sufficient grass
seed to supply all in full, provided that after all approved applications
for said grass seed in any county are supplied, if there be a surplus
the same shall be sold by direction of the board of county commissioners and the sum received therefor shall be turned over to the
county treasurer who shall give his receipt therefor and the same shall
be placed on file in the office of the county auditor and the said
sum so received by said treasurer shall be by him paid over to the
state treasurer who shall receipt for the same to the said county
treasurer, and said sum so received by the said state treasurer shall
be placed to the credit of the general fund of this state.

See. 8. The county auditor of each county shall, as soon as the
board of county commissioners shall have performed the duty pre-
scribed in the preceding section, issue to each applicant an order directed to the person who shall be designated by the board of county
commissioners to distribute such grass seed for the number of bushels and kind of grass seed to which each applicant shall be entitled,
and upon presentation of the same to the person so designated to distribute such grass seed, he shall deliver to said applicant the amount
and kind of grass seed named in such orders. And such county
auditor shall keep a record in a book kept for that purpose to be
provided at the expense of the county, of the names to whom such
orders have been issued, and the amount and kind of grass seed
specified in such order.

See. 9. Any person or persons who shall, contrary to the provisions of this act, sell, transfer, take or carry away, or in any manner
dispose of the grass seed or any part thereof, furnished by the state
as provided in this act, or who shall use any of said grass seed for
any other purpose than of seeding his meadow, shall be guilty of a
misdemeanor and upon conviction thereof, before any justice of the
peace, having jurisdiction, shall pay a fine of not less than ten dollars
nor more than one hundred dollars, or be imprisoned in the county
jail for a term of not exceeding ninety days.

See. 10. The provisions of this act shall apply only to actual bona
fide residents of the county affected thereby.

See. 11. This act shall take effect and be in force from and after
its passage.

CORRESPONDENCE.

THE following letters are merely inserted to show something of the character of the work devolving upon the commission, and represents fairly the hundreds received of like nature:

I note your letter requesting information as to aid given people at Sandstone.

If you will send us a list of the people whom you have on the ground there, and of others as fast as they come in, we will send you complete information as to what has been done for them by this office.   Yours truly,

H. H. HART,

I wish to acknowledge receipt of your favor of October 18th, enclosing copy of a letter under that date to Hon. Charles A. Pillsbury, of Minneapolis, giving an outline of your work and the progress that had been made up to that time. I am very glad to know that at that date you were in fairly good shape, and I trust that the progress which has been made since then has been so good that you can now look forward to at least the beginning of the end of your work so far as the commission is concerned. As the season is progressing it is a satisfaction to know that these poor people are beginning to be sheltered in their homes and that they will be protected from the rude blasts of the coming winter.

Very truly yours,

N. G. NORTON.

Would you be kind enough to inform me, if possible, if the members of a family by the name of Ekstrom were among those who perished in the recent fire at Hinckley. The family consisted of Andrew and Maren Ekstrom, husband and wife, and a son, Gustav, who was about eighteen years of age. This inquiry comes from a daughter of the old folks, who lives in Norway. She has had several letters

SIR DONALD SMITH, K. C. B.

returned, and therefore she fears that they were among the unfortunate. Kindly try to ascertain what has become of those people, and very much oblige,   Yours very truly,

E. H. HOBE,

We have pleasure in informing you there is no such name as Ekstrom on the death list, nor is it on the list of fire sufferers.

Truly yours,
CH. ARVOLD.

I write you to make inquiry about feeding young stock and horses that was saved from the fire of September 1st, 1894. Please let me know as soon as possible and oblige.

E. C. BUEL,

In behalf of the Presbyterian Church of this place we take the liberty of addressing you, hoping the commission, through you, will be able to afford us help in building a church. At time of fire we had a nice church, and being close to the woods, we were unable to get insurance, consequently it was a total loss, and having lost all our own property we can not do much towards building. At the present time we are short $400, or a little more, of completing building. Now, if you can help us, say $300, I think we can raise balance from outside friends. We are very truly yours,

J. S. LYNDS, Trustee.
M. BULLIS, Trustee.
GEORGE WILKES, Trustee.
ANGUS GUNN, Deacon.

I appeal to you for help. We have had a great deal of help but we can not cultivate our land without a team and implements to work with and seed to sow. We thought with five cows that we would be able to get along without more help, but it takes pretty near all the milk money to feed the cows and horse. The horse we have for the keeping this winter. I shall lose it in plowing time. I do not know what to do unless you help us to make a payment on a team. I shall have to quit selling milk, and my husband is not able to do hard work. We have to build fences and I shall have to hire help, and am unable to pay for it. We did not get any breaking done last fall. Mr. Miller has dropped us long ago and our supply is all gone except flour. I am willing and able to work, but with all my efforts I cannot feed and clothe them as they should be. I have four young children and a crippled husband to work for. I drive every morning to town, four miles and one-half, with the milk and leave my baby, one year old, at home.   Respectfully yours,

LOUISE C. BILADOE.

I am in receipt of your letter of March 9th inclosing petition from Gilbert, Morrison county, and will take immediate steps to look into the matter.

The state commission some time ago gave temporary relief to the fire sufferers in Morrison county, and the funds at their disposal will not admit of their giving any considerable additional relief. I hope, however, that we may be able to give them necessary relief in the line of seed.   H. H. HART.

WINDHOM, MINN., Sept. 4, 1894.

GOV. KNUTE NELSON:

I wired you today to "Draw on me for one hundred dollars, as token of partial sympathy for the fire sufferers. Pledge same amount from Glencoe."   Yours truly,

S. H. REED.

LAKEFIELD, MINN., Oct. 24, 1894.

MR. KENNETH CLARK, ST. PAUL:

You will find enclosed an order for ten dollars ($10) which is sent to you for the relief of the "fire sufferers." The pupils, not the teachers, of the Lakefield school, set on foot the idea of having an entertainment for the benefit of the fire sufferers, and as they could not find a more worthy cause, the teachers have helped as far as possible in the entertainment. The sum is small, and yet it is not, for a village of this size, but we hope it will benefit some one.

MISS FLORA GALBREATH, Principal.

MEDALIA, Oct. 23, 1894.

MR. PILLSBURY:

We have a large lot of bedding ready for the "fire sufferers." Will you please tell me whom to send it to for distribution?

Very respectfully,

MRS. WILLIAM BROWN.

GRAND RAPIDS, MICH., Oct. 12, 1894.

KENNETH CLARK, ESQ.:

I enclose a draft on Chicago for two hundred dollars for the "Relief of Fire Sufferers'" fund. This is contributed by the Misses Isabella C. Wood and Lorraine F. Wood, daughters of the late Ransom E. Wood, of this city, and who now reside in Europe.

Yours truly,   J. F. BAARS, Cashier.

APPLETON, MINN., Sept. 4, 1894.
MR. C. A. PILLSBURY:

Enclosed please find check for $25 to add to the relief fund for the Hinckley sufferers. It is small, but well meant.

Yours truly,

A. K. PEDUM.

SHATTUCK SCHOOL, FARIBAULT, MINN., Sept. 13, 1894.
MR. KENNETH CLARK:

I have just returned from Chicago, and find the enclosed letter from a manufacturing company in Virginia, from which we purchase our cadet cloth. The piece of goods has also arrived and I send it to your address by the United States Express. I am sure it will gratify my merchant if his gift is acknowledged from your office. With admiration for the noble work you and your associates are doing for their sufferings, I am

Yours very truly,

JAMES DOBBIN.

CHARLOTTESVILLE, VA., Sept. 5, 1894.
REV. JAMES DOBBIN:

The terrible loss of life and suffering, resulting from the fires in a portion of your state, appeals to our sympathies most earnestly, and as clothing will be needed, we decide to send a piece of goods for the benefit of the homeless survivors. Casting around for some one to send it to, in the absence of any suggestion in the telegrams about the fires as to who is chairman of the relief committee, I conclude to forward to you, with the request that you will see that it reaches its proper destination, and oblige. Most truly yours,

H. C. MARCHENT, President.

CANNON FALLS, MINN., Sept. 5, 1894.
I have just wired you, "Draw on village of Cannon Falls, donations of village and citizens, three hundred and fifty dollars ($350). More will follow." We hope to send some more within a few days.

Very truly,

DR. H. E. CONLEY, Mayor.   CLIFF W. GRESS, Cashier.

CHICAGO, Sept. 6, 1894.
With sympathy for the sufferers by the great fire in the state of Minnesota, I send the amount of the enclosed check.

Yours truly,

(Check $100.)   J. H. M'VICKER,

President of McVicker's Theater Company.

CARLISLE, ARK., Sept. 8, 1894.
Enclosed please find Pacific Express order for $6.75 (six dollars

MRS. ELIZA TOWERS AND SON.

and seventy-five cents), sent by citizens of our little village to help relieve suffering of the unfortunates at Hinckley. Not being able to find out names of chairman of relief committees, we send this to you, knowing that it will be applied to uses for which it is sent, as soon as though sent to relief committee. Our villages is small, but we send our little mite, and ask God's blessing on your unfortunate people.
Yours truly,
J. H. CUSHING,
C. H. OSBORN.

OMAHA, NEB., Sept. 8, 1894.

Please accept the enclosed two dollars for the use of the fire sufferers and oblige.
MR. AND MRS. I. BOYD.

LOS ANGELES, CAL., Sept. 9, 1894.

In reading the "Los Angeles Times" I saw your name mentioned. It was in reference to your going to Sandstone to look over the burnt district to see what help was needed. My heart goes out in sympathy with those sorrowing ones in those towns where the fires have occurred, and how I wish I had plenty of money to send to you, to use for these needy ones. Enclosed you will find postoffice order for $5. It is small, I know, but it will help a little.
Kindly yours,
MISS MARY CONSIDINE,
Pasadena, California.

CANNON FALLS, MINN., Sept. 10, 1894.

I ship you today by the Minneapolis & St. Louis Railway two boxes of clothing for fire sufferers, and more will follow in a day or two. I had no means of knowing how to ship, further than direct to you. We have raised about $450 in cash besides clothing.
S. S. LEWIS,
Chairman Relief Committee.

SAUK CENTER, MINN., Sept. 11, 1894.

Advise me where to ship bedding and clothing for sufferers.
P. LAMB.

FAIRFAX, MINN., Sept. 10, 1894.

Enclosed please find draft for sixty-five dollars and thirty-five cents, forty dollars and thirty cents of which was given by private subscriptions, and twenty-five out of village treasury, to be given to the dear people who are suffering from the recent fire. Praying that God may bless the small donation to them, and also encourage others to do the same, they have our prayers and sympathy. Please send me a receipt for the same.

Yours on behalf of the citizens of Fairfax,
REV. E. WILLIAMS.

MANKATO, MINN, Sept. 11, 1891.

Enclosed please find draft for one hundred and forty dollars from the ladies of Mankato, for the fire sufferers of Hinckley. A benefit entertainment given last night, of which the ladies had charge, raised the above amount. We send this right to you, and trust it may relieve some poor soul in distress and need. We know of no better committee to send it to.

Yours very respectfully,
MRS. W. B. CRAIG.
Chairman of Committee.

BYRON, MINN., Sept. 11, 1884.

Yesterday I presented to my congregation the claims of the fire sufferers, and asked them to give an offering, which they cheerfully did. Enclosed you will find my check for $30 as a contribution from the congregation of the Byron Methodist Church.

Please acknowledge. Sincerely,
REV. W. E. KING, Pastor.

OWATONNA, Sept. 14, 1891.

I have this day deposited, subject to your order, one hundred and forty-five dollars ($145) to be used for the relief of sufferers at Hinckley. We should be glad if this could be used for home building. I also hold, subject to your order, one car of merchandise, flour and furniture. Please advise me. Very truly,
JAMES A. CHAMBERLAIN.

WAHPETON, N. D., Sept. 15, 1891.

I take pleasure in sending you herewith on behalf of Turn Verein Norwaerts and the citizens of Wahpeton, draft No. 17,326, of $103.85, for the relief of the Minnesota fire sufferers. The above amount represents the net proceeds realized at a "Relief Ball," held under the auspices of the members of the Turn Verein Norwaerts, for the Minnesota fire sufferers. Respectfully yours,
CHARLES G. BADE.

ELBOW LAKE, MINN., Sept. 17, 1894.

The Ladies' Aid Society, of the Presbyterian Church of this place, have packed a box of clothing, bedding, etc., for the fire sufferers of Hinckley. As treasurer of the relief committee, we would like to have some information as to the place of sending, and to whom it may be addressed. The box is in readiness, and will be sent immediately upon receipt of information.

Yours, in the interest of the afflicted,

MRS. JAMES GODWARD,

President Ladies' Aid Society.

VERNON CENTER, MINN. Sept. 18, 1894.

The W. C. T. U., of Vernon Center, ship you today ten sacks of flour, one sack potatoes, one sack beans, one sack corn, six sacks, two boxes and one parcel of bedding and clothing, and inclose within this $8.50 check, which we trust you may receive in good order, and would like it to have been a much more liberal contribution.

Respectfully,

MRS. JENNIE R. BABCOCK.

MINNEAPOLIS, MINN., Sept. 20, 1894.

Herewith find account sales of Martin & Wyman, together with their check, duly indorsed, calling for $478.10, same being proceeds of sale of care No. 17,128, received from the citizens of Warren, Marshall County Minnesota, for the benefit of the sufferers caused by the late fire at Hinckley and vicinity, for which you will kindly sign the enclosed receipt and duplicate, and return same to this office, and much oblige.   Yours truly,

C. M. AMSDEN.

"Philadelphia, Sept. 5, 1894.—As mayor of Philadelphia and chairman of the citizens' permanent relief committee, I beg to convey to you the sympathy of this community with your people for the great loss of life and property occasioned by the terrible forest fires, and to request that you advise me as to the exact condition of affairs in that afflicted district, what relief is being given, and whether assistance is needed from sources outside of your state.

"EDWIN S. STUART,

Mayor of Philadelphia."

The same telegram was sent to Hon. George W. Peck, governor of Wisconsin.

B. W. DAVIS.

CAPT. W. R. BOURNE.

LONDON, ENGLAND, Sept. 4, 1894.

Deeply sympathize with sufferers by fire and am sending you today five thousand dollars for their relief.

DONALD SMITH.

LEMSFORD, ENGLAND, Sept. 6, 1894.

Have cabled Turnbull to send five thousand dollars in aid of relief fund. MOUNT-STEPHEN.

LONDON, ENGLAND, Sept. 6, 1894.

My wife sends you today one thousand dollars for relief fund.

SMITH.
Bank of Montreal.

MONTREAL, Sept. 7, 1894.

Will you kindly make over the enclosed check for $500 to the committee, as a contribution towards the relief of those who have so sadly suffered in the recent fires in Minnesota.

Yours sincerely,

R. B. ANGUS.

LETTER FROM POET LONGFELLOW'S SISTER.

CAMBRIDGE, MASS.

DEAR MR. WILKINSON:

Your letter has been received. I hasten to send you check enclosed for $100, which I hope will aid you in your church building in the fire district. The fires have been terrible in your midst.

Wishing you continued happiness and prosperity in your blessed work. I am Cordially yours,

MARY L. GREENLEAF.

MONTREAL, May 7, 1895.

I greatly regret that there has been so much delay in sending you the photographs of my husband and myself you kindly desire to have, but I had no photograph of myself in the house, and it is only within these few days back I have recovered sufficiently from a severe illness to be able to sit for one. They are forwarded by this mail, and I trust will still be in time for your purpose. It is hardly necessary I should say to you how glad we were to have had it in our power to contribute somewhat to the fund for the relief of the sufferers from fire in Minnesota, whose condition was heart-rending. We know how sympathetic our good friends Mr. and Mrs. J. J. Hill at all times are, and that their efforts and generous kindness in the particular case to which you refer should have been exerted to the fullest extent is only what we, and all who have the privilege of their acquaintance would have expected of them.

Thanking you much for your kind consideration, believe me to be, my dear sir, Very sincerely yours,

ISABELLA S. SMITH.

Dear Brother: I am glad to hear of the good work you are doing for the fire sufferers. You can use $250 I have had sent from a friend in the East. Only need must be considered; we must do our best to assist all sorts and conditions of men. Truly yours,

H. B. WHIPPLE.
Bishop of Minnesota.

ADVENTURES.

THE Hinckley fire, like all other great scourges, brought to light the true nature of men and women who seek to make calamity a means of gain. There were persons who sought to obtain relief at different places and here and there those who tried hard to make people think that they, before the fire, had been very well off, in fact "fixed in a way that left nothing to be desired!" All of which their neighbors never knew and which they themselves never told the county assessor. There were well-to-do people, about whose circumstances there could be no doubt, who felt that they should be dealt with according to what they had lost. "I want my share," said one; "divide up and I shall be satisfied; I lost twenty times as much as Smith lost." Such a method would have left the homeless in destitution. There was no possible plan of making up every man's loss; to do so would have taken millions of dollars. The man who lost least, who had a family and stayed at his old home, got relatively most.

Then there appeared the festive tramp who had been in the fire, came near being burnt up and was begging his way "to home, back East." One such got a good suit in Minneapolis, but came to a full stop when he, one fine morning, called upon a gentleman who was on the citizens' committee, told his story and was informed that if he were a real fire sufferer, he should be sent to his intended destination when asked to come to headquarters he had another engagement!

The ladies of the houses to which men like this came had read through blinding tears the sad stories of hair breadth escapes, and the tenderest emotions of their souls were moved and they were not afraid to express their interest in the woe begone tales such men could tell. "Were you in the fire?" "Yes, m'am; I lived two miles and a half above Hinckley. Lost my sister an' cousin an' a young lady as I was to have made my wife. All gone! I as was in a good place at work on a farm with Mr. Anderson, as is now dead, an' his wife in the hospital, have to beg to get back to my folks back East." To his friend round the corner: "This will give us both a cigar and something to drink. I tell you as this fire racket works well!"

One man asked aid who had eleven hundred dollars in the bank. One man came and said to Mr. Pillsbury: "I should think you would not keep such people as K., who is not very respectable, never had a good character." Mr. Pillsbury said: "I suppose these people were in the fire, lost all they had and are penniless and homeless?" "Yes, of course." "Well," said he, "this money was not all given by saints. Much of it was given by those who do not call themselves over religious. We shall ask no questions on such matters; we shall try to see that all have a place in which to live and that they have enough to eat, and clothes suitable to wear."

Right minded folks will see the wisdom of this plan.

Then there were men who passed through the fire who desired to have it thought they played a noble part, when men who were with them know that nature had not designed to make them prominent in the annals of courage. There was here and there a professional man or a tradesman, whose desire for cash got the better of his generous instincts, not to say sense of justice; but such was the exception. The cases where the adventurer and swindler got an advantage or made gain are few and unimportant, scarcely worth a name or place in this work except to show that selfishness will work, even when sadness is at its saddest.

WHAT CORPORATIONS DID.

THE work of the state commission and of all the committees was greatly helped by the splendid generosity of the corporations which had interests in the regions over which the fire passed. From the start the aid was prompt and given in a most cheerful spirit. In looking at this fact another must also be kept in view. The corporations were the heaviest losers. The St. Paul and Duluth Railway had buildings to erect and permanent way to repair for a distance of twenty miles. They put in more than twenty-two thousand ties under the rails, and of course, had to replace all the steel rails warped and otherwise damaged by fire. They had one train burnt so that nothing was left of value. They had the loss of much traffic for a time and paid the wages of all persons who in their employ sustained damage. There is no such thing as covering all this by insurance. The Great Northern Railway had thirty miles of track to repair and the Kettle river bridge to build anew. This bridge is more than three hundred feet long and a hundred and forty feet high. Timber suitable for many parts of this work was not on hand in Duluth at the time of the fire, but was being cut. In a few hours three hundred men were put to work on the bridge. It took them nine days to get it ready for service. They worked every possible hour, night and day. The master mechanic, Mr. Whyte, the master carpenter, Mr. Finlayson, and General Manager Mr. Farrington kept vigilant oversight of what was being done. Mr. S. Hill and Mr. J. J. Hill from time to time overlooked the work. The intention was to make a better bridge than the one burned ever was and the result justifies the design. The road repaired, wherever possible, was ballasted with stone from the quarries at Sandstone. It is intended to use this material all along the line so as to give durability and prevent dust. These two railways had to employ a small army of men for a long time and the mathematical precision with which the whole work was done was the admiration of all who

FREDERICK WEYERHAUSER.

saw it. The telegraph connections being repaired at a very early stage in the reconstructive work, gave means of communication with all parts of the railway systems. The wires could be tapped at any place and messages sent for men or material and thus time and labor were saved. It was in scenes like these when to railway officials every moment was of value, when a thousand things pressed for prompt attention that the heads of these corporations gave ready ear and whole souled help to the needs of those who had lived along their line and carried goods and people free; in fact all who were in the fire, their relatives who went to visit and friends who went to help them from September to November tenth, 1894. To this they added large gifts, as the report of the state commission shows The telegraph companies also joined the noble throng of those who desired to assist, and sent messages of all kinds free. When it is recorded that the man who had only a dollar was ready to share it and the poor farmer who had little, to divide it, and the newsboy to give of his gain and the rich man of his plenty, we also must tell that corporations, which are often abused and said to have no souls, in this great holocaust behaved as if they were all soul. The following resolutions were sent to President Samuel Hill, of the Eastern division of the Great Northern road, and A. B. Plough, general manager of the St. Paul and Duluth road.

Dear Sir:—The Minnesota State Relief Commission has now practically completed its work and I am instructed to extend to you in behalf of the commission their hearty thanks for the numerous courtesies which they received at your hands, all of which are warmly appreciated.

I am instructed also to emphasize what has already been said by the commission in its printed report by way of appreciation of the generosity and promptness with which you have responded to every call on behalf of the sufferers by forest fires. In the opinion of the commission nothing has been left undone by your company which could possibly have been expected of them under the circumstances. By your promptness and energy you have prevented much suffring and have added largely to the ability of those people to provide for themselves.

By order of the State Commission. H. H. HART,
Secy. of the Commission.

The telegraph companies also received well merited thanks and the resolution printed below shows in what form they were sent to I. McMichael, Esq., superintendent of the Western Union and to Harry A. Tuttle, Esq., general superintendent North American Telegraph Company.

Dear Sir:—The Minnesota State Relief Commission has now practically completed its work, and I am instructed to express to you their grateful appreciation of the generosity of your company in extending the free use of the lines to the commission. This privilege greatly facilitated the work of the commission and enabled them to operate much more efficiently and promptly than they otherwise could have done. I am, dear sir,

Yours respectfully,   H. H. HART,
Secy. State Relief Commission.

WISCONSIN.

The year 1894 will be lo   remembered in this state for its terrible forest fires. Not since the Pesthigo fires have there been such devastation. The intense heat and the scarcity of rain made the forests almost like a kiln, so that when once fire began it was always most difficult and often impossible to keep it in check. The experience gained by woodsmen and lumber men make them experts in dealing with forest fires, but all the knowledge and the resources of man availed little against the sweeping flames which are driven like an overwhelming flood by a strong wind, leaving destruction and death in its path. All the summer fire had been feared and looked for and by the end of July it was said not less than five million dollars worth of pine had been destroyed. The attention of men engaged in the lumber business had been called to this fact in the Mississippi Valley Lumberman of August third, by Mr. F. F. Morgan, who asked the help of that able paper to treat the matter exhaustively. All was done which was possible to do, but disaster was not averted. Fire extended over a space nearly fifty miles wide. The northern line of fire being about forty miles south of Superior. Hamlets and villages and towns shared the same fate. Phillips was burned on the 27th of July and the loss of life would have been great had it not been for the fact that the inhabitants escaped by taking train to the places of safety in which they found refuge. The John R. Davis Lumber Company was heaviest loser in a commercial point of view. Mr. B. W. Davis, manager, deserves great credit for his brave help of all in sorrow who could be assisted. Governor Peck wired help and on Sunday morning reached Phillips with a train and provisions of all kinds. He soon saw how appalling the damage was. Phillips, which with its more than two thousand people, looked bright and fair on Friday morning, on the Sunday after lay a heap of ruins. The people burned out at Phillips received help from Merrill, Rhinelander, Wausau. Portage. Superior. High Bridge. Mellen,

A BIG LOAD OF LOGS.

Stevens Point, Chicago, Milwaukee, Eau Claire, Fond du Lac. The
E. P. Allis Company of Milwaukee, sent $100. Major Up-
ham came with a committee from Marshfield and brought several cars
loaded with provisions, which were very welcome to the homeless
people. The dead, twelve in number, rest in peace in the midst of
scenes which were so familiar to them. A switch engine took 20
cars full of people twelve miles out of danger.

Mason, a small town on the Omaha road in Bayfield county, was
also the scene of a destructive fire Friday night. The plant of the
White River Lumber Company, a Weyerhauser interest, managed by
John A. Humbird, was entirely destroyed. The loss included the
saw mill, planing mill, about 33,000,000 feet of lumber and many
houses of employes. The loss to the White River Lumber Company is about $700,000, on which there was insurance to the amount
of $300,000. Mr. Humbird was seen in St. Paul and, in conversa-
tion with a representative of The Lumberman, stated that everything was so dry and was cleaned up so thoroughly that there was
hardly a bushel of ashes left. The camps of the Thompson Lumber
Company at White River were also burned, as was also the headquarters of the Ashland Lumber Company at Shores Landing.

The Barronett Lumber Company's entire plant was consumed.
W. R. Bourne, of the Barronett Lumber Company, who went up to
that town immediately upon receipt of the news of the fire, telegraphed the Milwaukee Sentinal that his company loses about 13,-
000,000 feet of lumber and O. A. Ritan & Co., about 1,000,000 at
Grand Lake. The Barronett Lumber Company also lost its mill,
thirty-five houses and all its property at Barronett, valued at about
$275,000. The insurance on the lumber was $115,000. About fifty
familes lost everything. O. A. Ritan Co.'s loss is estimated at $45,-
000. The Barronett Lumber Company's mill was insured to the
amount of $20,000 making its total insurance $135,000. The loss
at Barronett is estimated to be about as follows:

13,500,000 feet of lumber	$130,000
13,000,000 shingles	19,000
4,000,000 lath	5,000
Saw mill	40,000
Planing mill	10,000
Boarding house	3,000
Three barns	2,000
Dry sheds and shingle sheds	1,000

General View of Log Gang.

Store, office and stock 13,000
Windmill 2,000
Blacksmith and carpenter shop and tools 10,000
Logging sleds 7,000
Dwelling houses 20,000
200 tons hay and sheds 3,000
10,000 cords of slabs 10,000
Total loss $275,000

In view of the fact that the state is paying for the cultivation of trees; that the lumber supply is being so rapidly lessened, while the increase of demand has grown five times in less than sixty-five years; that forest fires raged in the great timber states of Michigan, Wisconsin and Minnesota; that towns like Mason, Phillips, Barronett, Shell Lake and many others in Wisconsin either were destroyed or came so near being destroyed as to terrify all the country round, is it not wise to take in hand seriously the question of prevention of fires? It does not sound much to hear that Shell Lake, for instance, suffered by fire, but it means much to the men who owned mills, to men who worked in them and cut sixteen million feet of lumber in a year, to Mrs. Towers, who had to drag her son out of bed when he had typhoid fever, to take him to the barn and throw water upon him, while she also saw her home burn to the ground. These forest fires mean that wake will be followed by want. It is of no use for the lumbermen to look for efficient help from legislatures in the prevention of disastrous fires. The men engaged in the cutting and sale of timber could raise a fund of five thousand dollars a year by giving twenty dollars each and the railways give transportation to a man, who could do more to prevent fires than has ever been yet done. As long as all kinds of refuse is left and the forests are unenclosed and every man can do in them pretty much as he will, we shall in dry seasons have calamity. Calamity which will move the very souls of men of all classes and in all lands. In the reports of relief we see this set forth. Henry Irving sends $500 to the fire sufferers, which it appears was not required in Wisconsin. Lord Mountstephen, of London, sends $5,000 to Minnesota, and Sir Donald Alex Smith and Lady Smith send six thousand dollars. Poor newsboys give of their cents. All this is more than noble, but we should see to it that the possibility of such need never again rises, if this can be.

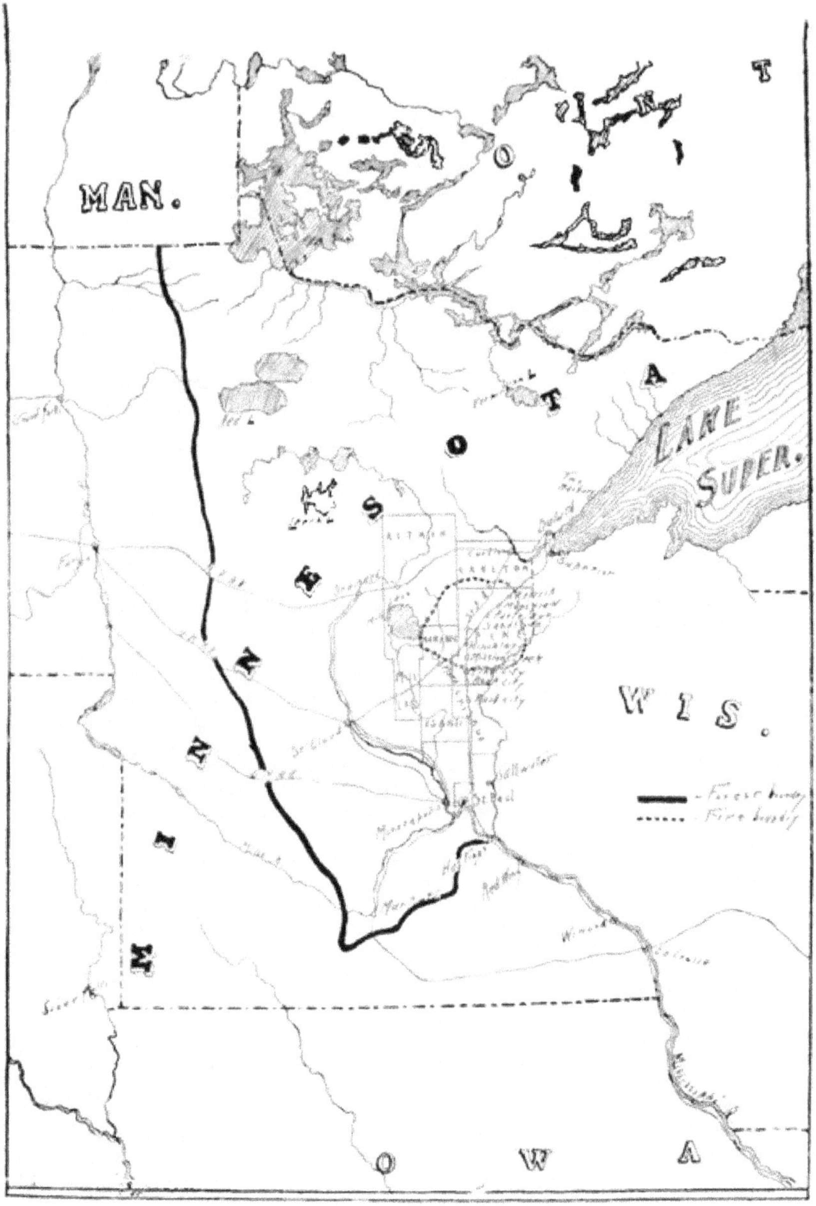
MAN.
MINNESOTA
LAKE SUPER.
WIS.

CONTENTS.

ILLUSTRATIONS AND PHOTOGRAPHS.

C. A. PILLSBURY.

REPORT OF THE STATE COMMISSION.

FOR THE RELIEF OF THE FOREST FIRE SUFFERERS.

To His Excellency, Knute Nelson, Governor of Minnesota:

On Saturday, Sept. 1, 1894, occurred one of the most dreadful calamities which this country has ever seen. Owing to the long protracted drought, forest fires had prevailed in different localities for several weeks, but on that day the wind suddenly rose to a tornado, and a small fire which was burning near Brown's Hill spread with frightful rapidity, and was carried on the wings of the tornado over a district covering, probably, from three hundred and fifty to four hundred square miles. Almost without warning, the fire swept over the villages of Mission Creek, Hinckley, Pokegama, Sandstone, Finlayson and Miller. A furnace blast swept over the fated district and left behind it absolute devastation. Every building in Hinckley and Sandstone, with one or two unimportant exceptions, was completely destroyed. Nearly every farmhouse was destroyed, with barns, crops and supplies, and in most cases, live stock. The material loss will probably approximate $750,000, in addition to the timber destroyed, but this is a small matter compared with the dreadful loss of life. So sudden was the onset of the flames that the people could only rush from their houses and seek a place of refuge, without even an effort to save their household goods and personal effects. Four hundred and eighteen persons, comprising about one-sixth of the entire population of the burnt district, are known to have perished by a most frightful death in the flames. A great many families lost one or more members, and some families were wiped entirely out of existence. The charred bodies, in most cases unrecognizable, were gathered up and buried by tender hands after the fire.

The full record of the heroic and unselfish endeavors of the people to rescue one another from threatening death can never be fully written. Some perished while striving to save the lives of others. The charred and shriveled hands of others testify to their endeavors to save their friends. A few cool headed men at Hinckley saved many lives by urging the people to abandon everything and hasten to the gravel pit. At Pokegama, a little group of people, who lay stifling in a pool of water, were preserved largely by the efforts of

one man who went from one to another, drenching them with water
and encouraging them to hold out through three dreadful hours.

The conduct of the employes of the St. Paul & Duluth and Eastern
Minnesota railways cannot be too highly praised. Engineer Best
and Conductor Powers of the Eastern Minnesota remained stead-
fast at their posts, and made up a train for the rescue of the sufferers, with as much coolness as if they were doing ordinary work,
although they knew that every moment's delay diminished the
chances of their successful escape. Engineer Root, Fireman John
McGowan, Conductor Thomas Sullivan and Porter John Wesley
Blair of the St. Paul & Duluth road were equally faithful to their
trusts.

No less heroic were those unseen and unnoted examples of men
and women in farmhouses and scattered hamlets, who sacrificed
themselves in an effort to preserve the lives of others. "Greater love
hath no man than this, that a man lay down his life for his friends."

Before the flames had died away, news of the disaster had spread
abroad. A relief train was sent to Hinckley by the St. Paul & Duluth Railroad Company, with a corps of physicians, and the first
party of refugees was brought into Pine City about 2 o'clock Sunday morning, September 1st.

The highest praise is due to the citizens of Pine City for the
promptness and efficiency with which they met the emergency. On
Sunday morning, September 2d, without any previous warning,
nearly five hundred refugees poured into Pine City, a village of a
thousand inhabitants. A relief committee was immediately organized and systematic plans were adopted. When the relief train from
St. Paul, Minneapolis, Stillwater, White Bear and Rush City arrived
at seven o'clock Sunday evening, with blankets, clothing, provisions,
hospital supplies, and a military guard, they found literally nothing
to be done; all of the sufferers had been fed, an eating house had
been established, sleeping quarters had been provided in the court-
house, schoolhouse, and private families, and a hospital had been
organized for the sick. Considering the resources of the village
of Pine City, this was in our judgment the most extraordinary
achievement in the history of this calamity. The local committee
at Pine City continued in charge of the work of relieving and caring
for the fire sufferers at that place until the 9th of September, when
they requested the state commission to relieve them of the work, but
continued to assist the commission by their united and individual
counsel and assistance. The Pine City committee received and disbursed $2,522.00, part of which was from local contributions, and part
was sent in to the committee from the outside points. Mr.
James Hurley was chairman of the committee, and Hon. F. A.
Hodge was treasurer. Mr. Albert Pennington acted as storekeeper for receiving and distributing supplies, without compensation.
The use of the Seventh Day Adventist Church was generously furnished for a storehouse, and rooms were freely furnished by citizens for storehouses, offices, etc.

About two-thirds of the refugees from the fire were taken to Duluth and West Superior. Those who went to Superior were soon transferred to Duluth, where some twelve hundred people received at least temporary relief. The action of the people of Duluth was no less prompt and hearty than that of the people of Pine City. A relief committee was appointed, and the churches, the benevolent societies, the Odd Fellows and the Bethel entered heartily into the work. At the Pilgrim Congregational Church, the news came during the morning service that a large number of survivors were on their way to Duluth; the pastor pronounced the benediction forthwith and the people adjourned to the basement of the church to make preparations, and at four o'clock they were prepared to feed and lodge one hundred and twenty refugees. A room was stocked with clothing, a supply of hot water was obtained from the Spalding House for bathing purposes, and before night the unexpected guests were comfortably housed, clothed and cared for. Similar activity and efficiency were displayed by other churches and organizations. The local committee established headquarters with a force of clerks for the investigation and registration of each case. An eating house was established at the armory with accommodations for five hundred people, and complete arrangements for lodging and caring for these people were made at the Berkelman Block. A large number was cared for at the Bethel for a considerable time, and a considerable number in a building fitted up by the Odd Fellows.

When the State Relief Commission was established, the Duluth local committee undertook to continue the work of temporary relief —feeding, etc. The citizens of Duluth raised about $13,000 in cash, besides donations of lumber, clothing, provisions, etc., and the work was efficiently carried on. Employment was found for many of the fire sufferers in Duluth and vicinity, and nearly two hundred people were located. The rest were cared for until such time as they were prepared, either to return to their former homes in the burned district, or to locate elsewhere. The local committee was made up of the mayor and the best business men of the city, with Hon. E. C. Gridley as chairman. These gentlemen gave several weeks' time freely to the work. The churches of the city, under the leadership of such clergymen as Bishop James McGolrick, Rev. E. M. Noyes and Rev. Dr. Salter, did noble service.

The suffering by forest fires was not entirely confined to Pine county; great damage was caused by fires in Mille Lacs county and, although no lives were lost, three hundred and seventy people were sufferers by fire to a greater or less extent. In Carlton county also, a considerable number of people suffered serious loss by fires. Local committees were organized for the relief of these people at St. Cloud, Cloquet and Mora, all of which did efficient work. A considerable number of fire sufferers from the burned district were taken to St. Paul and Minneapolis, where they received most generous care at the hands of the local committees. The hospital facilities at Pine City proving inadequate, the more serious cases there were transferred to Minneapolis, where they were cared for by the hospitals, free of expense.

At about the same time with the Hinckley fire, forest fires occurred in the vicinity of New York Mills, Otter Tail county, and applications were subsequently made for assistance by the local relief committee. As it appeared that the need was greater than could be well met by the local organizations, a limited amount of aid was extended. Applications for relief were received also from Aitkin, Cass, Crow Wing, Sherburne, Todd and Wadena counties. Most of these applications were rejected, for the reason that upon investigation they did not seem to come within the province of the commission, but in a few cases of serious suffering, resulting from local forest fires, aid was extended.

At first it was impracticable to adopt a thorough system; the refugees came in, destitute of everything, and it was necessary, first of all, to feed the hungry and cloth the naked. Clothing was given out freely, according to the evident and immediate needs of the people, and all fire sufferers were fed, but after two or three days a systematic plan of registration was adopted, both in Duluth and Pine City. A system of issuing clothing and other supplies, on duly authorized requisitions, was adopted, and an effort was made to regulate the relief given, according to the needs of the individual.

It soon became apparent, owing to the magnitude of the disaster and the fact that the sufferers were scattered in so many different places, that it would be necessary to have some general agency established to oversee the work of caring for the sufferers. Accordingly, Governor Nelson, Sept. 3, 1894, appointed the State Commission for the relief of fire sufferers, under the following proclamation:

RELIEF PROCLAMATION.

Information of an official character has reached me that the villages of Hinckley, Sandstone, Mission Creek, and the neighboring towns and farms have been destroyed by forest fires; that hundreds of lives have been sacrificed, and suffering and destitution are on every hand; that the survivors of this terrible devastation are in immediate need of food, shelter and everything that makes existence possible.

This appalling disaster appeals to every heart of generous impulses, and the case is one that demands the immediate and liberal assistance of all good citizens of this state.

Now, Therefore, I, Knute Nelson, governor of the State of Minnesota, in view of this awful calamity which has befallen our people, and by virtue of the authority in me vested, do hereby appeal to all liberal and public-spirited citizens, to all municipalities and to all religious and benevolent institutions of this state, to take immediate action toward securing contributions for the relief of the prevailing distress.

I hereby appoint the following State Commission, authorized to receive contributions of money and supplies, and to spend and disburse the same:

C. A. Pillsbury, of Minneapolis; Kenneth Clark, of St. Paul; Charles H. Graves, of Duluth, Matthew G. Norton, of Winona, Hastings H. Hart, of St. Paul.

In Witness Whereof, I have hereunto set my hand and caused to be affixed the great seal of the State of Minnesota, at the capitol, in the city of St. Paul, this 3d day of September, A. D. 1894.

KNUTE NELSON.

F. P. BROWN, Secretary of State.

The commission organized at St. Paul, Sept. 5, 1894, by electing C. A. Pillsbury, chairman, Kenneth Clark, treasurer, and H. H. Hart, secretary, and requested Governor Nelson to act as a member of the commission, to which he consented. It was agreed to proceed immediately to visit Hinckley, Duluth and Pine City, in order that the commission might ascertain what was neccessary to be done. The commission visited Duluth, Sept. 6, 1894, where they found the work of the local committee thoroughly and efficiently organized, and after a full conference, it was agreed that the Duluth local committee should continue to care for the immediate wants of all fire sufferers in Duluth, but that the work of permanent relief should be delegated to the State Relief Commission. They visited Hinckley and Pine City, Sept. 7th, and it was agreed there, as in Duluth, that the local committee should undertake the temporary relief of the fire sufferers, while the work of permanent relief should be delegated to the State Commission. On Sept. 11th, however, at the request of the Pine City local committee, the State Commission assumed charge of both permanent and temporary relief at that place. The Pine City committee co-operated heartily with the State Commission at every point, and the most satisfactory relations existed between the two agencies. As soon as practicable, the headquarters of the commission were removed from Pine City to Hinckley, for convenience in superintending the work of locating and building for the fire sufferers.

As soon as the news of the disaster spread, supplies of all kinds began to pour in from every direction in great quantities. Clothing (new and second hand), bedding and furniture, flour and groceries, meats, bread, milk, medicines and hospital supplies poured in abundantly. The warehouse facilities at Hinckley and Pine City were so inadequate that it was necessary to establish depots of supplies at Minneapolis and St. Paul, where the donations could be assorted and classified and forwarded in suitable quantities as needed. The larger part of the supplies from abroad were sent to St. Paul, where the work of assorting and classifying them was admirably systemized by the local committee, thus making the goods much more useful than they would otherwise have been. Careful accounts were kept of the quantities and estimated values of the goods received. The values of the donated supplies that passed through the St. Paul warehouse is estimated at $22,000. That this valuation was not fictitious, was shown by the fact that a dealer in second-hand clothing offered $5,000 for the clothing on hand at one time.

Considerable clothing and other supplies were shipped directly to Hinckley and Pine City. All of the railroad companies and express companies carried these supplies free of charge.

The popular proverb says that "corporations have no souls," but an exception must be made in favor of the St. Paul & Duluth Railroad Company and the Eastern Minnesota Railway Company. The officers and employes of these corporations were unremitting in their efforts to assist the work of relief, and, although making strenuous efforts to repair the immense damage suffered by the roads and to restore traffic, they did not hesitate to attend to the transportation of fire sufferers and supplies for their relief in preference to their own business. Nothing was left undone that could be done by either of these companies, and the requests of the commission were honored in all cases. All of the railroad companies centering in the Northwest, as well as the express companies, furnished free transportation for supplies. The Western Union Telegraph Company and the North American Telegraph Company placed their facilities at the disposal of the commission, without limit and without charge.

The commission would have been glad to make due acknowledgment for all supplies received, but this is impossible, for the reason that a large proportion of the packages afforded no clue to the names, or even the residence of the senders, and the goods being carried free, were not accompanied, in many cases, by the usual freight bill. Even five carloads of flour were received without indications of the source from which they came.

In addition to the large quantities of second-hand clothing, etc., the following donations were received, which were equivalent to cash:

From citizens of Duluth, lumber	$775.00
From citizens of Minneapolis, lumber	2,650.00
From citizens of Winona, lumber	1,200.00
From citizens of St. Paul, lumber	75.00
From citizens of Anoka, lumber	500.00
From citizens of Stillwater, lumber, value estimated	200.00
From Cloquet Lumber Company, lumber	130.00
Total lumber donations	$5,590.00
From citizens of Mankato, pork	$135.00
From citizens of Shakopee, stoves, flour and pork	550.00
From citizens of Grand Forks, two cars flour	700.00
From citizens of Moorhead and other places not reported, five cars of flour	1,750.00

From J. M. Danelz, Swift Falls, flour...		76.00
From merchants of Minneapolis, new merchandise		855.00
From Potter Palmer, Chicago, new suits of good clothing and blankets..		300.00
From Montgomery, Ward & Co., Chicago, 300 pairs excellent shoes, delivered by express to each recipient		750.00
From citizens of Atwater, one car wheat, sold and acknowledged as a cash donation...	$269.59	
From citizens of Warren, one car wheat, sold and acknowledged as a cash donation	478.10	
Total (not including wheat)		$10,700.00

CASH RECEIPTS AND DISBURSEMENTS.

(See Exhibits "A" and "B.")

The treasurer of the commission has received cash as follows:

From foreign countries, England and Canada.................................	$11,600.00
From the United States, except Minnesota....................................	14,711.19
From Minnesota	70,147.50
Total cash donations	$96,458.69
From sales of lumber and material to fire sufferers....................	2,018.15
Cash borrowed by the commission	15,000.00
Total cash received	$113,476.84

Disbursements.

Cash allowances to individual fire sufferers....................................	$23,294.61
Building material and labor erecting buildings................................	35,322.33
Outfitting families—clothing, furniture, hardware, etc.........................	22,238.61
Temporary relief—provisions, feed, medical attendance, etc..................	14,848.42
Miscellaneous expenditures—labor, cows, plowing, freight, etc.............	4,073.20
Administration—salaries and expenses of agents, clerks and storekeepers.	5,136.73
Total disbursements...	$104,813.95
Leaving in the treasurer's hands December 31, 1891..........................	*8,662.89

*The treasurer has disbursed, since Jan. 1, 1895, $3,926.16, leaving a balance on hand, Jan. 21, 1895, of $4,706.72.

In addition to the cash received and disbursed by the State Commission, the local committees in different parts of the state have received and disbursed money for the relief of fire sufferers, as follows: (See Exhibit "C.")

TEMPORARY RELIEF BY LOCAL COMMITTEES.

Minneapolis, by Hon. Wm. H. Eustis, mayor................................	$3,652.46
St. Paul, temporary relief by the local committee............................	1,500.01
Pine City, temporary relief, burials, etc., by the local committee...........	1,372.72
St. Cloud, local committee, relief of sufferers at Milaca and Pokagama...	1,254.46

Stillwater, local committee, relief extended by local committee direct to
fire sufferers at Hinckley and vicinity..................................... 2,800.00
Cloquet, local committee, relief extended to fire sufferers in Carlton
county 989.85
Mora, local committee, relief extended to fire sufferers (no report)...... ......
Duluth, local committee, temporary relief, feeding, lodging, clothing, etc. *11,850.00
White Bear, local committee, cash expended (in addition to $196.17, sent to
Pine City) 116.24

Total..................... .... $23,565.74

*Approximate estimate, detailed report not yet received.

It appears, therefore, that the total cash disbursements for the relief of the sufferers by fire so far as reported up to December 31,
1894, were $128,409. The entire cash value of the relief extended
may be estimated as follows:

Cash disbursed by the State Relief Commission.................... ....$104,844
Lumber, flour, etc., handled by the State Commission............. 9,700
Second-hand clothing, etc., handled through the St. Paul and Minneapolis
warehouses 22,400
Second-hand clothing, etc., shipped direct to Pine City and Hinckley (esti-
mated) 3,900

Total value of the cash and supplies handled by the State Commission.$140,544

Cash disbursed by the local committees at Minneapolis, St. Paul,
Duluth, Pine City, St. Cloud and Stillwater........................ $23,566
Second-hand clothing, etc., distributed by these committees, esti-
mated 7,434

Total value of cash and supplies distributed by local committees...... $31,000

Estimated value of free transportation furnished by St. Paul &
Duluth Railroad and the Eastern Minnesota Railway.............. $11,200
Estimated value of free transportation furnished by other railroads.. 2,000

Total free transportation............... .... $13,200

Grand total estimated value of relief furnished to fire sufferers........$184,744

It will be noted that the total administration expenses of the State
Commission in distributing relief to the amount of $140,544 (not in-
cluding railroad transportation which might very properly have been
added), was $5,157, which is 3.7 per cent.

The foregoing statement is very far from covering the total value
of the relief extended to the fire sufferers, much of which cannot be
measured in dollars and cents. The personal services of leading
citizens of St. Paul, Minneapolis, Duluth, Pine City, Rush City, St.
Cloud, Mora, Hinckley and New York Mills were freely given; and

in some cases for weeks, and even months, without reward. The St.
Paul & Duluth Railroad Company gave an extension of time on all
its land contracts, and in addition thereto credited up on the contract
of each purchaser the entire value of the improvements placed upon
his land by the State Commission as a cash payment. The amount
thus allowed to 28 settlers was $3,629. In many cases this credit
wiped out all, or nearly all of the indebtedness under the contract,
leaving the purchaser owner of his land in fee simple. Markham &
Kelsey, at Pokegama, gave an extension of time on all their contracts and donated to each purchaser a small tract of land in fee
simple on which to place his buildings. Laird & Boyle, of Mission
Creek, John D. Ludden, F. A. Hodge, and other land owners, made
liberal concessions to fire sufferers holding contracts with them.
The Western Land Company canceled a mortgage on a widow's lot
in order to give her a clear title to her home. The Sandstone Townsite Company sold lots to sufferers at $25 each, donating in each
case a piece of ground 48x50 feet in fee simple on which to build.
The Minneapolis Trust Company donated lots to all fire sufferers
who wished to build on the new townsite in Sandstone. About 50
beautiful building lots were so donated. Mr. James J. Hill, besides
a cash donation of $5,000, offered 5,000 acres of land in 40-acre tracts
to fire sufferers, conditioned only upon actual settlement upon the
land. The Rutledge Lumber Company offered employment to 20
heads of families and the citizens of Rutledge donated the funds to
purchase a lot for each family. These lots were finely located,
within one block of the school-house, and the fire sufferers who went
to Rutledge were generously treated.

In deciding upon the principles to be followed in the work of relief, as indeed in the entire work of the commission, there has been
complete unanimity among the members of the commission. In
every case they have been able to reach a unanimous conclusion.
Having decided upon the general rules to be followed, the details
of the work have been committed to the agents of the commission,
and individual cases have not usually been considered by the commission except where the agents were in doubt as to what course
should be pursued.

The commission decided, in the first place, that it was not its
province to act as an insurance agency, or to undertake to make
good the losses of fire sufferers; but that their action must be regu-
lated by the necessities of the case, rather than by the magnitude of
the loss. At the same time, it was the view of the commission that
they ought not as a rule to extend aid to such an extent as to make
the individual much better off than he was before the fire, unless it
was necessary to do so in order to prevent absolute suffering.

The commission regarded themselves as the agents of the donors
in extending friendly aid to those who had been overtaken by a
mighty, but temporary, misfortune. The sufferers by fire were, almost without exception, industrious, self-supporting people and they

felt that aid ought to be extended in a neighborly and friendly spirit, and in such a manner as not to impair the self-respect or the independence of the recipient. The agents of the commission were instructed to maintain this attitude towards these unfortunate people. This seemed to us the more important, for the reason that in addition to the loss of all their possessions and the physical and nervous shock produced by the terrible ordeal through which they had passed, many of them mourned the loss of dear friends and were deeply sensitive and sore-hearted.

We have considered it a matter of chief importance to render such assistance as should restore these people to a condition of self-support and relieve them as speedily as possible from a dependent condition; and it gives us much pleasure to report that in most cases the relief given has been instrumental in accomplishing this result, and that a large majority of the people who have been assisted are now in a position of self-support. It has been a cause of grief to the commission to see some of the people who were at first unwilling to accept any aid with which they could dispense, gradually lose their spirit of independence and become willing, and even eager, to take all they can get. It is a great misfortune when what is intended to assist the unfortunate becomes an actual damage to them.

We were of the opinion that no form of relief could be more helpful than employment; accordingly, we instructed our agents to employ fire sufferers to the fullest possible extent. The following is a statement of the amounts paid for salaries and wages, showing what proportion was paid to fire sufferers:

	Amounts Paid.	Paid Sufferers.
Workmen on buildings	$8,921.55	$3,248.10
Cash building allowances	1,553.61	1,553.61
Laborers	1,514.90	1,350.90
Cookhouse crews	655.88	289.58
Stockyard crews	311.00	311.00
Administration, salaries	4,857.75	1,217.01
Totals	$17,814.69	$7,970.29

It will be seen that of the $2,480 paid laborers, cookhouse and stockyard crews, $1,950, or 80 per cent., was paid to fire sufferers, and of the $10,475 paid workmen on buildings, $4,800, or 48 per cent., was paid to fire sufferers. Of the $4,857 paid for administration, $1,217, or 25 per cent., was paid to fire sufferers. And of the total amount, $17,814.69, paid out for services of all kinds, $7,970.29, or 45 per cent., was paid to fire sufferers.

The completeness of the loss and the resulting destitution, together with the near approach of winter, increased the greatness of the need; and the agents of the commission were instructed to pursue a generous policy and to err, if at all, on the side of liberality.

It was the desire of the commission to secure, if possible, to the beneficiaries the permanent enjoyment of the donations of their fellow citizens. The secretary of the commission, therefore, was instructed to employ a competent attorney and to make sure, as far as possible, that those for whom houses were built either owned their ground in fee simple or had such liberal contracts as would give a reasonable assurance that they would be able to secure title to their land. Land companies and owners of land were induced to extend their contracts so as to give ample time to purchasers. Squatters were assisted to procure land of their own, and it is believed that almost every house built by the assistance of the commission is a secure possession to its occupant.

The commission felt that they ought to encourage the people as far as their circumstances would admit, to return to their former homes, but where a removal seemed imperative they ought to facilitate it as far as possible. In those cases where it was evident that the people must go elsewhere in order to maintain themselves, it was decided to make a cash allowance, amounting usually to from $20 to $25 for each member of the family, but varying somewhat according to their peculiar circumstances. Able-bodied men were fitted out with a suit of clothes and a small amount of money.

For those who decided to remain in the burned district it was necessary to provide shelter, and the following general rules were adopted in dealing with them: People who had fire insurance were notified that the commission would not undertake to build houses for them unless they furnish satisfactory evidence that the money received for fire insurance was so far consumed in meeting pressing debts that they were not able to make such provision for themselves as the commission was making for others. For people who had homes of their own before the fire, the commission decided to build a frame house, 16x24 feet, boarded on the studding, then papered and covered with drop siding on the outside. These houses were built one-story or a story and a half high, according to the size of the family. It was found that many of the people had before the fire only a small house or "shack," representing in many cases a very small cost. To such people building material was furnished to the value of from $40 to $100, to enable the individual to build for himself. In many cases the commission furnished carpenters to assist in building such small houses. In the case of single men it was decided not to build houses for them unless they owned houses before the fire; but in the case of married men, even though they had no house before the fire, it was decided to render some assistance in building (usually from $50 to $75), providing it was made clear that they intended to live in the burned district, for the reason that there were no houses to rent, and it was necessary for them to have shelter. In two or three cases the commission built houses for young men who were not strictly entitled to them, for the reason that they had intended marrying before the fire; which intention has since been carried out.

As far as possible, the commission insisted that whatever buildings were constructed by their assistance should be located either on land owned by the individual in fee simple, or on land for which he had a liberal contract which would enable him to secure his home within a reasonable time. Homesteaders on government land were treated as though they owned the land. The cost of the material used in the construction of the ordinary houses built, 16x24 feet, with posts 8, 12 or 14 feet, was from $95 to $150. In a few cases of widows with large families, more expensive houses were built. As very few of the fire sufferers had teams it was necessary to deliver the lumber on the ground, and in some cases this involved a heavy expense, owing to the lack of bridges and the damage to corduroy roads by the fire. The estimated cost of the carpenter work on such houses was $35 per house, and those fire sufferers who preferred to do their own work received a cash allowance of $35 for the work. In practice it was found that the cost of the carpenter work considerably exceeded $35 per house.

The following is a list of articles of furniture, etc., furnished by the State Commission to a family of five; the outfit was increased or diminished, according to the size of the family:

Furniture—Three bedsteads; 3 w. w. springs; 3 excelsior mattresses: 3 pair pillows; 12 wood chairs; 1 rocker; 1 drop-leaf table.

Hardware—One No. 9 stove; 1 heating stove; 5 joints pipe; 1 elbow; 1 iron kettle; 1 fry pan; 1 tea kettle; 1 coffee pot; 1 dishpan, 2 milk pans; 1 sauce pan; 1 boiler; 1 washboard; 1 dipper; 1 water pail; 6 knives and forks; 12 spoons; 6 teaspoons; 1 basting spoon; 1 wash basin; 1 butcher knife; 1 drip pan; 1 dust pan; 1 broom; 2 flat irons; 1 one-gallon can; 1 axe; 1 buck saw; 1 shovel; 1 hammer.

Crockery—Twelve plates; 6 pint bowls; 12 cups and saucers; 6 tumblers; 1 ten-inch platter; 2 seven-inch vegetable dishes; 1 glass water pitcher; 1 salt and pepper; 1 glass lamp; 2 chambers.

Bedding—Four blankets; 2 comforters; 52 yards sheeting; 15 yards toweling.

The following is a list of rations issued to a family of five for three months: Four hundred lbs. flour; 7 lbs. coffee; 2 lbs. tea; 40 lbs sugar; 2 lbs. baking powder; 2 lbs. soda; 1 bu. beans; 20 lbs. rice; 20 lbs. fish; 20 bars soap; 4 pkgs. yeast cakes; 5 sacks salt; 1 pkg. matches; 1 bluing bottle; 15 lbs. lard; 100 lbs. pork; 4 gals. syrup; 20 lbs. crackers; 2 boxes pepper; 5 lbs. breakfast food.

The following is a list of rations issued to a family of five for thirty days: Two hundred lbs. flour; 3 lbs. coffee; 15 lbs. sugar; lb. tea; 1 lb. baking powder; 1 lb. soda; 1-2 bu. beans; 10 lbs. rice; 8 lbs. fish; 10 bars soap; 2 pkgs. yeast; 2 sacks salt; 1 pkg. matches; 6 lbs. lard; 1 bottle bluing; 45 lbs. pork; 2 pails jelly; 1 gal. syrup; 8 lbs. crackers; 1 box pepper; 3 lbs. breakfast food.

tration of the sufferers by fire.   Blanks were carefully prepared for use at Duluth, Pine City, Hinckley, Sandstone and Milaca.   A detailed record was made of each case, showing the names and ages of members of the family, social condition, residence before the fire, losses by fire, property before the fire, property saved, insurance and other resources, needs and desires, reference and address of friends, together with a record of the assistance given.   In order to secure an accurate registration and avoid imposition, fire sufferers who had a large acquaintance in the burned district were employed to assist in the registration.   The local committee at Hinckley, and other citizens of Hinckley, Pokegama, Mission Creek, Sandstone and Pine City, rendered great service in securing an accurate and reliable registration.   The St. Cloud committee took charge of the registration at Milaca, which was performed in the most accurate and systematic manner.

Exhibit "E," appended to this report, comprises a complete list of all persons registered by the commission, showing the number resident in the burned district, the number non-resident, the number who received assistance, and the number who received no assistance.   The following is a summary of the registration:

DISTRICT.	Number of Registered.	Individuals Included.	Resident in Fire District at Time of Fire.	Not Resident at Time of Fire.	Received Relief.	Received no Relief.
Hinckley	440	1,038	910	128	921	117
Vicinity of Hinckley	58	183	171	12	181	2
Sandstone	152	498	418	80	420	78
Pokegama	36	131	105	26	129	2
Mission Creek	33	75	69	6	67	8
Sandstone Junction and Mill r	21	69	69	....	69	....
Finlayson	28	94	85	9	85	9
Partridge	19	59	53	6	39	20
Rutledge	3	14	14	....	11	3
Mora	11	56	56	....	28	28
Kerrick	4	9	9	....	9	....
Scattering	33	123	86	37	67	56
Total for Hinckley district	818	2,350	2,045	304	2,026	323
Mille Lacs county	89	370	370	....	370	....
Carlton county	33	123	122	1	70	54
Otter Tall county	18	89	89	....	75	14
Morrison county	10	46	46	....	46	....
Wadena county	7	36	36	....	36	....
Aitkin county	13	55	55	....	....	55
Cass county	3	13	13	....	13	....
Total registration	1,011	3,081	2,775	305	2,636	445

The foregoing registration includes: Single men, 344; single women, 33; widows, 49 (whose families include 145 persons); widowers, 59 (whose families include 143 persons); orphans, 4. The number of widows created by the fire was 21. The number of widowers created was 22. The number of farmers registered in the Hinckley burned district was 151, and in the outlying counties was 164, making a total of 314 farmers.

It will be observed that out of the 3,082 persons registered 305 were non-residents at the time of the fire. Most of these are members of families where the head of the family was in the burned district. For example, Fritz Droel, foreman in the mill of the Brennan Lumber Company, who was burned to death, left a family at Eau Claire. Wis., to whom some assistance was given. Louis Chambers, formerly resident in South Dakota, had come into the burned district and had taken a piece of land, on which he was building a house. He had removed his furniture, team and effects, and his family in South Dakota were awaiting the completion of the house in order to remove to Minnesota. He was destroyed by fire with all his property, and his family were left destitute in South Dakota. They received assistance and are included in the registration. Thomas Henderson, residing at Pine City, was at work with his two sons in the burned district. The sons were burned to death and the father's hands were terribly burned in trying to save them, disabling him for several months, and his family received relief, although non-resident.

Some people received relief from the commission who lost neither houses, stock nor provisions, for the reason that their means of a livelihood was destroyed. Most of the people aided at Milaca were of this class, having lost hay, wood, logs, ties or timber, which they expected to sell for the support of their families during the coming winter.

In registering more than a thousand cases, most of them at a distance from the scene of the disaster, it is probable that some imposition was practiced, but we do not believe that one case in one hundred was of this class. The question whether aid should be given in particular cases was often a difficult one, especially where the loss was comparatively small. It is possible that aid may have been refused in some deserving cases, but we have endeavored to err, if at all, on the side of liberality; and if after careful inquiry there seemed reasonable ground for extending relief, it has been done.

The legislature has appropriated the sum of $20,000 to reimburse the commission for $15,000 advanced by them and to make necessary temporary provision, pending the consideration of the question whether any additional relief will be necessary. By Feb. 1, 1895, the commission will have expended all, or nearly all, of the $15,000 borrowed by them. We are now feeding about 600 people, including farmers' families, widows' families and villagers out of work. We are endeavoring to cut off these families as fast as they at-tain the possibility of self support, but we anticipate that it will be necessary to feed about 600 people until May 1st, and to feed about 400 people (families of farmers, widows, etc.) until August 1st, at a cost of about $6,800. We are now feeding about 50 cows, and we estimate the cost of feeding these cows for three months from February 1st, at about $600. We are now feeding about 15 teams, and we estimate the cost of feeding them for six months at $600, making a total probable expenditure for temporary relief of $8,000.

The commission has been unable to decide whether additional permanent aid should be extended to these people. About 90 cows were burned in the fire; the commission has given out 25 cows and has given assistance toward the purchase of 10 more, making a total of 35 cows. There are twenty or thirty additional families to which a cow would be a great blessing, but the commission did not see their way clear with the means at their disposal to furnish them.

It is almost impossible to carry on farming without some kind of a team. A few enterprising men have succeeded in obtaining teams for themselves, and in two or three cases the commission has assisted farmers in obtaining teams in lieu of other assistance. If the commission had had the means they would have been glad to furnish those who lost teams with assistance towards purchasing a team to the extent of, say, $50, provided that this donation would have enabled them to purchase teams. The objection to this plan is, that it would increase the disproportion of the amount of the relief given to the recipient, as compared with others. If such teams were purchased it would be necessary to feed them until harvest; otherwise the owners would have to leave their farms in order to earn feed.

The commission has considered seriously the question of distributing forty or fifty sewing machines. Means to purchase sewing machines have been furnished to a few women who were accustomed to earn a livelihood by sewing; but others of this class have not been supplied, and many women who have large families are greatly in need of a sewing machine. Several cases have been brought to our notice of those who have already purchased machines on the installment plan at from $40 to $60 each. The commission could purchase good reliable sewing machines delivered at Hinckley for about $15 each. A list of possible recipients was made up, but the sewing machines were not purchased, on account of the limited amount of funds available.

With the opening of spring seed will be an important item to the farmers. The chief crops of these farmers are potatoes, hay and garden vegetables. Large tracts of timber land have been burned almost clear. The commission distributed about five hundred bushels of winter rye in the fall of 1894, to be sown on such land, which was done with good promise of success. Most of the farmers are desirous of sowing timothy and red top on such lands. The seed ought to be sown just before the snow melts in the spring.

Some of the farmers want to sow oats with the grass seed, in order to get the benefit of the crop. This ground has been practically cleared by the fire, and with comparatively little labor can be brought under cultivation, but if neglected, will speedily grow up to weeds and underbrush.

The commissioners cannot lay claim to infallibility. They have doubtless made some mistakes, but if they have not made mistakes in more than one case in ten out of the 1,011 cases dealt with they will be satisfied. It must be borne in mind that they had to deal with people scattered over a large extent of territory, and that the work has been done by no less than ten different agents, besides the several local committees and it could not be expected that all of these agents would be able to pursue an absolutely uniform line of action. In Hinckley alone there have been four different agents in charge at different times.

The commission does not claim that its distribution of funds and supplies has been strictly equitable; it was impossible in the nature of the case that it should be so. When the work began it was not known either how much means would be available or how many people would have to be assisted. It was estimated at the outset that about 200 people were dead, that about 1,200 to 1,500 people might require assistance, and that about $75,000 would probably be realized from donations. The event proved that more than 400 people were dead, that more than 2,000 people have required assistance and that the cash donations passing through the hands of the state commission were $96,500, in addition to nearly $25,000, received and disbursed by the different local committees.

Many of the fire sufferers were unable to return to the burned district because of the impossibility of earning a livelihood there. For such persons a cash allowance was necessary, but in making such allowances it was necessary to exercise caution in order to insure having means to help those who remained.

In the distribution to those who remained it was impossible to exercise strict equality; widows with dependent children had to receive more in proportion than able bodied men with families; men who were sick or injured by fire or out of work received more assistance in proportion than others. As a rule, the farmers received more in proportion than the villagers, for the reason that most of the villagers were able to obtain employment for the support of their families, while many of the farmers must be assisted until they can raise a crop. Even among the farmers an equal distribution was impracticable. The commission distributed twenty-five cows to them who seemed to need them most; with each cow went necessarily about $15 worth of lumber for a stable and about $20 worth of food, making a total value of about $60 to $65, and this one item would make a difference of that amount in the aid extended to two families, both, perhaps, equally deserving.

These illustrations will show the difficulty attending the work of relief. Even with the most equitable distribution many inequalities must prevail. The previous condition of the fire sufferers and the scale of living to which they were accustomed made a great difference in the value of the relief. An expenditure of $150 or $200 would place one family in a better position than ever before, while an expenditure of $250 or $300 would leave another family in poorer circumstances than ever before, with a complete absence of those articles of comfort and refinement to which they have been accustomed. Under these circumstances it is not a surprise to the commission that there should be feelings of discontent and jealousy. It could hardly be otherwise, and we find as a matter of fact that in nearly every case of public disaster and distribution of relief similar complaints have arisen; they have to be accepted as a natural tendency of human nature.

Owing to the magnitude of the work and the extent of territory embraced, the commission found it necessary to have responsible agents for carrying on the work. Mr. H. H. Hart, a member of the commission, and secretary of the state board of corrections and charities, was made secretary of the commission and was given a general oversight of its work. Mr. J. G. Howard of Duluth, on recommendation of the Duluth local committee, was appointed as general superintendent of construction, with entire charge of the work of building houses in the burned district, the purchase of lumber and building materials, the employment of carpenters, etc. Mr. Howard pushed the work energetically and made every effort to provide shelter for the people before winter set in, giving most of his time to the work for two months without compensation. Mr. Geo. D. Holt, secretary of the associated charities of Minneapolis, was appointed as agent at Duluth and was subsequently transferred to Hinckley. He was succeeded as agent at Duluth by Mr. C. E. Holt, who had charge of the registration and permanent relief of all fire sufferers who were located at Duluth, including most of the people from Sandstone and vicinity and a part of those from Hinckley. Mr. James F. Jackson, secretary of the associated charities at St. Paul, was sent to Pine City as the representative of the St. Paul local committee. At the request of the commission the associated charities at St. Paul consented that he should act as the agent of the commission, first at Pine City and afterwards at Hinckley. His work was thoroughly satisfactory, and it was a matter of regret when his duties called him back to St. Paul after five weeks' service. Mr. H. D. Davis of Hinckley, general manager of the Brennan Lumber Company, acted as agent at Hinckley at the request of the Pine City relief committee until he was relieved by Mr. G. W. Marchant at his own request, owing to the demands of his business. Mr. Davis served without compensation and with entire satisfaction. Mr. G. W. Marchant was appointed as agent at Hinckley on account of his experience in caring for the sufferers by cyclone at Sauk Rapids. He was peculiarly adapted to the work, but found it necessary to withdraw after three weeks' service on account of his private business. He was succeeded temporarily by Mr. Jackson and permanently by Geo. D. Holt, who is still in the service of the commission as agent at Hinckley. Mr. N. J. Miller of Duluth, was appointed as agent at Sandstone, where he not only attended to the relief of the fire sufferers, but also took charge of building operations, and some fifty-five houses were built under his direction. Mr. Miller has performed his difficult duties to the entire satisfaction of the commission and is still in charge of affairs at Sandstone. Rev. Wm. Wilkinson of Minneapolis, acted as the agent of the commission at Pokegama. Mr. Wilkinson went to the relief of the people of Pokegama on the day after the fire and devoted himself indefatigably to the inetrests of the sufferers there, transporting supplies on hand cars, clothing the needy, burying the dead—even using the shovel and the ax with his own hand. The people of Pokegama were fortunate in finding such a faithful and disinterested friend, who devoted himself heart and soul to their interests without thought of reward.

Rev. David Morgan, superintendent of the St. Paul Bethel, acted as a special agent of the commission for the investigation of applications for relief from remote points. In this capacity he visited Pokegama, Brainerd, Aitkin, New York Mills and Little Falls. His reports were marvels of brevity and good sense, and for this work he received no compensation beyond his actual expenses. Mr. R. A. Hoyt of St. Paul, visited New York Mills and Milaca in behalf of the commission on similar service.

The commission was fortunate in obtaining the services of Mr. Christian Arvold of Rochester, formerly auditor of Blue Earth county, as accountant. Mr. Arvold proved thoroughly competent and worked early and late, not only in the discharge of his ordinary duties, but also in befriending and assisting the fire sufferers, and in interpreting for Swedes, Norwegians, Germans, Danes and Icelanders.

It will be seen that the commission chose as its agents men specially qualified for this service by training and experience in similar work, and the results have shown the wisdom of this course in guarding against imposition and avoiding experiments.

The members of the St. Cloud local committee, after rendering efficient aid to the fire sufferers at Pokegama, generously undertook the entire charge of the fire sufferers in the vicinity of Milaca. They cared for 377 people, expending $1.254 of their own money, and $4.133 furnished by the state commission. In addition to this sum, the state commission furnished new winter underclothing, etc., to the value of $760, which was distributed by the St. Cloud committee, who acted as our agents.

The Duluth local committee acted as agents of the state commission in the purchase of family outfits, clothing, furniture and provisions, which were supplied by local dealers on recommendation of our Duluth agent.

Members of the Pine City local committee acted as agents of the commission in disbursing funds and handling supplies at that place.

The local committees of St. Paul, Minneapolis, Duluth, Stillwater, Cloquet, Mora and White Bear disbursed funds raised by them for the relief of fire sufferers in such ways as seemed to them for their best interest. These committees have furnished us statements of their work, which are appended hereto.

To the best of our knowledge no member of any of these local committees has received any compensation for his services, unless one or two paid clerks employed at Duluth or St. Paul may have been members of local committees.

We have made application to the department of agriculture to furnish seed for these people, and Hon. A. R. Kiefer has introduced a bill into congress, authorizing the department of agriculture to furnish such seeds, but the department of agriculture has been unable to inform us whether seed can be furnished.

We have received a petition for the building of a schoolhouse at Sandstone Junction, to cost about $200. We have already furnished assistance for building school houses at Sandstone, Mission Creek and Pokegama, and having investigated this application, we think it should be granted.

The Duluth local committee raised about $13,000 in cash for the benefit of the fire sufferers, in addition to large quantities of clothing and provisions, which were used for the temporary relief of those who went to Duluth. Up to Nov. 15, 1894, the Duluth committee had expended about $10,000 in cash for the benefit of fire sufferers. Nearly two hundred people had located in Duluth and vicinity, many of whom were likely to require further assistance, and the Duluth local committee felt that they ought to reserve the remainder of their funds for future contingencies for the care of these people.

A joint meeting of the state commission and the Duluth local committee was held at Hinckley, Nov. 20, 1894, and the following minute was adopted: "It was mutually agreed that the Duluth local committee shall take active charge of cases of fire sufferers in that vicinity, and if they find it necessary to expend, not exceeding $1,500, including doctor bills, before January 15th next, they shall report it to the state commission, who will include this amount in their deficiency report to the legislature."

The Duluth local committee incurred expenditures for temporary relief, hospital bills and medical attendance for fire sufferers from Nov. 15, 1894, to Jan. 18, 1895, amounting to $1,896.80. They reported that at that date they had still under their care 135 people, for whom they are likely to incur more or less expense in the future. The state commission, therefore, respectfully recommends that the legislature include in any appropriations for the further assistance of fire sufferers, $1,500, to reimburse the Duluth local committee in part for the expense thus incurred.

One of the pressing needs of the burned district at the present time is assistance in replacing bridges and repairing roads. All of the bridges were destroyed by fire, and many miles of corduroy and peat roads have been literally burned up. The county has suffered heavily in consequence of the fire, by loss of taxes, and there is need of assistance from the state. The estimated cost of replacing the burned bridges and repairing the roads is $5,000, and we would respectfully recommend that an appropriation be made for that purpose.

Should the legislature deem it proper to provide for the items above mentioned, viz., additional temporary relief, assistance in purchasing teams, cows and sewing machines, grass seed, oats, seed potatoes, a schoolhouse at Sandstone Junction, an appropriation for roads and bridges and for reimbursing the Duluth committee, the total amount required will be about $21,500.

It has been and will be the aim of the commission so to distribute the means which have been placed in their hands as to help these unfortunate people to a position of self support at once, and we most earnestly recommend that, should the legislature see fit to grant additional relief, it be given immediately, and be so distributed as to enable the people to provide for themselves in future. We think that the work of relief should be finally closed up at the earliest possible date—not later than May 1, 1895.

Sept. 2, 1894, by order of the governor, per Tams Bixby, private secretary, eighty tents were shipped to Pine City by Capt. W. H. Hart, brigade quartermaster of the national guard of the state of Minnesota. Sixty-five of these tents were subsequently shipped to Hinckley, and were used by the fire sufferers at Hinckley, Sandstone, and other points.

These tents are the property of the United States government, and the national guard are responsible to the United States government for them.

The most of these tents were in use from sixty to ninety days. They were carefully inspected by Adjt. Gen. H. Muehlberg, Capt. W. H. Hart and D. E. Clark, storekeeper of the state relief commission, as a board of survey, and they submitted the following report respecting the condition of these tents:

We, a board of survey, have made inspection of the national guard tents, which were used by the relief commission at Pine City and the Hinckley fire district, and we find their condition as follows:

18 tents unfit for further use by the national guards; a total loss at $18.50
  each $333.50
12 tents badly damaged, estimated cost of repairs, at $11 each 132.00
31 tents damaged, estimated at 50 per cent. of value, $8.50 each 263.50

15 tents badly soiled, estimated cost of cleaning, $5 each	75.00
4 tents short	74.00
Tent pins short	32.00
	$910.00
15 canteens, $1.27 each	19.00
Total	$929.00

HERMAN MUEHLBERG,
Adjutant General.

W. H. HART,
Captain and Brigade Quartermaster.

D. E. CLARK,
Storekeeper State Relief Commission.

Adjutant General Muehlberg is of the opinion that the tents above mentioned as a total loss well be rejected by the United States government when they are called for. The tent poles are on hand, but are useless, for the reason that the government now issues conical tents instead of wall tents.

Three of the four tents short will probably be recovered, but their condition is not known.

We respectfully recommend that an appropriation of $930 be made, payable to the order of the governor, for the purpose of replacing such of these tents as cannot be used for the national guards, and repair such as are in need of repair; and that those tents which are condemned for further use on the part of the national guard of the state of Minnesota, be placed in charge of the military store-keeper, to be used in case of any similar emergency in the future.

The state relief commission has on file in the office of the treasurer accounts and vouchers in detail of all funds received and disbursed by them, together with a record of supplies received and issued, and a record of the relief given to each fire sufferer. We would respectfully request that the joint committee of the legislature appoint a sub-committee, or employ a competent expert to examine the books and vouchers of the commission in detail, and report of the committee. Mr. Christian Arvold, the accountant of the commission, will be at the service of the committee at any time, and will afford them whatever information they may require.

We submit herewith, as a supplement to this report, Exhibit "A," an abstract of the report of our treasurer; Exhibit "B," a list of cash donations received; Exhibit "C," a list of houses built and lumber donations; Exhibit "D," an abstract of the reports of the several local committees; Exhibit "E," a list of all persons registered by the commission.

Should the governor or the legislature desire any information with refernece to the work of the commission not contained in this report, we shall take pleasure in furnishing it.

We desire, in conclusion, to extend our thanks to Your Excellency, to the legislature, and to the multitude of contributors for the generous confidence reposed in us. We have endeavored to discharge this sacred trust in the spirit in which it was confided to us.

All of which is respectfully submitted.

CHARLES A. PILLSBURY,
KENNETH CLARK,
CHARLES H. GRAVES,
MATTHEW G. NORTON,
HASTINGS H. HART,
                                          Commissioners.

EXHIBIT A.

SUMMARY OF THE TREASURER'S REPORT.
KENNETH CLARK, TREASURER.

Receipts.

Donations from foreign countries	$11,600.00
Donations from United States, except Minnesota	14,711.19
Donations from Minnesota	70,147.50
Total cash donations	**$96,458.69**

Proceeds of Sales of Building Material, etc.

Collected by George D. Holt, agent at Hinckley	$875.25	
Collected by N. J. Miller, agent at Sandstone	965.41	
Collected by J. G. Howard, superintendent of construction	176.46	
		$2,018.15
Loan		15,000.00
Total cash receipts		**$113,476.84**

Disbursements.

Per receipted vouchers on file with the treasurer, and classified as follows:

Cash Allowances to Individual Fire Sufferers

Through Hinckley office	$13,326.99	
Through Duluth office	4,031.12	
Through St. Paul office	1,052.50	
Through Minneapolis office	661.50	
Through St. Cloud office (Milaca)	4,132.70	
		$23,204.61

Cost of Buildings Erected.

Lumber	$20,970.51	
Hardware, brick and lime	3,576.71	
Cash allowances for compo. board	300.00	
		$24,847.22
Labor of workmen on buildings, teamsters, etc.	$8,921.55	
Cash allowances for labor to parties building their own houses	1,553.61	
		$10,475.16
Total cost of buildings		**$35,322.38**

Outfitting.

Dry goods, shoes, clothing, blankets......... .... $6,567.46
Furniture and bedding............. .... 3,412.98
Crockery..... .... 808.68
Hardware, stoves, farming tools and implements......... 4,412.88
Housekeeping outfits ordered in Duluth.................... 6,275.31
Dry goods for Milaca fire suffers per St. Cloud com-
mittee..... .... 760.30
————— $22,238.61

Temporary Relief.

Provisions $8,635.33
Board of fire sufferers..... .... 1,413.68
Wages of cookhouse crews.......................... 655.88
————— $10,704.89
Hay, feed and seed $2,508.07
Wages of stockyard crew..... .... 311.00
————— $2,819.07
Medical attendance and nursing.................... 939.46
Temporary relief in St. Paul........................ 325.00
————— $14,848.42

Miscellaneous Disbursements.

Twenty-five cows purchased................................ $644.50
Plowing 598.30
Freight and transportation paid...................... 715.57
Sundry expenses 599.93
Wages paid laborers... .... 1,514.90
————— $4,073.20

Administration.

Salaries of agents, clerks, storekeepers, warehouse employes and expense of delivery teams.................... $4,857.75
Expenses paid 298.98
————— $5,156.73

Total disbursements to December 31, 1894................................ $104,843.95

Cash balance in treasurer's hands..................................... *$8,632.89
*Disbursed from Jan. 1st to Jan. 21st, $3,926.16; balance, Jan. 21, 1895, $4,706.72.

EXHIBIT B.

STATEMENT OF CASH DONATIONS RECEIVED BY THE MINNESOTA
STATE COMMISSION FOR THE RELIEF OF FIRE SUFFERERS.
FROM FOREIGN COUNTRIES.

ENGLAND.

London; Lord Mount Stephen................ .... $5,000.00

CANADA.

Montreal; Sir Donald Smith........ ....'.............. $5,000.00
"   Lady Donald Smith.. 1,000.00
"   R. B. Angus................................... .... 500.00

Niagara Falls; per mayor, through St. Paul committee............   100.00

                                                        $6,600.00

      Total from foreign countries...... .... $11,600.00

FROM THE UNITED STATES (EXCEPT MINNESOTA.)
ARKANSAS.

Carlisle;   citizens $3.75

CALIFORNIA.

Pasadena;   Mary Considine $5.00

COLORADO.

Denver; J. A. Wannis................................. .... $5.00

CONNECTICUT.

Bridgeport; Union Metallic Cartridge Co., per St. Paul committee	$100.00
Hartford; National Fire Insurance Co., per St. Paul committee...	100.00
New Haven; Winchester Repeating Arms Company, per St. Paul committee...........	200.00
L. Candee & Co., one-fifth of $1,000, per St. Paul committee..	200.00
Naugatuck; Goodyear Metallic Rubber Shoe Co., one-fifth of $1,000, per St. Paul committee......	200.00
South Woodstock; Sunday-school boys..............................	2.00

                                                          $802.00

FLORIDA.

Winter Park; Mrs. Berndon...	$20.00
Manatee; A. E. Stebbins..................................	7.65

                                                          $27.65

GEORGIA.

Macon; Mr. and Mrs. I. Block.. $5.00

ILLINOIS.

Aurora Sunday-school; to Pine City committee, $5 (see page 28)..		
Batavia; Horace N. Jones.. ..	$5.00	
Big Wood Sunday-school; to Pine City com. $1.77 (see page 28)...		
Champagne; Rev. D. W. Dresser, per St. Paul committee.........	5.00	
Chicago; Bradner, Smith & Co,......................................	100.00	
" Tribune subscription list................................	100.50	
" J. C. McVicker...............	100.00	
" W. K. Ackerman, city comptroller........................	719.55	
" W. K. Ackerman, city comptroller........................	359.78	
" Germans of Chicago, per George Benz......... $1,000.00		
" Germans of Chicago, per George Benz........ 1,100.00		
" Germans of Chicago, per George Berz........ 991.20		
	————	$3,091.20
" Subscribers to "Hemelandet," per St. Paul committee.	2.00	
" C. M. Wilkes, per St. Paul committee...................	35.00	
" T. A. Gardner, per St. Paul committee.................	1.00	
" L. D. Sherman, per St. Paul committee..................	10.00	
Durand; Magens Swenningsen.........	36.00	
Hingland Park; Presbyterian church..............................	35.00	

Oak Park; Royal League and Royal Arcanum councils, per
 St. Paul committee........... .... 29.00
Plymouth; Congregational church.......................... 12.10
Riverside; Citizens........... .... 104.85
Rock Island; L. E. West............................... 5.00
Waukegan; A. D. Stilson...... .... 1.00

                   $4,741.98

IOWA.

Ayrshire; F. H. Henry, per Minneapolis committee..................$ 5.00
Bellevue; Citizens 39.50
Clarksville; Citizens, per Minneapolis committee...................... 22.00
Decorah; Citizens, per St. Paul committee........................... 200.00
Grinnell; C. Newton 75.50
Osclan; John Johnson ....:.......... 10.10
Sioux City; S. J. Beals 10.00
 Dr. Hukins & Bro., to Pine City com. $10 (see page 35.).......

                   $362.10

KANSAS.

Fort Scott; B. T. McDonald .... $ 5.00
Kearney; M. E. Dulebohn 1.60
Pleasant Valley; Y. P. S. C. E. 17.00
Reserve; Women of R. C. 19.58

                   $42.58

LOUISIANA.

Rustan; A. W. Rogan $1.00

MARYLAND.

Brookville; per Bishop H. B. Whipple $7.00
St. Barskotsman Parish; St. John's Church 6.00

                   $13.00

MASSACHUSETTS.

Boston; J. H. Salter, Jr. $10.00
 G. M. Lee, per St. Paul committee 50.00
 Boston Rubber Shoe Co. (by Kellogg, Johnson & Co.), per
  St. Paul committee 500.00
 United States Rubber Co. (one-fifth of $1,000), per St. Paul
  committee 200.00
 American Rubber Co. (one-fifth of $1,000), per St. Paul com.... 200.00
Holyoke; Massasoit Paper Co. (through Bradner, Smith & Co.).. 25.00
Roxbury; W. A. Blossom (Exalted Ruler), per St. Paul com'te :.. 100.00

                  $1,085.00

MICHIGAN.

Grand Rapids; J. Wool.... .... $200.00

MISSOURI.

Emmetstown; Rev. W. T. Brand (by Bishop Gilbert) per St.
 Paul committee $14.00
St. Louis; Liggett Myers Tobacco Co., per St. Paul committee.... 100.00

                  $114.00

MONTANA.

Ft. Keogh; Sunday school, per St. Paul committee...................	$3.23
Eighty-two U. S. Soldiers, per St. Paul committee..............	43.30
Other contributions, per St. Paul committee	1 00
Red Lodge; Howard Watson	2.50

$46.03

NEBRASKA.

Omaha; Mr. and Mrs. R. A. Boyd $2.00

NEW HAMPSHIRE.

Gorham; D. L. Hitchcock, per Minneapolis committee $25.00

NEVADA.

Citizens $91.69

NEW YORK.

Albany; C. A. Hageman		$ 2.00
Fourth Presbyterian church		114.21
Cambridge citizens to Pine City committee, $5 (see page 39)		
Fairport; De Land & Co.	$41.52	
De Land & Co	51.20	
Per St. Paul Committee.		
De Land & Co. (by Griggs, C. & Co.)	56.52	
De Land & Co. (by J. H. Allen & Co.)	55.02	
De Land & Co. (by Noyes Bros. & Cutler)..............	41.52	
De Land & Co. (by S. & W.)	55.02	
Per Minneapolis Committee.		
De Land & Co. (by Geo. R. Newell & Co.)..............	56.72	
De Land & Co. (by A. Kelly & Co.)	54.20	
De Land & Co. (by Winston F. & Co.)...................	40.90	
		455.42
Church & Co. (by Geo. R. Newell & Co.)		125.00
John Dwight		125.00
Hudson; Dr. G. E. Benson		25.00
Le Roy; "Friend," per Minneapolis committee		20.00
New York; "The Times," per John R. Douglass		15.00
Horace White		125.00
F. Robert Magee		25.00
Henry L. Stimson		5.00
M. C. Miller		5.00
"Evening Post" Publishing company	80.00	
"Evening Post" Publishing company	16.00	
"Evening Post" Publishing company	5.50	
		101.00

Per St. Paul Committee.

Austin Corbin	500.00
J. C. Carter	250.00
New York Life Insurance company	1,000.00
New York Mutual Life Insurance company	500.00
E. H. Scott	2.00
Henry E. Noyes	25.00

Arnold, Constable & Co. (by T. C. Field) 250.00
J. McCreary & Co. (by T. C. Field) 100.00
Lee, Tweedy & Co. (by T. C. Field) 100.00
Chas. B. Landon & Co. (by T. C. Field) 100.00
Teft, Weller & Co. (by T. C. Field) 100.00
Dunham, Buckley & Co. (by T. C. Field) 100.00
E. L. Jeffray (by T. C. Field) 100.00
Willis & Gebt (by T. C. Field) 100.00
John S. Brown & Sons (by T. C. Field) 50.00
Meyer, Jonasson & Co. (by T. C. Field) 50.00
E. T. Mason & Co. (by T. C. Field) 50.00
J. C. Locke & Potts (by T. C. Field) 100.00
John Ruszits Fur Co. (by T. C. Field) 100.00
S. H. De Forest 10.00
John Dwight & Co. 125.00
New York Stock Exchange 1,100.00
Church & Co (by Geo. R. Newell & Co.) 125.00
Spencerport; John Merz, per Minneapolis committee........ 2.27

Total from New York state $6,084.90

NORTH DAKOTA.

Castleton; "Traveling Man" .... $ 2.00
Deepe; Mary Orgene 2.00
Drayton; W. C. T. U. 5.75
    W. C. T. U. 5.00
Gardner; Congregational Parsonage 40.00
    People of Gardner 16.00
New Salem; "Cash," per St. Paul committee.................. 5.00
Lisbon; Citizens 20.00
Tower City; Rich. L. Howell, per St. Paul committee 25.00
Wahpeton; Citizens and Turn Verein 103.85

                                                                $224.60

OHIO.

Berea $50.00
Cincinnati; A Davis & Co. (through George R. Newell & Co.,
    per Minneapolis committee) 25.10
Cleveland; C. F. Thwing 10.00
Lennox; King's Daughters, per St. Paul committee 8.00
Toledo; Commercial Club 5.00

                                                                $96.00

OREGON.

Mt. Tabor; "Cash" .... $ 5.00
Portland; Swedish Society "Lumea" 38.90

                                                                $43.00

PENNSYLVANIA.

Erie; J. H. Bliss $250.00
    "Cash," per St. Paul committee 5.00

Glenn; Martin Chevalier	5.00	
Philadelphia; Irene C. Faunce	10.00	
Wiseman & Wallace, per St. Paul committee	50.00	
		$320.00

RHODE ISLAND.

Woonsocket; Woonsocket Rubber Co., 1-5 of $1,000, per St. Paul committee		$200.00

TENNESSEE.

Columbia; John E. Greer		$4.00

TEXAS.

Fort Worth; Dr. A. P. Brown		$5.00

VIRGINIA.

Newport News; Robert Storker, of U. S. Navy		$15.00

WASHINGTON.

Seattle; G. Hanens, per St. Paul committee		$1.00

WISCONSIN.

Bayfield; J. H. Wing	$100.00	
Pepin; "Cash"	5.00	
Phillips; Presbyterian church	10.00	
S. H. Murphy	10.00	
Point Douglass; Episcopal church	10.00	
		$135.00
Total from the United States except Minnesota		$14,711.19

CONTRIBUTIONS FROM MINNESOTA.

Ada; Citizens	$243.50	
Norwegian Lutheran church	18.21	
		$261.71
Aitkin; Citizens		108.11
Albany; Citizens		26.00
Albert Lea; Citizens	$1,104.76	
Village	250.00	
C. P. Kiel, Sr	5.00	
		1,359.76
Alden; Citizens		64.10
Alexandria; Gov. Knute Nelson	$100.00	
Citizens	50.00	
Citizens	28.00	
		178.00
Rev. H. B. F. Lansem, to Pine City com., $15 (see page 38.)		
Almon; W. C. T. U.		5.00
Amboy; Citizens	$110.75	
Citizens	10.75	
		121.50
Anoka; Citizens	$68.56	
Citizens	16.00	
		84.56
Appleton; A. K. Pederson	25.00	
St. Margaret's Guild	42.00	
		67.00

Aretander; Citizens 67.00
Ashland; Dodge county, per St. Paul committee 100.00
Atwater; Dahl & Peterson (car of wheat sold) 369.59
Audubon; Citizens 61.65
Austin; J. Hoban $1.00
    Geo. Hirsch 10.00
    W. Elder 5.00
    Citizens of Mower County....................................... 250.00
    Citizens of Austin 250.00
                                               516.00

Bald Eagle; J. J. Leary, to Pine City com. $1 (see page 38)........
Barnesville; I. O. O. F. 95.75
Batavia; L. A. Kenney (see Batavia, Ill.) 5.00
Battle Lake; Citizens 25.25
Beaver Creek; Citizens 51.00
Belgrade; Claus Jorgerson, per Minneapolis committee 1.00
Belle Plaine; Citizens $50.00
    Citizens 17.00
    Catholic church of the Sacred Heart 41.60
                                               108.00

Belmont and Des Moines; Norwegian farmers 15.50
Bethany; Rev. Philip Gritensohn 20.00
Benson; A. N. Johnson 10.00
Big Lake; Citizens 25.75
Blue Earth; Presbyterian church $42.31
    M. E. Church 33.13
                                               75.44

Blooming Prairie; Citizens 50.00
Brainerd; Citizens 100.00
Brandon; Citizens 50.00
Brighton; Citizens 49.30
Browns Valley; Ladies 38.62
Byron; Congregational Byron Methodist church $30.00
    M. E. Church 6.00
    Village 25.00
                                               61.00

Cambridge; Citizens $67.50
Camp Release; Citizens, per Minneapolis committee................. 9.25
Cannon Falls; Village $350.00
    Village 100.00
                                               450.00

Canton; Citizens 20.00
Carver; Village Council and friends 160.00
Chaska; Village 150.00
Chatfield; Citizens 170.00
Chowan; Citizens, per Minneapolis committee 15.00
Christiana; Congregation; 23.10
Claremont; Y. P. S. C. E. 10.00

Clinton Falls; Baptist Church		12.45
Cloquet; Citizens, $989.85 received and disbursed by local committee (see page 39.)		
Cold Springs; Citizens		79.00
Cottage Grove; Citizens		164.25
Crookston; Citizens	$163.95	
Presbyterian Sunday school	12.07	
School children	23.67	
		199.69
Delhi; Presbyterian church		23.00
Delano; Citizens		125.00
Des Moines (see Belmont.)		
Detroit; H. E. Sargent	$100.00	
St. Luke's church	15.00	
Mrs. J. K. West	10.00	
		125.00
Dexter; Citizens		35.60
Duluth; received and disbursed by local committee, $11,850 a.....		
Dover; Citizens, per H. Brown		137.40
Dundas; Citizens of Dundas and vicinity	$125.00	
Citizens of Dundas and vicinity	40.00	
		165.00
Echo; Village		52.50
Elbow Lake; Citizens		114.00
Elizabeth; Village council		50.00
Elk River; Y P. S. C. E. of Union church	$41.57	
Village	60.00	
		101.57
Excelsior; Citizens		153.30
Fairmont; Village		100.00
Fairfax; Citizens and Village		65.35
Faribault; M. E. Church	$12 00	
Circuit M. E. Church	23.50	
Citizens	890.91	
		926.44
W G. Le Crone, to Pine City committee $7, (see page 38)..		
Farmington; F. C. Davis		200.00
Farwell; Citizens	$93.70	
Citizens	5.25	
		98.95
Fergus Falls; Citizens		250.00
Fisher; Citizens	$156.00	
School children	5.00	
R. H. Bain	2.50	
		163.50
Fort Snelling; Company B, Third Infantry, U. S. A., per St. Paul committee		23.00
Garden City; Baptist church, per Minneapolis committee		11.00

a Amount estimated; no report received.

Glencoe; A. H. Reed	$100.00	
Village	50.00	
St. P. and St. Luke's church	37.00	
St. Peter and Paul Church	3.00	
A. J. Brechet (per St. Paul committee)	1.00	
		$191.00
Glenwood; Women's Union Missionary Society	$28.41	
Women's Union Missionary Society	.60	
		29.01
Graceville; Citizens		111.50
Grand Rapids (see Grand Rapids, Mich.)		
Green Isle; Brendam's Church		29.15
Good Thunder; Citizens		47.55
Hancock; Citizens		24.00
Halstead; Citizens		86.25
Harmony; Citizens	$138.36	
T. Sanderson	3.00	
		141.36
Harris; Village, to Pine City committee, $100 (see page 38)		
Citizens, to Pine City committee, $37.75 (see page 38)		
P. H. Stolberg, to Pine City committee, $100 (see page 37)		
Hastings; City	$500.00	
St. Boniface church	$25.00	
		525.00
Hawley; Citizens	$94.10	
Citizens	5.75	
		99.85
Hay Creek; Citizens	$20.50	
Citizens	5.75	
		26.25
Hayfield; H. Bock		5.00
Henderson; Citizens		128.25
Heron Lake; Citizens		145.00
Hitterdal; Norwegian Lutheran church		15.56
Hutchinson; Citizens, Hutchinson and vicinity	122.60	
Citizens	2.00	
		124.60
Houston; Citizens		175.00
Ironwood; Camp M. W. of America No. 2381		10.00
Isanti; P. E. Fredin, to Pine City committee, $2 (see page 38)		
Janesville; Citizens		110.06
Jordan; Business men	$105.00	
A. O. U. W.	20.75	
Masonic Lodge of King Hiram	30.00	
		155.75
Kasota; Citizens (per Minneapolis committee)		56.00

Kasson; Village $200.00
   Mrs. W. S. Carslow 5.00
                                                              205.00

Kenyon; German Lutheran church, per Minneapolis committee... $8.75
   E. Rehnke 250.00
                                                              258.75

Kingston; Citizens, per Minneapolis committee 25.00
La Crescent; I. O. G. T. Lodge 25.00
Lake City; Village 250.00
Lake Andrew; Citizens 24.35
Lake Crystal; Citizens 100.00
Lake Elmo; Citizens, per St. Paul committee $25.29
   Mrs. D. T. Murphy, per St. Paul committee 1.00
                                                              26.29

Lakefield; School children 10.00
Lake Park, Nannenstad & Wangenstein $5.00
   Citizens 40.00
                                                              45.00

Lakeville; Citizens (through C. H. French) $25.00
Lanesboro; Citizens 59.50
La Prairie; Village 25.50
Le Roy; Citizens, per Minneapolis committee.................... 46.33
Le Sueur; Citizens $125.45
   Catholic church 31.25
                                                              156.70

Lindstrom; Citizens, to Pine City committee, $84 (see page 38) .
Litchfield; Village 200.50
Little Falls; Mrs. Sophia Hirter, per St. Paul committee......... 1.00
Long Prairie; Village $50.00
   A. O. U. W. 20.00
                                                              70.00

Long Lake; Citizens 19.88
   Citizens .... .12
                                                              20.00

Luverne; Citizens 139.52
Madelia; Citizens 204.00
Mankato; Mankato Lodge No. 225, B. P. O. Elks, per St. Paul
     committee $50.00
   Ladies of Mankato 142.00
   F. F. Holm 3.00
   Citizens 365.00
                                                              560.50

Mantorville; Village 100.00
Maple Plain; Citizens, per Minneapolis committee...... .... 15.00
Mapleton; A. O. U. W.. $10.00
   Citizens 126.00
                                                              136.00

Minneapolis; Thos. A. Matthews (per St. Paul commimttee) $5.00
Frank Spencer 5.00
Democratic state convention delegates 294.26
Scandinavian relief committee 1,563.97
Wholesale merchants' discount on merchandise 13.47
Minneapolis relief committee 25,890.16
    Total contributed from Minneapolis 27,771.86
Deduct: Disb'sed by Mayor Eustis for tire sufferers (see p. 9) 3,652.46
                             24,119.40

Money Creek; Miss G. Brown $1.00
Miss Olive Holland 5.00
J. Holland 5.00
                             11.00

Montevideo; Business men 40.75
Montgomery; Village 178.00
Monticello; Relief committee 59.50
Moorhead; Citizens 414.00
Mountain Lake; A. O. U. W. 10.50
New Prague; Citizens 180.00
New Trier; Citizens 80.00
New Ulm; August Schell $25.00
Carl W. A. Krook 10.00
Citizens 200.00
A. O. U. W. 25.00
Maennerchor 10.00
Citizens 172.00
Congregational church 50.00
                             492.00

North Branch; Citizens, $100, to Pine City committee (see p. 28).
Northfield; Citizens 600.00
North St. Paul; Village (per St. Paul committee) 21.50
Norwood; Citizens 70.00
Nylla; Citizens 5.00
Ortonville; Citizens $66.50
First Congregational church 4.25
                             70.75

Oslo; Dodge county, M. J. Ellingson $5.00
Owatonna; per Rev. J. R. Chamberlain $148.50
Citizens 32.25
                             180.75

Pelican Rapids; Citizens $100.00
W. C. T. U. 5.00
                             105.00

Perham; I. O. O. F. $25.00
Village 100.00
Sunday school children 1.00
                             126.00

Pine City; Relief committee, sundry donations received (see pages
    38, 39) $2,521.79
    Disbursed by local committee $1,372.72
    Returned money furnished by St. Paul local com-
      mittee (see page 36) 500.00
    Citizens, $10.50, to Pine City committee (see page 38)..——— —— 1,872.72
                                                649.07

Pine Island; Citizens $51.00
    Citizens 45.50
    Citizens 1.70
                                                9? 70

Pipestone; Daily Star relief fund $40.00
    Daily Star relief fund 32.21
    Citizens 25.16
                                                97.37

Plainview; Ladies of the Liberal League $33.71
    Churches 45.00
                                                78.71

Prairieville; Citizens 5.00
Preston; Base ball benefit 60.75
Prior Lake; L. J. Gossel 2.00
Quincy; Town of Quincy 50.10
Redwing; Dr Chas. N. Hewitt $25.00
    City 500.00
    Scandinavian Benevolent Society 25.00
    "Cash" 2.00
                                               552.00

Redwood Falls; J H. Bowers $5.00
    Citizens 30.00
    Citizens 39.27
                                              74.27

Renville; Citizens 113.08
Rice's; Village 100.00
Richland; M. E. Church $10.75
    Baptist church 14.10
                                               24.85

Rochester; City $500.00
    Citizens 444.50
                                              944.50

Rosemount; Citizens $73.75
    Dan Carroll 2.00
                                              75.75

Royalton; Citizens 45.00
Rush City; Village, to Pine City committee, $250 (see page 39).
Rushford; Citizens $101.00
    Citizens 1.00
                                            102.00

Rutledge; Rutledge Lumber Co. (discount) 7.74

Employes Rutledge Lumber Co., to Pine City committee, $100

Employes Rutledge Lumber Co., to Pine City committee, $175

Sacred Heart; Citizens 50.75

St. Charles; Citizens $100.00

   A. O. U W (per St Paul committee) 10.00
                                                            ———   110.00

St. Cloud; $1,254.46 rec'd and disb'd by local com. (see p. 40).....

St. Henry; Citizens 3.50

St. Hilaire; Ladies' Aid society 25.90

St. Louis Park; Citizens (per Minneapolis committee)...............   56.00

St. James; Citizens 280.48

St. Paul; Officers Germania Life Insurance Co...................... $100.00

  Conheim Bros. 25.00

  B. C. Lindquist 5.00

  K. M. Bowler 10.00

  Sharood & Crooks 109.25

  Thomas Wilson, Sept. 5 ....   50.00

  Thomas Wilson, Sept. 22..   50.00

  J. Rowe 20.00

  J. J. Hill 5,000.00

  Supreme Lodge Knights of Pythias of the United States......   250.00

C. S. Ross, Turn Verein 150.00

  "Cash" 15.00

  "Cash" 25.00

  George H. Edgerton 20.00

  "Cash" 1.00

G. C. Jacobs 3.00

  Stranger 1.00

  Builders' Exchange 25.00

  "Friend" 25

  Aurelius Bros. 5.00

  Isidor Rose 25.00

  J. S. Proctor 5.00

  H. M. Barnet, manager excursion to Hinckley...................   50.00

  Employes West Publishing Co......................................   117.50

  Engineer Best and Conductor Powers, of Eastern Minn. Ry...   5.00

  Children's Home Finder, by E. P. Savage 5.00

  Loyal Legion of Temperance, by Mrs. L. L. Maire 2.50

  D. Morrison, of Duluth 1.00

  Mrs. Dapron 1.00

  Wholesale merchants (discount on merchandise) 119.62

  St. Paul relief committee 15,325.54

  St. Paul relief committee (per Pine City relief committee)......   500.00

  St. Paul relief committee (per J. F. Jackson)...................   45.00

                                                                   ———

    Total contributed from St. Paul $23,086.66

Deduct: Disbursed for fire sufferers by local committee (see
  page 9) 1,539.01

           — —— 21,577.05

W. P. Broughton, to Pine City committee, $25 (see p. 39)......

St. Peter; C. F. Brown $5.00

 "Fats and Leans" Base Ball 231.00

 Citizens 115.77

           — — —   282.37

St. Thomas; Catholic Church 21.00

Sauk Center; City and citizens 32.40

Sleepy Eye; Village 25.00

South Wilton; Sunday school 7.79

Springfield; "Concert" 28.40

Soudan (see Tower).

Spring Valley; Citizens 279.80

Stillwater; Citizens, to Pine City committee, $20 (see page 39).

 P. Huntoon, to Pine City committee, $5 (see page 39).

 $2.80 received and disbursed by Stillwater local committee

Stewart; Village Council $70.00

 Citizens 55.00

           — —— —   125.00

Sturgeon Lake; A. H. Clark, $5.00, to Pine City committee (see

 Geo. E. Cunningham, $5.00, to Pine City committee (see

 F. Chimielewski, $5.00, to Pine City committee (see p. 39).

Taylors Falls; to Pine City committee, $24.00 (see page 39).

 Hon. A. F. Anderson, to Pine City committee, $5 (see

Tower and Soudan; Citizens 402.48

Thief River Falls; Norwegian Lutheran Evangelical church 15.58

Vernon Creek; W. C. T. U. 8.50

Wabasha; Citizens 100.00

Waconia; Citizens 150.00

Warren; Car wheat sold at 70 cents per bushel 478.10

Waseca; People $79.42

 Churches 94.50

           ————   173.92

Wasioja; Mrs. Mary Mason $1.25

 Township of Wasioja, per St. Paul committee..................   100.00

           ————   101.25

Watertown; Citizens 78.55

Waterville; Citizens $50.85

 Citizens 17.00

           ————   67.85

Watson Creek; Sewing society 9.89

West Duluth; S. A. Ebert, to Pine City committee, $25 (see

White Bear; South Side Sunday school, per St. Paul committee...   .55
    Citizens, to Pine City committee, $196.17 (see page 39).
    A. L. Linau, to Pine City committee, $5.00 (see page 39).
White Earth; Citizens 41.50
Willmar; Village $182.00
    Citizens 25.15
                                                 207.15
Windom; J. H. Clark 60.00
Winona; Citizens 1,500.00
Worthington; Citizens 28.33
Wykoff; Citizens 32.00
Wylie; Citizens 14.50
Wyoming; Citizens, to Pine City committee, $83 (see page 39).
Young America; A. S. Malmgren 60.00

    Total from Minnesota $79,147.50

EXHIBIT C.

RECAPITULATION OF HOUSES ERECTED AND ALLOTMENTS OF LUMBER MADE TO FIRE SUFFERERS.

Locality.	House No. 2.	House No. 1.	Lumber Allotments.	Public Buildings.	Total.
Hinckley village	33	6	7	1	47
Hinckley vicinity	8	6	10	......	34
Sandstone village	50	5	2	3	60
Sandstone vicinity	2	2	2	......	6
Pokegama	4	4	3	......	11
Mission Creek	1	7	3	......	11
Sandstone Junction	4	5	5	......	14
Finlayson	5	7	2	......	14
Miller	1	1	2	......	4
Partridge	1	......	3	......	4
Grindstone Lake	2	......	1	......	3
Pine City vicinity	2	......	1	......	3
Rutledge	2	......	......	......	2
Brown's Hill	......	......	1	......	1
Rush City	1	......	......	......	1
Totals	96	53	6	4	215

EXHIBIT D.

REPORT OF PINE CITY LOCAL COMMITTEE.

Receipts.

Illinois; Sunday-school at Aurora $5.00
    Sunday-school at Bigwood.......................................   1.77
                                                 $6.77

Iowa, Dr. Hukins & Bro.. .		10.00
New York; Citizen of Cambridge...................................		5.00
A. P. Noyes		2.50
P. A. Guthrie...		1.00
"Unknown"		1.00
Mr. and Mrs. R. F. Paxton.......................................		5.00
Mrs. W. De Hart		1.00
Alexandria, Minn.; Rev. H. B. F. Lansem........................		15.00
Bald Eagle; P. Leary...		1.00
Harris; P. H. Stalberg...	$100.00	
Citizens of Harris......................................	37.75	
illage of Harris	100.00	
		237.75
Faribault; W. C. Le Crone		7.00
Isanti; P. E. Fedlue..		2.00
Lindstrom; Citizens...		83.00
North Branch; Citizens..		100.00
Rutledge; Rutledge Lumber Company...............................	$100.00	
Employes of Rutledge Lumber Company....................	175.00	
		275.00
St. Paul; local committee.......................................	$500.00	
W. B. Broughton	25.00	
		$525.00
Rush City; Village		250.00
Stillwater; Citizens..	$250.00	
P. Huntoon	5.00	
		255.00
Sturgeon Lake; A. H. Clark	$5.00	
George E. Cunningham	25.00	
F. Chimielowski	5.00	
		35.00
Taylors Falls; Citizens...	$354.00	
Aug. F. Anderson......................................	50.00	
		414.60
West Duluth; L. A. Elbert.......................................		25.00
White Bear; Citizens	$196.17	
A. L. Lienau	5.00	
		201.17
Wyoming; Citizens...		85.00
Total receipts		$2,521.79

Disbursements.

Paid orders drawn by Pine City relief committee for relief of fire sufferers............	$1,372.72	
Paid Kenneth Clark, treasurer State Relief Commission, account St. Paul local committee	500.00	
Paid Kenneth Clark, treasurer State Relief Commission...........	649.07	
Total disbursements		$2,521.79

REPORT OF THE CLOQUET LOCAL COMMITTEE.
Receipts.

Cash contributions $989.85

Disbursements.

Lumber purchased for fire sufferers in Carlton and Pine counties.	$506.76
Merchandise purchased for Carlton county sufferers................	361.83
Freight paid on same	31.14
Cash to Cromwell fire sufferers......................................	60.00
Expenses of the committee	30.12

Total disbursements $989.85

Additional contributions of lumber, clothing, groceries, furniture,
etc., distributed to fire sufferers................................. 900.00

REPORT OF THE STILLWATER LOCAL COMMITTEE.
Receipts.

Cash contributions... $3,000.00

Disbursements.

To Pine City local committee......................................	$200.00
Expended for the relief of fire sufferers...........................	2,800.00

Total disbursements $3,000.00

Additional contributions of lumber, provisions and clothing, distributed to fire sufferers 3,000.00

REPORT OF THE WHITE BEAR LOCAL COMMITTEE.
Receipts.

Cash donations $159.50

Disbursements.

To Pine City local committee	$196.17
Expended for relief of fire sufferers................................	146.24
Balance subject to order of State Relief Commission..............	17.09

Total disbursements $159.50

The above report does not include donations of provisions, clothing, etc.

REPORT OF ST. CLOUD LOCAL COMMITTEE.

ST. CLOUD, Minn., Dec. 26, 1894.

Hon. C. A. Pillsbury, Chairman Minnesota State Fire Relief Commission, Minneapolis, Minn.

Dear Sir:—At the request of your Honorable Commission, the St. Cloud Committee entered upon the duties assigned to it in distributing the relief to the suffering settlers at and around the village of Milaca, who lost property in the recent disastrous forest fires, and beg herewith to submit a complete report of the aid extended in that locality.

TREASURER'S STATEMENT.

Receipts.

From State Fire Relief Commission	$4,132.50
Cash contributions	1,254.46
Total receipts	$5,386.96

Disbursements.

Net amount expended for Milaca sufferers	$4,529.47
Goods bought and sent to Pokegama	414.90
Caring for Joseph Zonyca (Pokegama sufferer) at St. Raphael's Hospital, St. Cloud	142.02
Expenses of committee, agents' salaries, clerk hire and rent	300.57
Total disbursements	$5,386.96

The clothing and provisions contributed by the citizens of St. Cloud and the clothing shipped by the State Commission to Milaca are not included in the above statement, but were distributed among the needy sufferers gratuitously.

While we have aimed to do equal and exact justice to all, we may have failed in some cases through unreliable information, although we have been very careful to pass upon no application until investigated by our own agent and approved by him, and then submitted to the local relief committee at Milaca and in turn approved by it.

Believing that we could better serve the interests of the sufferers by furnishing them with such goods as they needed, bought by us at wholesale prices for cash, than to give them money to use in their limited market, we rented a vacant store building in the village of Milaca, shipped in staple goods—consisting mostly of groceries and supplies—and placed in charge of the station thus established Mr. John F. Jerrard, of this city, who proved well qualified for the position.

We have paid out less than $200 to the sufferers in money, furnishing them nearly the full amount of their allowance in goods at cost, charging nothing for freight or the handling of the goods. You will notice from this report that we have expended in relief $1,254.46 in excess of the amount received from your commission, which was paid from a fund contributed by the citizens of St. Cloud and vicinity.

In this connection we will state that we bought goods to the amount of $414.90, which, with one carload of contributed goods, we took to Pokegama on the 3d day of September, being the first relief from the outside brought into that locality. Subsequently another carload of provisions, building material, tools and clothing was sent to Pokegama which was placed at their own disposal.

On September 3d we also left at Pokegama a crew of men who searched the country, and, with the aid of the Rev. William Wilkinson, who arrived later, gave burial to seventeen bodies at the expense of our committee.

In addition to the aid rendered these people at Milaca, as enumerated in the following schedules, your commission sent a large amount of clothing there, on which our committee paid the freight and our agent, Mr. Jerrard, assisted the Milaca committtee in distributing the same.

As many of these sufferers live in the woods, we did not deem it advisable to build all frame houses and buildings, but furnished only such material as could not be obtained in the surrounding timber, and, in our opinion, they are all comfortably housed. The amount expended in this direction was about $1,000.

It is our judgment that a large number of these Milaca people will need seed and farming utensils in the spring with which to carry on their farming operations, and we presume that the legislature will take proper action in the premises.

We wish to acknowledge the valuable assistance and hearty co-operation of the local committee at Milaca which contributed immediate relief to many of the sufferers previous to the action taken by us.

The expenses of distribution of relief will be between five and six per cent, and we believe that we have very nearly succeeded in satisfying the sufferers in that locality, and trust that our efforts will receive the approval of your honorable commission.

(Signed by)   H. J. ANDERSON, President;
ALVAH EASTMAN, Secretary;
JOHN COATES,
JOHN DE LES,
J. F. BRADFORD,
St. Cloud Local Committee.

EXHIBIT E.

LIST OF SUFFERERS BY FOREST FIRES SEPTEMBER, 1894, REGISTERED BY THE STATE RELIEF COMMISSION.

NOTE.—The registration is intended to include all of the fire sufferers, whether they received relief or not. Under "received relief" are included all who received relief, however small in amount, consisting, in some cases, only of railroad transportation or a few articles of clothing.

"w" Indicates widow or widower.

HINCKLEY FIRE DISTRICT.
HINCKLEY.

Name	Persons included.	Present at time of fire.	Not present time of fire.	Received relief.	Received no relief.
Nels Parsons	7	7	....	7	....
Chas. Lund	4	4	....	4	....
Wm. Kelly	5	1	4	5	....
L. H. Clow	6	6	....	6	....
B. L. Clow	1	1	....	1	....
Nels Wingren	4	4	....	4	....
John McNamara	1	1	....	1	....
Eske Norton	1	1	....	1	....
Oscar Hanson	1	1	....	1	....
Jos. Cloutier	.	1	....	1	....
Carl La Brass	1	1	....	1	....
Jas. O. Burse	3	2	1	3	....
Chas. Borg	2	2	....	2	....
Frank Beckwith	2	1	1	2	....
Chas. Fraser	1	1	....	1	....
Henry Carter	1	1	....	1	....
Chas. Carter	1	1	....	1	....
Mary Hanson	1	1	....	1	....
Hans Wingren	1	1	....	1	....
Andrew Nelson	7	7	....	7	....
Rev. A. Holmgren	3	1	2	3	....
John E. Hanson	5	5	....	5	....
James Rowley	1	1	....	....	1
Nat Richner	1	1	....	1	....
Nicholas Paulson	1	1	....	1	....
Louis Uhlin	1	1	....	1	....
Albert Schlussler	3	3	....	3	....
August Schlussler	2	1	1	....	2
Wm. Ricketson	5	5	....	5	....
Martin Anderson	1	1	....	1	....
Victor Borg	1	1	....	1	....
Samuel Richards	1	1	....	1	....
Fred Anderson	1	1	....	1	....
Ole Johnson	1	1	....	1	....
Jos. Lund	1	1	....	1	....
w. Hans Paulson	1	1	....	1	....
w. John Bean	2	1	1	2	....
John Gustafson	1	1	....	1	....
Nels Benson	1	1	....	1	....

NAME.	Persons included.	Present at time of fire.	Not present time of fire.	Received relief.	Received no relief.
Gust Bjork	2	2	....	2	....
John Espenbach	4	1	3	1	3
Peter Jensen	1	1	....	1	....
O. L. Setterlund	1	1	....	1	....
C. I. Bray	1	1	....	....	1
Peter Clint	4	4	....	4	....
C. A. Carlson	1	1	....	1	....
Peter Hokanson	3	3	....	3	....
w. Mrs. Otto Olson	1	1	....	1	....
w. Mrs. John Westerlund	1	1	....	1	....
w. Nels Frisk	1	1	....	1	....
Joseph Barden	8	8	....	8	....
Chas. Larson	4	4	....	4	....
w. Mrs. Chris. Tornell	1	1	....	1	....
w. Mrs. Lucy Michelmore	1	1	....	1	....
Hans Hokanson	2	2	....	2	....
w. Lyddy Detheck	1	1	....	1	....
Fred Bergquist	1	1	....	1	....
Jennie Irish	1	1	....	....	1
w. Dan Donahue	3	3	....	3	....
Robert Dowling	3	3	....	3	....
w. W. B. Grissinger	2	2	....	2	....
w. Martin Martinson	2	2	....	2	....
L. A. Beeman	3	3	....	3	....
Ted Warberton	5	5	....	5	....
Anthony Anderson	2	2	....	2	....
w. Wm. Beemis	1	1	....	1	....
Andrew Johnson	1	1	....	1	....
W. H. Nowark	1	1	....	1	....
John Stanchfield	9	9	....	9	....
w. John Hawley	8	8	....	8	....
F. A. Gustafson	2	2	....	2	....
Adolph Anderson	1	1	....	1	....
John Marigan	3	3	....	3	....
Nels Setterquist	1	1	....	1	....
Albert Fraser	5	5	....	5	....
Andrew Nelson	4	4	....	4	....
Eric Nelson	1	1	....	1	....
M. L. Elsmore	1	1	....	....	1
C. M. Johnson	1	1	....	1	....
Michael Marigan	1	1	....	1	....
C. A. Duff	3	3	....	3	....
w. Mrs. Mary McNeil	3	3	....	3	....

NAME	Persons included.	Present at time of fire.	Not present time of fire.	Received relief.	Received no relief.
Geo. Lott	3	3		3	
H. A. Schmaling	3	3		3	
E. J. McEachron	6	6		6	
John Erickson	4	4		4	
Ole Rosdahl	7	7		7	
Jos. Tew	9	9		9	
Jos. Kronenberg	7	7		7	
Thos. Reppl	1	1		1	
Peter Dahlstrom	1	1		1	
Gus. Martinson	1	1		1	
Nels Anderson	4	4		4	
Hilma Johnson	1	1		1	
John W. Stockholm	5	5		5	
Wm. Craig	3	3		3	
w. Mike Connor	3	3		3	
Wm. Barrett	1	1		1	
w. Mrs. Mary Booth	3	3		3	
w. Benj. Sweet	5	5		5	
J. M. Currie	5	5		5	
John Larson	1	1		1	
Peter Palm	1	1		1	
C. A. Almquist	1	1		1	
Peter Flinn	2	2		2	
Sam. Newland	1	1		1	
R. A. Freeman	1	1		1	
w. John Blanchard	2	2		2	
Aaron Olson	5	5		5	
Emil Olson	2	2		2	
Soren Johnson	1	1		1	
Andrew Peterson	1	1		1	
Andrew Stone	3	3		3	
Mike Dunn	3	3		3	
Newman Ewings	1	1		1	
Allen Wight	3	3		3	
Pat Connaker	9	2	7	2	7
Louise Heisler	1	1		1	
Tena Heisler	1	1		1	
J. Fitzgerald	1	1		1	
Stella Bishop	1	1		....	1
w. A. E. Craig	2	2		2	
Henry Richards	9	9		....	9
Carl Vanhooven	1	1		1	
Geo. J. Morast	2	2		2	

NAME.	Persons included.	Present at time of fire.	Not present time of fire.	Received relief.	Received no relief.
Orville Cox	3	3	....	3	....
E. D. Mitchell	6	6	....	6	....
Chas. McKean	1	1	....	....	1
w. Lee Webster	1	1	....	1	....
D. McLaren	1	1	....	1	....
James Riley	1	1	....	1	....
w. Douglas Greeley	3	1	2	3	....
C. R. Lonergan	1	1	....	1	....
Mrs. Mary Norton	6	2	4	6	....
S. G. Hallman	2	2	....	2	....
John Vanderbeek	5	5	....	5	....
Horace Gorton	1	1	....	1	....
Mrs. Ella Thompson	2	2	....	....	2
w. Mike Lynch	3	3	....	3	....
Frank Baumchen	1		....	1	....
Dan McIver	6	6	....	6	....
Wm. Schmaling	1	1	....	1	....
Jos. Williams	8	8	....	8	....
w. Peter Johnson	1	1	....	1	....
Frank Morgan	3	3	....	3	....
w. Chas. Nystrom	1	1	....	1	....
Anton Colberg	1	1	....	1	....
Henry Garberg	1	1	....	1	....
Louis Nelson	2	2	....	2	....
Peter Gustafson	1	1	....	1	....
Stiner Peterson	1	1	....	1	....
Fred Hanson	1	1	....	1	....
James Hanley	1	1	....	1	....
John Frisk	1	1	....	1	....
John Nelson	1	1	....	1	....
Nels Cox	1	1	....	1	....
Thomas O'Gorman	9	9	....	9	....
Garrett Corrigan	3	1	2	3	....
H. P. Hanson	1	1	....	1	....
Noble Wilson	1	1	....	1	....
Andrew Anderson	4	4	....	4	....
Andrew Granstrom	4	4	....	4	....
w. Herman Stehnke	3	....	3	3	....
John Hogan	2	2	....	2	....
w. M. Hammond	1	1	....	....	1
J. O. Coffin	4	4	....	4	....
Henry Coffin	2	2	....	2	....
Geo. D. Bartlett	1	1	....	1	....

Name.	Persons included.	Present at time of fire.	Not present time of fire.	Received relief.	Received no relief.
w. Nels Nelson	1	1	....	1	....
Pat Lawless	3	3	....	3	....
John Brennan	9	9	....	9	....
Phillip Baumchen	1	1	....	1	....
C. J. Johnson	1	1	....	1	....
Jos. Russell	2	2	....	2	....
Nels Mortenson	6	6	....	6	....
John McGinnis	1	1	....	1	....
John H. Nelson	1	1	....	1	....
Carrie Peterson	1	1	....	....	1
Ole Johnson	1	1	....	1	....
w. Geo. W. Roach	3	3	....	3	....
Thos. Campbell	1	1	....	1	....
James Cummins	1	1	....	1	....
John Lindstrom	1	1	....	1	....
M. L. Miller	4	4	....	4	....
John Luchsinger	6	6	....	6	....
J. T. Clark	1	1	....	1	....
w. Mary Cathcart	1	....	1	1	....
Nellie McGowan	1	1	....	1	....
Phil. Barrett	3	3	....	3	....
w. Mrs. Nancy Murphy	4	4	....	4	....
James Duff	5	5	....	5	....
Clara Turgeon	1	1	....	1	....
Hans Olson	4	4	....	....	4
J. H. Willard	1	1	....	1	....
Dr. E. L. Stephan	1	1	....	1	....
Wm. Dunn	1	1	....	....	1
w. Mrs. Sarah Barry	6	....	6	6	....
Emil Bjork	1	1	....	1	....
Wm. Cathcart	4	4	....	4	....
H. S. Bartlett	1	1	....	1	....
D. S. Scott	5	5	....	5	....
Chas. Lind	3	3	....	3	....
Chas. Olson	5	5	....	5	....
Eva Hopkins	1	....	1	....	1
A. Williams	1	1	....	1	....
Hjalmer Lundborg	1	1	....	1	....
W. F. Gray	3	3	....	3	....
Joe DeMarsh	1	1	....	1	....
Chas. Lawson	2	2	....	2	....
J. T. Craig	2	2	....	2	....
w. Mrs. Henry Hanson	7	7	....	7	....

Name.	Persons included.	Present at time of fire.	Not present time of fire.	Received relief.	Received no relief.
James Morrison	2	....	2	2	....
Rev. Peter Knutson	2	2	....	2	....
S. W. Anderson	4	4	....	4	....
Alex. Cameron	2	2	....	2	....
Pat. Glennon	1	1	....	1	....
Mich. Marooney	1	1	....	1	....
H. W. Miller	7	7	....	7	....
Chas Warner	1	1	....	1	....
James Farrigan	1	1	....	1	....
Wm. J. Hughes	6	6	....	6	....
John Sjoquist	3	3	....	3	....
Isidore Cohen	5	1	4	5	....
Ida Larson	1	1	....	....	1
Luther Trotter	1	1	....	1	....
Charles Swanson	1	1	....	1	....
Benj. C. Bartlett	7	7	....	7	....
w. Mrs. Axel Hanson	4	4	....	4	....
James Jordan	8	8	....	8	....
Ernest Leske	5	1	4	....	5
J. H. Young	5	5	....	5	....
R. C. Saunders	1	1	....	....	1
A. C. Hay	1	1	....	1	....
Louis Davis	1	1	....	1	....
John Welch	1	1	....	1	....
D. Brennan	7	7	....	7	....
Mike Carlson	1	1	....	1	....
August Lindborg	1	1	....	1	....
Jos. Carl	1	1	....	1	....
w. Mary M. Pratt	3	....	3	....	3
John Westman	1	1	....	1	....
Larry Murphy	1	1	....	1	....
Frank Lord	4	1	3	1	3
Thos. W. Bartlett	1	1	....	1	....
John Brodie	1	1	....	....	1
Oscar Knowlton	1	1	....	....	1
John Miller	2	2	....	....	2
w. John Cathcart	1	1	....	1	....
Geo. Nevers	7	7	....	7	....
Al Olena	1	1	....	....	1
May Vaughn	1	1	....	1	....
John Armstrong	1	1	....	1	....
w. John McNamara	4	4	....	4	....
John K. Anderson	5	5	....	5	....

Name.	Persons included.	Present at time of fire.	Not present time of fire.	Received relief.	Received no relief.
Andrew Carlson	4	1	3	1	3
Alfred Socky	1	1	....	1	....
J. E. Welsinger	1	1	....	....	1
John Roach	1	1	....	....	1
Pat. Hogan	1	1	....	1	....
Nelson Henry	4	4	....	4	....
w. Mrs. Fritz Droel	6	....	6	6	....
Wm. Jordan	2	2	....	2	....
Joe Riley	2	2	....	2	....
Chas. Enge	1	1	....	1	....
Mike Garity	2	2	....	....	2
Paul Cornier	1	1	....	1	....
w. Mrs. Cecelia Johnson	2	2	....	2	....
H. Niblette	1	1	....	1	....
Ed. Mason	1	1	....	1	....
w. B. A. Larson	3	3	....	3	....
August Borg	2	2	....	2	....
R. J. Hawley	1	1	....	1	....
Andrew Campbell	1	1	....	1	....
Otto Skamser	1	1	....	1	....
C. J. Nelson	4	....	4	....	4
Mrs. Ida Janda	1	1	....	1	....
Freda Grandberg	1	1	....	1	....
Delore Fortin	1	1	....	1	....
w. John Braff	4	4	....	4	....
Chas. Bjorklund	1	1	....	1	....
w. Sam Estes	1	1	....	1	....
Ed. Carlson	1	1	....	1	....
Nels Anderson	8	8	....	8	....
James Love	2	1	1	2	....
Albert Lundgren	1	1	....	1	....
Christ. Dolmseth	1	1	....	1	....
J. T. Hawley	1	1	....	1	....
James Vishert	1	1	....	1	....
Wm. Vishert	1	1	....	1	....
E. L. Neslund	1	1	....	1	....
Frank Jensen	1	1	....	1	....
John Anderson	1	1	....	1	....
Walter Scott	4	4	....	4	....
J. F. Larson	1	1	....	1	....
Axel Rosdahl	1	1	....	1	....
Peter Nelson	5	....	5	5	....
Geo. Turgeon	1	1	....	1	....

Name.	Persons included.	Present at time of fire.	Not present time of fire.	Received relief.	Received no relief.
Elmer Torberson	1		1	1	
Rich. Underwood	1	1		1	
w. Mrs. Nels Nelson	6	6		6	
Joe Wigue	1	1		1	
Paul Johnson	1	1		1	
Dr. D. W. Cowan	1	1		1	
Albert Erickson	1	1		1	
John Peterson	3	3		3	
John Anderson	1	1		1	
Andrew Peterson	1	1		1	
w. Mrs. Claire Turgeon	4	4		4	
A. Richner	2	2		2	
Joe Savoy	6	6		6	
Mrs. Johanna Gustafson	2	2		2	
Hans Toite	1	1		1	
Josephine Turgeon	1	1		1	
Geo. Parish	1	1		1	
Anton Larson	7	7		7	
Frank Decoursey	2	2		2	
Richard Nesbitt	1	1		1	
A. F. Murray	1	1			1
Rebecca Sandberg	1	1		1	
Sadie Henry	1	1		1	
Albert Nelson	1	1		1	
Thomas Lane	3	3		3	
Emma Olson	1	1		1	
Louis Lundy	1		1	1	
Aaron Gustafson	1		1	1	
Mary Anderson	1	1		1	
Frank Murray	1	1		1	
Wm. Fitzsimmons	1	1		1	
Peter Cox	1		1	1	
w. John Sullivan	1		1		1
Moses Cohn	7		7	7	
Ed. Mickelson	1	1		1	
w. Mrs. Charlotte Hansen	1	1		1	
Xavier Bone	2	2		2	
Eric Johnson	1	1		1	
Mons Cleveland	1	1		1	
Wm. Johnson	1		1	1	
Chas. Olin	1	1		1	
Kate Nelson	1	1		1	
John Brothen	1	1			1

Name.	Persons included.	Present at time of fire.	Not present time of fire.	Received relief.	Received no relief.
Mike O'Gara	1	1	....	1	....
T. Sparemell	1	1	....	....	1
Jesse Gilman	1	1	....	1	....
Robert Johnson	1	1	....	1	....
Frank Swenson	1	1	....	1	....
Ole Hanson	4	1	3	....	4
w. Hannah Risberg	5	5	....	5	....
Albert Wickstrom	1	1	....	1	....
Wm. Carlson	1	1	....	1	....
M. A. Stroinsky	1	....	1	....	1
Wm. Lee	1	....	1	....	1
Harry Olson	1	1	....	1	....
G. J. Albrecht	4	4	....	4	....
Chas. O. Anderson	7	7	....	7	....
Chas. Peterson	3	3	....	3	....
Peter Peterson	2	2	....	2	....
M. S. Collins	1	1	....	....	1
w. Mrs. John Burke	4	4	....	4	..
Ben Nelson	4	1	3	1	3
Henry Maps	1	....	1	1	....
Joe Fournier	1	....	1	1	....
John Hopkins	1	....	1	....	1
C. Warberton	4	1	3	1	3
Mrs. W. M. Stevens	3	....	3	....	3
Dennis Dunn	1	1	....	1	....
O. Rasmusson	1	1	....	1	....
T. J. Sweeney	1	....	1	....	1
w. Marinda Ricketson	1	1	....	1	....
Martin Westrud	7	7	....	7	....
Christ Peterson	4	4	....	4	....
Christ Britton	2	2	....	2	..
Annie Hintz	1	1	....	1	....
Helen Peterson	1	1	....	1	..
H. D. Davis	8	1	7	....	8
August Walden	1	1	....	1	..
Oscar Anderson	1	1	....	....	1
Jos. Arndt	1	1	....	1	....
Jesse Badgeron	2	....	2	2	....
Louis Bedard	7	7	....	7	....
Otto Berg	1	1	....	1	....
Victor Borg	1	1	....	....	1
Albert Borg	1	1	....	1	....
Victor Carlson	4	4	....	4	....

Name.	Persons included.	Present at time of fire.	Not present time of fire.	Received relief.	Received no relief.
w. Andrew Carlson	1	1	....	....	1
James T. Fairchild	1	1	....	1	....
James Flemming	3	3	....	3	....
Ole Frederickson	1	1	....	....	1
James W. Green	8	8	....	8	....
Sim Green	1	1	....	....	1
Andrew Gunderson	10	10	....	10	....
Hugo Gustaison	1	1	....	1	....
Conrad Gustafson	1	1	....	1	....
Clara Hanson	1	1	....	1	....
w. Mary Hanson	4	4	....	4	....
Frank Howard	1	1	....	1	....
Marta Hanson	1	1	....	1	....
Alex. Iverson	6	1	5	1	5
J. Peter Jenson	1	1	....	1	....
Anton Johnson	1	1	....	1	....
August Johnson	1	1	....	1	....
Mary Knowles	1	1	....	1	....
Rev. E. J. Lawler	1	1	....	1	....
Dr. Inez A. Legg	1	1	....	1	....
Martin Halmaas	1	1	....	1	....
Frank Miller	5	5	....	5	....
T. A. Miller	3	1	2	1	2
Mrs. Laura Miller	2	2	....	1	1
Thos. Maroney	3	3	....	3	....
Simon Nelson	1	1	....	1	....
John J. Oitelie	2	2	....	2	....
w. Andrew Olson	5	5	....	5	....
Christ. Olson	5	5	....	5	....
Christ. Olson	1	1	....	1	....
John Olson	5	5	....	5	....
Nels Olson	3	3	....	3	....
Michael O'Neil	1	1	....	1	....
John Potterud	4	4	....	4	....
Fred Robinson	1	1	....	1	....
Mary Robinson	1	1	....	1	....
Chas. Sleight	3	3	....	3	....
Cecelia Stockholm	2	2	....	2	....
Martin Sletten	4	1	3	1	3
O. H. Svastuen	5	5	....	5	....
Annie Swanson	1	1	....	1	....
Emily Swanson	1	1	....	1	....
Chris. J. Skamser	4	4	....	4	....

Name.	Persons included.	Present at time of fire.	Not present time of fire.	Received relief.	Received no relief.
John Sletten	5	5	....	5	....
w. Mrs. Chas. Strum	3	3	....	3	....
Tollef Thompson	1	1	....	1	....
Andrew Torgerson	3	3	....	....	3
Ole Torgerson	2	2	....	2	....
Louis Ronneberg	1	1	....	....	1
Wm. Nixon	4	....	4	4	....
Emma Molin	1	1	....	1	....
Joseph Kroll	1	1	....	1	....
Swan Anderson	1	1	....	....	1
Chas. Swanson	5	5	....	5	....
John Wald	1	1	....	1	....
Chas. Waliberg	1	1	....	1	....
Totals	1038	910	128	921	117

HINCKLEY VICINITY.

Name.	Persons included.	Present at time of fire.	Not present time of fire.	Received relief.	Received no relief.
Dan'l Hoffman	6	6	....	6	....
Herman Lindau	8	8	....	8	....
w. George Weireter	1	1	....	1	....
Fred Pino	1	1	....	1	....
Swan Johnson	4	4	....	4	....
F. T. Russell	3	3	....	3	....
Otto Will	2	2	....	2	....
A. L. Holm	6	6	....	6	....
Simon Benton	2	2	....	2	....
Carl Jencke	9	9	....	9	....
C. A. Peterson	4	1	3	4	....
Thomas Henderson	7	1	6	7	....
A. G. Lindblad	4	4	....	4	....
Swan Johnson	1	1	....	1	....
Peter Gustafson	3	3	....	3	....
John Best	4	4	....	4	....
Christian Best	1	1	....	1	....
Wells De Long	2	2	....	2	....
Nels A. Wicklund	5	5	....	5	....
E. O. Rask	4	4	....	4	....
John Bergman	5	5	....	5	....
Andrew Rask	1	1	....	1	....
Archie McGowan	4	4	....	4	....
Chas. Peterson	10	10	....	10	....
Ernst Weser, Jr	1	1	....	1	....
John Nelson	1	1	....	1	....

Name.	Persons included.	Present at time of fire.	Not present time of fire.	Received relief.	Received no relief.
John Patrick	4	4	....	4	....
Chas. J. Johnson	8	8	....	8	....
Andrew Nelson	1	1	....	1	....
Ernst Weser, Sr	2	2	....	2	....
Henry Hundertmark	1	1	....	1	....
Samuel Neil	4	4	....	4	....
Robert D. McDonald	1	1	....	1	....
w. Noble Sherman	1	1	....	1	....
Jos. Almsberger	5	3	2	5	....
Axel Peterson	1	1	....	1	....
A. W. Peterson	2	2	....	2	....
w. John Peterson	4	4	....	4	....
Emil Worp	1	1	....	1	....
James Sexton	1	1	....	....	1
Chas. Barriau	1	1	....	1	....
Christ. Sexton	1	1	....	1	....
Jerry Sexton	1	1	....	1	....
Dennis Sexton	1	1	....	1	....
Mike Fitzgerald	6	6	....	6	....
Frank Haney	1	1	....	1	....
Gustav Wentz	1	1	....	1	....
Phillip Heist	1	1	....	....	1
John Tenquist	5	5	....	5	....
w. Mary J. Doremus	7	7	....	7	....
w. Mrs. Christiana Cane	3	3	....	3	....
Chas. Holmstrom	9	9	....	9	....
M. C. Dean	1	1	....	1	....
James Oredson	1	1	....	1	....
Louis Paulson	3	3	....	3	....
w. Mrs. Louis Chambers	1	....	1	1	....
H. Gender	4	4	....	4	....
John Lundburg	1	1	....	1	....
Totals	183	171	12	181	2

SANDSTONE.

Martin Nelson	1	1	....	1	....
w. August Anderson	1	1	....	1	....
John Nelson	1	1	....	1	....
A. G. Johnson	1	1	....	1	....
Frank Westergreen	1	1	....	1	....
Otto Stafverfeldt	2	2	....	2	....

Name.	Persons included.	Present at time of fire.	Not present time of fire.	Received relief.	Received no relief.
An l. Lund		1	....	1	....
Ralph Rasmusson	1	1	....	1	....
William Lindeke	1	1	....	1	....
George Friesendahl	1	1	....	1	....
Hans Kruse	6	6	....	6	....
Ernst Hogan	2	2	....	2	....
J. W. Concannon	2	2	....	2	....
Peter Ogren	4	1	3	1	3
William Severt	1	1	....	1	....
James Carroll	3	3	....	3	....
Charles F. Anderson	6	6	....	6	....
Peter Jones	5	5	....	5	....
Albert Glassow	5	5	....	5	....
w. Angus Gunn	5	5	....	5	....
Christ. Heisler	4	4	....	4	....
Herman Gast	1	1	....	1	....
R. A. Smith	3	3	....	3	....
Stephen O'Neil	10	10	....	10	....
Mike Bresnahan	1	1	....	1	....
George Sutherland	1	1	....	1	....
Charles Gustafson	5	1	4	1	4
Charles Peterson	1	1	....	1	....
w. Ole Englund	2	1	1	1	1
Gus Stenwall	1	1	....	1	....
Joe Hagelin	1	1	....	1	....
C. Staples	4	1	3	4	....
Charles Feldt	5	1	4	1	4
Gust Peterson	1	1	....	1	....
Charles Pearson	1	1	....	1	....
W. O. Pleas	7	7	....	7	....
M. Fitzsimmons	1	1	....	1	....
Octavo Dube	6	1	5	6	....
Charles Upstrom	1	1	....	1	....
Olaus Holm	4	4	....	4	....
W. W. Jessmer	5	5	....	5	....
Peter Lund	3	3	....	3	....
M. Bullis	5	5	....	5	....
Ole Anderson	4	4	....	4	....
Thomas McCoy	1	1	....	1	....
August Rouvell	2	....	2	....	2
Thomas Rorek	1	1	....	1	....
Carl Eliason	1	1	....	1	....
John Monson	6	1	5	1	5

NAME.	Persons included.	Present at time of fire.	Not present time of fire.	Received relief.	Received no relief.
E. O. Stenmark	7	1	6	7	....
Gus. Falk	2	2	....	2	....
John Falk	4	4	....	4	....
Nels Flykt	1	1	....	1	....
William Lindblom	3	3	....	3	....
George Meader	3	3	....	3	....
Peter Peterson	4	4	....	4	....
Manda Falk	1	1	....	1	....
Gus Holmquist	1	1	....	1	....
August Pearson	1	....	1	1	....
N. W. Thompson	1	1	....	....	1
Axel Westin	7	7	....	7	....
Ed. Halverson	6	6	....	6	....
Nels Sjolander	1	1	....	1	....
Eric Wallin	4	4	....	4	....
John H. Friesendahl	8	8	....	8	....
Neils Bjorklund	5	....	5	....	5
John Gjertson	4	4	....	4	....
Ole Swanson	3	1	2	....	3
Frank Hammerstad	4	4	....	4	....
w. Ed. Linehan	6	6	....	6	....
J. E. Erickson	9	9	....	9	....
w. Magnus Ortenblal	2	2	....	2	....
John S. Lynds	4	4	....	4	....
J. P. Runnell	3	2	1	3	....
C. Kaljander	8	1	7	1	7
Henry Wallin	3	3	....	3	....
w. Thomas Madisen	1	1	....	1	....
John Sundin.	3	3	....	3	....
Ed. Peterson	1	1	....	1	....
Eric Olson	5	1	4	1	4
Victor Gjertson	3	3	....	3	....
Gust Gjertson	1	1	....	1	....
Eric Hanson	1	1	....	1	....
B. Bjorklund	3	3	....	3	....
Matt Hakinson	7	7	....	7	....
Mary Regan	1	1	....	1	....
Gust E., Möll	3	3	....	3	....
N. P. Johnson	5	5	....	5	....
Nestor Koski	4	4	....	4	....
Isaac Hassoo	2	2	....	2	....
w. Gust Anderson	1	1	....	1	....
E. Torell	1	1	....	1	....

NAME.	Persons included.	Present at time of fire.	Not present time of fire.	Received relief.	Received no relief.
Hans Hanson	6	1	5	1	5
Noe Mireau	4	4	....	4	....
Andrew Anderson	4	4	....	4	....
Eric Anderson	5	5	....	5	....
Charles Anderson	1	1	....	1	....
Ole Berglin	0	0	....	0	....
Peter Degerstrom	5	5	....	5	....
w. Edward Edstrom	1	1	....	1	....
Caroline Erickson	1	1	....	1	....
John Erickson	1	1	....	1	....
John P. Flood	7	7	....	7	....
Daniel J. Forin	4	4	....	4	....
Thomas W. Finn	5	5	....	5	....
Oscar Flood	1	1	....	1	....
George Gardner	2	2	....	2	....
Hugh Glenn	8	8	....	8	....
w. Anna Goldahl	3	3	....	3	....
Christ. Hanson	6	6	....	6	....
Hilda Hawkinson	1	1	....	1	....
w. John Hops	1	1	....	1	....
Eric Johnson	5	5	....	5	....
Albert Johnson	1	1	....	1	....
Andrew Kaleen	2	1	1	1	1
Johanna Kindlund	1	1	....	1	....
John Koepi	1	1	....	1	....
David Lafebore	0	0	....	0	....
Solomon Lundborg	1	1	....	1	....
Harry Madison	1	1	....	1	....
Jennie Madison	1	1	....	....	1
w. Christine McElroy	2	2	....	....	2
Mauritz Mokato	7	1	6	1	6
Gust Nelson	4	4	....	4	....
E. P. O'Sell	5	5	....	5	....
John O'Neil	1	1	....	1	....
Gust Peterson	4	4	....	4	....
Dennis Prenevost	1	1	....	1	....
John Robinson	7	7	....	7	....
John Raud	1	1	....	1	....
James Steward	3	3	....	3	....
Harvey Staples	9	9	....	9	....
Charles Sjolander	2	2	....	2	....
George Wilkes	5	5	....	5	....
Emil Nelson	1	1	....	1	....

NAME.	Persons included.	Present at time of fire.	Not present, time of fire.	Received relief.	Received no relief.
Swan Johnson	4	1	3	1	3
w. Andrew Hofilen	3	3	....	3	....
C. G. Bergstrom	1	1	....	1	....
Edward Crepau	1	1	....	1	....
w. Mrs. Maggie Swanson	6	6	....	6	....
Thomas O'Neil	1	1	....	1	....
w. Christine Nelson	3	3	....	3	....
w. Mrs. Anna Nyberg	4	4	....	4	....
C. A. Carlson	6	....	6	1	5
A. J. Johnson	6	1	5	1	5
Thomas Handley	1	1	....	1	....
w. Mrs. Johnson	1	1	....	1	....
A. J. Johnson	1	....	1	....	1
Aaron Anderson	9	9	....	1	8
L. W. Johnson	2	2	....	....	2
Andrew Frederickson	7	7	....	7	....
Samuel Warman	3	3	....	3	....
Patrick Regan	5	5	....	5	....
Totals	468	418	80	420	78
Indianapolis; A. Donnely					$1.00

POKEGAMA.

NAME.	Persons included.	Present at time of fire.	Not present, time of fire.	Received relief.	Received no relief.
M. L. Seymour	4	1	3	4	....
I. C. Baty	3	3	....	3	....
W. N. Carver	2	2	....	2	....
C. F. Collier	4	4	....	4	....
Mrs. L. Calhoun	1	1	....	....	1
Reuben Osternick	7	1	6	7	....
W. W. Braman	2	2	....	2	....
A. Berg	6	6	....	6	....
w. Mrs. Mary Whitney	3	3	....	3	....
w. Robert Barnes	2	2	....	2	....
Joseph Gonyea	11	1	10	11	....
Samuel Misel	4	4	....	4	....
Charles Smith	5	5	....	5	....
Thomas Racine	5	5	....	5	....
W. N. Thompson	1	1	....	1	....
Joe Coblin	1	1	....	1	....
C. W. Kelsey	7	7	....	7	....
Dr. C. A. Kelsey	6	6	....	6	....
Hans Nelson	6	6	....	6	....
Charles N. Ward	3	3	....	3	....

Name.	Persons included.	Present at time of fire.	Not present time of fire.	Received relief.	Received no relief.
Joseph Frame	7	7	....	7	....
John Johnson	4	4	....	4	....
Emil Johnson	1	1	....	....	1
John Powers	1	1	....	1	....
Frank Littengarver	1	1	....	1	....
Jake Greenberg	1	1	....	1	....
J. L. Boucher	3	3	....	3	....
Joseph Sipris	2	2	....	2	....
Israel Rosenberg	4	4	....	4	....
Abram Chapman	7	1	6	7	....
Gustav Ellison	1	1	....	1	....
David Frame	1	1	....	1	....
Henry Nelson	1	....	1	1	....
H. Shapiro	5	5	....	5	....
B. Finer	4	4	....	4	....
Mrs. Raphael	5	5	....	5	....
Totals	131	105	26	129	2

MISSION CREEK.

Name.	Persons included.	Present at time of fire.	Not present time of fire.	Received relief.	Received no relief.
Axel Halgren	2	2	....	2	....
Oscar A. Peterson	3	3	....	3	....
John Sexton	2	2	....	2	....
John Turner	2	2	....	2	....
W. Peter Norberg	2	2	....	2	....
Swen Swenson	1	1	....	1	....
L. G. Johnson	3	3	....	3	....
P. H. Nyberg	1	1	....	1	....
Gust Sandquist	1	1	....	1	....
John Berg	2	1	1	1	1
Peter Bergman	1	1	....	1	....
E. S. Wallace	2	1	1	1	1
G. D. Edlund	4	4	....	4	....
Frank Sexton	1	1	....	1	....
A. G. Moberg	1	1	....	1	....
Charles Johnson	1	1	....	1	....
Joseph Sexton	1	1	....	1	....
H. S. Rice	1	1	....	1	....
Eric Nelson	4	4	....	4	....
Ed. J. Boyle	3	3	....	3	....
J. T. Smullen	1	1	....	1	....
John De Shaw	1	1	....	1	....
Fred Baudrau	1	1	....	1	....

NAME	Persons included.	Present at time of fire.	Not present time of fire.	Received relief.	Received no relief.
Joseph Boyle	1	1	....	1	....
G. W. Hambleton	1	1	....	1	....
C. A. Johnson	4	4	....	4	....
Frank Kapinos	4	4	....	4	....
Hans H. Sieger	6	6	....	....	6
Adolph Anderson	4	4	....	4	....
Carl Hagelund	6	6	....	6	....
J. F. Walsten	6	2	4	6	....
August Myren	1	1	....	1	....
Amy Armstrong	1	1	....	1	....
Totals	75	69	6	67	8

SANDSTONE JUNCTION AND MILLER.

NAME	Persons included.	Present at time of fire.	Not present time of fire.	Received relief.	Received no relief.
M. E. Greenfield	3	3	....	3	....
Andrew Hanson	1	1	....	1	....
w. Louis Mottorz	1	1	....	1	....
Paul Flamstrom	1	1	....	1	....
William Jacob	1	1	....	1	....
Charles Peterson	1	1	....	1	....
John H. Samuelson	11	11	....	11	....
John Derosier	2	2	....	2	....
C. F. Johnson	1	1	....	1	....
Peter Prenevost	6	6	....	6	....
Gust Malm	2	2	....	2	....
A. L. Thompson	4	4	....	4	....
Peter Chelman	1	1	....	1	....
Eric Troolin	10	10	....	10	....
w. Henry Lind	1	1	....	1	....
Peter Bilado	6	6	....	6	....
w. John Westerlund	1	1	....	1	....
John Bjorklund	7	7	....	7	....
Alfred Anderson	4	4	....	4	....
Sievert Haglin	4	4	....	4	....
Charles Strumberg	1	1	....	1	....
Totals	69	69	....	69	....

FINLAYSON.

NAME	Persons included.	Present at time of fire.	Not present time of fire.	Received relief.	Received no relief.
w. Mary Murphy	1	1	....	1	....
w. Mrs. Murray	1	1	....	1	....
P. A. Orman	7	7	....	7	....
Andrew Hokka	.	3	....	3	....

Name.	Persons included.	Present at time of fire.	Not present time of fire.	Received relief.	Received no relief.
H. G. Tyler	2	2	....	2	....
John L. Cowing	1	1	....	1	....
John Krebs	5	5	....	5	....
William Stoll	3	3	....	3	....
Fred Kunzli	1	1	....	1	....
C. W. Harris	5	5	....	5	....
E. C. Buel	1	1	....	1	....
George Foley	5	1	4	5	....
Charles Brown	1	1	....	1	....
John Wytenbach	4	4	....	4	....
A. G. Crocker	3	3	....	3	....
Arne Anderson	6	6	....	6	....
John Greenley	5	5	....	5	....
Charles Willis	1	1	....	1	....
James Carman	7	7	....	7	....
Fred Nelson	4	4	....	....	4
Martin Greenley	7	7	....	7	....
Albert G. Cramer	1	1	....	1	....
w. Anna J. Cheney	1	1	....	1	....
William O'Connor	6	1	5	1	5
w. Anna McCloud	2	2	....	2	....
Christian Ramm	6	6	....	6	....
Joe A. Carman	1	1	....	1	....
C. A. Crocker	4	4	....	4	....
Totals	94	85	9	85	9

PARTRIDGE.

Name.	Persons included.	Present at time of fire.	Not present time of fire.	Received relief.	Received no relief.
John W. Lynch	2	2	....	2	....
Pat Kane	1	1	....	1	....
L. G. Johnson	6	6	....	....	6
John Sopher	6	6	....	6	....
Dan Bovington	2	2	....	2	....
J. W. Alexander	5	5	....	5	....
Tim O'Niel	6	6	....	....	6
James Woodard	2	2	....	2	....
Hogan Hoganson	6	1	5	6	....
Gust Taylor	1	1	....	1	....
w. Nels E. Nelson	1	1	....	1	....
Charles Alexander	1	1	....	....	1
John A. Johnson	6	6	....	....	6
Reuben Quarterman	3	3	....	3	....
William Williams	1	1	....	1	....

Name.	Persons included.	Present at time of fire.	Not present time of fire.	Received relief.	Received no relief.
L. Saunders	1	1	....	....	1
Henry White	2	2	....	2	....
Hugh McKenzie	5	5	....	5	....
John Jackson	2	1	1	2	....
Totals	59	53	6	39	20

RUTLEDGE.

Name.	Persons included.	Present at time of fire.	Not present time of fire.	Received relief.	Received no relief.
Adolph Schepstedt	4	4	....	1	3
John Israelson	1	1	....	1	....
Emil Larson	9	9	....	9	....
Totals	14	14	....	11	3

MORA.

Name.	Persons included.	Present at time of fire.	Not present time of fire.	Received relief.	Received no relief.
Nels Sjodin	9	9	....	....	9
John Selin	4	4	....	4	....
Gust Carlson	4	4	....	....	4
Eric Erickson	3	3	....	....	3
Nels Sall	9	9	....	9	....
Fred Lebenthal	4	4	....	....	4
Henry Lebenthal	4	4	....	....	4
W. F. Geddes	3	3	....	....	3
P. E. Person	11	11	....	11	....
Andrew Swenson	4	4	....	4	....
C. W. Whitney	1	1	....	....	1
Totals	56	56	....	28	28

KERRICK.

Name.	Persons included.	Present at time of fire.	Not present time of fire.	Received relief.	Received no relief.
Andrew Gillberg	2	2	....	2	....
Gustav Sandborg	4	4	....	4	....
Swan Lingren	1	1	....	1	....
Josephine Peterson	2	2	....	2	....
Totals	9	9	....	9	....

SCATTERING.

Name.	Persons included.	Present at time of fire.	Not present time of fire.	Received relief.	Received no relief.
Edw. Hanson	1	1	....	....	1
William Smith	4	1	3	4	....
William Holbrook	5	5	....	5	....
E. W. Fisk	1	....	1	1	....
Eric Sanberg	2	2	....	....	2

Name.	Persons included.	Present at time of fire.	Not present time of fire.	Received relief.	Received no relief.
Isaac Toolson	1	1	....	1	....
Julius Cooper	1	1	....,	1	....
Frank Karas	6	6	....,	6	....
Anton Ludwig	1	1	....	1	....
Stekl	5	1	4	....	5
James Byers	5	5	....	....	5
Ed. McLeod	1	1	....	1	....
C. H. Furman	6	....	6	6	....
Andrew Jackson	9	9	....	9	....
H. S. Austin	3	1	2	1	2
William Wisdom	6	1	5	....	6
Melvin Guptill	3	....	3	....	3
James J. Warner	5	5	....	....	5
J. B. Butler	8	....	8	....	8
T. E. Ryan	3	3	....	....	3
Louis Sakovitz	7	7	....	7	....
Ole H. Olson	7	7	....	7	....
Evan Hanson	1	1	....	1	....
A. E. Rian	1	1	....	1	....
John Young	1	1	....	1	....
A. Webber	3	....	3	....	3
Ludwig Olson	5	5	....	....	5
w. Mrs. Mary Norman	1	1	....	1	....
Henry Nelson	3	3	....	3	....
Alexander Bee	5	5	....	....	5
Mathey Molner	5	5	....	5	....
John W. Stafford	3	1	2	....	3
J. A. Tasker	4	4	....	4	....
Totals	123	86	37	67	56

MILACA COUNTY.

Andrew Johnson	9	9	....	9	....
C. L. Anderson	4	4	....	4	....
Charles Hoaglund	10	10	....	10	....
Peter Anderson	3	3	....	3	....
Carl Clausen	5	5	....	5	....
Gust Lundberg	4	4	....	4	....
John Lund	5	5	....	5	....
Elias Jackson	6	6	....	6	....
Olaf Pierson	3	3	....	3	....
w. Matilda Peterson	3	3	....	3	....
Peter Erickson	3	3	....	3	....

Name.	Persons included.	Present at time of fire.	Not present time of fire.	Received relief.	Received no relief.
William Johnson	4	4		4	
Gust Sjostrom	7	7		7	
A. Bostrum	5	5		5	
Herman Nelson	5	5		5	
August Johnson	3	3		3	
Frank Bergstrom	3	3		3	
Carl E. Carlson	1	1		1	
Gust Kilburg	4	4		4	
H. C. Darholt	8	8		8	
K. C. Moland	5	5		5	
Nels Johnson	3	3		3	
Peter Turnquist	10	10		10	
John Hakenson	6	6		6	
E. W. Stromberg	4	4		4	
Peter Hanson	1	1		1	
John Wilkstrom	10	10		10	
Andrew Holmquist	5	5		5	
Charles W. Hedblad	1	1		1	
John B. Heron	7	7		7	
Peter Johnson	4	4		4	
Jacob Salberg	2	2		2	
James Udstrand	1	1		1	
F. A. Francine	3	3		3	
F. Hendrickson	2	2		2	
John Peterson	4	4		4	
A. D. Crosby	4	4		4	
Nicholas Erickson	6	6		6	
Carl Anderson	9	9		9	
Andrew A. Wass	4	4		4	
L. B. Baxter	2	2		2	
Andrew Johnson	3	3		3	
w. Mrs. C. A. Anderson	4	4		4	
C. O. Stromburg	3	3		3	
Carl Johnson	1	1		1	
Ole Sundberg	7	7		7	
Stephanus Peterson	5	5		5	
J. G. Eglund	2	2		2	
James Johnson	6	6		6	
Mrs. M. J. Bullis	3	3		3	
B. E. Larson	1	1		1	
B. E. Schedline	6	6		6	
Frank Haidlund	7	7		7	
Nels Hanson	2	2		2	

Name	Persons included.	Present at time of fire.	Not present time of fire.	Received relief.	Received no relief.
A. P. Johnson	1	1	....	1	....
Lars Larson	8	8	....	8	....
John Lindman	7	7	....	7	....
John Daline	3	3	....	3	....
Andrew Sand	4	4	....	4	....
Andrew K. Wass	3	3	....	3	....
Charles Wigman	3	3	....	3	....
Carl Turnquist	3	3	....	3	....
P. A. Lekburg	1	1	....	1	....
Alfred Sandstrom	4	4	....	4	....
Charles Nord	2	2	....	2	....
Lars Lode	1	1	....	1	....
Ben Jacobson	1	1	....	1	....
Ole Anderson	7	7	....	7	....
Peter Olson	6	6	....	6	....
Eric Blomberg	6	6	....	6	....
N. P. Anderson	5	5	....	5	....
Herman Carlson	3	3	....	3	....
Charles Erickson	6	6	....	6	....
P. M. Lindberg	5	5	....	5	....
John M. Anderson	4	4	....	4	....
Nels Oreyson	1	1	....	1	....
Oscar Osborner	1	1	....	1	....
A. P. Olson	1	1	....	1	....
Charles Palmquist	5	5	....	5	....
Alfred Ahlquist	6	6	....	6	....
John Erickson	10	10	....	10	....
John Enghold	1	1	....	1	....
Henry Berg	5	5	....	5	....
Olaf Peterson	1	1	....	1	....
August Blomberg	7	7	....	7	....
Gust Pearson	1	1	....	1	....
G. A. Arnely	5	5	....	5	....
C. E. Newberg	4	4	....	4	....
Samuel Nelson	1	1	....	1	....
Totals	370	370	....	370	....

CARLTON COUNTY.

Name	Persons included.	Present at time of fire.	Not present time of fire.	Received relief.	Received no relief.
Nettie Ameson	2	2	....	2	....
Louis Amans	1	1	....	1	....
Alexander Bolanger	5	5	....	....	5
Benjamin Beck	1	1	....	....	1

NAME.	Persons included.	Present at time of fire.	Not present time of fire.	Received relief.	Received no relief.
Frank Buschert	11	11	....	11	....
William Cool	4	4	....	4	....
Edward P. Duffy	5	5	....	5	....
Oscar Dotten	3	3	....	3	....
Amasa Dotton	9	9	....	....	9
Barbara Ehr	1	1	....	1	....
George Flaugher	1	1	....	1	....
August Johnson	1	1	....	1	....
Anton Johnson	1	1	....	1	....
John Kajander	4	4	....	....	4
Joseph Lavallee	2	2	....	1	1
Alexander La Blanc	1	1	....	....	1
John Lindquist	3	3	....	....	3
w. Louis Lundgren	2	2	....	....	2
Charles Morse	4	4	....	....	4
John Miller	7	7	....	7	....
Peter Morrison	2	2	....	2	...
Aldrich Mattinen	3	3	....	....	3
Horace Paine	9	9	....	....	9
Herman Skart	5	5	....	....	5
E. Terrien	2	1	1	1	1
W. T. Wright	4	4	....	4	....
George Wright	5	5	...	5	....
Isaac Walli	9	9	....	9	....
w. Woodbury Whitten	1	1	....	1	....
William Holm	4	4	....	4	....
w. D. Trepannier	4	4	....	1	3
John Stave	2	2	....	....	2
L. B. Sawyer	5	5	....	5	....
Totals	123	122	1	70	53

OTTER TAIL COUNTY.

NAME.	Persons included.	Present at time of fire.	Not present time of fire.	Received relief.	Received no relief.
Charles Olgreen	7	7	....	7	....
John Wullolle	7	7	....	7	....
M. Mattson	5	5	....	5	....
James Johnson	4	4	....	4	....
H. Haatafa	11	11	....	11	....
H. Tanny	2	2	....	2	....
M. Ekonon	2	2	....	2	....
F. Paavola	6	6	....	6	....
H. Lehtiner	6	6	....	6	....
I. Lindstrom	2	2	....	2	....

Name	Persons included.	Present at time of fire.	Not present time of fire.	Received relief.	Received no relief.
W. Pickett	4	4	....	4	....
Unnamed family	3	3	....	3	....
Unnamed family	3	3	....	3	....
Unnamed family	3	3	....	3	....
w. Mrs. Johanna Nelson	2	2	....	2	....
H. Henderson	8	8	....	8	....
C. G. Granstrom	6	6	....	....	6
P. Berglov	8	8	....	....	8
Totals	80	80	....	75	14
MORRISON COUNTY.					
w. Mr. Hasch	1	1	....	1	....
Mr. Martin	2	2	....	2	....
E. Weedmark	3	3	....	3	....
H. Durenland	6	6	....	6	....
Hans Isaacson	7	7	....	7	....
F. Granstrom	4	4	....	4	....
G. Nelson	7	7	....	7	....
A. Granstrom	4	4	....	4	....
Andrew Mulenander	5	5	....	5	....
R. Pettis	7	7	....	7	....
Totals	46	46	....	46	....
WADENA COUNTY.					
W. H. Gaines	9	9	....	9	....
w. Abigael Feilder	2	2	....	2	....
J. C. Peterson	6	6	....	6	....
Russell Witheral	2	2	....	2	....
George Witheral	7	7	....	7	....
Carl Worm	7	7	....	7	....
Henry Henrickson	3	3	....	3	....
Totals	36	36	....	36	....
AITKIN COUNTY.					
Knute Engstrom	5	5	....	....	5
Gust Williamson	5	5	....	....	5
Chris Opgaard	6	6	....	....	6
Joe Johnson	3	3	....	....	3
John Larson	2	2	....	....	2
Charles Johnson	4	4	....	....	4

Name.	Persons included.	Present at time of fire.	Not present time of fire.	Received relief.	Received no relief.
E. Johnson	4	4			4
A. Halberg	4	4			4
Christ Knutson	4	4			4
Ole Barge	5	5			5
Hans Peterson	5	5			5
G. O. Brown	6	6			6
Frank Rathburn	2	2			2
Totals	55	55			55
CASS COUNTY.					
O. W. Caldwell	4	4		4	
w. Hattie V. Sims	4	4		4	
w. Rosa A. Bennett	5	5		5	
Totals	13	13		13	

www.ingramcontent.com/pod-product-compliance
Lightning Source LLC
Chambersburg PA
CBHW031815270326
41932CB00008B/426